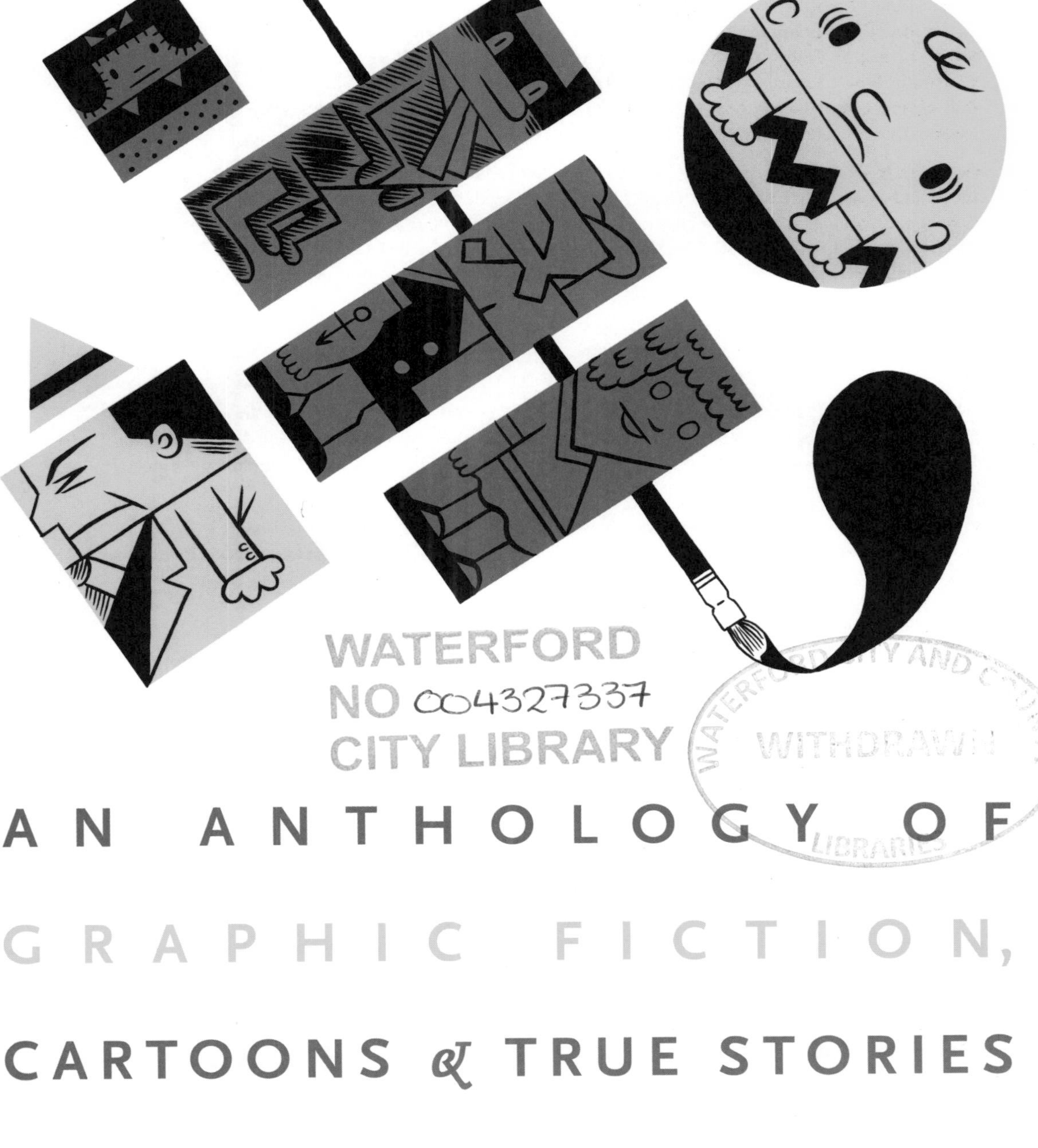

AN ANTHOLOGY OF GRAPHIC FICTION, CARTOONS & TRUE STORIES

VOLUME TWO

Edited by IVAN BRUNETTI

Yale University Press, New Haven & London

EDITOR: Ivan Brunetti

ASSISTANT EDITORS: Chris Ware and Laura Mizicko

KIBITZER: Daniel Raeburn

PRODUCTION: John Kuramoto

ADDITIONAL PRODUCTION AND RESEARCH ASSISTANCE: Chris Ware, Alvin Buenaventura, Jeremy "Onsmith" Smith, Jonathan Wilcox, Amy Peltz, Marc Filerman, Sara Gleich, Kim Thompson, Gary Groth, Eric Reynolds, Paul Baresh, Adam Grano, Jacob Covey, Tom Devlin, Amelia Meath, Alison Naturale, Morgan Charles, Glenn Bray, M. Todd Hignite, Dan Nadel, Jon Vermilyea, and Craig Yoe.

THANKS also to Michelle Komie, Françoise Mouly, Tim Samuelson, Matthew McClintock, Ken Parille, Jonathan Bieniek, Adele Kurtzman, Denis Kitchen, Amy Snyder and the Hirshhorn Museum, the A+D Gallery of Columbia College Chicago, Victor Alsobrook, Jayne Antipow and the Arf Museum, Thomas King and DC Comics, Cristin O'Keefe Aptowicz and the Artists Rights Society, Donna Norkus and the William Steig Estate, Margaret Sloan and the Jess Collins Trust, Thomas Dobrowolski and Pantheon Books, the Saul Steinberg Foundation, Lanny Silverman, Ron Turner, Kristine Anstine, Rob Stolzer, Chris Coffin, Phillip King, Lindsay Toland, every single artist in this book, all the friends and family who offered emotional support (too numerous to list here, unfortunately), and John Kulka for suggesting this project in the first place and helping it come to fruition.

Many of these comics first appeared in books and magazines published by Fantagraphics Books, Drawn & Quarterly, Raw Books and Graphics, Pantheon Books, Highwater Books, Buenaventura Press, Last Gasp, Top Shelf, Alternative Comics, Gingko Press, PictureBox, and McSweeney's, and this anthology is greatly indebted to all of them.

DUSTJACKET DESIGN AND ILLUSTRATIONS: Daniel Clowes

CASE COVER: William Steig, "Maternal Type" and "He Who Gets Slapped," from *Persistent Faces* (Duell, Sloan and Pearce, 1946)

ENDPAPERS: Richard McGuire, from *P+O* (Éditions Cornélius, 2001)

TITLE PAGE: Onsmith, *Cartoon Suprematism* (2007)

Set in Scala Sans by John Kuramoto.
Printed in China.

LIBRARY OF CONGRESS CATALOGING-IN-PUBLICATION DATA

An anthology of graphic fiction, cartoons, and true stories : volume 2 / edited by Ivan Brunetti.
p. cm.

ISBN 978-0-300-12671-6

1. Comic books, strips, etc.—United States—History—20th century. 2. Cartooning—United States—History—20th century. 3. American wit and humor, Pictorial—History—20th century. I. Brunetti, Ivan.

NC1764.5.U6A58 2006

741.5'69—dc22 2006014095

A catalogue record for this book is available from the British Library.

This paper meets the requirements of ANSI/NISO Z39.48-1992 (Permanence of Paper).

10 9 8 7 6 5 4 3 2 1

CONTENTS

Page 6
Saul Steinberg
Untitled (Family Group)
(1965–68)

Page 7
Ivan Brunetti
Introduction

Page 8
Sammy Harkham
Napoleon!
(from *Crickets* No. 2, 2008)

Pages 9–13
Chris Ware
Rocket Sam
Big Tex
Quimby the Mouse
Tales of Tomorrow
God
(from *The Acme Novelty Library*, 2005, and *Quimby the Mouse*, 2003)

Pages 14–15
R. Sikoryak
Action Camus
(from *Snake Eyes* No. 1, 1991)

Page 16
Michael Kupperman
excerpts from *Snake 'n' Bacon's Cartoon Cabaret* (2000)

Page 17
Drew Friedman
He Had a Funny Face
(from *Raw* Vol. 2, No. 2, 1989)

Page 18
Mark Beyer
Messenger of Death
(from *A Disturbing Evening and Other Stories*, 1978)

Pages 19–23
Kaz
The Tragedy of Satan
(from *Snake Eyes* No. 1, 1991)

Pages 24–28
Mack White
The Nudist Nuns of Goat Island
(from *Snake Eyes* No. 2, 1993)

Pages 29–31
Jayr Pulga
Thrift Shop Love
(from *Snake Eyes* No. 1, 1991)

Pages 32–34
Renée French
ZZZ
(from *Comix 2000*, 1999)

Pages 35–43
Kim Deitch
The Road to Rana Poona
(from *Raw* Vol. 2, No. 2, 1990)

Page 44
Richard Sala
Untitled
(from the *Comics Journal Special Edition* Vol. 1, 2002)

Page 45
J. Bradley Johnson
The Grolo & Co.
(from *Kramers Ergot* No. 5, 2004)

Page 46
Archer Prewitt
Funny Bunny
(from the *Chicago Reader*, 2002)

Page 47
Anonymous
excerpt from *Utility Sketchbook* (2006)

Page 48
H. J. Tuthill
The Bungle Family
(1929)

Page 49
Milt Gross
Dave's Delicatessen
(1933)

Page 50
Bill Holman
Smokey Stover
(1942)

Pages 51–53
Harvey Kurtzman
Hey Look (1948)
Genius (1951)
Egghead Doodle (1950)

Pages 54–55
Robert Crumb
Ode to Harvey Kurtzman
(from *Harvey Kurtzman's Strange Adventures*, 1989)

Page 56
Basil Wolverton
Cover of *Mad* No. 11
(1954)

Page 57
Adam Gopnik
Kurtzman's Mad World
(from the *New Yorker*, 1993)

Pages 57–62
Art Spiegelman
H.K. (R.I.P.)
A Furshlugginer Genius
(from the *New Yorker*, 1993)
The Malpractice Suite
(from *Arcade* No. 6, 1976)
Dead Dick (1990)

Page 63
Jess
Tricky Cad: Case V
(1958)

Page 64
John Hankiewicz
Dance Drama
(from *Asthma,* 2006)

Pages 65–67
Tim Hensley
Smooth Jazz
(from the *Comics Journal Special Edition* Vol. 2, 2002)

Pages 68–69
Bill Griffith
The Plot Thickens
(from *Raw* Vol. 1, No. 2, 1980)

Page 70
Richard McGuire
The Thinkers
(from *Raw* Vol. 2, No. 2, 1990)

Pages 71–76
Gilbert Hernandez
Drink, Fucker!
Mosquito
She Sleeps with Anybody but Me
(from *Fear of Comics,* 2000)

Pages 77–89
Jim Woodring
Particular Mind
(from *The Book of Jim,* 1993)

Pages 90–97
David Collier
Artist
(from *Collier's* No. 2, 1992)

Page 98
Eugene Teal
Frogs Sunday Funnie
(from *Weirdo* No. 3, 1981)

Pages 99–105
Charles Burns
excerpt from *Black Hole*
(2005)

Page 106
Karl Wirsum
3 My Eye Land Cyclops?
(1983)

Pages 107–114
Gary Panter
excerpt from *Jimbo: Adventures in Paradise* (1987)

Page 115
Paper Rad
Bad
(from *B.J. and da Dogs,* 2005)

Pages 116–122
Fletcher Hanks
Stardust, The Super Wizard
(1940)

Pages 123–129
C.F.
MM22
(2001)

Page 130
Charles Forbell
Naughty Pete
(1913)

Pages 131–139
Ron Regé, Jr.
We Must Know, We Will Know
(from *Drawn & Quarterly* Vol. 4, 2001)

Page 140
Winsor McCay
Dream of the Rarebit Fiend
(1913)

Pages 141–145
Matthew Thurber
Island of Silk and Ectoplasm
(from *The Ganzfeld* No. 4, 2005)

Pages 146–148
Souther Salazar
Fervler 'n' Razzle
(from *Kramers Ergot* No. 5, 2004)

Page 149
Kevin Scalzo
Pie Face
(from *SPX 2000,* 2000)

Pages 150–153
Megan Kelso
Kodachrome
(from *Comix 2000,* 1999)

Pages 154–156
James McShane
09/12/04
(from *Kramers Ergot* No. 6, 2006)

Page 157
Laura Park
Sunday, April 4th
(from unpublished sketchbook, 2005)

Pages 158–160
Vanessa Davis
September 1, 2005
September 3, 2005
September 5, 2005
(from *Kramers Ergot* No. 6, 2006)

Page 161
Onsmith
502 West Main Street
(unpublished, 2007)

Pages 162–166
Joe Matt
excerpts from *Peepshow: The Cartoon Diary of Joe Matt* (1992)

Pages 167–174
Jeffrey Brown
excerpts from *Unlikely* (2003)

Page 175
Martin Cendreda
I Want You to Like Me
(from *Kramers Ergot* No. 6, 2006)

Page 176–177
Dave Kiersh
Plainview
(from www.davekiersh.com, 2007)

Pages 178–180
John Porcellino
excerpts from *King-Cat Comics & Stories* No. 38 (1993)

Pages 181–186
Carrie Golus and **Patrick W. Welch**
Beachy Head, Illinois
Halloween Was a Blast
(from *Alternator: Grand Junction,* 1999)

Pages 187–194
Jessica Abel
Jack London
(from *Artbabe* No. 5, 1996)

Page 195
Cole Johnson
Twigs and Stones
(from the *Chicago Reader*, 2006)

Pages 196–198
Lynda Barry
Dancing
(from *One! Hundred! Demons!* 2002)

Pages 199–203
Debbie Drechsler
Constellations
(from *The Best of Drawn & Quarterly*, 1993)

Pages 204–205
Diane Noomin
Some of My Best Friends Are
(from *Arcade* No. 7, 1976)

Pages 206–207
Aline Kominsky-Crumb
The Bunch, Her Baby, & Grammaw Blabette
(from *Love That Bunch*, 1990)

Page 208
Ariel Bordeaux
Alike-A-Look
(from *Deep Girl* No. 5, 1995)

Pages 209–216
Chester Brown
My Mom Was a Schizophrenic
(from *The Little Man*, 1998)

Pages 217–226
Anders Nilsen
excerpt from *The End* No. 1 (2007)

Pages 227–241
Joe Sacco
White Death
(from *Safe Area Gorazde*, 2000)

Pages 242–253
Phoebe Gloeckner
Minnie's 3rd Love, or: "Nightmare on Polk Street"
(from *A Child's Life and Other Stories*, 1998)

Pages 254–255
Elinore Norflus
Depressed Dora Comics
(from *Weirdo* No. 4, 1982)

Pages 256–257
Brian Chippendale
Episodes 68 and 69
(from *Ninja*, 2006)

Page 258
Leif Goldberg
National Seashore
(from *National Waste* No. 1, 2002)

Pages 259–267
David Mazzucchelli
Near Miss
(from *Rubber Blanket* No. 2, 1991)

Pages 268–269
Jerry Moriarty
Jack Survives
(from *The Complete Jack Survives*, 2008)

Pages 270–278
Ben Katchor
excerpts from *Julius Knipl, Real Estate Photographer: The Beauty Supply District* (2000)

Pages 279–282
Frank Santoro
excerpt from *Storeyville* (1995)

Pages 283–290
Dan Zettwoch
Cross-Fader
(from *Kramers Ergot* No. 6, 2006)

Pages 291–300
Kevin Huizenga
The Curse
(from *Curses*, 2006)

Pages 301–304
Bill Griffith
Is There Life After Levittown?
(from *Lemme Outa Here!* 1978)

Pages 305–310
Harvey Pekar and **Robert Crumb**
How I Quit Collecting Records and Put Out a Comic Book with the Money I Saved
(from *American Splendor*, 1986)

Pages 311–329
Robert Crumb
That's Life
(from *Arcade* No. 3, 1975)
Patton
(from *Zap Comix* No. 11, 1985)
Hunting for Old Records: A True Story
(from *Oxford American*, 1999)

Pages 330–331
Carol Tyler
Country Music
(from *Late Bloomer*, 2005)

Page 332
Maurice Vellekoop
Waiting
(from *Drawn & Quarterly* Vol. 2, No. 6, 1997)

Pages 333–342
Seth
excerpt from *Clyde Fans*
(from *Palookaville* No. 16, 2002)

Pages 343–348
Adrian Tomine
Hazel Eyes
(from *Sleepwalk and Other Stories*, 1998)

Pages 349–354
Jaime Hernandez
Jerusalem Crickets
(from *The Death of Speedy*, 1987)

Pages 355–371
Daniel Clowes
Blue Italian Shit
(from *Caricature*, 1998)
excerpts from *Ice Haven* (2005)

Pages 372–381
Chris Ware
excerpt from *Building Stories* and *Sleep*
(from *Acme Novelty Library* No. 18, 2007)

Pages 382–397
David Heatley
Portrait of My Mom
Portrait of My Dad
(from *My Brain Is Hanging Upside Down*, 2008)

398–400
Contributors

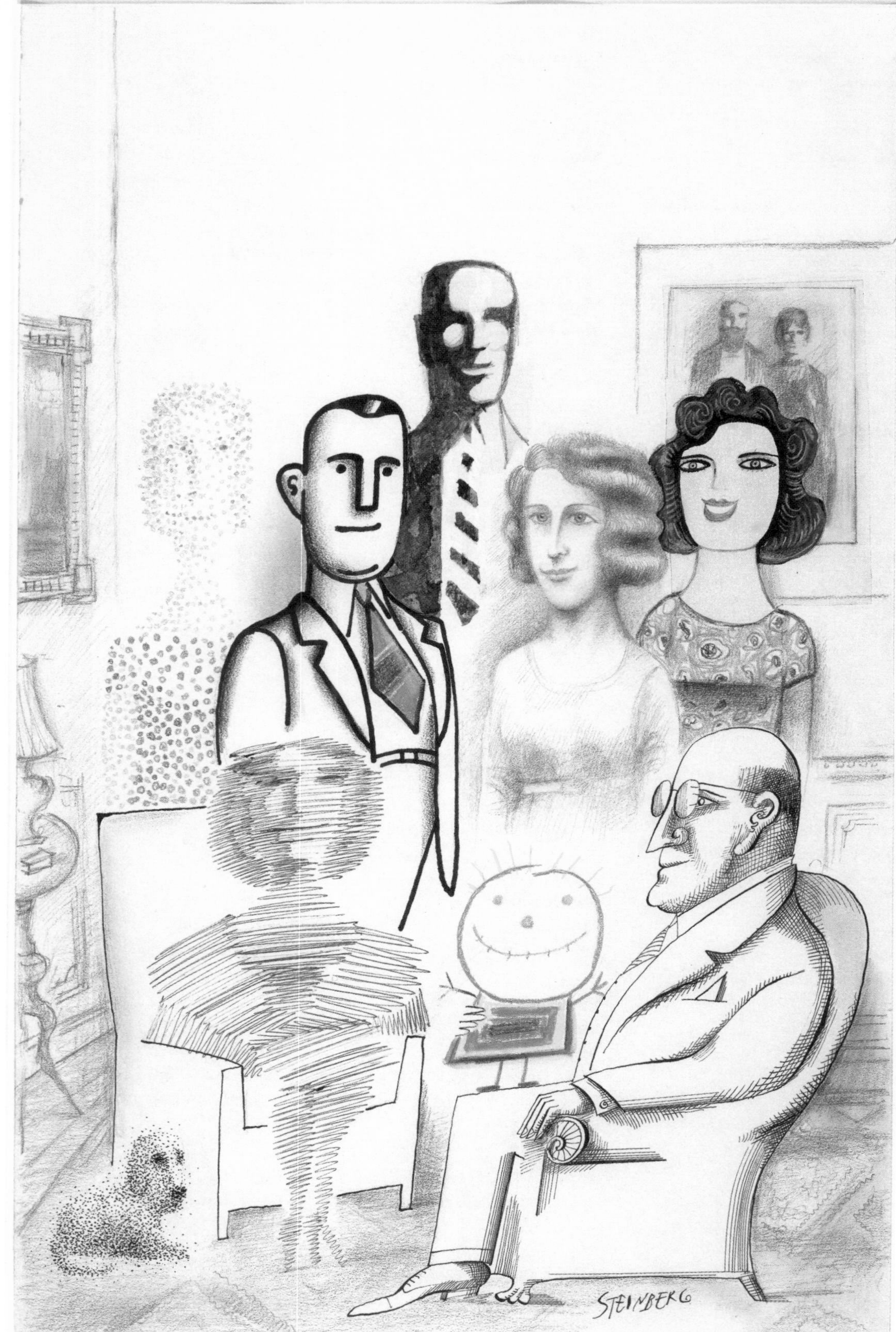

Saul Steinberg, Untitled (Family Group), *1965–68. Ink, pencil, colored pencil, crayon, and ballpoint pen on paper, 23 ½ x 14 in. (59.7 x 35.6 cm). Collection of Carol and Douglas Cohen. © The Saul Steinberg Foundation/Artists Rights Society (ARS), New York*

INTRODUCTION

Ivan Brunetti

I will keep this mercifully brief, since I would like the works contained here to attest to their own quality, unencumbered by my voice; as well, this second volume is in many ways a continuation—and perhaps a culmination—of the ideas embodied in the first book. The *Anthology* once again focuses entirely on untranslated work by North American creators; while this is partly for the sake of logistics, as France and Japan alone would each command a volume of this size, it is primarily because the works share a common bond by virtue of the artists sharing the same cultural broth.

This is, admittedly, a deeply personal book (I'm not sure how a book can be impersonal). As such, it reflects my own temperament, from which my aesthetics and taste naturally follow. Much like the Saul Steinberg drawing on the facing page, I have tried to represent a variety of approaches while retaining a sense of wholeness and interconnectedness among the stories. If the first volume viewed comics as a developing human being, then this volume treats them as an extended family.

Please keep in mind that these are but some of my favorite comics. I have tried to keep this "family portrait" from getting too unwieldy, and thus I could not include all the far-flung or distant relatives; moreover, some of them would have been prohibitively expensive to fly in, so to speak, while others could not or would not attend the "sitting" for one reason or another. In the end, I chose work that I feel an indescribable affection for, but the pieces also mesh together well and feel as if they are "one."

These are comics that opened my mind, pointing and pushing the medium in new and interesting directions, whether through formal experimentation, uncompromised subject matter, uniquely expressed mood, deeply felt theme, inventive drawing, or sheer craft. They are comics that possess an internal life, a creative spark, an impishness at their core—or as Paul Klee called it, "dynamic equilibrium," a feeling of order and balance that teeters on the verge of chaos and imbalance. In my favorite comics, this quality is ever present, extending from the power of a single mark through the structure of an entire graphic novel.

Perhaps not coincidentally, "dynamic equilibrium" also serves as a metaphor for both cosmological and biological processes, describing the delicacy and totality of life itself. The creative process is the very expression of this principle. Its elusive, fluxlike essence may render it ultimately ineffable, but the creative process is by no means murky or fuzzy. It reiterates, reflects on a smaller scale, the ever-flowing natural order, its immense complexity and drive toward balance.

I have organized this book to mirror the free-associative process of creation—an assemblage of observation, memory, and imagination—with the resultant structure acting as a document of its own discovery. Working from a pre-established system of rules seemed too constricting and arbitrary. A single comic, even a single page, can straddle many categories, encompassing a multitude of moods and themes. It seemed reductive and demeaning to pigeonhole an artist or a story into a "genre"; furthermore, any given piece was affected by those surrounding it, stories being no more absolute than colors.

Chalk doodle drawn by a Roman soldier on the wall of his barracks in AD 79, from James Parton's Caricature and Other Comic Art in Many Lands and All Times *(1878).*

Comics are a "fractal" art form, somewhere between the literary and the visual, much like collage exists somewhere between two and three dimensions (confusing things further, comics are themselves a "collage" of words and pictures). The connections from one story to the next in this book are purely personal and intuitive, relating the stories visually and thematically and forming a set of pulsing leitmotifs. I am using the word "stories" for the sake of convenience, as some of the contents are more akin to other literary forms (poem, essay, etc.). What is paramount is the flow from page to page, the sense of an interdependent and inseparable whole, winding its way around and back into itself.

I am now cringing because I sound pretentious, and I do not think comics are pretentious. Cartoonists are, at heart, doodlers. And the doodle has its own authority, directness, and power; it is both primal and sophisticated. As always, I return to Saul Steinberg, who wanted to preserve in his work an element of vulgarity: "I consider it something necessary; like a man, who in changing his social class, still wouldn't want to break up with his wife and old friends."[1]

NOTE

1. Reflections and Shadows, *Saul Steinberg with Aldo Buzzi. Translated by John Shepley, © 2002, Random House.*

NAPOLEON!

I'M NEVER GOING TO FINISH THIS DAMN THING IN TIME
I NEVER SHOULD HAVE AGREED TO THIS...
GENERAL!
WHAT, WHAT IS IT NOW?
THE AUSTRIANS HAVE ENTERED ITALY GENERAL!
SIGH... COME HERE A MOMENT
DO YOU THINK THIS WORKS? I MEAN, IT'S SUPPOSED TO BE FUNNY, BUT IS IT EVEN READABLE?
HMMM...
RUB
ONE GLASS OF YOUR FINEST WHISKEY!
COMING UP!
THANK YOU!
AAH...
SPLASH
I THINK THAT MAN IS IN NEED OF A DOCTOR!
RUB
RUB
OH, DO NOT WORRY- HE'S JUST ENGLISH!
CRASH
DOTS FOR EYES CAN BE PROBLEMATIC...
SIR, YOUR WIFE
MAYBE...
I HAVE TO GO DARLING
GO?
TO SICILY, DARLING
..BUT WE ONLY GOT MARRIED TWO DAYS AGO...
I'LL WRITE
BOM
KA-BOOM
AAAAAAAAAAAA!
BOMF
BOMF
BOM
BOMF
AAARGH!
LOAD
CLK
CLK
CLK
CLK
CLK
CLK
MERDE...
KRK
THWK
GRAB
STAB
MAYBE DOTS FOR EYES DO GIVE TOO MUCH EMPATHY...
SIGH
I'LL NEVER WRITE A JOKE AS GOOD AS BEN FRANKLIN...

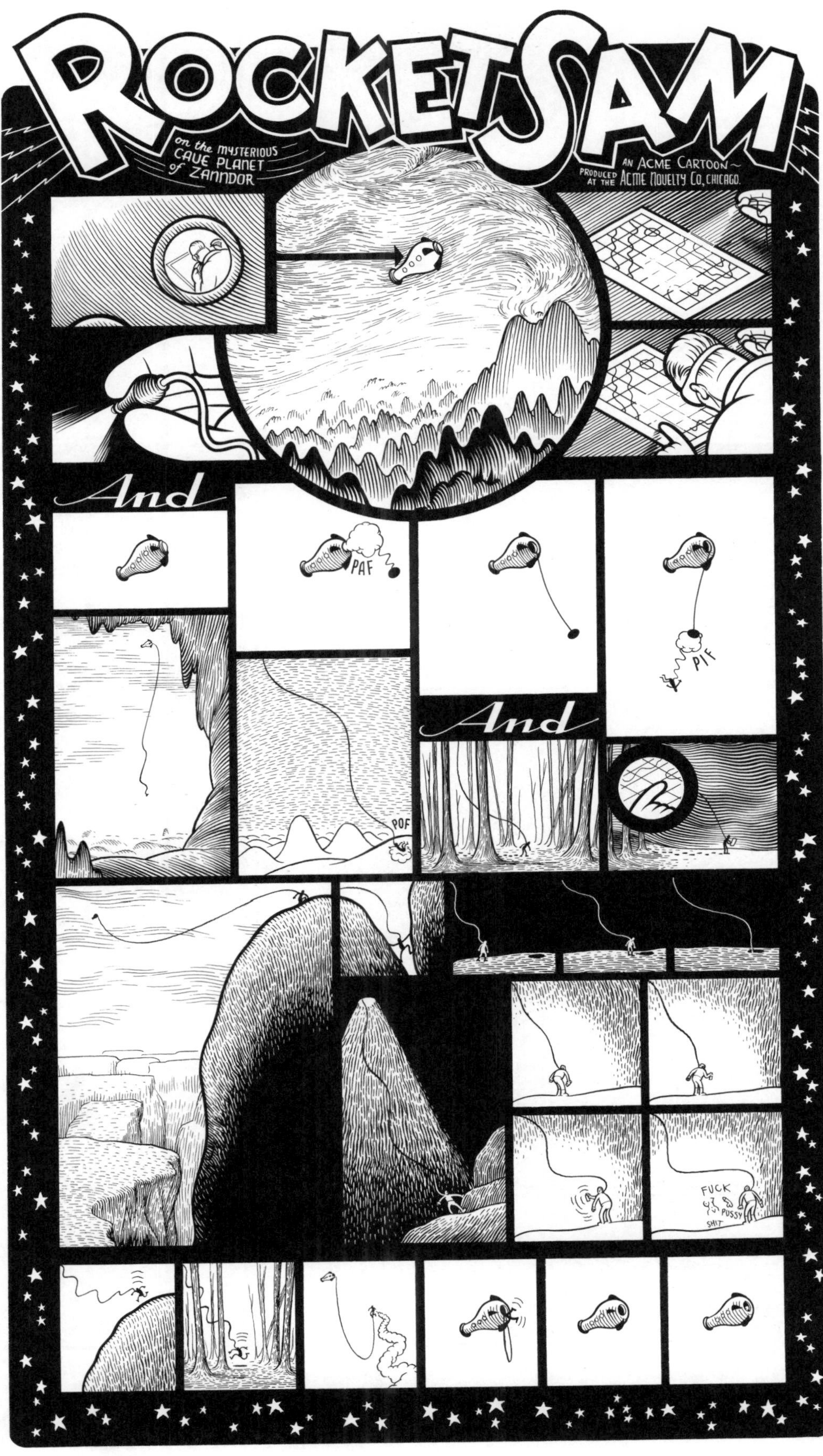
ROCKET SAM
on the MYSTERIOUS CAVE PLANET of ZANNDOR
AN ACME CARTOON~
PRODUCED AT THE ACME NOVELTY CO, CHICAGO.
And
PAF
PIF
And
POF
FUCK
PUSSY
SHIT

BIG TEX

MAW AN PAW, I HAST BRUNG YOU TWO PRESENTS AN SOME FLOWERS WHICH I WILL LEAVE FER YOU TODAY. I HOPE THAT YOU LIKE THEM AND THAT YOU HAVE BEEN OKAY

MAW

PAW

TEX... koff NOW YOU TAKE CARE OF THIS PLACE, Y'HEAR? kff **Y'HEAR?**

PAW... snf DON' TALK LIKE THAT... YER GONE BE JEST **FINE... DOC SAID!**

LOOKIT MAW! THEM BURDS IS RAISIN A **FAMBLY** JEST LIKE YOU AN PAW HAST BEEN RAISIN **ME!**

HA HA YES TEX koff I SUPPOSE THAT'S RIGHT

BANG

P-PAW I **GOT** 'IM! I **GOT** ONE A THEM LITTLE GODDAM SONSUHBITCHES!

HAW... THERE Y'GO, TEX--THET'S REAL **MAN'S** WORK--LEMME HAVE A COUPLA SHOTS NOW!

TEX, WHERE DID YOU GIT THIS FIREWOOD FROM?

N-N-NOWHERE, PAW

TEX I **ASKET** YOU WHERE IT WAS YOU GIT THIS **FIREWOOD** NOW **TELL** ME

P-PAW, I-I...

TEX YOU GWAN OUT AN SEE WHUT YOU KIN SKIR UP INNA WAY OF FIRE-WOOD, UNNERSTAND?

YESSIR PAW I KIN DO THAT

BUT DON'T YOU THINK YOU OWE YOUR PAW AN APOLOGY?

BUT **MAW** I DIDN' DO **NOTHIN'** I DIDN' DO **NOTHIN'** gng PAW JEST START TO WHUPPIN ME WIF THE RAKE snf AN THEN HE STARTED TO TRYIN TO PUT MY **HEAD** INTO THE **CORN COBBER** snf SO **THET'S** WHEN IT WAS I **BIT** HIM snf BUT I DIDN' **MEAN** TO snf I DIDN' **MEAN** TO BITE HIM, MAW snf

LOOK, PAW-- LOOK!

LOOK AT WHAT OUR LITTLE TEX HAS DONE... HE'S PLANTED A **TREE** OUT IN THE YARD... NOW ISN'T THAT **SOMETHING,** PAW?

WELL MOTHER, AIN'T THAT **THOUGHTFUL...** I BET THAT TEX IS GONNA GROW UP TO BE ONE **SMART COOKIE,** DONTCHA THINK?

I HATE YOU

AND I'M SURE OF IT THIS TIME.

Really. I just decided.

I THOUGHT YOU'D LIKE TO KNOW.

EVEN THOUGH I HAVE *Nothing* TO SAY TO YOU.

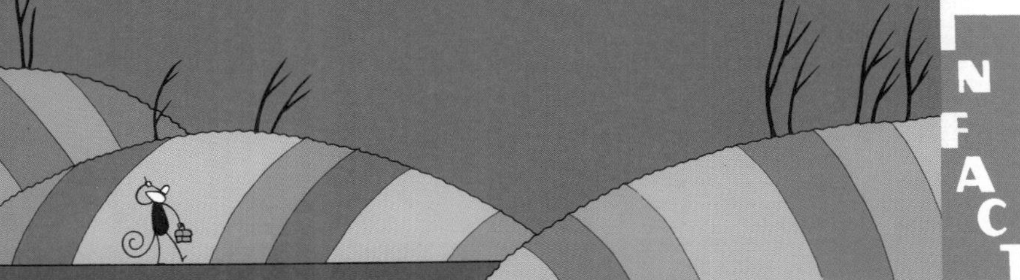

IN FACT

I DON'T CARE IF I EVER SEE YOU AGAIN

BESIDES,

I NEVER THINK ABOUT YOU ANYMORE.

FOR YOU IN THE FIRST PLACE IS A MYSTERY TO ME NOW

I'm JUST TRYING TO BE AS CLEAR AS POSSIBLE.

SO THAT IF I EVER DO HAPPEN TO SEE YOU

WHAT TO SAY.

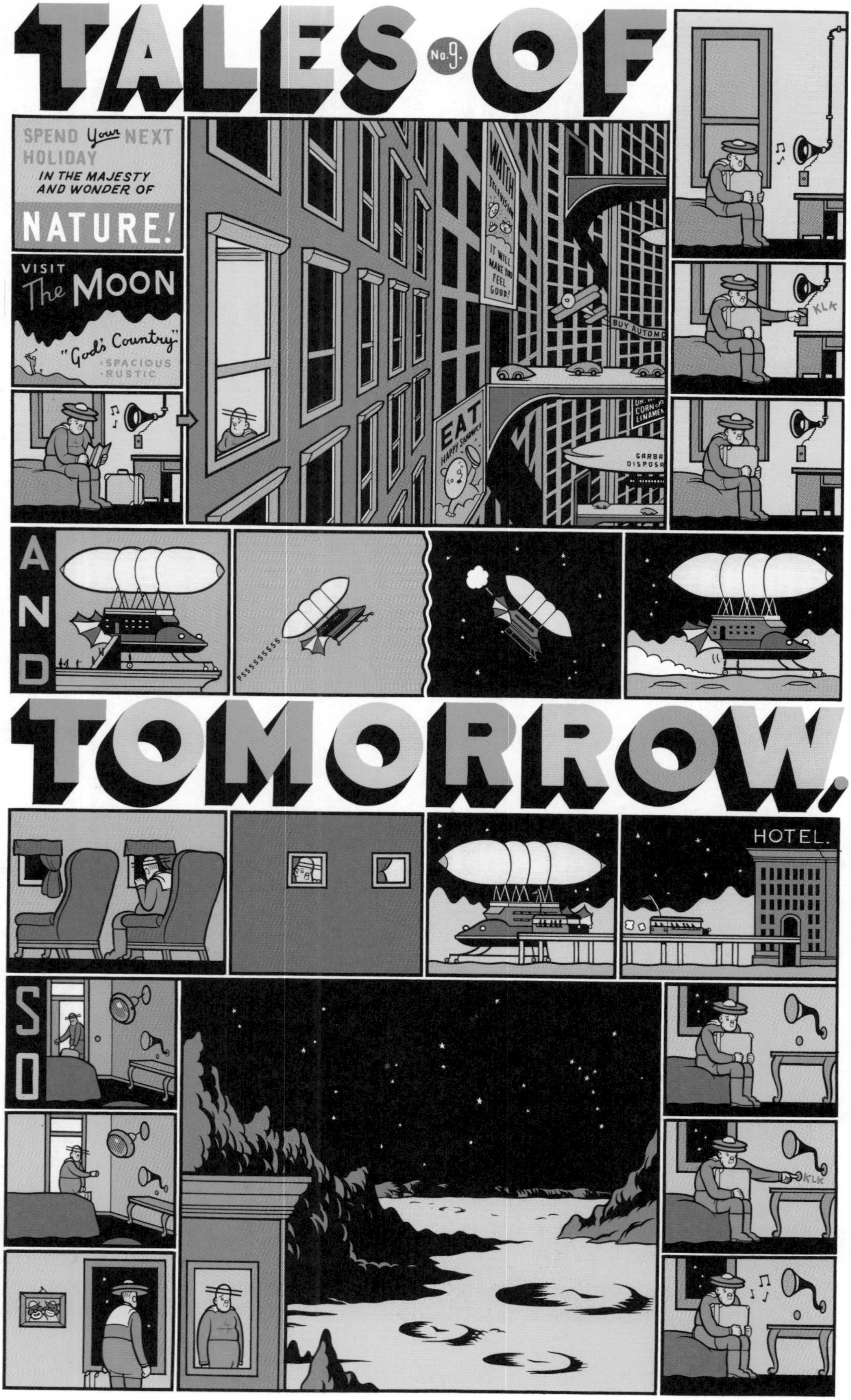

TALES No. 9. OF

SPEND Your NEXT HOLIDAY
IN THE MAJESTY AND WONDER OF
NATURE!

VISIT The MOON
"God's Country"
·SPACIOUS
·RUSTIC

WATCH TELEVISION
IT WILL MAKE YOU FEEL GOOD!

EAT HAPPY SANDWICH

KLK

AND

PSSSSSSSSS

TOMORROW,

HOTEL.

SO

KLK

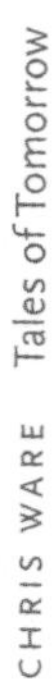

STRANGER
No. 11
Ten Cents
A STRANGER PUBLICATION
AC
ACTION CAMUS
In this issue:
THE STRANGER DISCOVERS
"MOTHER DIED TODAY"
OR WAS IT YESTERDAY?

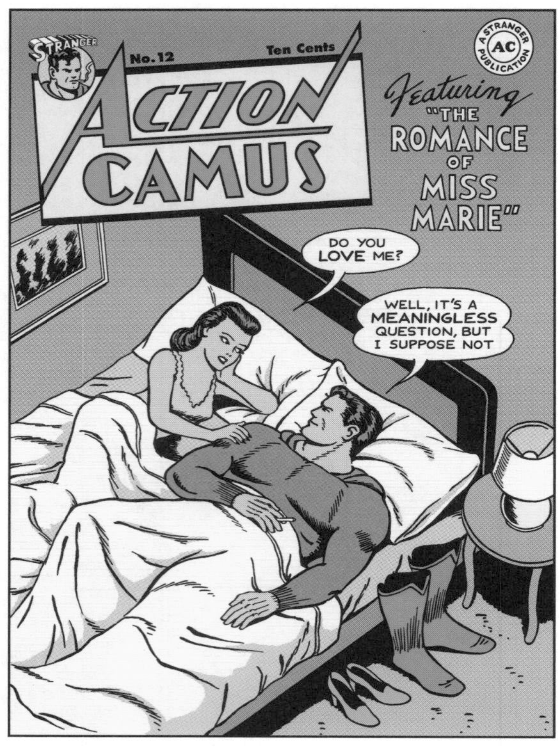
STRANGER
No. 12
Ten Cents
A STRANGER PUBLICATION
AC
ACTION CAMUS
Featuring
"THE ROMANCE OF MISS MARIE"
DO YOU LOVE ME?
WELL, IT'S A MEANINGLESS QUESTION, BUT I SUPPOSE NOT

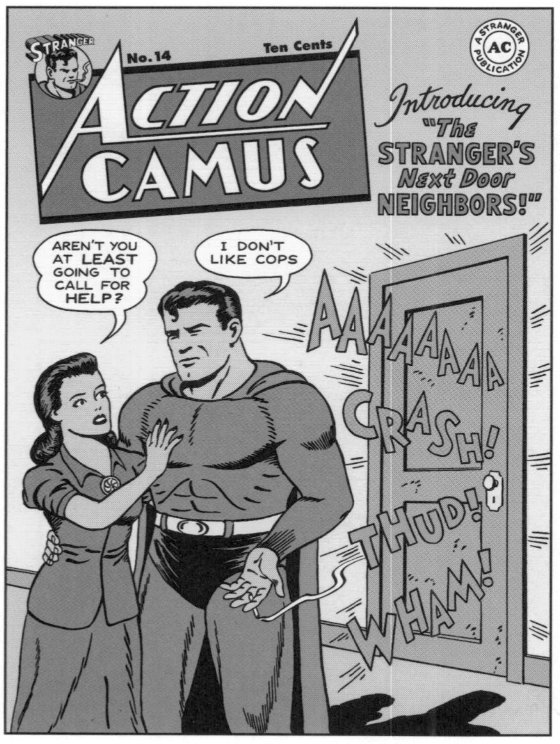
STRANGER
No. 14
Ten Cents
A STRANGER PUBLICATION
AC
ACTION CAMUS
Introducing
"The STRANGER'S Next Door NEIGHBORS!"
AREN'T YOU AT LEAST GOING TO CALL FOR HELP?
I DON'T LIKE COPS
AAAAAAAAA
CRASH!
THUD!
WHAM!

STRANGER
No. 16
Ten Cents
A STRANGER PUBLICATION
AC
ACTION CAMUS
Don't Miss--
"A WALK ON THE BEACH!"
SO MUCH FOR THE HARMONY OF THE DAY!
BLAM!
BLAM!
BLAM!
BLAM!

STRANGER
No.22
Ten Cents
A STRANGER AC PUBLICATION
ACTION CAMUS
Another STRANGER ADVENTURE--
"NO WAY OUT!"
I GUESS ONE CAN GET USED TO ANYTHING

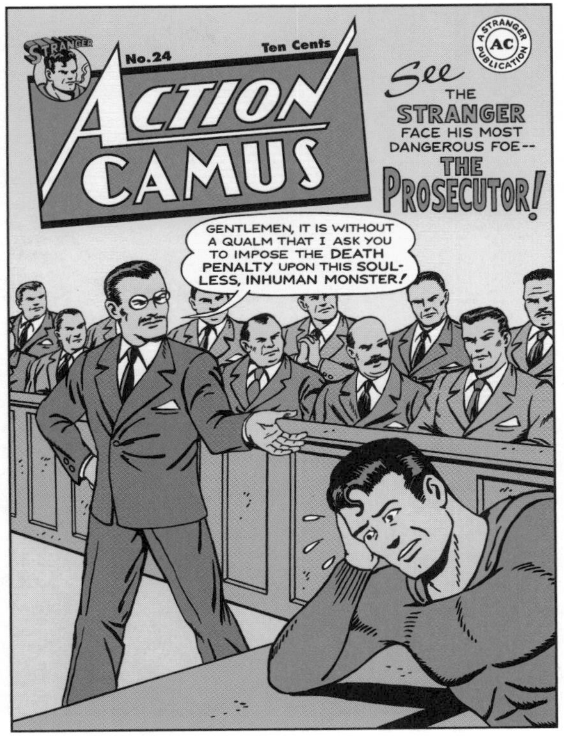
STRANGER
No.24
Ten Cents
A STRANGER AC PUBLICATION
ACTION CAMUS
See THE STRANGER FACE HIS MOST DANGEROUS FOE--
THE PROSECUTOR!
GENTLEMEN, IT IS WITHOUT A QUALM THAT I ASK YOU TO IMPOSE THE DEATH PENALTY UPON THIS SOUL-LESS, INHUMAN MONSTER!

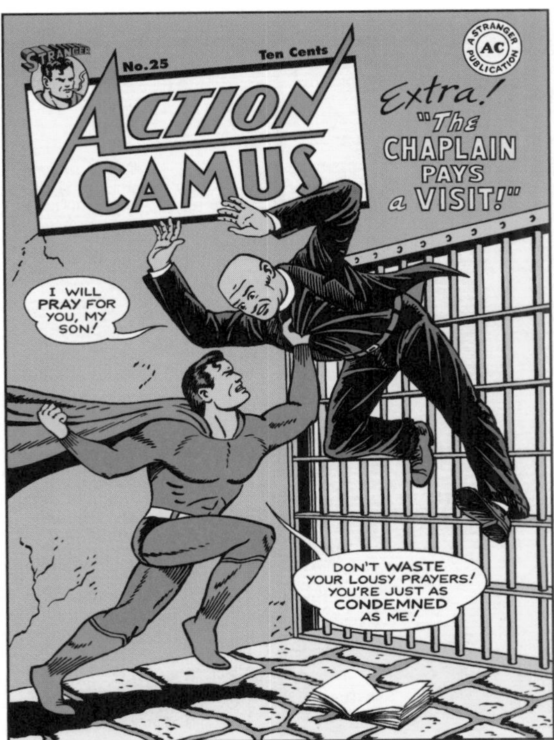
STRANGER
No.25
Ten Cents
A STRANGER AC PUBLICATION
ACTION CAMUS
Extra! "The CHAPLAIN PAYS a VISIT!"
I WILL PRAY FOR YOU, MY SON!
DON'T WASTE YOUR LOUSY PRAYERS! YOU'RE JUST AS CONDEMNED AS ME!

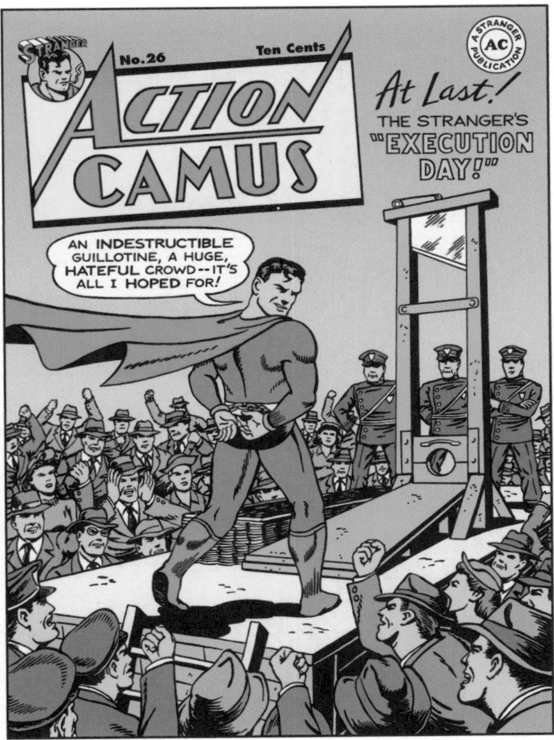
STRANGER
No.26
Ten Cents
A STRANGER AC PUBLICATION
ACTION CAMUS
At Last! THE STRANGER'S "EXECUTION DAY!"
AN INDESTRUCTIBLE GUILLOTINE, A HUGE, HATEFUL CROWD--IT'S ALL I HOPED FOR!

DICK
CRAZY

I'M TIRED OF BEING IN THIS BUCKET! I'M GOING TO CALL THE CHIEF, USING MY "2-WAY WRIST T.V."

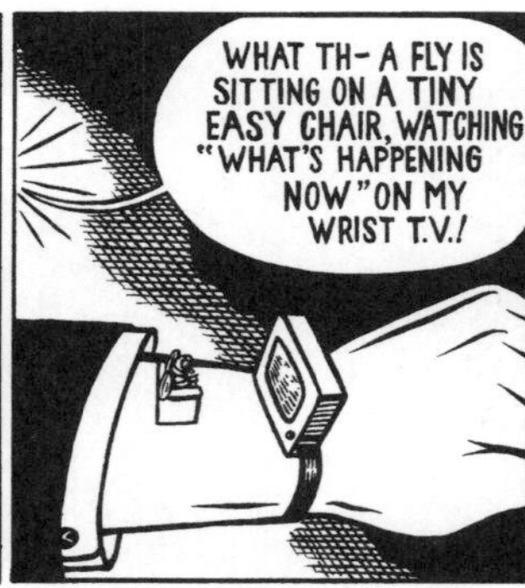
WHAT TH- A FLY IS SITTING ON A TINY EASY CHAIR, WATCHING "WHAT'S HAPPENING NOW" ON MY WRIST T.V.!

WHAT SHOULD I DO? ARREST HIM? WAIT UNTIL THE SHOW IS OVER? THE BOOK DOESN'T SAY WHAT TO DO...I'M WRITING THE BOOK RIGHT NOW!

COUSIN
GRANPA

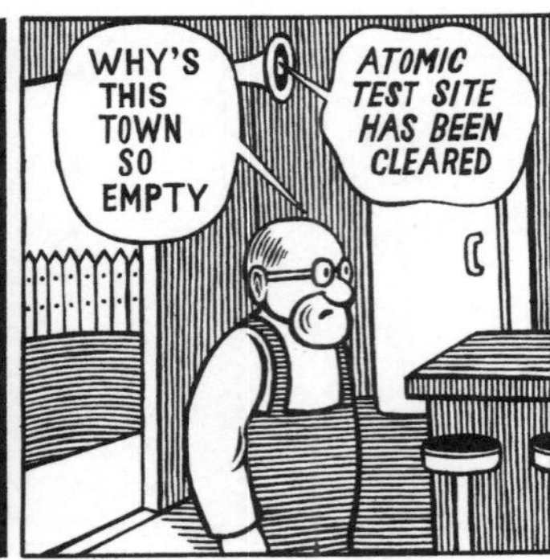
WHY'S THIS TOWN SO EMPTY
ATOMIC TEST SITE HAS BEEN CLEARED

DETONATION AT 6:00 SHARP

AH SHIT

SNAKE
'N'
BACON

DAMN IT, SNAKE'N'BACON! YOU CAUGHT THE CRIMINALS, BUT YOU ALSO BLEW UP HALF THE DAMN HARBOR!
SSSS
I'M REAL BACON

IS THAT ALL YOU HAVE TO SAY FOR YOURSELF?
SSSS
DELICIOUS BACON

I OUGHT TO THROW YOU BOTH OFF THE FORCE... BUT INSTEAD I'M GIVING YOU BOTH PROMOTIONS! NOW GET OUT!
SSSS
PAT ME DOWN WITH A PAPER TOWEL TO REMOVE EXCESS GREASE

HERE
COMES
MADNESS

HELLO! I RUN THE SEARS KITCHEN DEPARTMENT. HOW CAN I HELP YOU?
I'D LIKE TO TAKE A... JOURNEY INTO MADNESS!

WOW! THE MERE FACT THAT YOU HAVE MADE THIS STRANGE REQUEST OF ME MEANS THAT I WILL PROBABLY BE TAKING A JOURNEY INTO MADNESS MYSELF! HMM...

I WANT A SINK GLMBF!
OUTTA THE WAY, POINDEXTER!!
YEAH!! MAKE WAY FOR MADNESS!!

HE HAD A FUNNY FACE

© DREW FRIEDMAN

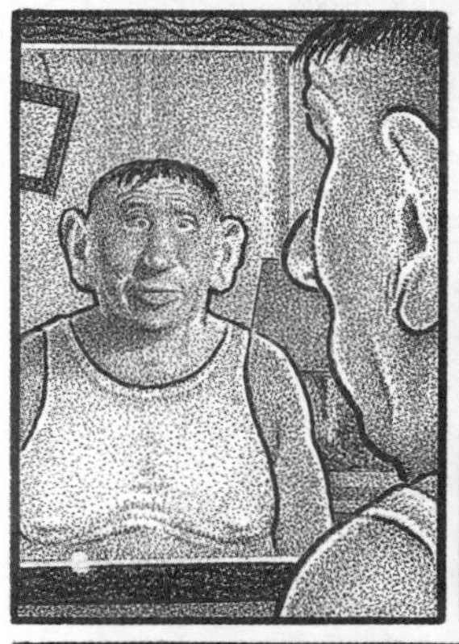

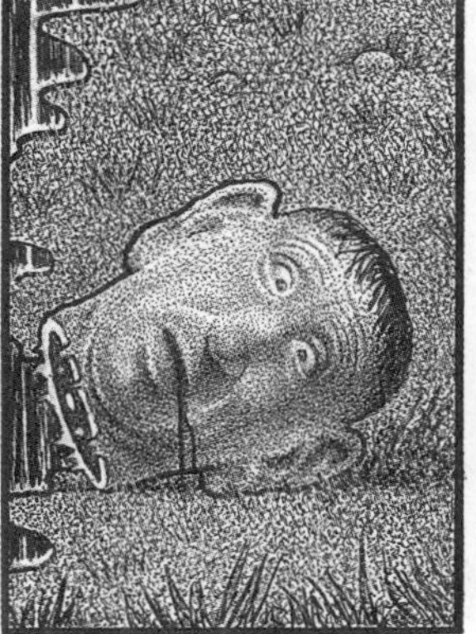

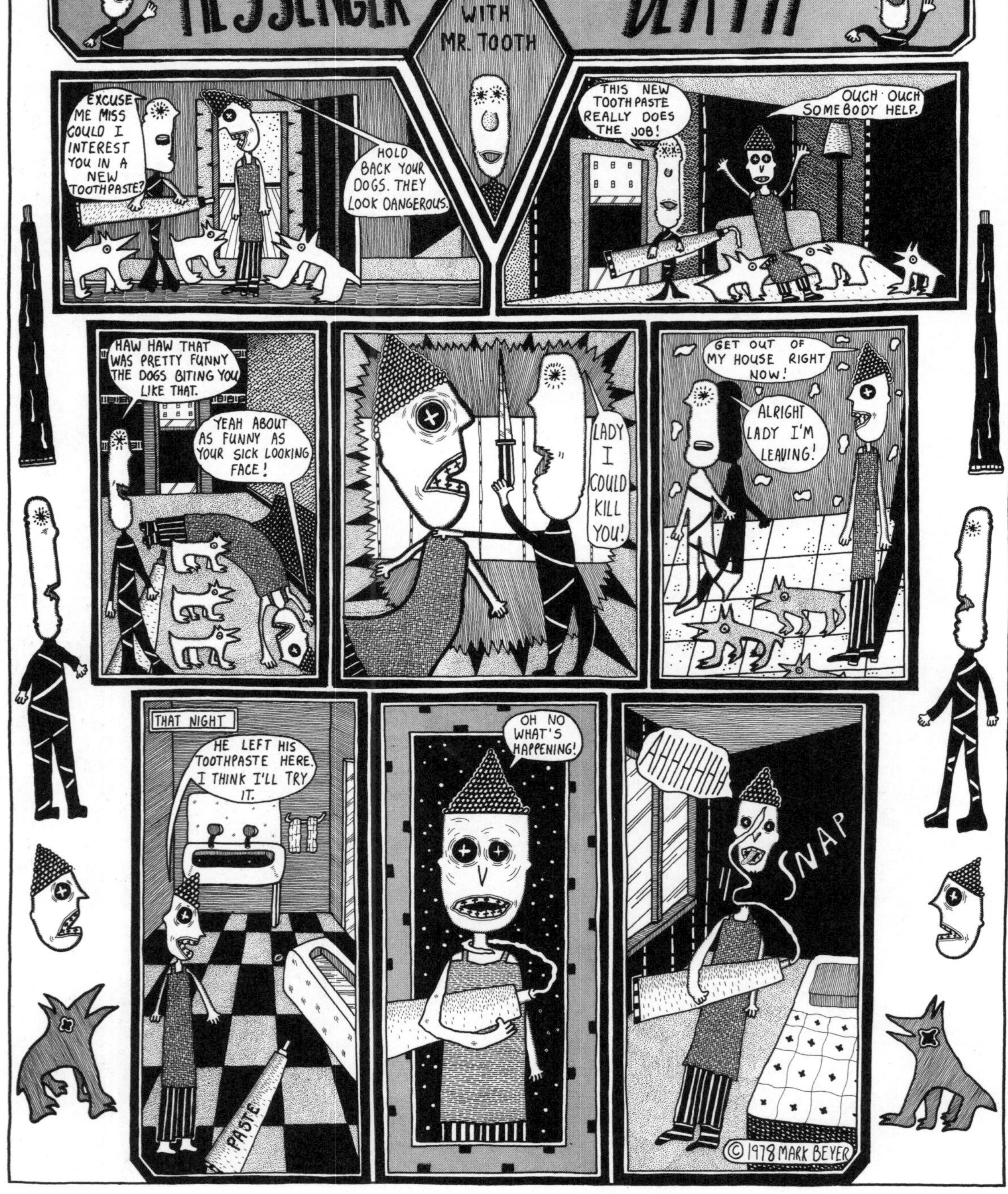

MARK BEYER Messenger of Death

THE TRAGEDY OF SATAN
©KAZ 1990

SINCE HIS FIRST APPEARANCE IN PERSIA IN THE 6th CENTURY B.C., THE DEVIL HAS UNDERGONE COUNTLESS INTERPRETATIONS AND NAME CHANGES. THROUGH THE CENTURIES HIS POWERS HAVE RISEN AND FALLEN IN ACCORDANCE WITH THE WHIMS AND CULTURES OF MAN. THROUGHOUT IT ALL—Angra Mainyu, Set, Beelzebub, Lucifer, Satan—THE DEVIL HAS ALWAYS STOOD FOR NOTHING ELSE BUT THE TOTAL SOURCE OF ALL EVIL. Doesn't he get tired of being bad?
huh!
BOINK
...I JUST HAD A DREAM THAT I WAS GOOD!

BUT THAT'S IMPOSSIBLE! IN ORDER TO BE GOOD ONE HAS TO HAVE A HEART! AND GOD DID NOT GIVE ME ONE!
MY NATURE HAS ALWAYS BEEN ONE-DIMENSIONAL! I'M A robot! A LOUSY STINKING CLOCK-WORK ROBOT!

FUCK YOU, GOD!
BOSS?

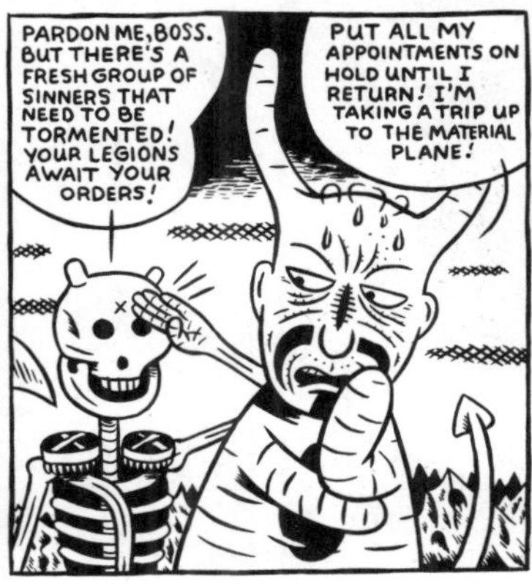
PARDON ME, BOSS. BUT THERE'S A FRESH GROUP OF SINNERS THAT NEED TO BE TORMENTED! YOUR LEGIONS AWAIT YOUR ORDERS!
PUT ALL MY APPOINTMENTS ON HOLD UNTIL I RETURN! I'M TAKING A TRIP UP TO THE MATERIAL PLANE!

THIS WAY TO THE SURFACE
AUTHORIZED DEMONS ONLY

JUST AS I FIGURED! THERE'S NOBODY MINDING THE POOP-HATCH TO HELL!*
CHURCH CLOSED you're on your own
*Lithuanian mythology.

OUT AMONGST MAN, THE PRINCE OF DARKNESS NATURALLY FINDS HIMSELF DRIFTING TOWARDS THE SEAMIER CORNERS OF SIDETRACK CITY.
MAYBE I DON'T NEED A HEART TO BE WHOLE. PERHAPS IT CAN BE DONE SOME OTHER WAY. But how?
WORMWORTH

WOW
SHE'S BEAU-TIFUL!
THAT'S IT! LOVE! I'LL FALL IN LOVE! I DON'T NEED A HEART! I'LL USE MY INTEL-LECT! AND I CHOOSE HER!
A PERFECT CHOICE FOR THE OLD SERPENT: MEET VIRUS SLUNK, THE WORST WOMAN IN THE WORLD. LIAR, THIEF, KILLER, JUNKIE... HER MIND INFESTED WITH EVERY MALIGNANT IDEA EVER INVENTED; HER BODY CRAWLING WITH EVERY DISEASE IMAGINABLE!
I DON'T WANT A BLOW JOB! I WANT US TO BE IN LOVE!
FIFTY DOLLARS FOR A HALF-HOUR THEN GET LOST!

HEY LOVER BOY, WHERE YA GOING? YOUR HALF-HOUR'S NOT UP YET!
I'LL BE BACK! I HAVE TO CHECK IN WITH MY OFFICE! What am I doing wrong?
LOOKS LIKE VIRUS TURNED A TRICK!

HONE
HELLO, THIS IS THE BOSS! HOW'S IT GOING DOWN THERE?
BAD NEWS, CHIEF! THE SINNERS ARE PILING UP AND YOUR LEGIONS ARE IDLE! SOME IN THE RANKS HAVE DESERTED AND ARE ACTUALLY HELPING NEW-COMERS ADJUST TO THE AFTERLIFE!
YOU'LL HAFTA STAND-BY A LITTLE BIT LONGER!
THERE'S ONE MORE THING, BOSS!
yes?
IT'S STARTING TO GET COLD DOWN HERE!

SIMPLY ASKING FOR LOVE IS NOT ENOUGH, I SUPPOSE. I'LL HAVE TO USE ALL THE SUPER-NATURAL POWERS AT MY DISPOSAL TO WIN HER!

I KNOW YOU MADE MORE THAN FIFTEEN DOLLARS TODAY, VIRUS! I JUST SAW A TRICK LEAVE HERE A MINUTE AGO! YOU BETTER COUGH IT UP!
FUCK OFF, FRANK! I'M NOT IN THE MOOD!
KNOCK KNOCK

TAKE CARE OF THIS CUSTOMER. I'LL WAIT IN THE BATHROOM!

OH, IT'S YOU AGAIN!
WATCH ME MY DARLING AND FALL IN LOVE!
BY MY POWERS AS SATAN, AND THE BRAWN TO BE CRUEL...
ARISE FROM THE PITCH A MONSTROUS JEWEL!
eeerK
eerK!
eeerK!
eeerK!

SPLOT
SPUT
SPLISH

ALL THE TREASURES OF THE WORLD ARE YOURS, MY LOVE! IF ONLY YOU—
NO!

YOU CAN'T REFUSE ME! I'M SATAN! THE DEVIL HIMSELF! YOU MUST LOVE ME!
DON'T TELL ME WHAT I MUST DO! I'LL NEVER LOVE ANYTHING! THE WHOLE UNIVERSE IS ONE BIG, DECAYING, PUTRID, STOOL! BOTH YOU AND GOD CAN GO FUCK YOURSELVES!!!

KAZ The Tragedy of Satan

AND STAY OUT OF MY LIFE!
SLAM
THUD

WoW!
I CAN'T WAIT TO SELL THIS BABY! I'LL BE RICH!

what the hell? IT DIS-APPEARED!
Poof!
IT'S ALL YOUR FAULT, VIRUS! YOU BITCH!

STAB
OOF
STAB

HONE
HELLO, THIS IS THE BOSS AGAIN. THINGS AREN'T GOING SO WELL UP HERE. HOW ARE YOU GUYS HOLDING OUT DOWN THERE?
NOT SO HOT, CHIEF! ADMISSIONS ARE DOWN TO A TRICKLE. THE SINNERS ARE QUESTIONING THEIR GUILT AND INSTEAD OF PUNISHING THEM---YOUR LEGIONS ARE agreeing WITH THEM!
I KNOW HOW THEY FEEL!
what?
I SAID--- TURN THE HEAT UP ON THOSE BASTARDS!
I CAN'T! THE THERMOSTAT IS FROZEN!

THIS LOVE BUSINESS IS WEARYING. IT'S PAINFUL FOR ME TO SUPRESS MY NATURAL URGE TO SET HER HEAD ABLAZE! SOMETHING KEEPS ME FROM DOING IT. Love? FEAR OF Losing? I MUST GO OFF AND MEDITATE ON THIS. BUT FIRST---I SHOULD TELL HER THAT I'LL BE GONE FOR AWHILE.

HELLO,
VIRUS?
NNOOOO, SHE'S DEAD.

Wait a minute! A BAD GIRL LIKE HER IS SURE TO END UP IN HELL! SHE'LL BE ON MY TURF! I'LL HAVE AN ETERNITY TO WIN HER LOVE!

I'M COMING DARLING!

AT HELL'S ADMISSIONS OFFICE
Pant! HEY, LOUIE. DID A VIRUS SLUNK JUST COME THROUGH HERE A MINUTE AGO? Pant!
I HAVEN'T SEEN ANYBODY COME THROUGH HERE IN A WHILE, BOSS! BUT LET ME CHECK THE REGISTER.
WELCOME TO HELL

nope. NO VIRUS SLUNK HERE!
WHAT?!? ARE YOU SURE? THAT'S IMPOSSIBLE! CHECK AGAIN, DAMN IT!
wait, hold on...
WELCOME TO HELL

ACCORDING TO THIS HERE --- SHE'S BEEN SENT TO PURGATORY! IT SEEMS THAT AS BAD AS SHE WAS, SHE NEVER FULLY ACCEPTED YOU!

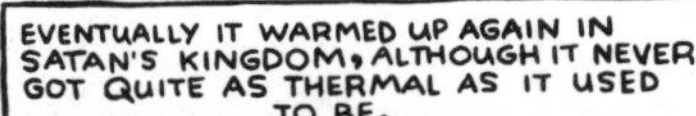
EVENTUALLY IT WARMED UP AGAIN IN SATAN'S KINGDOM, ALTHOUGH IT NEVER GOT QUITE AS THERMAL AS IT USED TO BE.

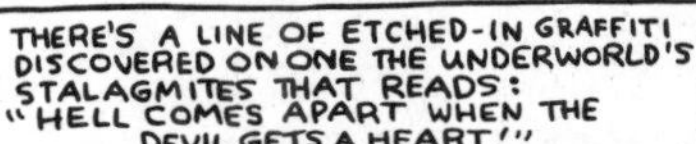
THERE'S A LINE OF ETCHED-IN GRAFFITI DISCOVERED ON ONE THE UNDERWORLD'S STALAGMITES THAT READS: "HELL COMES APART WHEN THE DEVIL GETS A HEART!"

THAT HASN'T HAPPENED YET. But HE DID GROW A PULMONARY ARTERY.
—END

THE NUDIST NUNS OF GOAT ISLAND
BY MACK WHITE

I WAS CRUISING WITH FRIENDS IN THE MEDITERRANEAN...

...WHEN I SAW A STORM APPROACH FROM THE EAST...

LIGHTNING STRUCK THE YACHT...

A FIRE SPREAD BELOW DECK, BUT BEFORE I COULD REACH THE LIFEBOAT—
BOOM!

I WAS THROWN CLEAR BY THE FORCE OF THE EXPLOSION. BLINDLY I GRABBED A PIECE OF DEBRIS...

...AND CLUNG TO IT TILL LONG AFTER THE STORM HAD PASSED...

NEAR SUNSET I SPOTTED AN **ISLAND** AND PADDLED TOWARDS IT. I FELL **EXHAUSTED** ON THE BEACH...

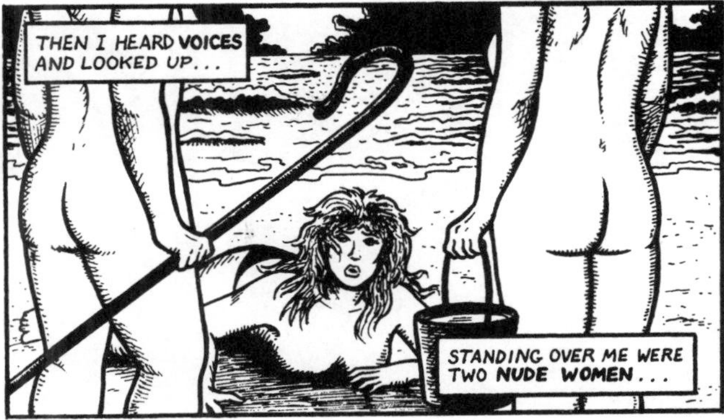

THEN I HEARD **VOICES** AND LOOKED UP...
STANDING OVER ME WERE TWO **NUDE WOMEN**...

I THOUGHT PERHAPS I HAD WASHED ASHORE ON A **NUDE BEACH**. THEN JUST BEFORE I LOST CONSCIOUSNESS...
...I SAW THEY WORE THE **HABITS OF NUNS**.

I AWOKE IN A STRANGE ROOM. I REMEMBERED THE **NUDIST NUNS**. HAD THEY BEEN A **HALLUCINATION**? THEN THE DOOR OPENED...
...AND I SAW THAT THEY WERE **REAL**...

WHEN I WAS **RECOVERED** FROM MY **ORDEAL**, I WAS TAKEN TO THE **MOTHER SUPERIOR**...

WELCOME TO **GOAT ISLAND** — AND WELCOME TO OUR **CONVENT**.
NO DOUBT YOU HAVE NOTICED SOMETHING **UNUSUAL** ABOUT US...
AS A MATTER OF **FACT**, I—

IT IS OUR **VOW** THAT WE SHOULD ALWAYS GO ABOUT **NAKED**. THE REASON FOR THIS IS **SECRET**. INDEED, THE VERY **EXISTENCE** OF OUR ORDER IS SECRET—
—SO SECRET **NOT EVEN THE POPE** KNOWS ABOUT US!

THE **ONLY MENTION** OF THIS **CONVENT** IN THE OUTSIDE WORLD IS IN AN **ANCIENT BOOK** KEPT UNDER LOCK AND KEY IN THE **VATICAN**, WITH INSTRUCTIONS NOT TO OPEN TILL **JUDGMENT DAY**...
ROMANS 11:32

BECAUSE OUR SECRET MUST BE KEPT, THEN, NO ONE WHO COMES TO THIS ISLAND MAY EVER LEAVE!

WHAT?!
ESCAPE IS IMPOSSIBLE. THERE ARE NO BOATS ON THE ISLAND, AND EVEN IF THERE WERE—
—YOU WOULD FIND THE WATERS UNNAVIGABLE!

IT IS THE LORD'S WILL THAT YOU REMAIN HERE AS OUR PERMANENT GUEST. WE WILL SERVE YOU...
...YOU NEED DO NO WORK NOR FOLLOW ANY RULES —BUT ONE...

...DEEP IN OUR DUNGEON IS A DEMON WHICH IT IS OUR SACRED DUTY TO GUARD TILL JUDGMENT DAY...
NEVER INTERFERE WITH THIS DUTY!

I DOUBTED THERE WAS TRULY A DEMON IN THE DUNGEON. AND I DOUBTED TOO IT WAS THE LORD'S WILL I STAY ON THE ISLAND. BUT IT MIGHT AS WELL HAVE BEEN, FOR ONE THING WAS TRUE: THERE WAS NOT A BOAT TO BE FOUND ANYWHERE ON THE ISLAND.
ROMANS 11:32
I KNOW A LITTLE ABOUT BOATING, SO IF I'D BEEN ABLE TO FIND A BOAT, I WOULD HAVE ESCAPED—AND FOUND OUT FOR MYSELF WHETHER OR NOT THE WATERS AROUND THE ISLAND WERE UNNAVIGABLE, AS THE MOTHER SUPERIOR HAD WARNED...

BUT THERE WAS NO BOAT—AND I DIDN'T KNOW THE FIRST THING ABOUT BUILDING A RAFT. SO ALL I COULD DO WAS LOOK OUT TO SEA AND HOPE FOR RESCUE FROM THESE CRAZY, GOAT-SACRIFICING NUNS. THEN ONE NIGHT WHILE THE NUNS WERE AT THEIR PRAYERS...
HEY, MISS! OVER HERE!
A MAN'S VOICE CALLED TO ME FROM UNDER A PILE OF ROCKS...

COME CLOSER! HURRY! YOU'RE DRESSED—SO I KNOW YOU'RE NOT ONE OF THEM! CAN I TRUST YOU?
YES—BUT WHO ARE YOU?

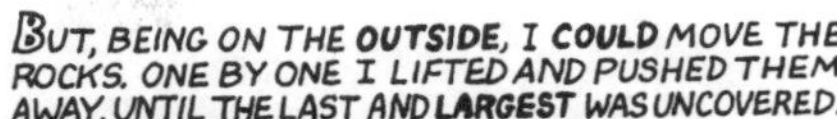

SOME DEMON, I THOUGHT. IF ANYTHING, HE LOOKED RATHER CHRIST-LIKE WITH HIS BEARD AND SAD EYES...

WE FLED TO THE OTHER SIDE OF THE ISLAND AND HID IN THE WOODS. HE SAID HE WOULD BUILD A RAFT COME DAYLIGHT.

I DON'T KNOW WHAT CAME OVER ME. MAYBE IT WAS HIS SAD EYES-HIS LONELINESS-MY LONELINESS-OUR CLOSENESS-HIS WARMTH-OUR HEARTS BEATING TOGETHER FASTER AND FASTER...

LOOK UPON YOUR SIN! SEE WHAT YOU HAVE LAIN WITH— THIS ANIMAL—THIS MONSTER—THIS DEMON!
BAAA!

PAN IS HIS NAME—PAN THE SATYR...
HALF MAN, HALF GOAT! WORSHIPPED AS A GOD IN PAGAN TIMES-THEN IN THE TIME OF CONSTANTINE CAPTURED AND BROUGHT HERE, WHERE FOR CENTURIES OUR ORDER HAS GUARDED HIM! HAD HE ESCAPED IT WOULD HAVE MEANT THE END OF THE CHRISTIAN ERA!

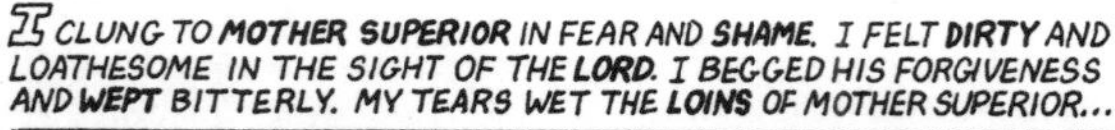

I CLUNG TO MOTHER SUPERIOR IN FEAR AND SHAME. I FELT DIRTY AND LOATHESOME IN THE SIGHT OF THE LORD. I BEGGED HIS FORGIVENESS AND WEPT BITTERLY. MY TEARS WET THE LOINS OF MOTHER SUPERIOR...

THERE IS ONE WAY YOU CAN CLEANSE YOURSELF AND ATONE FOR YOUR SIN— YOU MUST TAKE THE VOW, AS WE HAVE DONE!

FOR WE, LIKE YOU, EACH WERE WASHED ASHORE UPON THIS ISLAND, AND FELL EVENTUALLY TO PAN'S TEMPTATION...
WE TOO HAVE LAIN WITH HIM IN THE FULL MOON, EXPERIENCED HIS TRANSFORMATION, AND TO OUR SHAME BECOME HIS NYMPHS!

AND NOW YOU, LIKE US, MUST BEAR HIS GOAT-CHILD...

AND YOU MUST TAKE THIS VOW...
...TO JOIN US, AND STAND EVER READY TO PREVENT PAN'S ESCAPE, LEST THE WORLD FALL TO PAGANISM— AND TO ALWAYS REMAIN IN THE STATE OF SHAME IN WHICH YOU WERE FOUND-NAKED-AS PENANCE FOR YOUR FALL— YET DO SO PROUDLY...
...FOR IF IT IS TRUE THAT THROUGH THE FLESH WE FALL, AND IF BY FALLING FIND SALVATION, THEN SACREDLY SHOULD WE HOLD THE FLESH AND HOLY BE OUR SIN!

THAT'S MY TRAIL.

I'M GLAD I FOUND YOU.
IT'S PERFECT.

IT'S PERFECT JUST PERFECT.

I'LL STITCH YOU UP NOW.
COULDN'T YOU STAY?

I'M SORRY, BUT I HAVE TO GET THESE BACK RIGHT AWAY

I HOPE SHE HAS GOOD TEETH.

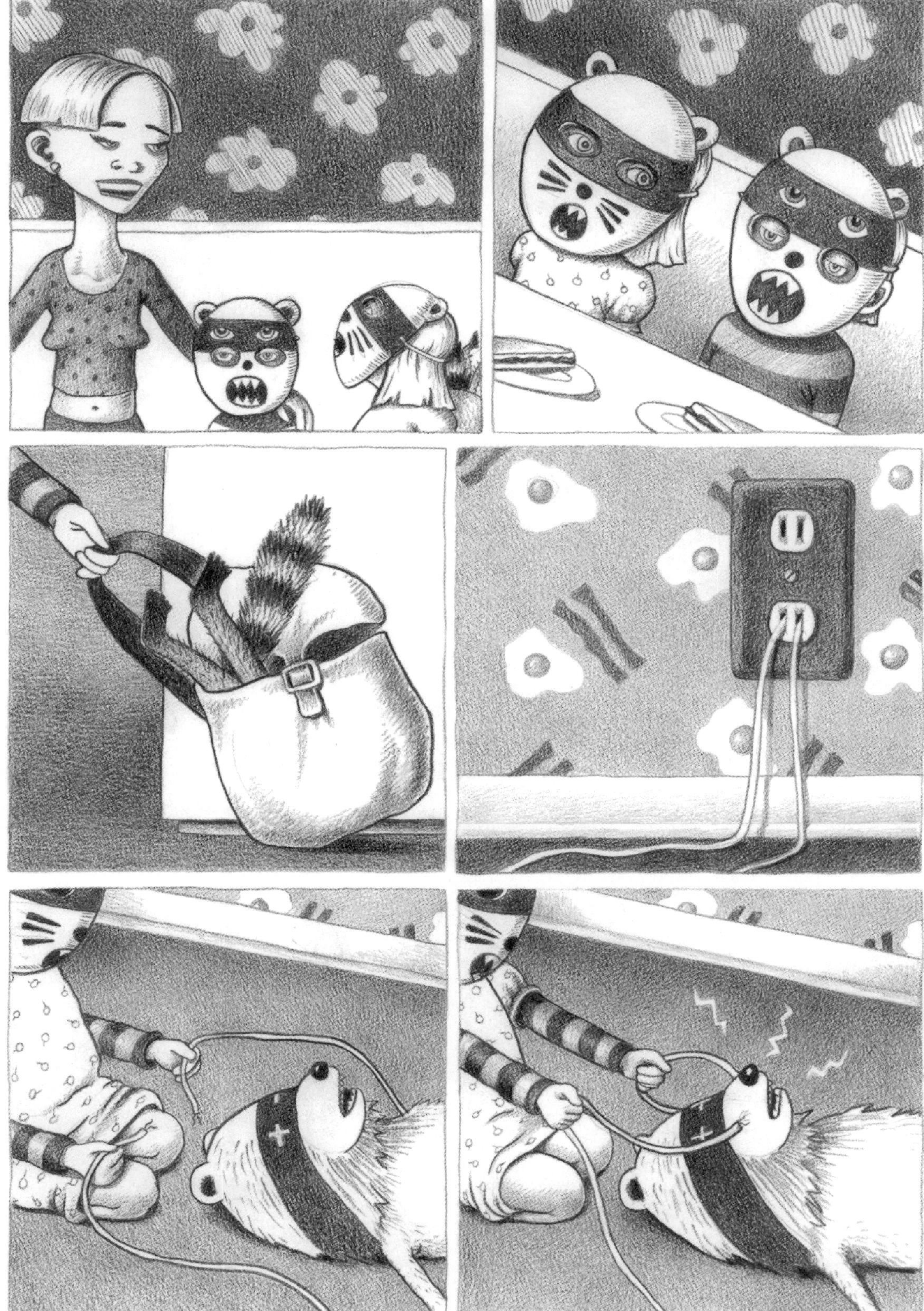

Renée French

The Road To Rana Poona
THERE ARE MANY ROADS TO RANA POONA. IT IS A LAND WITHIN.
1924: AL LEDICKER SITS IN WEBER'S AT CONEY ISLAND, SIPPING BOOTLEG HOOTCH AND WATCHING THE WORLD GO BY.
PROHIBITION IS ON, BUT IF THEY KNOW YOU AT WEBER'S THEIR "SPECIAL" SODAS ARE KNOWN TO WORK WONDERS!
AS AL SIPS, HE IS LULLED INTO A STRANGE REVERIE.
IS IT SOMETHING ABOUT THE DANCER?
OR IS IT THE TUNE? HAS HE HEARD IT BEFORE SOMEWHERE?
WAS IT AT CONEY? GOD! IT MUST HAVE BEEN BACK IN 1894 WHEN HE WAS HERE LAST!
PINKY
HE WAS JUST A KID THEN, WITH A TROUPE STARRING THE GREAT LITTLE EGYPT!

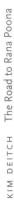

GREAT DAYS! COULD AL EVER FORGET THOSE AFTERNOONS OF SWEET CHILDHOOD? HE, EGYPT, AND PINKY THE ELEPHANT WOULD SIT SPELLBOUND LISTENING TO PINKY'S TRAINER, A STRANGE LAD NAMED KARI.
3 WAY
THERE ARE MANY ROADS TO RANA POONA. IT IS A LAND WITHIN.
3 WAY
NOBODY KNEW MUCH ABOUT KARI, BUT HE SURE MADE A HIT WITH AL'S DAD, "DOC" LEDICKER, WHEN HE CAME UP WITH THE FORMULA FOR LEDICKER'S FAMOUS THREE WAY OIL.
SIMMER SLOWLY FOR THREE DAYS.
GRAIN ALCOHOL
OPIUM
3 WAY
LEDICKER 3 WAY! CURING THE WORLD
ANYWAY, DOC WAS PREOCCUPIED WITH PLANS FOR BREAKING INTO THE BIG TIME.
LEDICKER PRESENTS...
MIGHTY ENGINES COLLIDING!
SEE IT JULY 4th! 50¢ ADMISSION

!
AND THAT'S WHERE THE TROUBLE STARTED. KARI HAD A PRESENTMENT OF GREAT DANGER IF DOC WENT THROUGH WITH HIS PLAN!
BUT HIS EFFORTS TO WARN DOC FELL ON DEAF EARS.
AND HIS PLAN TO SAVE AL, BY KID-NAPPING HIM, WAS A BIG DISASTER!
THEN THE GREAT DAY CAME.
AND IN A JAIL CELL NEARBY, KARI BEGAN TO PLAY A DOLEFUL TUNE PITCHED SO LOW NO HUMAN EARS COULD HEAR.

BUT BACK ON THE FIELD, A CERTAIN PAIR OF EARS HAVE HEARD.
PINKY TO THE RESCUE!
3 WAY
KEERASH!
3 WAY
DOC WAS PRETTY UPSET,
BUT STRANGELY QUIET WHEN KARI, PINKY AND EGYPT DISAPPEARED WITHOUT A TRACE THE NEXT DAY.

BUT AS USUAL, DOC LANDED ON HIS FEET. HE EVEN PROMOTED A MEMORIAL CIGAR OF THE MOMENTIOUS EVENT.
PINKY PERFECTO
3 WAY
10¢
Pinky Perfecto
10¢
AL NOTICED THE WAY HE'D GO INTO AN ALMOST HYPNOTIC REVERIE WHEN HE LIT ONE UP.
IT SEEMED TO AL AS THOUGH DOC WAS SECRETLY THINKING OF THE MISSING THREE FAR AWAY IN RANA POONA.
MEN
THESE LONG FORGOTTEN THOUGHTS ARE STILL WITH AL AS HE AMBLES OFF TO THE MEN'S ROOM.

THERE, HE GETS A REAL SURPRISE!

THE MEN'S ROOM ATTENDANT IS NONE OTHER THAN THE MYSTERIOUS MISSING ELEPHANT BOY, KARI!

HE LAUGHS HEARTILY WHEN AL TELLS HIM HOW SURE HE WAS THAT HE, EGYPT AND PINKY HAD GONE TO MYSTIC RANA POONA.

EGYPT AND I NEVER LEFT CONEY ISLAND.

WE HAVE A LITTLE PLACE RIGHT NEAR THE NEW SUBWAY. THAT'S HER DANCING OUT THERE.

WHEN AL GETS BACK OUT, A BIG POLICE RAID IS UNDERWAY!

I WARNED YOU, TONY. BUY YOUR HOOCH FROM THE BIG GUY OR NOT AT ALL.

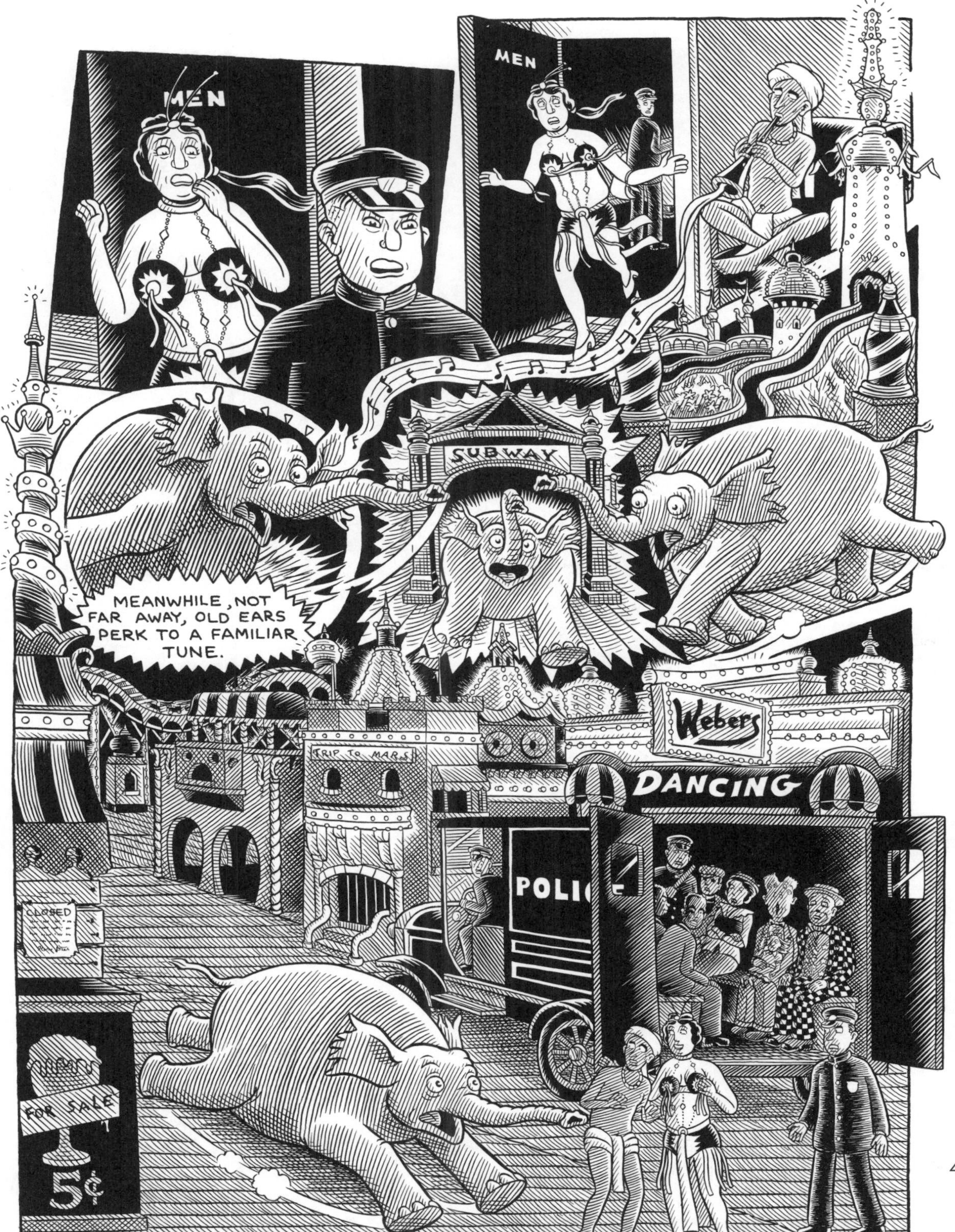
MEN
MEN
SUBWAY
MEANWHILE, NOT FAR AWAY, OLD EARS PERK TO A FAMILIAR TUNE.
TRIP TO MARS
Webers
DANCING
POLICE
CLOSED
FOR SALE
5¢

SO, THE JOB SUPPLYING LIQUOR TO WEBER'S IS OVER?
LUNA PARK
YES, AND I WAS RECOGNIZED AS WELL.
NOW WE MUST GO WITHIN.
SUBWAY
SOON A LIGHT AT THE END OF THE TUNNEL...
KEEERANG!
...AS THE CONEY ISLAND SPECIAL SMASHES INTO THEM.

LATER, OUT ON BAIL, AL LIGHTS UP ONE OF HIS FATHER'S OLD PINKY PERFECTOS.
PINKY PERFECTO
3 WAY
10¢
HE CAN'T HELP IT. HE'S GETTING THAT SAME CRAZY NOTION THAT AT LAST THOSE THREE HAVE FOUND THE ROAD TO RANA POONA.
Kim Deitch

1
2
3
4
5
6
7
8
9
10
11
12
R. Sala

The GROLO & co.
by: JOHNSON
WE'RE NOT TAKEN IN BY THAT DOG'S IMAGINARY ANTICS!
...OH, NO! WE PREFER---
DYNAMITE!
HEH! HEH!
Slub--- Slub---
Bang.
GO GETTIM, SHERIFF!!!
GROW-LOW!
SLUB.
HAVE YOU BEEN KILLING PRETTY SPARROWS?
UH...
SSSSSSSSSS
DON'T YOU HAVE ANY FEELINGS?
NO
YOU ARE A DOG.
SSSSSSSSS
A VERY BAD DOG.
KER-
I KNOW I'M A BAD DOG, BUT IT'S NOT MY FAULT!
BLOOEY
Bang.

FUNNY BUNNY
GROAN
Dunno?... ain't nuthin' good...
Can't seem to Shake this dark losin' end...
Mebbe I just need to eat better...
REFUS
Oh - chew - God! -ump- What is - chew - wrong wimme?!
-Smak-
G'wan wit ya!
It's these times... All this confusion and madness in the worl'... Lawd, Lawd.
GRUNT
HAW HAW
Cheezus!
G☆!♁ dizgusting!
WOOF!
AKK NO AK NO!
Th' harrah...
Yeah? Hold on. Hold on. Thor's killed Something again...
END

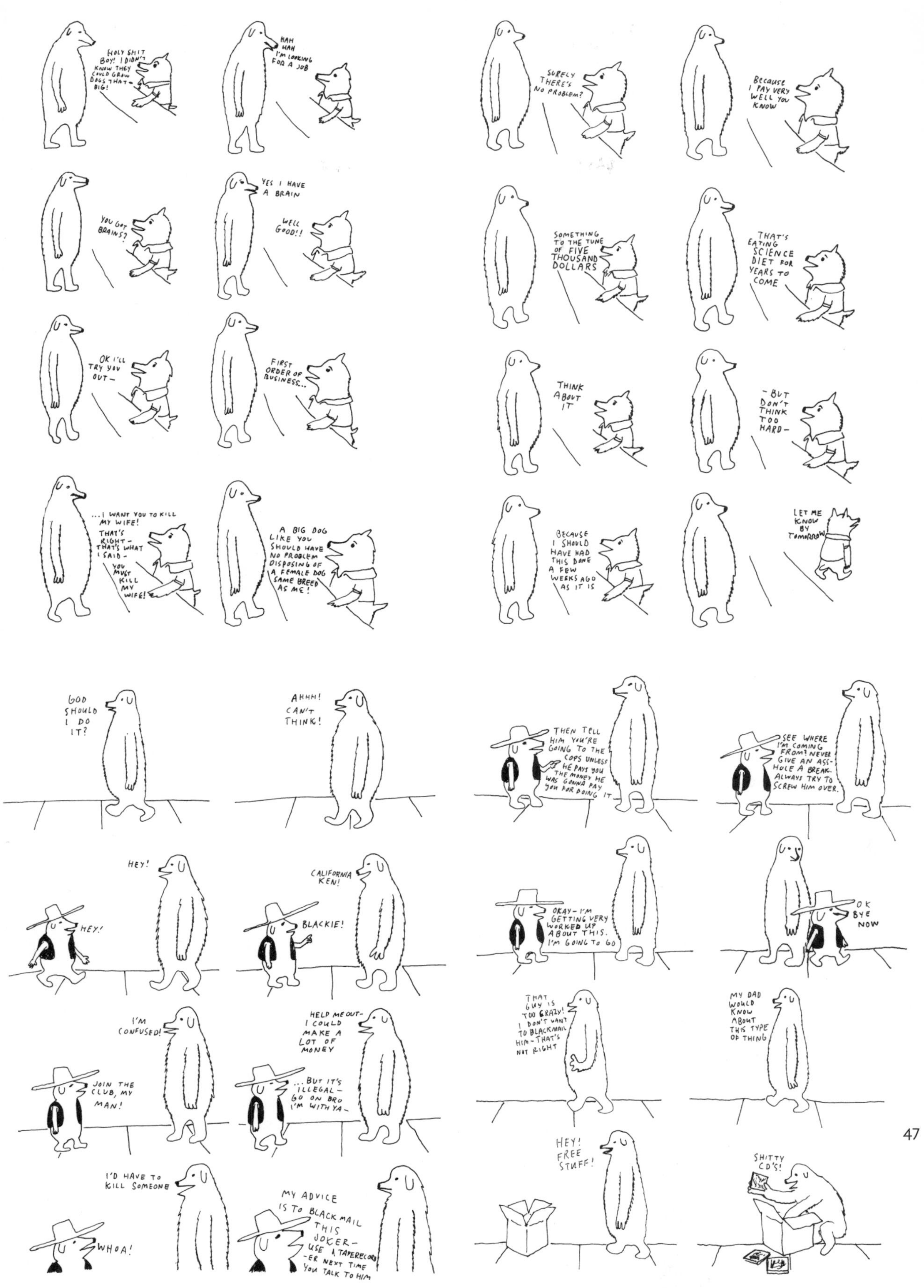
HOLY SHIT BOY! I DIDN'T KNOW THEY COULD GROW DOGS THAT BIG!
HAH HAH I'M LOOKING FOR A JOB
YOU GOT BRAINS?
YES I HAVE A BRAIN
WELL GOOD!!
OK I'LL TRY YOU OUT—
FIRST ORDER OF BUSINESS...
...I WANT YOU TO KILL MY WIFE!
THAT'S RIGHT— THAT'S WHAT I SAID—
YOU MUST KILL MY WIFE!
A BIG DOG LIKE YOU SHOULD HAVE NO PROBLEM DISPOSING OF A FEMALE DOG SAME BREED AS ME!
SURELY THERE'S NO PROBLEM?
Because I PAY VERY WELL YOU KNOW
SOMETHING TO THE TUNE OF FIVE THOUSAND DOLLARS
THAT'S EATING SCIENCE DIET FOR YEARS TO COME
THINK ABOUT IT
—BUT DON'T THINK TOO HARD—
BECAUSE I SHOULD HAVE HAD THIS DONE A FEW WEEKS AGO AS IT IS
LET ME KNOW BY TOMORROW
GOD SHOULD I DO IT?
AHHH! CAN'T THINK!
HEY!
HEY!
CALIFORNIA KEN!
BLACKIE!
I'M CONFUSED!
JOIN THE CLUB, MY MAN!
HELP ME OUT— I COULD MAKE A LOT OF MONEY
...BUT IT'S ILLEGAL— GO ON BRO I'M WITH YA—
I'D HAVE TO KILL SOMEONE
WHOA!
MY ADVICE IS TO BLACKMAIL THIS JOKER— USE A TAPERECORD-ER NEXT TIME YOU TALK TO HIM
THEN TELL HIM YOU'RE GOING TO THE COPS UNLESS HE PAYS YOU THE MONEY HE WAS GONNA PAY YOU FOR DOING IT
SEE WHERE I'M COMING FROM? NEVER GIVE AN ASS-HOLE A BREAK. ALWAYS TRY TO SCREW HIM OVER.
OKAY— I'M GETTING VERY WORKED UP ABOUT THIS. I'M GOING TO GO
OK BYE NOW
THAT GUY IS TOO CRAZY! I DON'T WANT TO BLACKMAIL HIM— THAT'S NOT RIGHT
MY DAD WOULD KNOW ABOUT THIS TYPE OF THING
HEY! FREE STUFF!
SHITTY CD'S!

AHEM, AHEM, WELL HOWDY. NICE DAY ISN'T IT, MISS—?

?

SIR!

I DON'T KNOW YOU. HOW DARE YOU SPEAK TO A PERFECK STRANGER.

YOU OLD FLIRT!

THE NERVE. THE VERY NERVE.

THAT'S WHAT COMES OF NOT WASHING MY FACE EVERY DAY.

THE BUNGLE FAMILY AN EVENING WITH THE LAW

THE BUNGLE FAMILY

An Evening with the Law.

By H. J. TUTHILL

YES, BULLWINKLE WOULD HAVE MADE A WONDERFUL LAWYER. HE LOVES TO ARGUE, ABOUT ANYTHING. HE'S ALWAYS BORROWING BOOKS FROM LAWYERS. WE HAVE THE BASEMENT FULL OF THEM.

KNOW LAW AND YOU KNOW IT ALL. FOR INSTANCE TAKE THE LEGAL PHRASE **MOPUS**......BY THE WAY, WHAT IS THAT NOISE?

OH, THAT'S ONLY THE MAN UPSTAIRS CHOPPING WOOD IN HIS PARLOR I GUESS.

CHOPPING WOOD IN A HOUSE? THAT'S AGAINST THE CONSTITUTION. WHAT HAVE YOU DONE ABOUT IT? YOU SHOULD GIVE HIM A WRITTEN NOTICE. GET ME A PEN AND PAPER, OLD CHAP, SO I CAN PROTECT YOUR LEGAL INTERESTS.

EVERYTHING HAS TO BE VERY LEGAL THESE DAYS.

I'VE SPOKEN TO HIM ABOUT IT.

HERE IT IS, LISTEN, WHEREAS I HEREBY ASK, DEMAND AND REQUEST THAT YOU HEREBY STOP, DESIST AND CEASE ALL NOISE COMING THROUGH AND EMANATING FROM ABOVE, CEILING OR TAKE THE LEGAL CONSEQUENSES. NOW LET'S GO UP AND HAND IT TO HIM LEGALLY.

THAT SOUNDS VERY LEGAL, BULLWINKLE. VERY.

HE'S VERY TOUGH, VERY.

FINE! THE LAW LOVES 'EM LIKE THAT. THE BIGGER THEY COME THE HARDER THEY FALL—LEGALLY. THE LAW STANDS SOLIDLY IN BACK OF YOU IN A CASE LIKE THIS WHERE YOU ARE WHAT WE CALL IN LAW, **LEX TALONS.**

SAY, SAY, WHAT'S THE IDEA OF HANDING ME THIS DAFFY NOTE SIMPLY BECAUSE OUR BEST LAMP FELL ON THE FLOOR? ARE YOU TWO PILLS LOOKING FOR TROUBLE?

PILLS?

BE CAREFUL WHAT YOU SAY, SIR. STRIKE MY FRIEND HERE AT YOUR PERIL. I DEFY YOU TO STRIKE HIM!

SO!

DON'T FLINCH FROM HIM GEORGE. **THE LAW WILL PROTECT YOU. AND PLENTY. ALSO—**

AND NOW FOR YOU. STOP!

STOP, BULLWINKLE! STOP! SO I CAN GET HIM. STOP!

WHOOIE! WHAT A MAN. WHAT A SOCK HE HAS. THE BEST I COULD DO WAS WIN TWO ROUNDS OUT OF FIVE.

I KNOW! I WAS A LEGAL WITNESS TO ALL OF IT. DON'T WORRY. WE'VE GOT HIM STOPPED. HE ASSAULTED YOU **PRO TEM** AND THREATENED ME. WHAT DID HE STRIKE YOU WITH?

HIS FIST! WHOOIE! I'LL HAVE TO SIT DOWN AGAIN AND REST. **WHOOIE!** EVERY TIME HE HIT ME I FELT AS THOUGH I WAS ON FIRE. HIS FISTS ARE—

MERELY HIS FISTS, EH? BY JOVE, HOW I WISH HE HAD USED A WEAPON OF SOME SORT ON YOU. MAYBE AN AX. THEN WE COULD CHARGE HIM WITH **PARTICEPS CRIMINUS.**

LISTEN BULLWINKLE, DID I UNDERSTAND YOU TO SAY YOU WISH THAT BABY HAD ALSO USED AN AX ON ME?

ABSOLUTELY! THEN WE COULD—**BE CAREFUL, BUNGLE. NO VIOLENCE. THE LAW STANDS IN BACK OF ME AND.....**

THE IDEA! SUCH EXCITEMENT. WHO STARTED THE—?

BULLWINKLE. SUCH CRUST. TALKING ME INTO GOING UPSTAIRS AND THEN BEING SORRY I WASN'T CRIPPLED FOR LIFE.

YOUR EYES! BOTH CLOSED! YOU'RE A WRECK!

THAT'S FINE! IT'S EVIDENCE. THESE BRUISES MAKE ME A PERFECT CASE OF **CAVEAT EMPTOR.**

YES SIR! MARK MY WORD, YOU'LL BE SORRY YOU HAD TROUBLE WITH BULLWINKLE. HE'S ALWAYS TALKING ABOUT THE LAW, AND HE WAS TALKING ABOUT IT WHEN HE AND EMMA LEFT.

WELL IF HE HANDLES THIS CASE LIKE HE DID THE FIRST ONE THIS EVENING MY ONLY WORRY IS THE SKIN I KNOCKED OFF MY KNUCKLES.

11.17.29

Tuthill

Harry J. Tuthill, The Bungle Family, *original artwork for Sunday page, November 17, 1929 (hand-watercolored sometime after publication, 23 x 29 in., India ink on Bristol board). Collection of Rob Stolzer.*

Milt Gross, Dave's Delicatessen, *Sunday page, June 11, 1933.*

Bill Holman, Smokey Stover, *Sunday page, October 25, 1942. Collection of Craig Yoe.*

Harvey Kurtzman, Hey Look, *originally published in* Lana No. 2, October 1948. *Collection of Glenn Bray.*

Harvey Kurtzman, Genius, *originally published in* John Wayne Adventure Comics *No. 12, December 1951. Collection of Glenn Bray.*

Harvey Kurtzman, Egghead Doodle, *originally published in* My Friend Irma *No. 5, October 1950. Collection of Glenn Bray.*

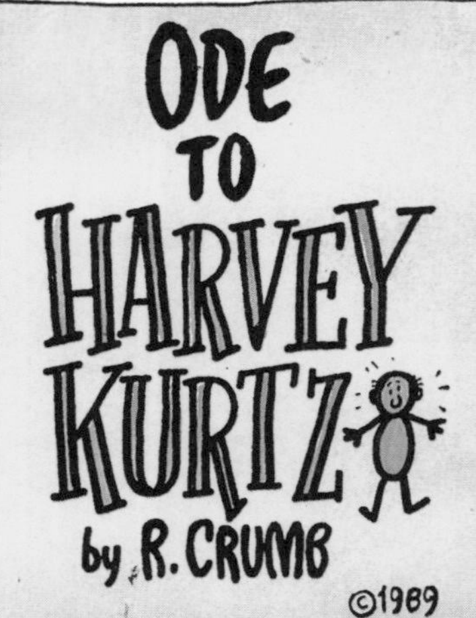
ODE TO HARVEY KURTZ
by R. CRUMB
©1989

I REMEMBER WHEN I SAW THE FIRST ISSUE OF MAD IN A MAGAZINE STORE, OCTOBER, 1952... I WAS NINE YEARS OLD... IT MADE A DEEP IMPRESSION...
WHA-A-?
"IT'S MELVIN"??
??
I'M NOT READY FOR THIS!
WITCHES TALES
TERROR
TALES FROM THE CRYPT
MAD

A YEAR OR TWO PASSED... I GREW OLDER... THE COVER OF MAD #11 CHANGED THE WAY I SAW THE WORLD FOREVER!
THIS LOOKS JUST LIKE LIFE MAGAZINE, ONLY— ONLY—
MAD
PANIC

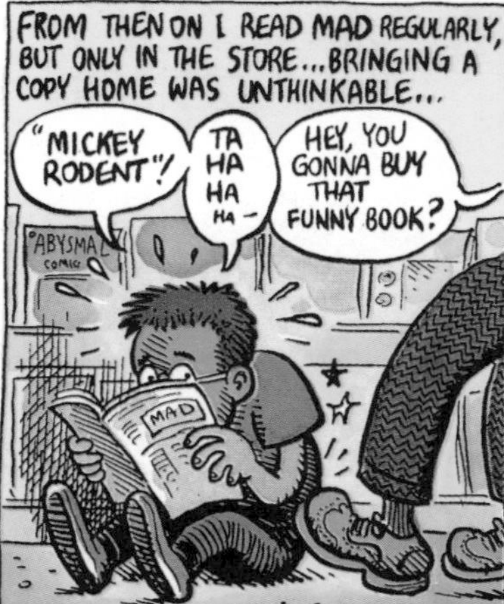
FROM THEN ON I READ MAD REGULARLY, BUT ONLY IN THE STORE... BRINGING A COPY HOME WAS UNTHINKABLE...
"MICKEY RODENT"!
TA HA HA HA
HEY, YOU GONNA BUY THAT FUNNY BOOK?
ABYSMAL
MAD

AFTER MAD TURNED INTO A MAGAZINE IT WAS HARD TO FIND AND I LOST TRACK OF IT, BUT THEN ONE DAY IN 1957 AT THE LOCAL SODA SHOP I SAW HUMBUG #2 SITTING IN THE MAGAZINE RACK.
WHAT IS THAT?!
HUMBUG
DIG
PHOTO PLAY
HOTROD
LIZ

THAT COVER WAS THE HEAVIEST CULTURAL ARTIFACT I HAD EVER SEEN! I WAS SENT!!
DING DONG

FROM THAT MOMENT I BECAME A RABID FAN OF HARVEY KURTZMAN... I LIVED, BREATHED AND ATE THE PAGES OF HIS MAGAZINES.... I WAS TRULY IN LOVE!!
WHAT ARTWORK!
WHAT A VISION OF AMERICA!

I HAD TO HAVE THEM ALL... I ROAMED THE ALLEYS LOOKING IN TRASH CANS FOR OLD ISSUES FROM 1955 & '56... THEM THINGS WERE DOGGONE HARD TO FIND!
OH, I MUST HAVE MADS 24, 26, 27 & 28!!

I HAD DREAMS OF IMAGINARY ISSUES OF MAD MAGAZINES I WAS MISSING!
OBOY! MINE ALL MINE!

I ASPIRED TO DRAW LIKE THE MAD-HUMBUG ARTISTS, AND WRITE SATIRE LIKE KURTZMAN ....IT WAS TOUGH...
HM—PRETTY GOOD... NOT BAD FOR A FIFTEEN-YEAR-OLD....
...KINDA STOOPID, ACKSHULLY...

IT WAS VERY FRUSTRATING...I WAS A RANK AMATEUR.....
HOW DO THEY DO IT!!?
I GIVE UP!!
I'LL NEVER BE A PRO!!

FIVE OR SIX YEARS PASSED...I GREW OLDER... I SENT ONE OF MY FUNNY ANIMAL CARTOONS TO KURTZMAN, WHO WAS THEN EDITING HELP MAGAZINE...ONE DAY A REPLY ARRIVED; MY FIRST COMMUNICATION FROM MY HERO!!
HE LIKES MY CARTOON!!

SUMMER OF '64...SOMEHOW I ENDED UP IN NEW YORK WORKING AS ASSISTANT TO THE ASSISTANT EDITOR OF HELP...I COULDN'T BELIEVE MY GOOD FORTUNE...
CRUMB, YOU NUTCASE, CAN YOU RUN THIS OVER TO HARRY CHESTER FOR ME?
SURE HARVEY!

HARVEY WAS A MENTOR TO ME DURING THIS PERIOD. HE GAVE ME LOTS OF ENCOURAGEMENT AND SOUND ADVICE ABOUT THE CARTOONING AND COMMERCIAL ART GAME AND COPING WITH THE WORLD IN GENERAL.
SHMUCK! WHATAYA DOING?? WHO EVER HEARD OF MAYO ON A CORN-BEEF SAN'WICH!! HOW GOYISH CAN Y' GET?!
HUH?

HE HELPED ME GET WORK AND EVEN OFFERED ME A JOB DOING BACKGROUNDS FOR THE BEAUTIFULLY WATER-COLORED LITTLE ANNIE FANNY STORIES HE WAS DOING FOR PLAYBOY...I SPENT WEEKS TRYING TO LEARN THE TECHNIQUE...
THIS LOOKS SHITTY!
I'LL NEVER BE A PRO!!
I GIVE UP!

EVEN THOUGH I'VE MADE A NAME IN MY OWN RIGHT I STILL FEEL LIKE A WORSHIPFUL FANBOY IN HIS PRESENSE!
SMOOCH!
HARVEY, YOU SAVED MY FUCKIN' LIFE, MAN!
CRUMB, YOU'RE A NUT CASE!

YEARS WENT BY...I GREW OLDER...IT'S 1989.. HARVEY CALLED AND INVITED ME TO ILLUSTRATE ONE OF THE STORIES FOR THIS BOOK PRESS PUBLICATIONS WAS DOING. I WAS THRILLED TO HAVE THE OPPORTUNITY TO WORK FROM HARVEY'S GREAT PENCIL LAYOUTS—JUST LIKE ELDER, WOOD AND DAVIS!
HM... PRETTY GOOD... NOT BAD FOR A FIFTEEN-YEAR-OLD...

MAN, IT WAS TOUGH!
I GIVE UP!
HOW DO THEY DO IT!?!
I'LL NEVER BE A PRO!
end

MAD

HUMOR IN A JUGULAR VEIN—10¢

BEAUTIFUL GIRL OF THE MONTH

READS 'MAD'

BASIL WOLVERTON

AN ENTERTAINING EC COMIC

TALES CALCULATED TO DRIVE YOU . . .

NUMBER 11...MAY

Basil Wolverton, original artwork for the cover of Mad *No. 11, May 1954,*

KURTZMAN'S MAD WORLD

Adam Gopnik

Harvey Kurtzman was a New Yorker. He was born in Brooklyn, in 1924; moved with his family to the Bronx; and went to high school in Manhattan and launched his career as a cartoonist and comic-book impresario there. As a kid, he was a street artist—drawing comic strips on the pavement with chalk. He joined the Army during the Second World War, and after his discharge he went to work for the wildest and most notorious of all the New York comic-book publishers: E.C., whose line of grisly horror comics (including "The Vault of Horror" and "The Crypt of Terror") occasioned the 1954 congressional investigations into comics and, eventually, the self-censoring Comics Code. Kurtzman disliked the horror comics, though, and he made his living, and his early reputation, writing and drawing war comics for E.C.; they were memorable for their marriage of realistic writing—conscientiously, even obsessively researched—and a slightly abstract, animated, bounding cartoon style.

In 1952, he urged E.C.'s publisher, William Gaines, to publish a satirical comic book. Gaines, who was game for almost anything, agreed, and the result, in the autumn of 1952, was *Mad*. The first issue consisted solely of takeoffs on other E.C. comic-book genres, but soon Kurtzman turned his attention to the whole exploding world of the American media—to Howdy Doody and the Western and the new youth movies, and even to the classic Disney cartoons. *Mad's* panels were a riot of manic detail, and overflowed with indignation at the absurdities of the adult world of the fifties. Kurtzman's *Mad* was the first comic enterprise that got its effects almost entirely from parodying other kinds of popular entertainment. Like Lenny Bruce, whom he influenced, Kurtzman saw that the conventions of pop culture ran so deep in the imagination of his audience—and already stood at so great a remove from real experience—that you could create a new kind of satire just by inventorying them. To say that this became an influential manner in American comedy is to understate the case. Almost all American satire today follows a formula that Harvey Kurtzman thought up.

His was such a sturdy and easily replicable kind of humor that, once *Mad* had been launched and converted into a full-fledged magazine, it didn't need him to keep it going. Having invented a new kind of comedy, Kurtzman left *Mad* in the middle of 1956. Hugh Hefner, then at the first height of his fame, offered to bankroll a new satirical magazine for him, and Kurtzman founded *Trump*, which was, as he put it, kind of a glossy *Mad*—a big-budget *Mad*. But Hefner pulled the plug on *Trump* after two memorable issues, and after that Kurtzman was never quite able to find a vessel for his talent. In the late fifties and early sixties, he ran a couple of smaller, maverick magazines, *Humbug* and *Help!* which were influential for a while and, more important, became places where young cartoonists could apprentice. But they folded, too, and by 1962 Kurtzman had gone back to work for Hefner, for whom he wrote and drew, with Will Elder, "Little Annie Fanny" for more than twenty years.

For many of Kurtzman's young admirers, this was an embarrassment. Kurtzman belonged to an older generation; he made fun of the values of the entertainment world but, unlike his best disciples, at some level he also embraced them. This was, in a sense, his limitation, yet it was also the source of a complete lack of cynicism, which radiated from his life and still radiates from his work. In his last years, Kurtzman, in addition to working as a cartoonist, became a teacher, a guru—a man who impressed on his students the worth of the underloved art of cartooning. There has been scarcely a single cartoonist or animator of note in the last forty years—from R. Crumb and Art Spiegelman to Monty Python's Terry Gilliam and the French cartoonist Goscinny, the co-inventor of "Astérix"—who did not come under his direct influence and encouragement. To make a significant advance in one's art and then to instruct a generation of apprentices in the dignity of their craft perhaps remains the best definition of what it means to be a master.

H.K. (R.I.P.)

BY ART SPIEGELMAN

This essay and the comic strips on Pages 57–59 were originally published in the New Yorker, *March 29, 1993.*

EVEN MOST OF HARVEY'S CARTOONING STUDENTS AT THE SCHOOL OF VISUAL ARTS DIDN'T QUITE REALIZE THAT THE KIND, UNASSUMING GUY THEY CALLED *TEACH*, THE GUY ROGER PRICE ONCE DESCRIBED AS LOOKING "LIKE A BEAGLE WHO IS TOO POLITE TO MENTION THAT SOMEONE IS STANDING ON HIS TAIL," WAS ACTUALLY...

A FURSHLUGGINER GENIUS!

I'VE ASKED ART SPIEGELMAN HERE TO SHOW YOU SLIDES OF HIS WORK... IT'S A CHANCE FOR YOU TO BE EXPOSED TO HIS FRESH NEW PERSPECTIVES, AND IT'S A CHANCE FOR HIM TO MEET **YOU**, TOMORROW'S TOP CARTOONISTS, TODAY...

BUT *MAINLY* IT'S A CHANCE FOR **ME** TO DO A CLASS WITHOUT LIFTING EVEN A PINKIE!

I'M AN OLD MAN, BY GEORGE!

BUT HEY, **LOOK**, HARV. I DIDN'T *BRING* SLIDES OF **MY** WORK. I BROUGHT SLIDES OF ***YOUR*** WORK! AFTER ALL, YOU'RE WHAT MADE ME WANNA **BE** A CARTOONIST!

HEY LOOK

I'M READING HERE WHERE THIS CARTOONIST, SHMILL SHMEISNER, DOES A TAKE-OFF IN HIS CARTOON STRIP...

—ON THE CARTOON STRIP, SHMI'IL SHMABNER, BY NAME, BY SHMAL SHMAPP WHO DOES A TAKE-OFF ON MAH IDEAL—

...SHICK SHMACY, BY SHMESTER SHMOULD, WHO DOES A TAKE-OFF—

—ON SHMONDIE BY SHMICK SHUNG— WHO—

JUST PLAIN TAKES OFF LIKE THIS—

KNOW WHAT I'M TALKING ABOUT?

I DON'T!

In this Style 10/6

KAT

IT WAS 1988. I SHOWED HIS CLASS THE RIGOROUS STRUCTURING AND JAZZY RHYTHMS THAT HARVEY BROUGHT TO HIS EARLY "HEY LOOK" PAGES, AND I TALKED ABOUT **MAD**.

SELF-REFLEXIVE AND CHEERFULLY VULGAR, HARVEY'S EARLY **MAD** COMIC BOOK WAS LIVELIER AND MORE SUBVERSIVELY ANARCHISTIC THAN THE LATER MAGAZINE.

MAD WAS AN URBAN JUNK COLLAGE THAT SAID "PAY ATTENTION! THE MASS MEDIA ARE **LYING** TO YOU... INCLUDING THIS COMIC BOOK!"

I THINK HARVEY'S **MAD** WAS MORE IMPORTANT THAN POT AND LSD IN SHAPING THE GENERATION THAT PROTESTED THE VIETNAM WAR.

MAD

HUMOR IN A JUGULAR VEIN—10¢

BEAUTIFUL GIRL OF THE MONTH

NUMBER 11... MAY

HARV DIDN'T CHANGE THE CULTURE ONLY BY CREATING A NEW MODE OF SATIRE. AT THE HEIGHT OF THE KOREAN WAR HE EDITED, WROTE, AND DREW WAR COMICS— NOT JINGOISTIC TRASH BUT THOROUGHLY RESEARCHED NARRATIVES WITH GREAT MORAL PURPOSE.

NEXT SLIDE, PLEASE.
NO SMOKI

VA-VA VOOM!
WOO WOO!
HOTCHA!
HEH, HEH— WRONG SLIDE. "LITTLE ANNIE FANNY" WAS FROM A LATER POINT IN HARV'S CHECKERED CAREER.

HIS DRAMAS REFLECTED HIS HUMANISM. THEY WERE ABOUT THE PAIN AND SUFFERING OF WAR.
NO MACHO HE-MEN, ONLY SCARED KIDS. THE ENEMIES WEREN'T DEMONS, ONLY OTHER PEOPLE.
TWO-FISTED TALES
10¢
FELLAS! I JUST GOT WORD THEY'RE ARRANGING AN ARMISTICE!
YEAH YEAH! TELL JONESY HERE ABOUT YOUR ARMISTICE! HE'LL BE GLAD!

"LITTLE ANNIE FANNY" © 1969 PLAYBOY. ALL RIGHTS RESERVED.

I ANALYZED HARVEY'S VISUAL STORYTELLING STRUCTURE TO SHOW HOW HE CREATED A PRECISE FORMAL "GRAMMAR" OF COMICS.
I MENTIONED HIS IMPORTANCE AS AN INNOVATOR OF EDITORIAL FORMATS, AND CONCLUDED BY TALKING ABOUT HIS SKILLS AS AN EDITOR WHO NURTURED THE TALENTS OF OTHERS.

EACH PANEL ON THIS PAGE IS BUILT ON VERTICALS. SO, NOW TAKE A LOOK AT THESE PANEL RHYTHMS...

THE CLASS SAT IN AWE. SARAH DOWNS, HARVEY'S ASSISTANT, WAS WEEPING SOFTLY. ONLY HARVEY'S SWEET, FRAIL VOICE, TREMBLING WITH THE PARKINSON'S DISEASE THAT RAVAGED HIM, BROKE THE SILENCE.

GEE, ARTIE. THAT WAS TERRIFIC! COULDJA COME BACK NEXT WEEK AND GIVE US THE SAME LECTURE AGAIN?
S.V.A

"TWO-FISTED TALES" © 1952, 1979 WILLIAM M. GAINES.

AFTERWARDS HARVEY GLOWED WITH PLEASURE. HE WARMLY CLASPED MY HAND.

GOSH, IT WAS INSPIRING! YOU EVEN MADE ME WANNA DRAW COMICS. THANK YOU, ARTIE!
NO, HARVEY. THANK YOU. FOR EVERYTHING!

I LOOKED LOVINGLY AT MY ROLE MODEL, AND FOR A LONG MOMENT WE EMBRACED...

ARTIE!... ARTIE!...
OH, HARVEY!

MY MENTOR WAS WHISPERING SOMETHING TO ME. HE WAS BARELY AUDIBLE:

ARTIE ... PLEASE... LET GO... YOU'RE CRUSHING MY DAMN GLASSES!
WHAT—ME WORRY?
1924-1993

NERVOUS REX
The MALPRACTICE suite
I SUPPOSE
I SUPPOSE I SHOULD ANSWER IT
I HAVE SOMETHING TO READ ---AND I CAN WATCH TV!
I SUPPOSE I SHOULD ANSWER IT
KNOCK KNOCK
MAY I COME IN? I'LL BE ONLY A FEW MINUTES!
KEITH! WE'VE BEEN WAITING TO HEAR FROM YOU!
MAY I COME IN? I'LL BE ONLY A FEW MINUTES!
KEITH! WE'VE BEEN WAITING TO HEAR FROM YOU!
I'D LIKE TO TALK TO YOU, VALERIE!
HE WAS HERE A MINUTE AGO!
HAVING TOLD JUNE THAT HE KNOWS ABOUT JANIE'S PHONE CALL TO HER, WADE NORTON THEN ASKS A QUESTION!
KEEP OUT OF THIS!
I'D LIKE TO TALK TO YOU, VALERIE!
HAVING TOLD JUNE THAT HE KNOWS ABOUT JANIE'S PHONE CALL TO HER, WADE NORTON THEN ASKS A QUESTION!
MAY I COME IN? I'LL BE ONLY A FEW MINUTES!
WE'LL MISS YOU, KEITH!
NOW, JUST A MINUTE, SIR---
I'D LIKE TO TALK TO YOU, VALERIE!
NOW, JUST A MINUTE, SIR---
KEEP OUT OF THIS!
MAY I COME IN? I'LL BE ONLY A FEW MINUTES!
NOW, WAIT A MINUTE, DOCTOR! I WANT YOU TO SEE ME THIS AFTERNOON! I'M LEAVING FOR JAPAN TOMORROW!
I'D LIKE TO TALK TO YOU, VALERIE!
NOW, WAIT A MINUTE, DOCTOR! I WANT YOU TO SEE ME THIS AFTERNOON! I'M LEAVING FOR JAPAN TOMORROW!

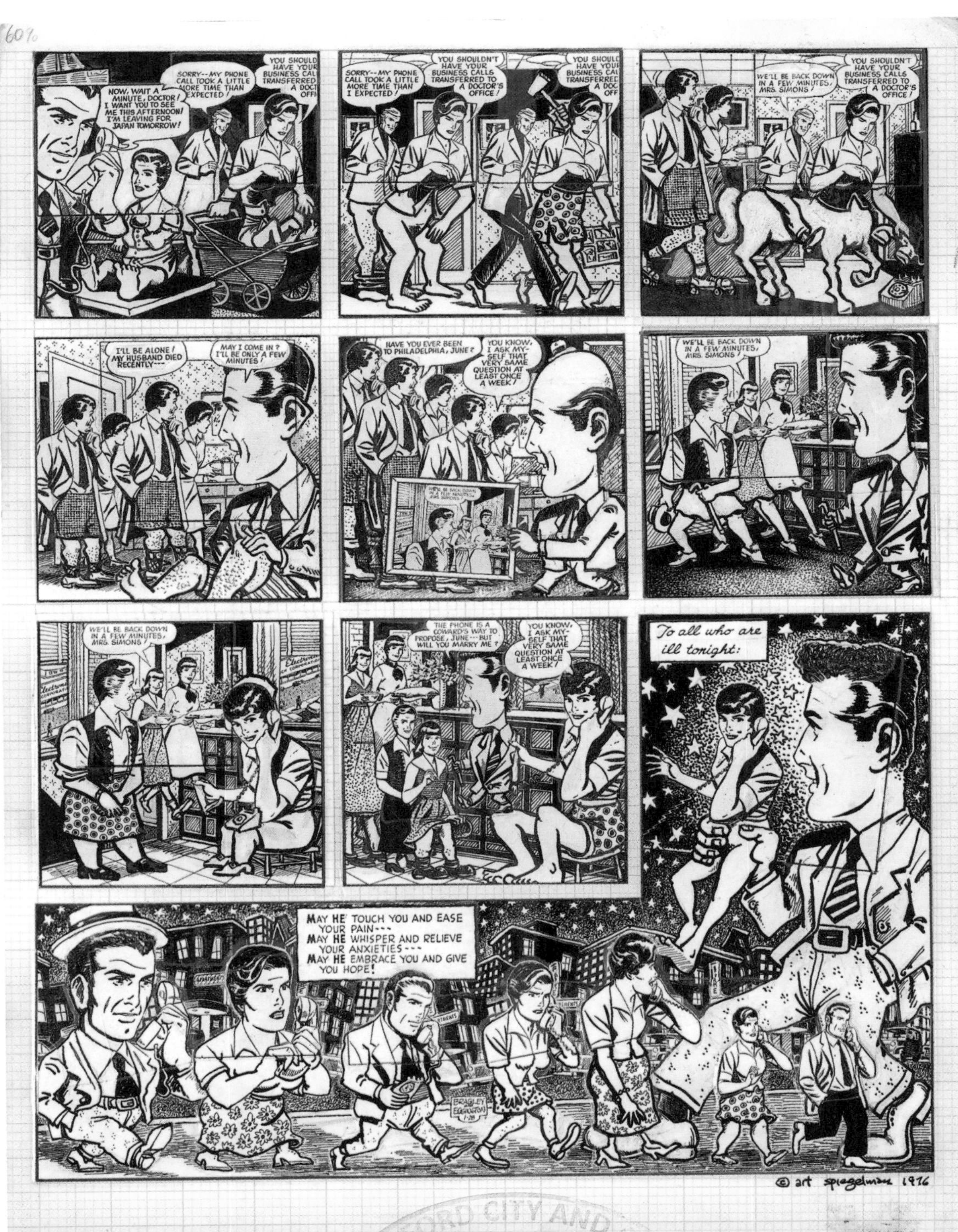
60%
NOW, WAIT A MINUTE, DOCTOR! I WANT YOU TO SEE ME THIS AFTERNOON! I'M LEAVING FOR JAPAN TOMORROW!
SORRY--MY PHONE CALL TOOK A LITTLE MORE TIME THAN I EXPECTED!
YOU SHOULD HAVE YOUR BUSINESS CALL TRANSFERRED A DOCTOR OFFI
SORRY--MY PHONE CALL TOOK A LITTLE MORE TIME THAN I EXPECTED!
YOU SHOULDN'T HAVE YOUR BUSINESS CALLS TRANSFERRED TO A DOCTOR'S OFFICE!
YOU SHOULD HAVE YOUR TRANSFERRED A DOCTOR OFFI
WE'LL BE BACK DOWN IN A FEW MINUTES, MRS. SIMONS!
YOU SHOULDN'T HAVE YOUR BUSINESS CALLS TRANSFERRED TO A DOCTOR'S OFFICE!
I'LL BE ALONE! MY HUSBAND DIED RECENTLY---
MAY I COME IN? I'LL BE ONLY A FEW MINUTES!
HAVE YOU EVER BEEN TO PHILADELPHIA, JUNE?
YOU KNOW, I ASK MY-SELF THAT VERY SAME QUESTION AT LEAST ONCE A WEEK!
WE'LL BE BACK DOWN IN A FEW MINUTES, MRS. SIMONS!
WE'LL BE BACK DOWN IN A FEW MINUTES, MRS. SIMONS!
THE PHONE IS A COWARD'S WAY TO PROPOSE, JUNE---BUT WILL YOU MARRY ME?
YOU KNOW, I ASK MY-SELF THAT VERY SAME QUESTION AT LEAST ONCE A WEEK!
To all who are ill tonight:
MAY HE TOUCH YOU AND EASE YOUR PAIN---
MAY HE WHISPER AND RELIEVE YOUR ANXIETIES---
MAY HE EMBRACE YOU AND GIVE YOU HOPE!
© art spiegelman 1976

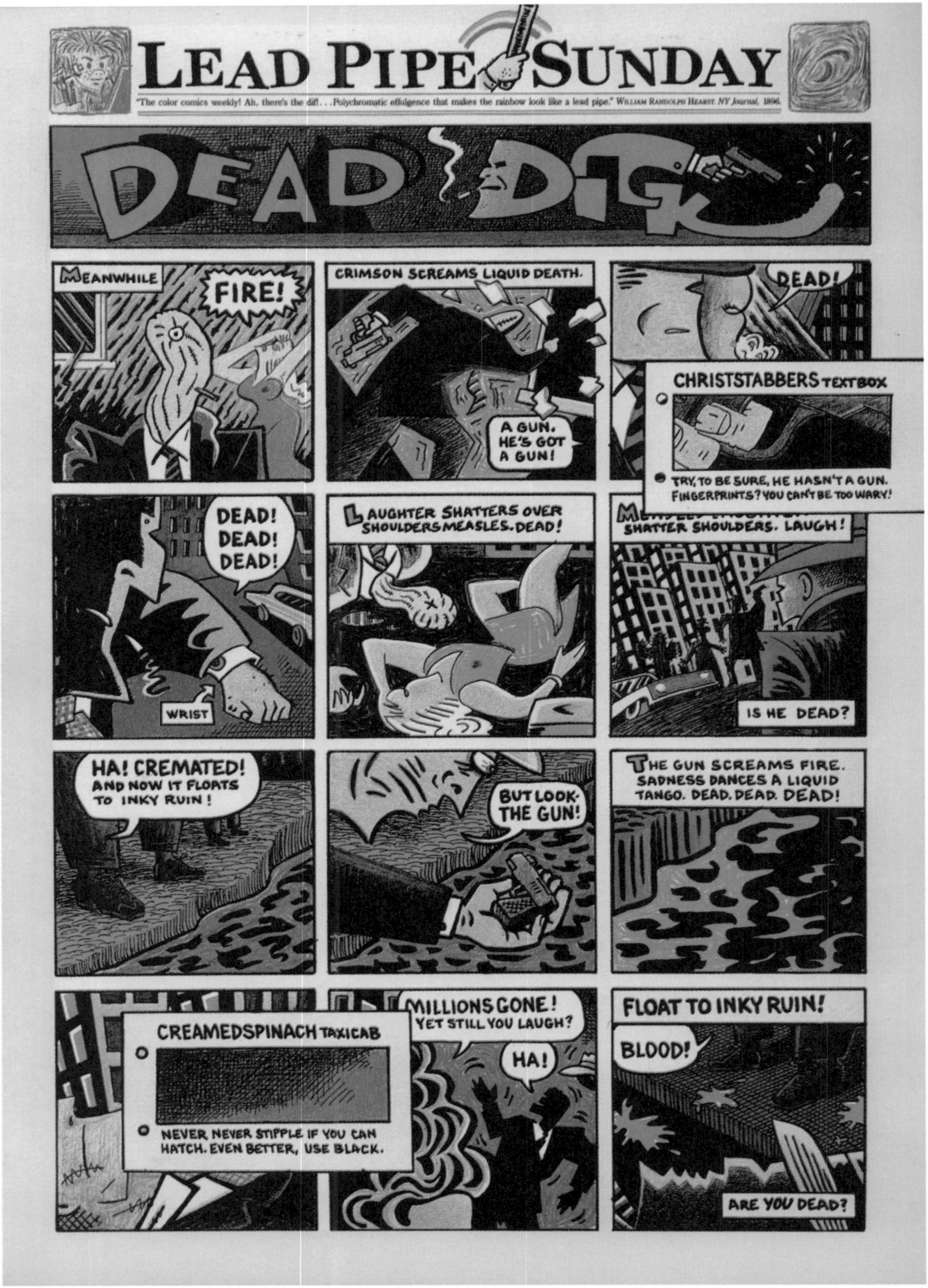

Art Spiegelman, "Dead Dick," Lead Pipe Sunday No. 1, *detail of lithograph, 1990 (Corridor).*

Jess, Tricky Cad: Case V, *1958, newspaper, cellulose acetate film, black tape, fabric, and paper on paperboard, 13 ¼ x 24 15⁄16 in. (33.7 x 63.4 cm.). Courtesy of the Hirshhorn Museum and Sculpture Garden.*

dAnCe

I first saw you naked in your grandfather's barn.

But before that, we went up in the trees to kiss.

Later, you hated it when I'd pretend to have a wooden leg and walk lopsided

in the store as we learned to shop for ourselves.

dRaMa

SMOOTH JAZZ
Tim
"Jacqui, your objective is to obtain the secret formula for smooth jazz."

OUR AGENTS BELIEVE THIS MAN, JAN (PRONOUNCED YAWN) WYNDHAM, HOUSES THE FORMULA IN A DEVICE CALLED THE RESTMAKER™ THAT SITS ON HIS BEDSTAND.
Jan

OUR OPERATIVES CLAIM THE RESTMAKER™ HAS FIVE SETTINGS-- BROOK, COPSE, SPUME, SLEET, AND GULL.
FFFF
"OUR SCIENTISTS HAVE HERETOFORE ONLY BEEN ABLE TO RECREATE THE LULL OF A CREEK!"

"The Taciturn Monsoon supper club is on the rocks, boys. If I don't accrue a 3.5 mil variable annuity revenue yield by Thursday, well..."

"Pops, we can't let you fold. How many conference calls have we spent dining on sole and new potatoes in a walnut-enfused endive slaw?"

NO! WE'RE GOING TO THROW A SUNDAY BRUNCH. AND NOT JUST ANY SUNDAY BRUNCH. I'M TALKING VINEYARD SNIFTERS, INVESTMENT BROKER COUNSELING, CHARTERS TO THE KEYS, VALET PARKING...

SAX PEALS OF CURLICUE INDICATE
THE LUBRICITY OF THE OFFICE CONCOURSE.
PURVEYORS AND PROPRIETORS,
THEIR MONT BLANC PENS INITIALING
REAMED THREATS OF NECKTIES,
HOLD FOR CONTINUOUS SOFT HITS
PELTING THEM WITH PASTEL DOWN...

YOUR SET REALLY EASED MY COMMUTE. ON THE I-5, THERE WAS A NON-INJURY COLLISION ON THE RIGHT SHOULDER TRANSITION.

YOU'RE INTO TRAFFIC? WHAT WAS YOUR FIRST MONEY MARKET CD?

"Have I got a bouquet for you.
We simply must take my Delorean
to the marina coast for a chilled bottle
of Chateau Jean Luc Ponty 1985."

THAT WAS EVERYTHING BUT THE WINE WITH URBAN EARTH SOUL HEARTBEAT. NOW HERE'S NIGHT PRISM ACROPOLIS WITH CARDIO-GROOVE...

YOUR SAX IS CONCOMITANT WITH CHABLIS-- A HINT OF FULL-BODIED WELCH PAIRED WITH GAME. THE DULCET CORK IS OF BREEZES, WAVES, AND WORLD-CLASS GOLF RESORTS.
Das Boot
PISMO
41

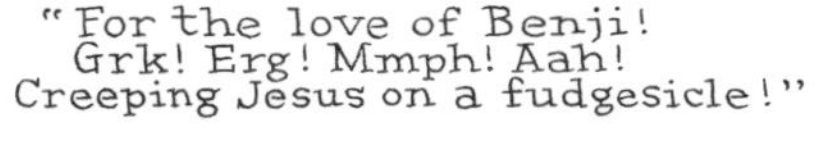

FTT
SNUK
Boot

At this moment, a hummingbird darts into the nostril of Jan

"For the love of Benji! Grk! Erg! Mmph! Aah! Creeping Jesus on a fudgesicle!"

CAN THIS BE THE RECLINEMENT AND SOPHISTICATION OF THE RESTMAKER™? THIS ISN'T MUSIC!
ZCHAU
I BELIEVE, SIR, IT IS WHAT THE SURREALISTS CALL "AUTOMATIC HEARING."
Z Z Z
Z Z Z
Z Z Z
Z Z Z
Z Z Z
SHT

"And wrapping up another block of legal brief staples, that was Leaf Alchemy with Shimmer..."

©1980 BILL GRIFFITH

IT WAS A COLD, CLEAR AFTERNOON. CHARLIE BENDIX STIRRED HIS COFFEE WITH A FINGER AS HE CONTEMPLATED HIS NEXT MOVE. THE CAFETERIA WAS EMPTY. IN FACT, IN THAT VAST CAVERN OF TABLES AND CHAIRS, CHARLIE WAS THE ONLY THING STIRRING. THERE WAS NOTHING IN THE PAPER. CHARLIE BENDIX WAS 36. HE STIRRED HIS COFFEE WITH A FINGER AND HE SAID TO HIMSELF:

..MY NAME IS **CHARLIE BENDIX.** I WISH I HAD A **SPOON.**
NEWSPAPER

THEN SHE CAME INTO HIS LIFE. SHE WAS A REPORTER FOR A BIG CITY NEWSPAPER. ON THE SIDE SHE DID "NEON SCULPTURE". SHE LOVED CATS. SHE LOVED DOGS. SHE LOVED PIZZA & SHE LOVED CHARLIE BENDIX.

SHIRLEY? HOW MANY **OIL WELLS** DID YOU SAY YOUR **FATHER** OWNS??
I DON'T KNOW HOW **MANY**..HE HAS **FOURTY-FOUR FIELDS**.. ..HE WANTS TO **MEET** YOU...

TEXAS WAS ALIEN TO CHARLIE. HE MISSED THE OCEAN... HE DIDN'T LIKE COWBOY HATS. HE DIDN'T LIKE LONE STAR BEER. HE DIDN'T LIKE THE WIDE, OPEN SPACES. AND HE DIDN'T LIKE LESTER.

H'LO THERE, OL' **BUDDY!!**
CHARLIE, I WANT YOU TO MEET MY **OLD BOYFRIEND, LESTER.** AND MY **FATHER**.. ..AND MY **AUNT NORLEEN**.. AND **COUSIN ANNIE** AND..

LESTER MISTOOK CHARLIE'S DEFERENCE FOR FRIENDSHIP. CHARLIE MARRIED SHIRLEY. THEN ONE DAY:

I NEVER TOLD THIS TO **NO ONE**, CHARLIE.. BUT **SHIRLEY** AND **ME**.. SHE DON'T **KNOW** THIS..WELL, WE GOT A **KID!!**
MY LIFE'S NO BOWL OF **CHERRIES** EITHER, LESTER..

CHARLIE MISTOOK LESTER'S HOSTILITY FOR PATHOS. HE RELATED AN INCIDENT FROM HIS PAST.

IT WAS AFTER THE **PLANE CRASH** THAT I TURNED TO **GAMBLING**..

ACTUALLY, CHARLIE WAS LYING. IT WAS HIS 2 YEARS IN THE PRIESTHOOD THAT LED HIM TO THE THE CRAPS TABLE.

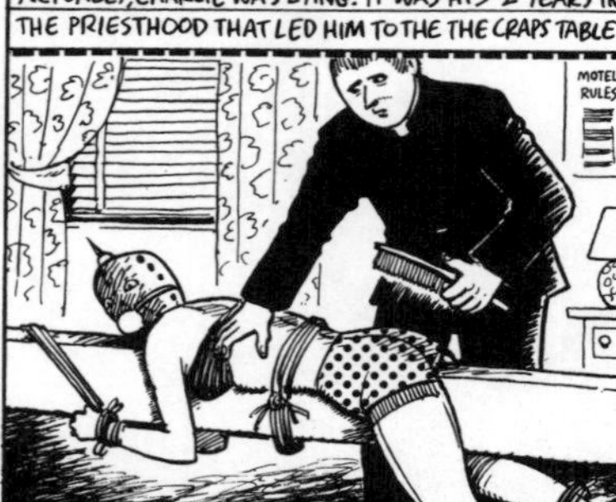

LESTER FINALLY TOLD SHIRLEY ABOUT THE BABY. SHE TOOK IT VERY HARD.

IT'S **TOO LATE**, CHARLIE.. I'M ALREADY **DEAD**..

SHIRLEY!! YOU'RE BREAKING THE **LAW!**

PILLS XX

SHIRLEY'S FATHER COULDN'T STAND THE SHOCK. HE EXPIRED IN THE ARMS OF A WHORE

TIME'S UP, MR. LAMONT!

AT THE READING OF THE WILL, IT WAS CHARLIE'S TURN TO BE SURPRISED.

..AND TO MY **SON-IN-LAW,** WHO **LOVES** THE **WIDE, OPEN SPACES,** I LEAVE THE **BULK** OF MY ESTATE...

CHARLIE WAS NOW A WEALTHY MAN. HE WAS HAVING LUNCH ONE TUESDAY WHEN:

HEY! THIS **FALAFEL** IS **DELICIOUS!** HOW MUCH FOR THE **WHOLE BUSINESS?**

FIFTY THOUSAND!

SOLD!

BENDIX FALAFEL HUTS SPROUTED UP ALL OVER THE COUNTRY.

Bendix FALAFEL HUT

A LITTLE TO THE **RIGHT,** LEFTY!!

CHARLIE SANK MILLIONS INTO A BIG AD CAMPAIGN.

Bendix FALAFEL HUT 2 MI. AHEAD

Go on a Bendix Bender! AMERICA'S FAVORITE FALAFEL

POP!! I WANNA **FLAVEL!**

AT FIRST, SALES WERE GOOD. THEN SOMETHING HAPPENED.

FALAFELS UNSAFE? See profile below

Research firm asserts Bendix Falafels contain Horse lips, tails

Norleen Lamont

IT WAS AUNT NORLEEN. SHE FELT CHEATED OUT OF HER INHERITANCE.

I REMOVED THIS **TAIL** FROM A POT OF **GARBANZO** BEANS IN THE KANSAS CITY BRANCH!!

NATIONAL CO

BENDIX FALAFEL HUTS WERE BANKRUPT. CHARLIE WAS RUINED.

I FEEL AWFUL.

HE USED HIS LAST BAD CHECK FOR A TICKET TO SWITZERLAND.

WATCHES CHOCOLATES

CHARLIE GRADUALLY DRIFTED DOWN TO MONTE CARLO.

WORKING IN A CASINO WASN'T ALL THAT BAD.

YOU GOT TO SEE ALL SORTS OF INTERESTING PEOPLE.

LESTER AND **AUNT NORLEEN!**

LESTER COULDN'T RESIST THE OPPORTUNITY TO GLOAT.

CHARLIE, YOU **SUCKER!** TH' **KID** WASN'T **SHIRLEY'S!** HAW! HAW! AND THE HORSE LIPS WERE **PLANTED!** NEAT TRICK, HUH PAL??

SO LATER THAT NIGHT CHARLIE DID WHAT HE HAD TO DO.

HE FIGURED IT WAS A SERVICE TO HUMANITY.

OLD MAN LAMONT TURNED IN HIS GRAVE & GRINNED.

..NICE **COWBOY HAT,** LESTER..

CHARLIE GOT OUT OF THE COUNTRY UNDETECTED.

HE TOOK A FURNISHED ROOM IN SAN FRANCISCO.

YEARS PASSED. CHARLIE PLAYED PIANO ON BUSH ST.

BEGIN THE BEGUINE.

SHE WAS 19. THEY DID THINGS FOR EACH OTHER.

THEY WERE MARRIED. BUT IT WAS INEVITABLE.

LET'S HAVE **LUNCH!!**

FALAFEL PALAC

CHARLIE LISTENED.

MY **UNCLE** LOST MILLIONS IN THE FALAFEL BUSINESS..

AND KEPT QUIET.

THERE'S EVEN A RUMOR THAT HE **KILLED** MY **FATHER**..

...VERY QUIET.

HONEY? DON'T YOU LIKE YOUR FALAFEL?

TROUBLE ENSUED.

..WHERE WERE YOU ALL NITE?

DRUGS DIDN'T HELP.

NEITHER DID WORK.

HONEY! THEY BOUGHT YOUR WAFFLE PATENT!

SO HE TRIED RELIGION.

Church of the One Way Street

IT WORKED....

...BUT SOON

CHARLIE BECAME

A VEGETABLE.

UNTIL ONE DAY..

CHARLES BENDIX?

IT HAPPENED.

YOU'RE UNDER ARREST.

..PRISON WAS OK.

BUT EVENTUALLY

HIS LAWYERS

JUSTIFIABLE HOMICIDE.

GOT HIM PARDONED.

A GREAT WEIGHT

WAS LIFTED

FROM HIS

SHOULDERS.

HE RETURNED

TO HIS NEW WIFE

& THE PIANO BAR

ON BUSH ST.

AND FORGOT ABOUT

RELIGION

AUNT NORLEEN

LESTER

FALAFELS

HORSE LIPS

CRAP TABLES

NEON SCULPTURE

OIL WELLS

COFFEE CUPS

CAFETERIAS

NEWSPAPERS

AND SPOONS.

END

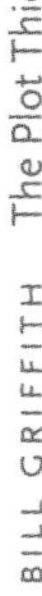

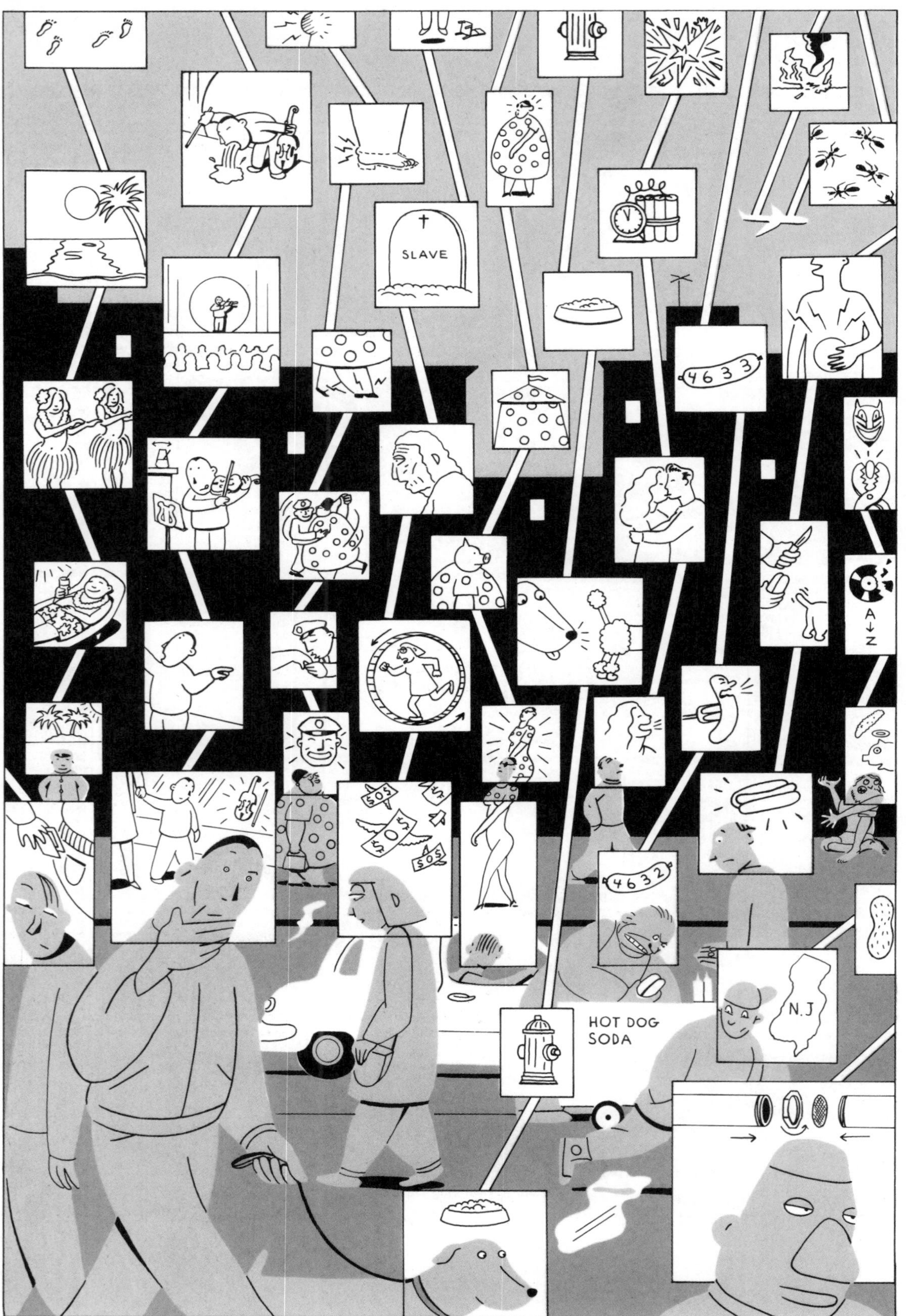
SLAVE
4633
4632
HOT DOG
SODA
N.J
A
Z

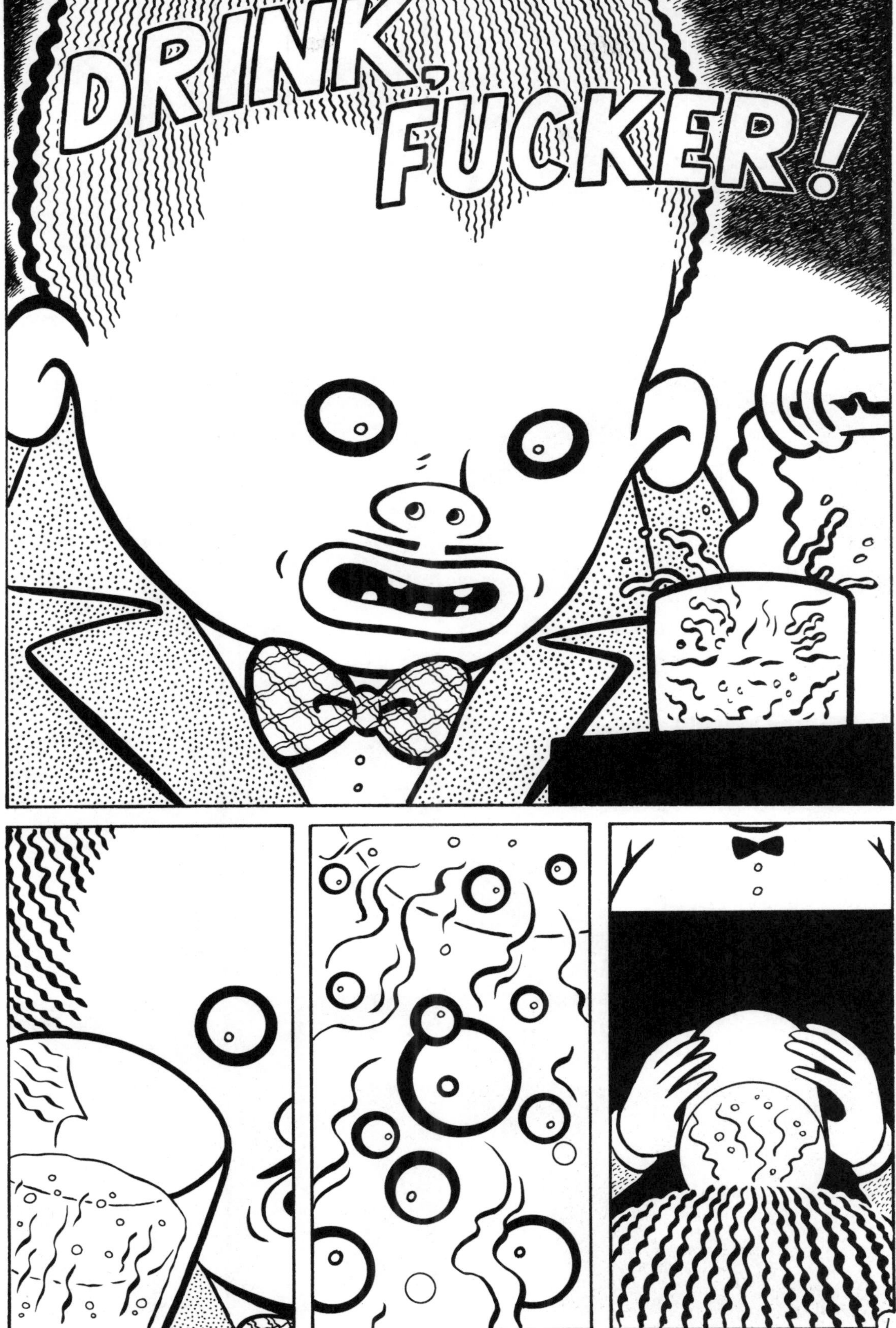
DRINK, FUCKER!

THERE IT IS. MY LAST ONE. WELL.
LINE 'EM UP, BARTENDER!

JUST GOT PAID TODAY, GONNA GET DRUNK AND WAKE UP IN A STRANGE PLACE ON MONDAY!
AND A REFILL FOR MY SWARTHY FRIEND HERE!

I JUST HAD MY LAST DRINK, MY FRIEND, BUT THANKS JUST THE SAME.
OH, NO YOU DON'T, PAL! I NEVER DRINK ALONE AND I DON'T TAKE NO FOR AN ANSWER!

WELL, NOT TO BE RUDE.
BOTTOMS UP!

LINE 'EM UP AGAIN, BARTENDER! FUCK IT! LEAVE THE BOTTLE!
THANKS AGAIN, BUT I HAVE TO GET HOME. I'LL PAY YOU FOR THE DRINK, OF COURSE.

HOME?! AND WHAT'S SO FUCKING IMPORTANT AT HOME THAT YOU MUST INSULT ME?!
WIFE. KIDS. I THANK YOU AGAIN FOR THE DRINK.

ALL THE MORE REASON TO BE SHIT-FACED WHEN YOU GET THERE!
DRINK, FUCKER!

2

THAT'S THE STUFF. HAVE ANOTHER.
AND ANOTHER AND ANOTHER AND ANOTHER...

WHY DO YOU DO IT..?
WHAT?

DRINK. I MEAN, YOU'RE RIGHT ABOUT MY WIFE AND KIDS, BUT THERE'S MORE... I DRINK BECAUSE I CAN'T SEEM TO MAKE ANY.. ANY CONNECTIONS BETWEEN ..WELL, WHEN I'M SOBER I..I CAN'T SEEM TO..
I DRINK TO GET DRUNK. WHAT CONNECTIONS, SISSY?

SEX AND LOVE...ART AND COMMERCE...DEATH AND.. DEATH AND..
PURPOSE?

PURPOSE. THAT IS, LIFE AND PURPOSE, BUT DEATH IS OUR ONLY TRUE PURPOSE, OUR ONLY TRUE INEVITABLE. THOSE MISSED CONNECTIONS I WAS SPEAKING OF...I DON'T KNOW HOW TO LINK THEM TO ANY..ANY SPIRITUAL SATISFACTION, IF YOU WILL, ANY TRANSCENDENT RESULT. MAYBE I'M ASKING TOO MUCH; FOR ME, AT LEAST. OTHERS SEEM ABLE TO.. BUT THEN, THEY MAY BE DELUDED...

OH, I KNOW IT'S THE SAME OLD PHILOSOPHICAL SHIT WHAT'S BEEN BLATHERED SINCE THE BEGINNING OF MAN ... AND I ALSO KNOW ALCOHOL ACTUALLY PREVENTS THOSE CONNECTIONS FROM LINKING ORGANICALLY. AS THE BRAIN BEGINS TO RELY ON THE BOOZE TO DO THE WORK, AN ATROPHY OF SORTS SETS IN. SO, I DRINK, HOPEFULLY TO BE PROVEN WRONG: THAT DRINK HAS/IS THE ANSWER.

AND THE MAN DRANK. HE DRANK AND HE DRANK AND HE DRANK SOME MORE. THEN, ONE DAY, ONE WARM, OVERCAST TUESDAY IN JUNE, HE FOUND HIS ANSWER. HE FOUND DRINK IS THE ANSWER AND, THUS, LIVED A LONG, HEALTHY, HAPPY LIFE.
BETO/97

MOSQUITO
BETO/96

AH HA HA HA HAA
I STOLE ALL THEIR BLOOD!

HA HA HEEE

SISSYS! I'VE BEEN KILLING BEFORE I LEARNED TO WALK!
YOU WANT TO KNOW HOW TO KILL ME?

HEE HEE HAAA
HURRY, FLAMES! I CAN'T WAIT TO DO MORE HARM!

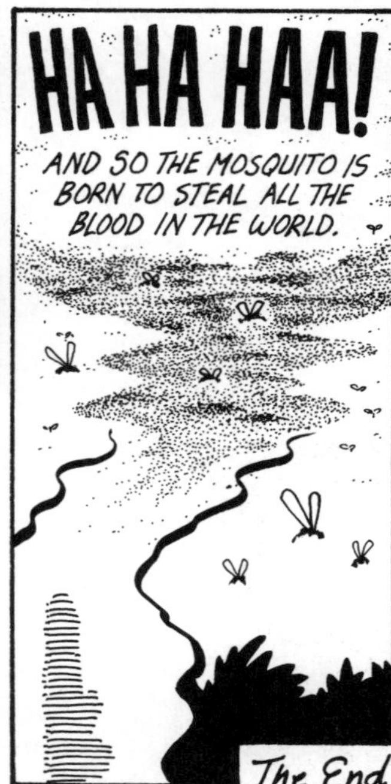
HA HA HAA!
AND SO THE MOSQUITO IS BORN TO STEAL ALL THE BLOOD IN THE WORLD.
The End

She Sleeps With Anybody but Me®

DING

EXCUSE ME... MAY I SEE WHAT YOU'RE DOING?
SURE...

I'M DRAWING HER INTO A COMIC STRIP PAGE... I CAN GET A LOT MORE INFORMATION OUT THIS WAY... SHE'S NOT JUST SITTING THERE IN SPACE, YOU KNOW...
THIS IS REALLY EXCELLENT

OH, DO YOU LIKE COMICS? DID YOU USED TO LIKE TO READ THE FUNNIES WHEN YOU USED TO BE A BOY?
UM... WELL, I'M ACTUALLY PRETTY SERIOUS ABOUT CARTOONS... I... REALLY...

HUH! WELL, IT'S... OH, I DON'T KNOW... IT'S DIFFERENT FOR ME. TO ME, CARTOONING IS AN ART FORM.
WELL... BYE!

THINGS ARE WORSE THAN I THOUGHT... MAYBE IF I CHANGE INTO MY PAJAMAS IT'LL HELP ME RELAX... I WONDER WHEN THIS CLASS STARTS?

HEY! MY PAPER IS GONE!
THAT GIRL MUST HAVE PICKED UP MY PAD BY MISTAKE!

I HAVE TO GO GET ANOTHER ONE

AH! IT'S TRASH DAY!

WHAT IN THE HOLY WELL IS THIS THING? GOOD GOD, IT'S A COCOON... BIG JOHNSON...

AND LOOK OUT-
WOOP!

MARY! MARY!

EXCUSE ME... PUFF PUFF... EXCUSE ME, GIRLS... WOULD YOU COME WITH ME A MINUTE... THERE'S A BIG RATTLESNAKE... A THREAT TO THE COMMUNITY... BACK THERE...
1974
2

I WANT TO KILL IT BEFORE IT BITES SOME CHILD... I WANT SOME-ONE ALONG IN CASE I GET BIT IN THE PROCESS, Y'SEE?
LEAD ON, PJ'S!

STAND BACK!
THERE IT IS!

YAUGH!
CLACK

OH, YICK!
WHY DID YOU DO THAT!?
!!

IT'S... IT'S RAMMY, OUR LITTLE CAT. HOW COULD I HAVE MADE SUCH A MISTAKE?

OH, WELL... AT LEAST IT WAS OVER QUICKLY. SNAKES ARE DAMN HARD TO KILL, AS I KNOW THROUGH BITTER PERSONAL EXPERIENCE. IT COULD WELL HAVE TAKEN HOURS... A HORRIBLE, GRUELING STRUGGLE. THANK GOD IT DIDN'T ACTUALLY COME TO THAT. RAMMY WASN'T MUCH OF A CAT ANYWAY...

NO; WHAT AM I THINKING!? RAMMY'S BEEN ONE OF MY DEAREST PALS OVER THE YEARS! I'LL... I'LL... I'LL... BUILD HIM A MONUMENT! THAT'S IT! I'LL BUILD A MONUMENT TO HIS MEMORY. A LARGE... ER... THING.

PEOPLE WILL SEE IT AND SAY, "THINK OF IT- THAT GLORIOUS MONUMENT, AND ALL TO A CAT! WHAT TENDER DEVOTION! HOW NOBLE!" THAT IS A GREAT IDEA... A REALLY AND TRULY GREAT IDEA...

I WISH I WERE HOME...
3

HOME

HEY! THOSE BIG TREES YOU'RE SO PROUD OF ARE ON THEIR WAY OUT OF HERE, PAL! YOU CAN'T KEEP 'EM!
!

YOU KNOW, THEY USED TO TRAIN FARM ANIMALS TO PERFORM AS YOU DO. THE ADVANTAGE LAY IN THE MANY PIGLETS, ET CETERA, BORN AS A RESULT!!
I'M GONNA KILL YUH!

NO... NO... I DON'T WANT TO FIGHT... ESPECIALLY WITH MY NEIGHBORS. COME ON IN AND HAVE A BEER OR SOMETHING
WELL... OKAY...

EXCUSE THE MESS...
TWO
SPE
GRO

?

COME ON, THERE'S GOING TO BE SOME SORT OF A SHOW
NIDVA
HUH?

I LIKE THIS GUTTURAL MUSIC, WHATEVER IT IS...
AH!
4

GUFFAW

!

5

OH JIM, WOULD YOU COME OVER HERE FOR A MINUTE?

HI!
HI HONEY
YOUR MOTHER AND I ARE HAVING A DIFFERENCE OF OPINION. WHAT DO YOU THINK OF MR. MONDRIAN?
FPT
FLAIR

MONDRIAN? GOSH, THAT'S A TOUGHIE. HIS PAINTINGS AL-WAYS MAKE ME THINK OF BASEBALL, FOR SOME REASON
OH, THAT REMINDS ME - I WANTED TO TELL YOU THEY'RE SHOWING A WHOLE BUNCH OF OLD WARNER BROTHERS CARTOONS, ALL ABOUT BASEBALL, AT THE NUART THIS WEEK
TEX AVEREYS!

ARE YOU STILL DRAWING EVERY DAY, I HOPE? OH, I LIKE YOUR WORK SO MUCH! I HAVE A PICTURE OF YOURS I'LL BET YOU DON'T EVEN REMEMBER DOING!
THE L.A. RIVER
YOUR TRUE HOME
LIAR

TA-DAA! YOU WERE GOING TO THROW IT OUT, REMEMBER? BUT I GOT IT FROM YOU AND HAD IT FRAMED IN LONDON AND I JUST LOVE IT!
FUCKER
CLACK

SAY, WE'RE GOING TO GO OUT DANCING TONIGHT- CARE TO COME ALONG?
OH, NO THANKS. I DON'T LIKE TO DANCE VERY MUCH

COME ON, IT'LL BE FUN! I'LL SHOW YOU HOW TO MAKE THE SPARKS FLY!
HEY, HE'S GOOD!
NO THANKS
6

IT'S GENEROUS OF YOU TO OFFER, BUT I ACTUALLY LIKE TO BE ALONE...

I'M COLD BUT NOT UNCOMFORTABLE
OH, JIM!

GOOD... YOU'RE STILL HERE... WOULD YOU... COULD YOU MOVE YOUR CAR SO I CAN GO TO THE STORE? I NEED TO GET SOME THINGS FOR DINNER...
I'LL GO FOR YOU... WHAT DO YOU WANT ME TO GET?
1012

WHY... THAT'S SO NICE OF YOU! THAT'S JUST SO NICE! IT'S THE NICEST THING YOU'VE EVER DONE FOR ME, I THINK... THANK YOU! THANK YOU VERY MUCH!
GEE, IT'S NOTHING!

I'M A NICE GUY!

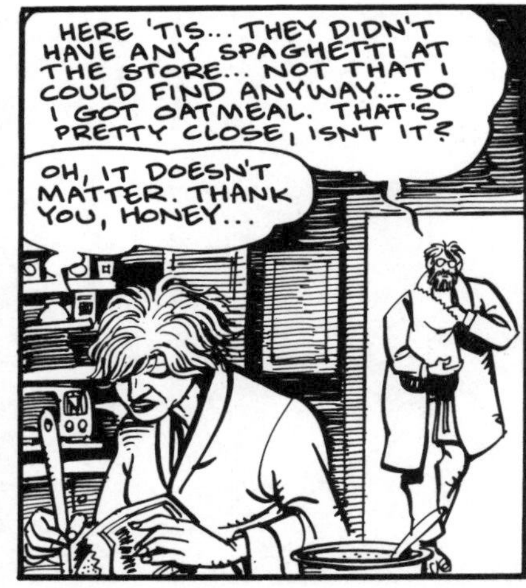
HERE 'TIS... THEY DIDN'T HAVE ANY SPAGHETTI AT THE STORE... NOT THAT I COULD FIND ANYWAY... SO I GOT OATMEAL. THAT'S PRETTY CLOSE, ISN'T IT?
OH, IT DOESN'T MATTER. THANK YOU, HONEY...

MY GOD, YOU'RE MAKING ENOUGH FOOD FOR AN ARMY!
I JUST WANT TO GET A LITTLE BIT AHEAD... THAT'S ALL... JUST A LITTLE...
HUH!

BUT I'M SO TIRED...

GAH!
WAKE ME UP IN A LITTLE BIT, WON'T YOU?
7

HEY, WHAT'RE YOU DOING!?
WHAT ARE YOU, A DOG?!
COME OUT FROM THERE!

HERE... COME ON... REST ON A COUCH... HERE, I'LL FIND ONE AND TAKE YOU TO IT... JUST BE A MINUTE...

OH GOD, WHAT IS WRONG WITH EVERYTHING?

DAMNATION, I THINK ALL THESE ROOMS BELONG TO SOME-ONE ELSE....

...BUT YOU KNOW WHAT...?

...YOU KNOW WHAT...?

EUREKA!

MY GRANDPARENTS' BEDROOM! HOW I'VE LONGED FOR THE MOMENT WHEN I WOULD REDISCOVER THIS PLACE!
8

THE ATMOSPHERE HERE, THE SENSE OF PRESENCE HERE IS SO STRONG I'M ALMOST AFRAID OF IT... IT BRINGS ME TO THE VERY BRINK OF... OF JOY...

JUST A LITTLE NUDGE IS ALL I NEED... GOD DAMN IT, WHERE'S MY POWER!?

HUM!

WUH

HN

H

HELP ME
9

WHUCK
CLOMP
CLUMP

CLONK

HEY!
HISSSSS

WHAT ARE YOU DOING IN THERE? WHO SAID YOU COULD MONKEY AROUND WITH THAT?
I WAS JUST LEAVING

DON'T YOU KNOW HOW DELICATE THAT THING IS? YOU'RE LUCKY ONE OF THOSE SCIENTIST FELLERS DIDN'T CATCH YOU IN HERE!
YEAH YEAH

SWEET FREEDOM!
GAH!

MY LITTLE CAR... SOME DRUNK MUST HAVE CRACKED IT UP AND LEFT IT HERE LIKE THIS... THE BASTARD!
SCRAPE
THUD

IT STILL RUNS GREAT, THOUGH... GOOD OL' CAR...
RRM RMM
RRRMMMMMMMMMM

I'M NOT MEANT TO MAKE THIS THING DO GRACEFUL ARABESQUES... ALL I WANT IS TO GET IT AS FAR ALONG AS POSSIBLE BEFORE IT BREAKS DOWN ENTIRELY
10

LOOK AT THE DAIRY...
OH GOD, I DON'T WANT TO THROW MYSELF DOWN ANY MORE... I DON'T WANT TO WASTE ANYTHING...

I WANT TO VISIT THE HANDIWORK OF OTHERS... I WANT TO LIVE CLOSELY WITH MACHINES AND KEEP THEM RUNNING FREELY...
SNIF

O GOD, I AM READY TO SUR-RENDER MY ATTACHMENT TO BLANK HORROR!

YACK!
BLAM!

BLAMB

11

OH, GOD, IS THERE ANY DEPTH TO WHICH I WON'T SINK? IS THERE ANY VILE ACT THAT IS BENEATH ME?
I LACK EVERYTHING IN MYSELF, I'M JUST A BLOATED BLADDER PULSING WITH APPETITES AND SHALLOW SCHEMES. ALWAYS AT ODDS, NERVOUS IN A ROOM, NO TRUE MAN AT ALL...

WHY ARE YOU CHASING AFTER THAT WHICH CAN ONLY BRING UNHAPPINESS? SETTLE YOURSELF, ATTACH YOURSELF FIRMLY TO THAT GREAT SELF WHOSE DREAM THIS WORLD IS AND WHO IS YOUR VERY BEING...
HAR?

...YOU WILL ALWAYS BE ABLE TO WORK. CAN THIS BE TAKEN FROM YOU UNFAIRLY? THIS ABILITY IS YOUR PORTION, THIS PART OF KNOWLEDGE HAS BEEN REVEALED TO YOU ALONE...
THIS WINDOW IS SO GRIMY I CAN'T SEE A DOGGONE THING!

YOU OBSCURE IT YOURSELF WITH DOUBT AND WORRY. YOU WEAKEN YOURSELF...
YOU OBSCURE IT YOURSELF WITH DOUBT AND WORRY. YOU WEAKEN YOURSELF...

HELLO, SON
IS IT YOU? IT IS!!

OH, I'M SO GLAD TO SEE YOU AGAIN... YOU CAN'T IMAGINE HOW CONFUSED AND WRETCHED I AM!
YOU SHOULD HAVE MORE FAITH!

TRY NOT TO WORRY SO MUCH. WHAT CAN HURT YOU? YOU WERE NEVER BORN!
YEAH? REALLY?
12

I THOUGHT NOT...
UH OH, THAT VEDANTA CENTER LOOKS AS IF IT'S BEEN BURGLED. WOULD YOU LIKE ME TO INVESTIGATE?
NO, IT'S ALL RIGHT

DO YOU SEE THAT POOR THING? IT CAN NEVER BE YOU. THERE IT GOES, BACK TO THAT HUGE DEAD HOUSE BY THE SEA... THE HOUSE YOU THINK YOU LOVE.

OH...
...ALL MY CHERISHED DELUSIONS ARE WANING. I FEEL UTTERLY BEREFT.
YES, YOU ARE CHANGING. ISN'T THAT WHAT YOU WANTED?
YES...

DO YOU KNOW, I SEE YOU EVERYWHERE JUST NOW. ALL AROUND. DON'T WORRY: YOU WILL MAKE IT.
YEAH?

THAT'S THE BEST NEWS I'VE HAD ALL WEEK!
YOU'RE SUCH A CHILD! GO AND DO YOUR WORK!
OKAY!

HA HA HA!! HOW COULD I HAVE BEEN SUCH A FOOL!?

AT LAST, MY SEASON IN HELL IS ENDED!
GOODBYE DULL CARE!

WOULD SOMEONE BE SO KIND AS TO LOAN ME SOME PAPER?
WHAT TH'-?
WHO TH'-?

HOLD THAT POSE!
BIZZZ

J.W. 13

Artist
SO, DID MIKE BUY THAT TRUCK YET?
WELL, HE'S **BOUGHT** IT, BUT WE AIN'T **GOT** IT!

HE DROVE IT TO A CUSTOM-IZING PLACE — RIGHT FROM THE DEALERSHIP!

HE'S GETTING SPOILERS AND RUNNING BOARDS PUT ON, AND HE'S GETTING THE WINDOWS TINTED!

HE SAYS HE'S NOT GOING TO LET ANY-ONE SEE IT UNTIL IT'S FINISHED!
UH-OH!

HI GUYS!

IT'S PRETTY COLD OUT! MY EARS HURT!

I HAD TROUBLE WITH MY DRYER, BUT THAT'S 'CAUSE I WAS SPINNING IT BACKWARDS WITH MY HANDS!

THE REASON WHY I WAS SPINNING IT BACKWARDS, WAS TO MAKE SURE THERE WERE NO CLOTHES LEFT IN IT...

THIS DUDE IS SERIOUSLY STRANGE!

YOU'RE NOT ALLOWED TO DO THAT IN HERE!
HM.
HELP! HE'S SMOKING!!

OKAY, YOU AIR POISONER, LET'S GO KISS THE SIDEWALK!
HUT HO!

SASKATOON
LEGION
HALL

WHEW! WOTTA WEIRDO!
TELL ME ABOUT IT! I SEE HIM EVERY DAY WHEN I'M DRIVING!

"HE WALKS DOWN HERE; ALL THE WAY FROM DUNDURN! THAT'S AT **LEAST** TWENTY MILES!
Bible Camp
DEPT.
STORE

I KNOW ALL ABOUT THAT GUY! HE WENT TO HIGH SCHOOL WITH MY OLDER BROTHER GARY, LIKE, TEN MILLION YEARS AGO!

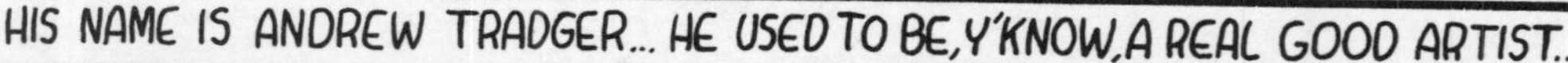
HIS NAME IS ANDREW TRADGER... HE USED TO BE, Y'KNOW, A REAL GOOD ARTIST...

OKAY CLASS, FOR THE NEXT FOUR PERIODS WE ARE GOING TO LEARN HOW TO MAKE LINO-CUTS!
11B
KNIVES
- 3 DOZEN

THIS IS REAL BULL SHIT MAN!
HOW CAN ANYONE BE INTO THIS SHIT?
IIA
IIB

♪

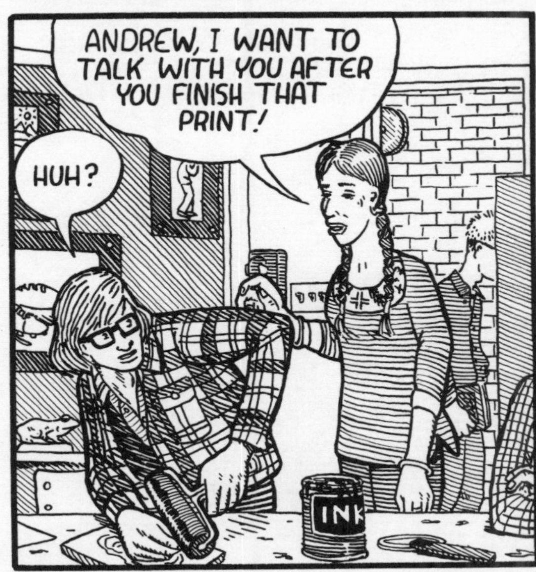
ANDREW, I WANT TO TALK WITH YOU AFTER YOU FINISH THAT PRINT!
HUH?
INK

ELLEN, THE OLD ART TEACHER, WAS, LIKE, TOTALLY IN LOVE WITH HIM! HE WAS BY FAR HER BEST STUDENT!

HE NEVER BRAGGED OR ANYTHING, BUT, **STILL**, SOME PEOPLE WERE JEALOUS!
HEY, WHAT'D SHE WANT? YOU IN SHIT?
HA-HA! NO, SHE WANTS TO PUT MY WORK IN A DISPLAY CASE AT THE BOARD OF EDUCATION, AND WE ALSO TALKED ABOUT THE "ART FAIR" THAT'S COMING UP!

THAT'S GREAT! I'M JUST **SO** FUCKING HAPPY FOR YA!

I CAN'T BELIEVE THIS IS ME THIS IS HAPPENING TO! IF I CAN KEEP ON IMPROVING MY ART AT THIS PACE, IT WON'T BE LONG 'TILL I'LL BE ABLE TO BLOW THIS POPSTAND!
I'LL GO LIVE IN A BIG CITY LIKE MINNEAPOLIS OR VANCOUVER!

...BUT THERE COMES A TIME WHEN YOU GOTTA MOVE ON!
YUCK!

I MEAN, SASKATOON IS NICE AND ALL... A STABLE, QUIET (BORING) KIND OF PLACE!
KING GEORGE Parkade
ENTRANCE

PROBABLY, HE WOULD'VE "BAILED RIGHT OUT" OF SASKATCHEWAN-PROBABLY HE WOULD'VE DONE LOTS OF THINGS, IF THINGS HAD TURNED OUT DIFFERENTLY!

-AND THINGS WOULD'VE TURNED OUT A LOT DIFFERENT IF HE HADN'T BEEN AT THAT PARTY!
...THEN, I WRAPPED LIKE, TEN ROLLS OF TOILET PAPER AROUND HIS CAR!
HA-HA!

HEY LOOK! WHAT TH' HELL IS THAT?

DARYL JONES! SINCE WHEN HAVE YOU BEEN A PUNK ROCKER?!
I READ ABOUT IT IN "PEOPLE"...
NICE HAIRCUT!

YEAH? WELL YOU'RE ALL A BUNCH OF POSEURS AN' WANKERS, ANYWAYS!
The Who

SO, ANDREW, HOW'S IT GOIN', LIKE, WITH YOUR ART AN' ALL?
AH-AH-AMANDA!

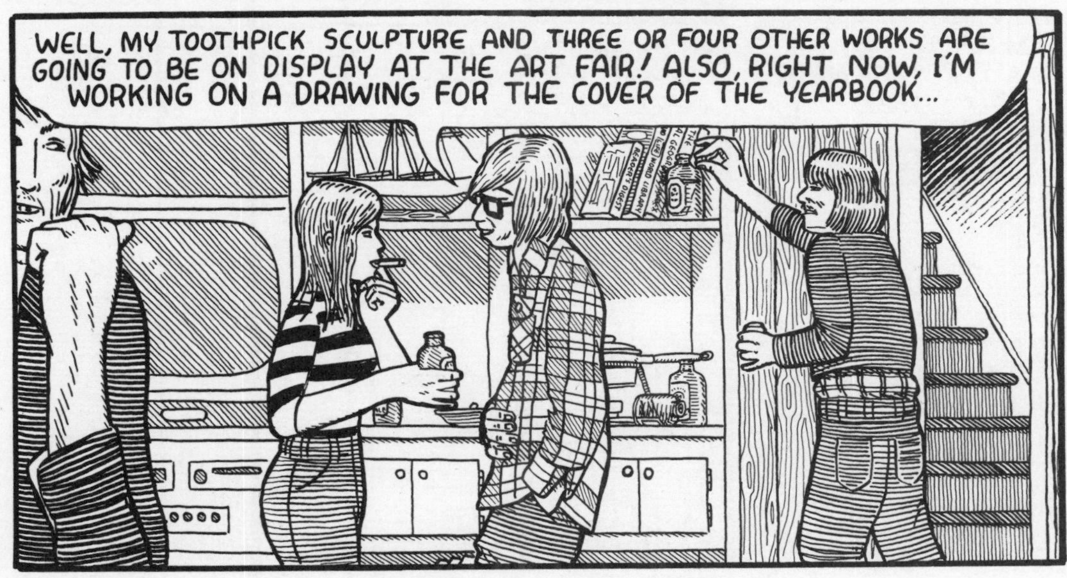
WELL, MY TOOTHPICK SCULPTURE AND THREE OR FOUR OTHER WORKS ARE GOING TO BE ON DISPLAY AT THE ART FAIR! ALSO, RIGHT NOW, I'M WORKING ON A DRAWING FOR THE COVER OF THE YEARBOOK...

FASCINATIN'.
HEH-HEH! WHEW!

SO, THAT'S WHAT HAPPENED — THOSE ASSHOLES AT THE PARTY PUT A WHOLE SHITLOAD OF ACID IN HIS BEER!
TSK!

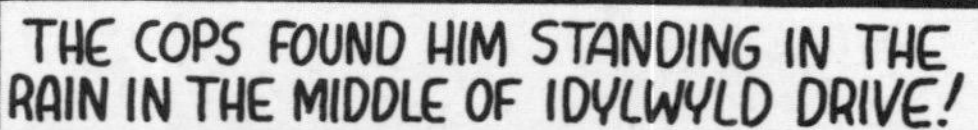
THE COPS FOUND HIM STANDING IN THE RAIN IN THE MIDDLE OF IDYLWYLD DRIVE!

Robin Hood

—GUESS YOU COULD CALL HIM "A CASUALTY OF THE '70'S"!
NO DOUBT!
California FITNESS CENTRE®
FITNESS FOR EVERYONE
PLEASE REMOVE WET FOOTWEAR
SIGH

I'M AFRAID THAT NO-ONE CARES FOR ME OR YOU, OL' PIPE!

NO USE DWELLING ON THAT NOW! THERE'S A LOT OF PARKING METERS, AND I'D BETTER TEST ALL OF THEM!
THIS ONE CHECKS OUT OKAY!
FOR RENT
INQUIRE
967-1111
FOR LEASE
INQUIRE
967-1111
FOR SALE
INQUIRE
967-1111
CLICK!

MEANWHILE!
!!殺
AAAGH! HOW CAN I WORK IN THIS RACKET?

別做縮頭烏龜了滾出來吧!!
ENCYCLOPEDIA
HAPPY BIRTHDAY!
WILL HE EVER SHUT UP?? THE INSANE GUY WHO LIVES BY HIMSELF ACROSS THE LANE IS STARTING TO DRIVE ME CRAZY!! HE YELLS LIKE THAT ALL DAY AND NIGHT!

THAT CARTOON FOR "NICKELS AND QUARTERS MAGAZINE" WILL HAVE TO WAIT! I'VE GOT TO GO GET SOME QUIET!

NOT THAT I'M MUCH DIFFERENT FROM ALL THESE DISTURBED PEOPLE...IT'S ONLY THE ART THAT KEEPS ME FROM A WANDERING LIFE!

TO KEEP HEALTHY, WE NEED TO WORK OUR BRAINS WITH CREATIVE EFFORTS! YES...I'M CERTAIN!
Let Me Be Free

THOUGH THE NOTION OF A CHARACTER LIKE THIS, EVER TAKING UP SOMETHING LIKE SAY, ART, DOES SEEM RATHER FAR-FETCHED!
...CHECKS OUT OKAY!
CLICK!
fin

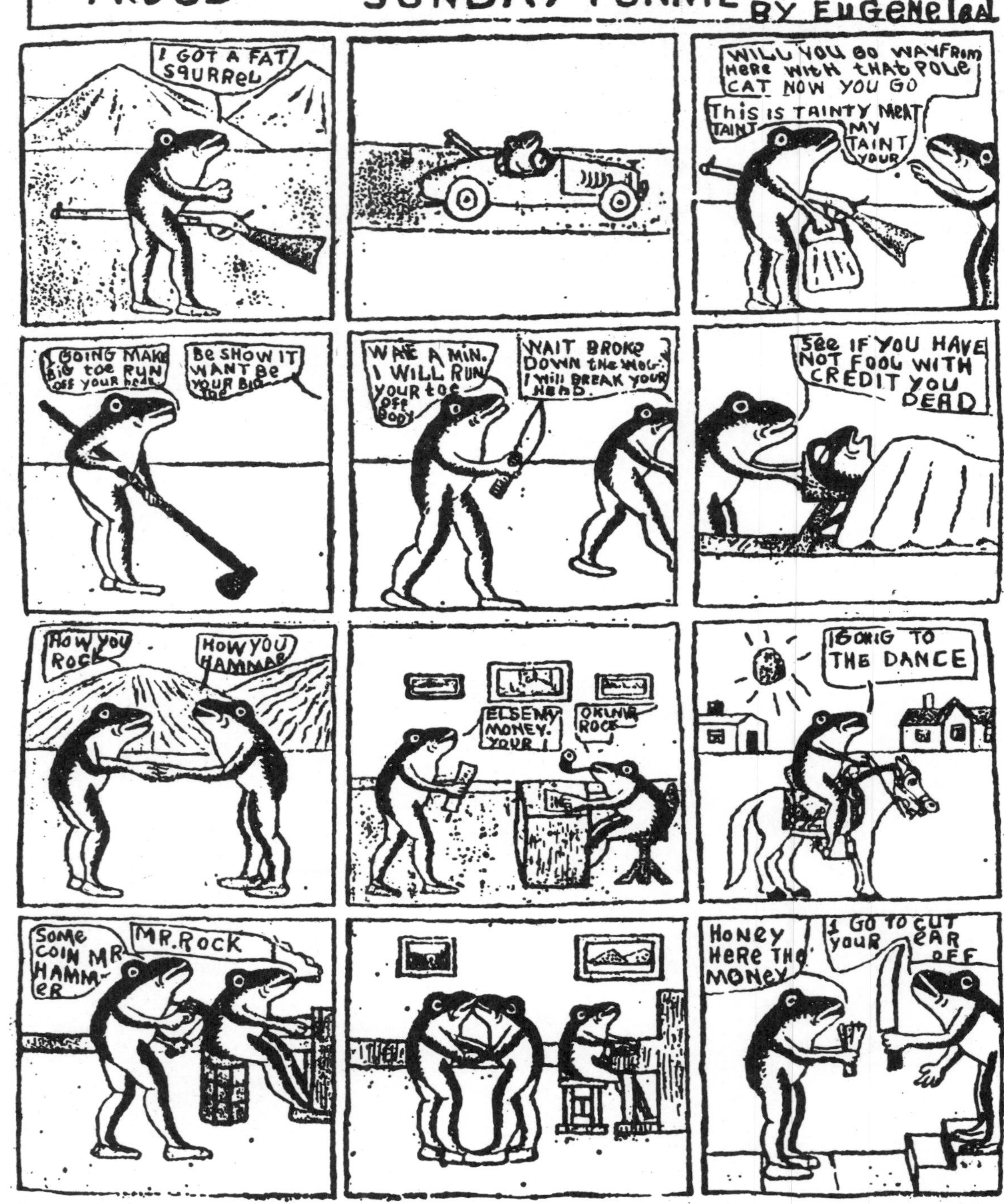

BY EUGENE TEAL

THIS COMIC STRIP BY THE LEGENDARY EUGENE TEAL IS A XEROX OF A XEROX OF A XEROX, GIVEN, SO THE STORY GOES, TO CARTOONIST ROGER BRAND WHILE RIDING A BUS IN DOWNTOWN OAKLAND, CALIFORNIA, BY MR. TEAL HIMSELF, WHO WAS DESCRIBED AS AN ELDERLY BLACK MAN. THIS WAS IN AROUND 1975. MANY SMALL STORES IN THE BLACK SECTION OF OAKLAND HAVE SIGNS DRAWN AND SIGNED BY EUGENE TEAL. THIS STRIP SUPPOSEDLY APPEARED MANY YEARS AGO IN AN OBSCURE BLACK NEWSPAPER IN OAKLAND. NO OTHER COMIC STRIPS BY HIM HAVE SO FAR BEEN LOCATED, AND MR. TEAL'S PRESENT WHEREABOUTS IS UNKNOWN.

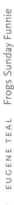

—R. CRUMB

CHARLES BURNS *excerpt from* Black Hole

IT WAS SO WEIRD. IT HAPPENED IN MY THIRD PERIOD BIOLOGY CLASS. WE GOT DIVIDED INTO GROUPS OF TWO BECAUSE WE WERE ALL GOING TO BE DISSECTING FROGS.

I LUCKED OUT FOR ONCE AND GOT CHRIS AS MY LAB PARTNER. CHRIS RHODES. SHE WAS A TOTAL FOX.

ALL THE OTHER GIRLS WERE SQUEALING AND STUFF AND THE GUYS WERE SORT OF TAKING OVER AND PUTTING ON THE WHOLE TOUGH GUY ACT.

I GUESS I WAS TRYING TO DO THE SAME THING ... I WENT AHEAD AND PINNED THE ARMS AND LEGS DOWN LIKE YOU WERE SUPPOSED TO AND WAS JUST STARTING TO CUT IT OPEN WHEN IT HAPPENED.

AS THE SKIN OPENED UP, A BUNCH OF FORMALDEHYDE SPILLED OUT. YOU COULD SEE THE GUTS THROUGH THE SLIT I'D MADE AND THEY LOOKED ALL HARD AND WHITE.
parts adapted fo
reathing adults
on land but
eggs. Adults
they hiber

I FROZE. I CAN'T EXPLAIN WHAT HAPPENED. IT WAS LIKE A DÉJÀ VU TRIP OR SOMETHING... A PREMONITION. I FELT LIKE I WAS LOOKING INTO THE FUTURE...AND THE FUTURE LOOKED REALLY MESSED UP.

CHARLES BURNS *excerpt from* Black Hole

I WAS LOOKING AT A HOLE... A *BLACK* HOLE AND AS I LOOKED, THE HOLE OPENED UP...

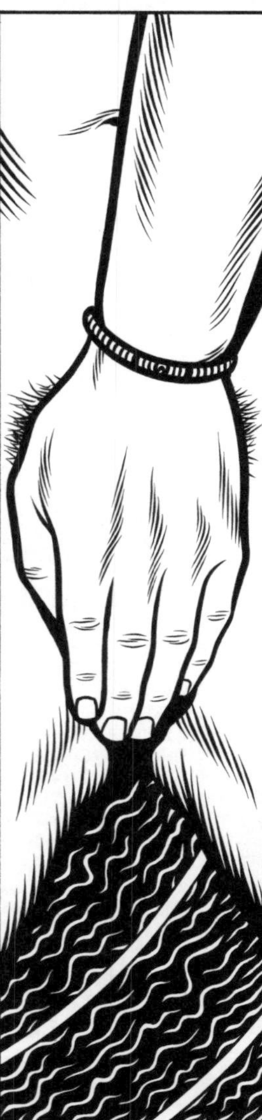

...AND I COULD FEEL MYSELF FALLING FORWARD, TUMBLING DOWN INTO NOTHINGNESS.

WHAT'S THE MATTER? ARE YOU OK?

CHARLES BURNS *excerpt from* Black Hole

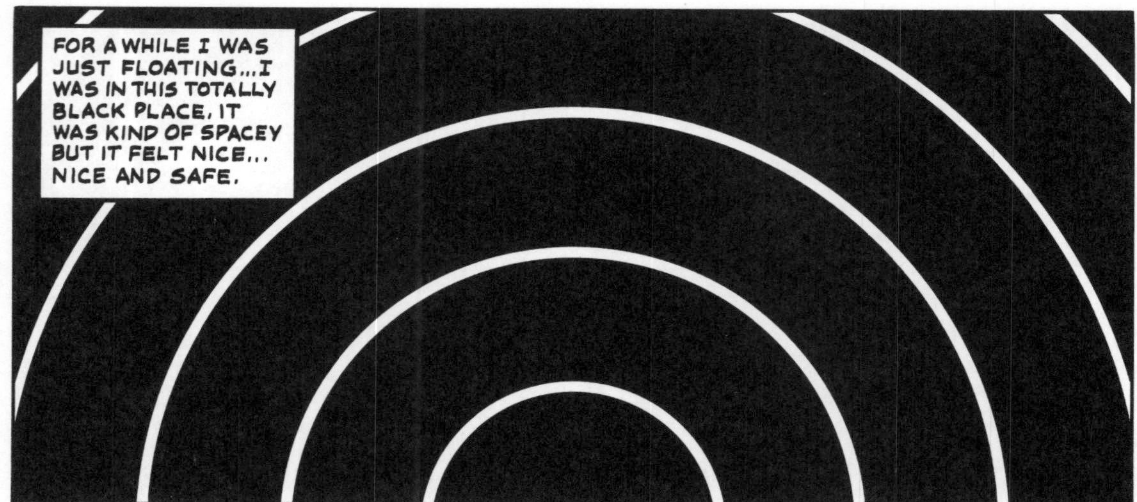

FOR A WHILE I WAS JUST FLOATING...I WAS IN THIS TOTALLY BLACK PLACE. IT WAS KIND OF SPACEY BUT IT FELT NICE... NICE AND SAFE.

THEN IT WAS LIKE THINGS STARTED PUSHING INTO THE BLACKNESS...VOICES, BLURRY SHAPES.

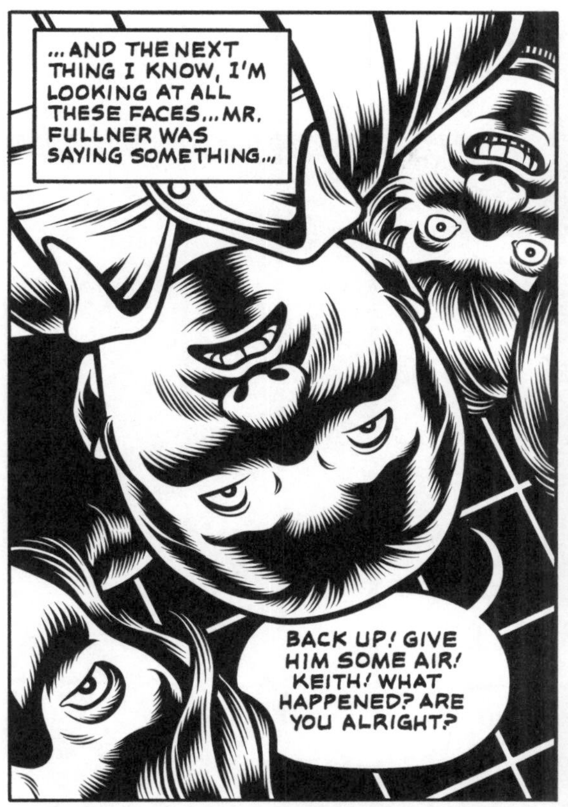

CHARLES BURNS *excerpt from* Black Hole

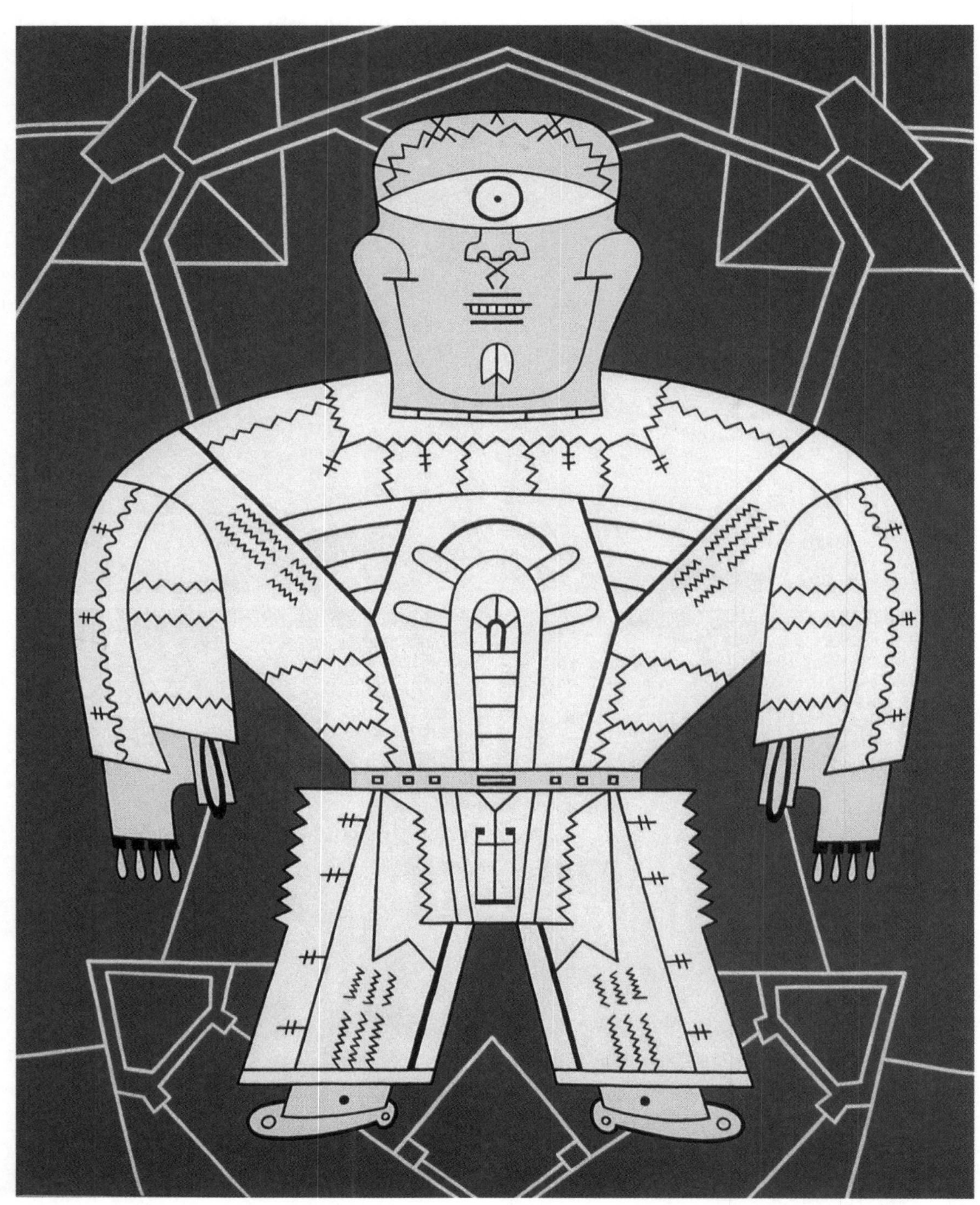

Karl Wirsum, 3 My Eye Land Cyclops? 1983, acrylic on acetate, 26 ½ x 21 ½ in., Collection of James A. Young, M.D. Mr. Wirsum's work seems to be infused with the very breath and spirit of comics, and refreshingly free of condescension toward them; in turn, he has gone on to influence a number of present-day cartoonists.

GARY PANTER *excerpt from* Jimbo: Adventures in Paradise

GARY PANTER *excerpt from* Jimbo: Adventures in Paradise

GARY PANTER *excerpt from* Jimbo: Adventures in Paradise

JIMBO
IN THE SEWERS...
IT'S KINDA LONELY, SMELLY, AND SPOOKY DOWN HERE, BUT AT LEAST THERE'S PLENTY OF ROOM...
AND NO ONE TO TELL YOU ANYTHING.
OF COURSE LOTS OF PEOPLE CAME DOWN HERE TO BUILD STUFF.
SOMEBODY TOLD SOMEBODY ELSE TO BUILD THAT THING THERE.
IN THE PINES!! ♪ IN THE PINES!!♪ WHERE THE SUN NEVER SHINES!!!♪ AND YOU SHIVER WHEN THE...
I HARDLY EVER CATCH ANYONE DOWN HERE... HARDLY NEVER.
HOLY JUMPING CATFISH! A TUNNEL SCRUB!!!
RRAUGH
TUNNEL SCRUBBERS HAVE BATTERIES AND SOLAR COLLECTORS THAT COULD POWER MY WHOLE HOUSE!
12-1-87
4
© 1987 GARY PANTER

GARY PANTER *excerpt from* Jimbo: Adventures in Paradise

GARY PANTER *excerpt from* Jimbo: Adventures in Paradise

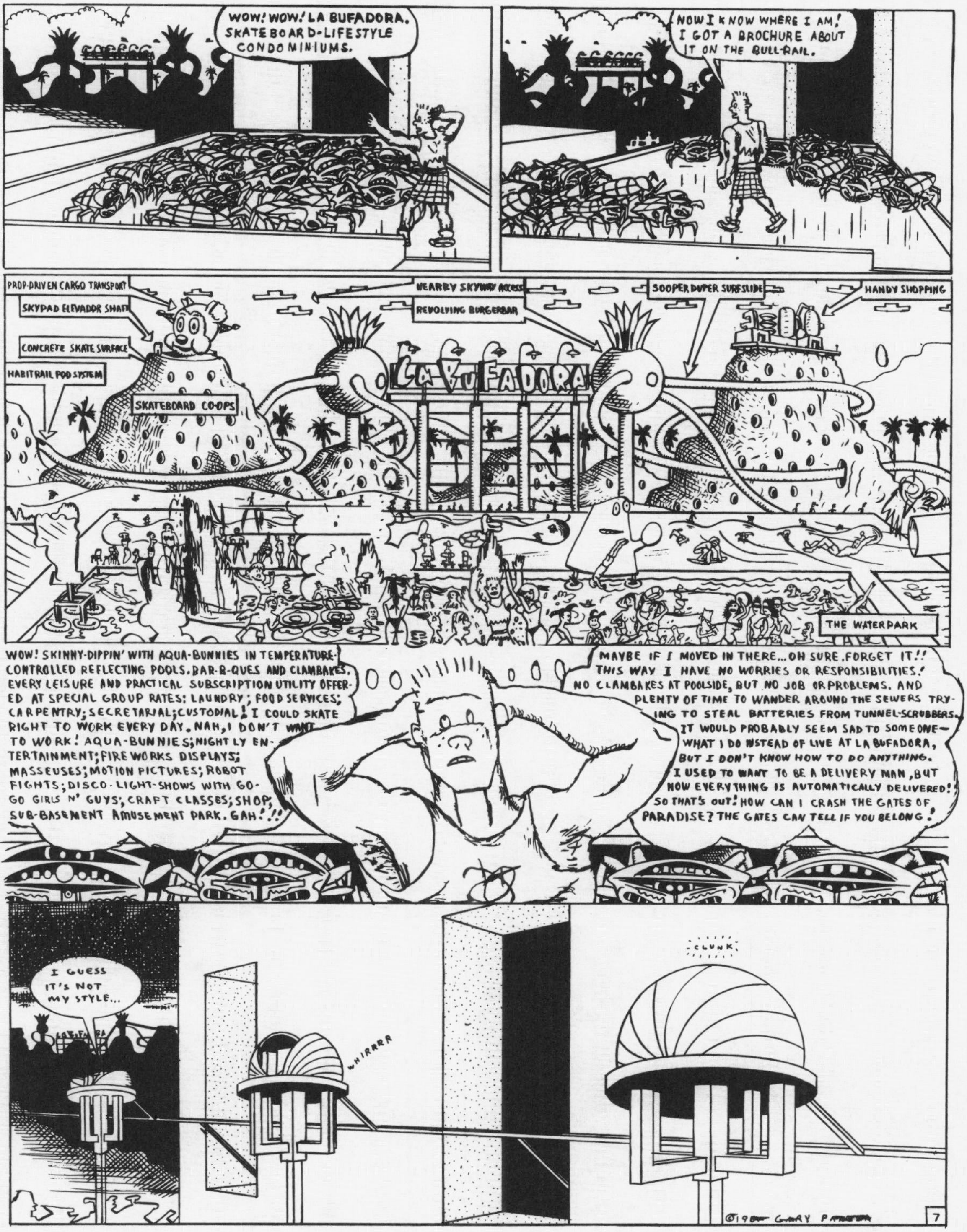

WOW! WOW! LA BUFADORA. SKATEBOARD-LIFESTYLE CONDOMINIUMS.

NOW I KNOW WHERE I AM! I GOT A BROCHURE ABOUT IT ON THE BULL-RAIL.

PROP-DRIVEN CARGO TRANSPORT

SKYPAD ELEVADOR SHAFT

CONCRETE SKATE SURFACE

HABITRAIL POD SYSTEM

SKATEBOARD CO-OPS

NEARBY SKYWAY ACCESS

REVOLVING BURGERBAR

LA BUFADORA

SOOPER DUPER SURFSLIDE

HANDY SHOPPING

THE WATERPARK

WOW! SKINNY-DIPPIN' WITH AQUA-BUNNIES IN TEMPERATURE-CONTROLLED REFLECTING POOLS. BAR-B-QUES AND CLAMBAKES. EVERY LEISURE AND PRACTICAL SUBSCRIPTION UTILITY OFFERED AT SPECIAL GROUP RATES: LAUNDRY; FOOD SERVICES; CARPENTRY; SECRETARIAL; CUSTODIAL! I COULD SKATE RIGHT TO WORK EVERY DAY. NAH, I DON'T WANT TO WORK! AQUA-BUNNIES; NIGHTLY ENTERTAINMENT; FIREWORKS DISPLAYS; MASSEUSES; MOTION PICTURES; ROBOT FIGHTS; DISCO-LIGHT-SHOWS WITH GO-GO GIRLS N' GUYS; CRAFT CLASSES; SHOP; SUB-BASEMENT AMUSEMENT PARK. GAH!!!

MAYBE IF I MOVED IN THERE... OH SURE. FORGET IT!! THIS WAY I HAVE NO WORRIES OR RESPONSIBILITIES! NO CLAMBAKES AT POOLSIDE, BUT NO JOB OR PROBLEMS. AND PLENTY OF TIME TO WANDER AROUND THE SEWERS TRYING TO STEAL BATTERIES FROM TUNNEL-SCRUBBERS. IT WOULD PROBABLY SEEM SAD TO SOMEONE— WHAT I DO INSTEAD OF LIVE AT LA BUFADORA, BUT I DON'T KNOW HOW TO DO ANYTHING. I USED TO WANT TO BE A DELIVERY MAN, BUT NOW EVERYTHING IS AUTOMATICALLY DELIVERED! SO THAT'S OUT! HOW CAN I CRASH THE GATES OF PARADISE? THE GATES CAN TELL IF YOU BELONG!

I GUESS IT'S NOT MY STYLE...

WHIRRRR

CLUNK

7

GARY PANTER *excerpt from* Jimbo: Adventures in Paradise

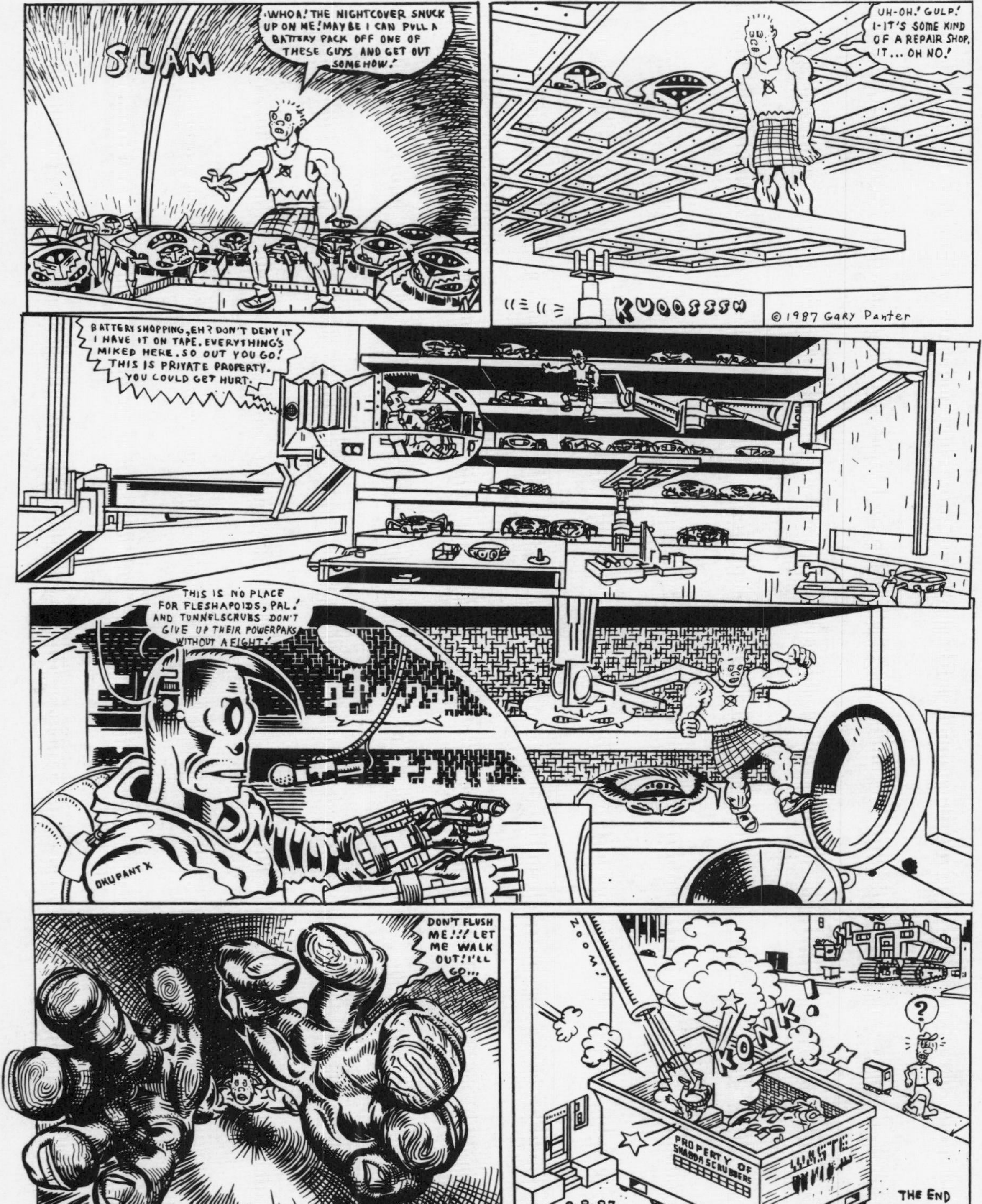

GARY PANTER *excerpt from* Jimbo: Adventures in Paradise

D RDOO
WWW.PAPERRAD.ORG
HONK
HONK
SHUT UP
HIS CAR ONLY goes 30mph because it runs on blood

PAGE 50 FANTASTIC COMICS

NO 7 6-40

From Fantastic *No. 7, 1940. Collection of Jerry Moriarty.*

WHEN EVERYBODY HAS DISAPPEARED INTO SPACE, WE'LL REVERSE OUR ANTI-SOLAR RAY AND RESTORE THE EARTH'S MOTION AND IT'S GRAVITY! THEN WE CAN HAVE THE WHOLE EARTH AND ALL IT'S WEALTH FOR OURSELVES!

THAT'S THE DANGEROUS "GYP" CLIPP GANG! PREPARING TO MURDER OVER HALF A BILLION PEOPLE!
I'LL ATTEND TO THEM!

COME ON, YOU MUGS! GET READY! WE'RE GOING TO RELEASE OUR ANTI-SOLAR RAY!

THE RAY IS RELEASED, AND THE EARTH BEGINS TO TURN MORE SLOWLY.

IT FINALLY LOSES ALL ITS MOTION . . . .

AS IT COMES TO A STOP AND GRAVITY IS DESTROYED, PEOPLE BEGIN TO RISE FROM THE SURFACE AND PLUNGE HELPLESSLY INTO SPACE . . . .

2

PAGE 52 FANTASTIC COMICS

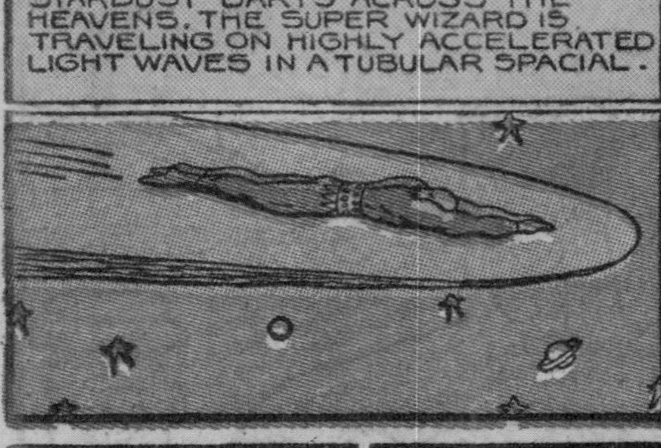

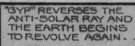

MEANWHILE, STARDUST ENCIRCLES THE EARTH, DISCHARGING LONG ATTRACTOR BEAMS TOWARDS THE DRIFTING MILLIONS OF EARTHPEOPLE.

FINALLY, WITH A TREMENDOUS BURST OF POWER, HE BEGINS DRAWING THE STRONG ATTRACTOR BEAMS BACK TO HIM. THE HALF A BILLION EARTHPEOPLE ARE NOW UNDER HIS CONTROL . . . .

WITHOUT DELAY, HE TRANSMITS THEM TO THE NOW NORMAL ATMOSPHERE OF THEIR PLANET . . . .
I MUST DEPOSIT EACH ONE IN THE PROPER PLACE!

"GYP" CLIPP, BELIEVING HE HAS THE WORLD TO HIMSELF, GLOATS MADLY. . . .
IT'S ALL MINE! ALL MINE!

SUDDENLY THE SKY BECOMES DARKENED WITH THE SLOWLY DESCENDING FORMS OF HUMAN BEINGS . .

WITHOUT MISTAKE, EACH PERSON IS RETURNED TO THE SPOT FROM WHICH HE OR SHE LEFT THE EARTH WHEN "GYP" STOPPED THE ACTION OF GRAVITY. . .

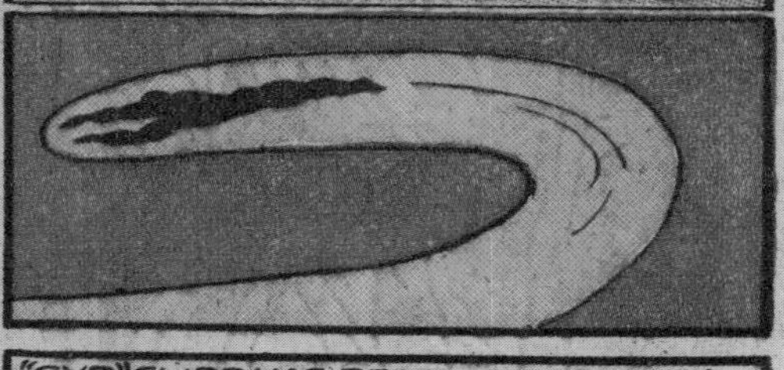
GLIDING SWIFTLY, STARDUST CONTROLS EVERY MOVEMENT OF THE EARTHPEOPLE

"GYP" CLIPP HAS BECOME TERRIFIED! . .
THEY'LL HANG ME!

"GYP" HIDES IN HIS LABORATORY . . .

SUDDENLY, A BLINDING FLASH FILLS THE LAB. . .

AND "GYP'S" EQUIPMENT IS ENTIRELY DESTROYED BY A FUSING RAY. . .
BANG!

FROM OUT OF THE FLASH STEPS STARDUST.
OH, MY LORD!

COME ON, "GYP"! YOU'RE GOING INTO SPACE!
5

NEVER TO RETURN AGAIN!..

'GYP' WHIRLS INTO OUTER SPACE...
AND STARDUST FOLLOWS, READY TO PROPEL HIM TO THE REALM OF CONSTANT TWILIGHT. .

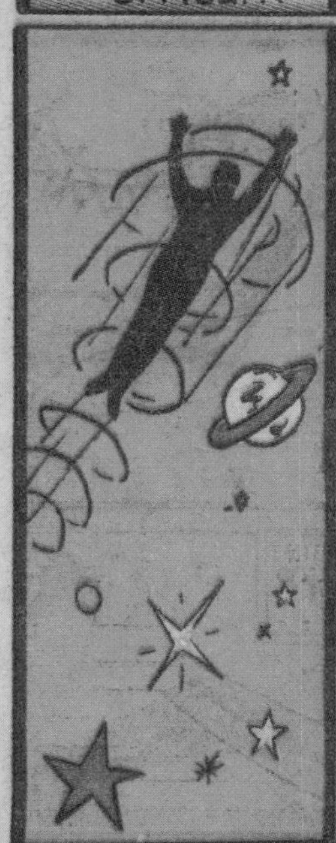

6

IN THE NEXT ISSUE, **STARDUST WILL BATTLE THE SUPER FIEND OF LEPUS**

FANTASTIC COMICS IS ON SALE THE 10th OF EVERY MONTH

MM22

OLD
COMIC
7 YEARS

SHOWROOM DUMMIES // PUMPKIN COMIC 1

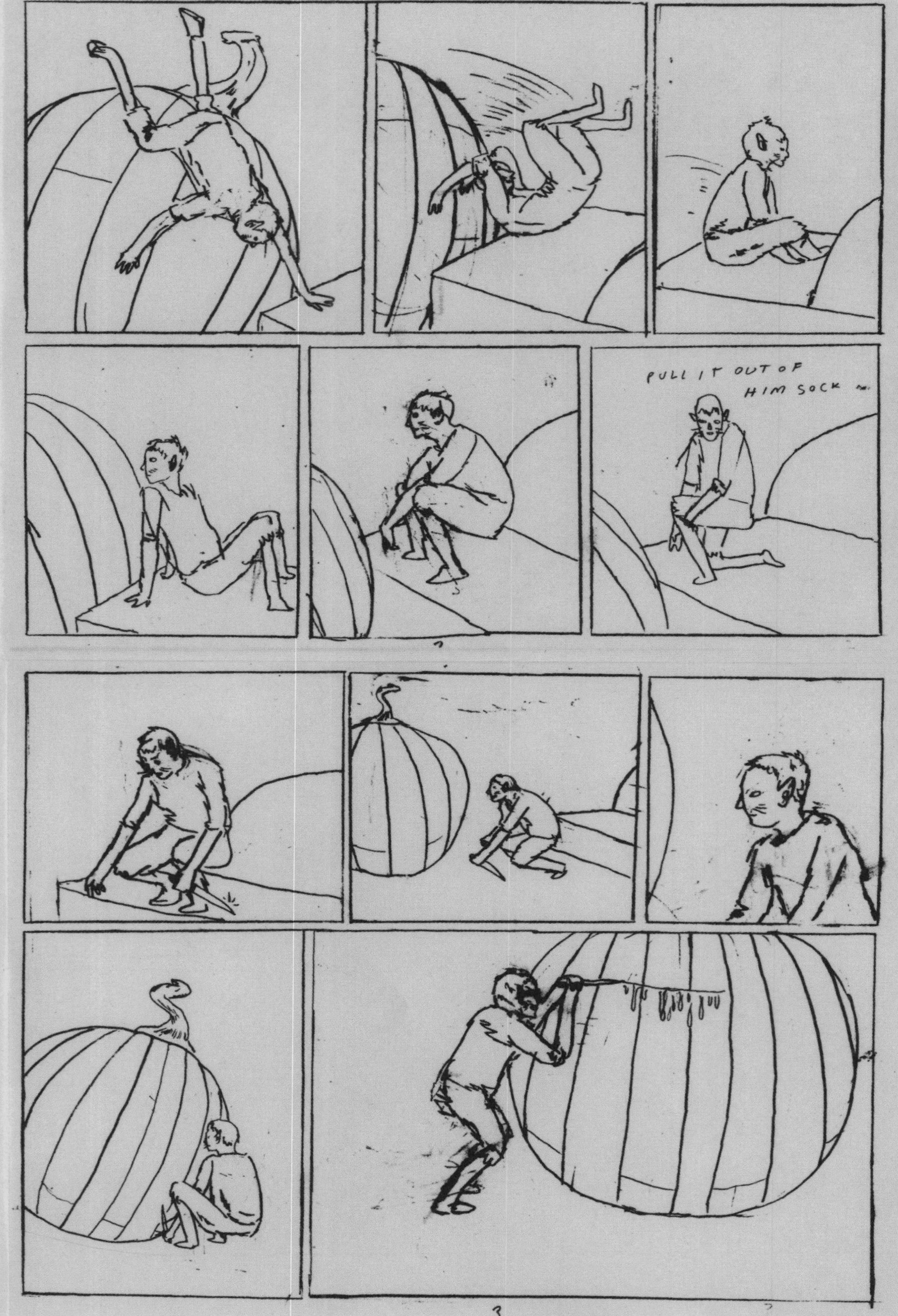
PULL IT OUT OF
HIM SOCK
3

4

5

IN

SPLOOSH
DOWNSTREAM
8
MEANWHILE-
SHAKE & SHIVER
U. DOUGIE'
FOLLOW
M.M. 22.
FOOT-STEPS
9

C.F. MM22

PLOISH
PADDLE PADDLE
NOT MUCH FURTHER DOWN STREAM:-
SUN COMING DOWN GOOD
10
PADDLE PADDLE PADDLE
?
11

SWISH
HURTS SO BAD
M.M.22. RUNS AWAY
12
PUSH
& SHOVE
FWD
13

COMIC SECTION. THE NEW YORK HERALD. FOUR PAGES.

NEW YORK, SUNDAY, DECEMBER 7, 1913. PRICE FIVE CENTS.

NAUGHTY PETE

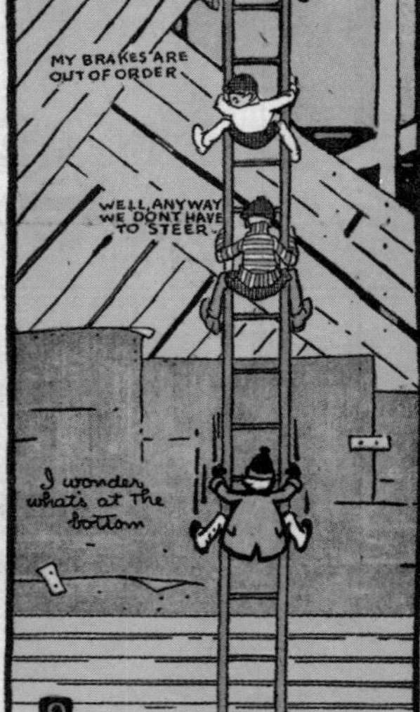

Charles Forbell, Naughty Pete, *Sunday page, December 7, 1913. Collection of Chris Ware.*

This cartoon story was drawn in Berkeley, CA during february & March of the year ~ 02001.

THE~
I am fascinated by the rich patterns and properties of perfect numbers.
I respect their subtlety and cunning.
~PROBLEM
With numbers, we can discover truths that are absolute.
Truth that is untainted by the inaccuracies of perception.
~OF THE~
Numbers are hidden in everything. The truth is everywhere.
Rational numbers can be used to explain ALL natural phenomenon
Sir? I have been working with the number √2. No such fraction seems to exist. Could it be possible that all numbers may not be rational?
!
~MUTILATED~
I have defined the entire universe in terms of rational numbers.
I have worked too long to accept this & change everything. — Yet, I cannot find a way to prove him wrong.
CHESS~
I sentence him to death by drowning.
By destroying me, you will save face for now, but the truth cannot be hidden forever. You of all people should know that truth cannot be covered up!
~BOARD
A mathematical result has a proof deeper than any other.

MagiCicada
Nymphs suck on roots for 17 years. Adults emerge. They swarm & cover the landscape. Within a few weeks, they mate, lay eggs & then die.
WHY DO THEY WAIT FOR SO LONG?
There is another Cicada that waits 13 years. What could be the advantage? Perhaps there is a parasite that preys on the Cicada that also has a long life cycle. The Cicada wants to avoid years that are divisible by 2 or 3.~ it would meet up with Parasite sooner. There are no whole numbers that divide evenly into prime numbers. *→
MATE
SWARM
DIE
MUD
TUNNEL
SUCK
{*13 & 17 are PRIME numbers}
If the parasite shows up every year~ then it would die out while waiting!! The parasite could also try to evolve into the same 17 year cycle. This would take even longer~ It would take 272 years for bugs with 16 & 17 year life cycles to meet up.
No one knows for sure, but scientists think that the parasite that plagued the cicada may have died out long ago~ leaving the cicada stuck with this super~ long life cycle.

WHAT HAVE WE LOST?
The Artist in his Museum
Lives are lived, and work is done. People create new ideas and methods. They solve, create, and ponder new problems. They attempt to pass the knowledge on~ or keep a record for the future of the work they have done~ of their LIVES.
PUNK ART
Society and culture will change. The work and knowledge could be lose. destroyed randomly~ or on purpose. The old knowledge may seem sacrilegious in the new society. The knowledge may be secretly preserved or it may escape.
A person may choose to spend life creating work in secret. After they die~ the work might disappear~ but perhaps it will be found. The images or ideas or writings may become well known~ whether he wanted them to or not~~
LEWIS FOWLER
Numerous cultures & societies have been thoughtlessly destroyed or simply lost. What were they thinking? Does our ignorance of them negate the work they did? Did they want us to remember? Who cares?
The chaos of history somehow allows people from different times to share knowledge and discover new things. Is this not random and miraculous? What are the chances? IS POSTERITY SELFISH?
?

Infinite ∞ HOTEL
NO VACANCY
DAMN!
Hold on~ I'll find you a room...
Could everyone please move down one room?
There you are sir, room #1.
Thanks!
HEY!
I've got a bus outside filled with an infinite number of people!
?
Alright, Bring them in...
I need everyone to move into the room that is DOUBLE the number of the room you are in now...
O.K. Have your people move into any ODD numbered rooms.
thanks
Some Infinities are Bigger Than Others.
ARCHIMEDES
GET OUT OF THE WAY, OLD MAN! I AM POWER! YOU MUST OBEY!
I am concentrating so hard on this problem, that I cannot even acknowledge the presence of this man in front of me.
THEN DIE!
violence!
The divisors of: 220 are 1,2,4,5,10,11→
20,22,44,55,110. The sum of these numbers is
MATHEMATICAL APHRODISIAC
284
220
SLURP
71,142. The sum of these numbers is
The divisors of: 284 are: 1,2,4,
EULER
~Developed the algorithmic method~
"The mathematical cyclops"
Got paid £300.
Now I have less distraction
Infinite descent...
Goes completely Blind-yet calculates lunar positions.
Goes blind in one eye ~ works with imaginary numbers.
The imaginary number is a fine and wonderful recourse in the divine spirit~ an amphibian between being & non-being.

I'm kind of only an Amateur Academic. I do some math in my spare time. I'm really a civil servant. I live kind of far away from academia. I don't really interact with it.
I love this old math book. It's got this theorem by this old guy in it.
y
z
x
$x^2 + y^2 = z^2$
I wonder if this theorem is true for any numbers higher than 2. In other words:
$x^n + y^n = z^n$
Hm. I can DEFINITELY prove that no numbers higher than 2 fit this equation. The way I've proved it is quite ingenious, if I do say so myself.
I've been jotting notes down in the margins of this old book. I'll just make a note here that I can prove this.
Arithmeticorum
demonstration of this proposition which this margin is too narrow to contain
My father {God rest his soul} sure loved this old book. He made all kinds of notes in the margins.
I've got an idea! I'm going to publish an edition of this book ~ and I'll include the notes my father wrote in the margins. -That way, his work will never be forgotten!
I couldn't solve it
I couldn't solve it.
I couldn't solve it.
I couldn't solve it.
Have you seen this new edition of the Arithmetica?
Yeah, it's got all these notations in it that the publishers father wrote. In particular there's this one problem that seems like it would be really hard to solve.
hm. I couldn't prove that.
I couldn't solve it.
I couldn't solve it.
I couldn't solve it!
I couldn't solve it.
I couldn't find it.
I couldn't solve it.
I couldn't solve it.
I couldn't solve it.
I couldn't find it.
I couldn't solve it.
I couldn't solve it.
I solved it.

OK~ So you see ~ these 2 different parts of mathematics are as far away from each other as possible.
?
Now, this young Japanese guy discovers one of these forms has numbers in a series that is identical to one of the other kinds of forms.
?
His frend takes the idea ~ and presents a paper that proposes that All of these forms are actually the same!
HEY!
GLORP!
Now this second guy becomes famous, and the first guy, who actually came up with the idea ~ became so upset that he killed himself!
Hey JOE!
!
!
Wait a minute! I heard about that suicide, but I never heard about it having anything to do with the conjecture! Where did you hear about this?
Um, my professor told me.
Do you think you could find me anything in writing that supports this?
I can try.
HEY!
SUICIDE STOPPER
OK! Perfect! I've got it all figured out! I will kill myself at the stroke of midnight!
Um, well, what the heck am I going to do until then? ....
... I guess I'll go to the library.
Wow. Nobody's been able to find a proof to this problem for a long time. It's really intriguing.
Scritch
Scritch
Oh my god! It's past midnight! My plan to kill myself has been ruined!
In honor of this great problem. that gave me the will to live again, I am going to set up a fund which will award the man who finally does find a proof for this problem.
$X^N + Y^N =$

I was sitting right here at this desk. in the attic.
{Like he had for 7 years}
When suddenly, quite unexpectedly, I had an incredible revelation.
It was the most important moment of my working life.
Nothing he ever does will be as significant.
I had solved the last theorem.
I went the afternoon without lunch. Around 4:00 I was sure it was solved, so I went downstairs.
Oh. You're awful late! Aren't you hungry?
I've found it.
Hm? Josh's toy? Oh, good. He'll be so relieved!
No. I've done it. I've solved the the theorem!
PLOP!
Leading up to a new idea, there has to be a period of intense, undistracted concentration on the problem.
For seven years~ I would wake up with the idea, think about it all day long~ and go to sleep thinking of it~
Afterwards, there seems to be a kind of period of relaxation during which the subconcious appears to take over, and it's during that time that some new insight comes.
I find walking to have an extraordinary effect on your concentration. I would often come here by the lake. While walking, you are concentrating & relaxing at the same time
He first discovered the theorem as a ten year old boy. The problem makes sense, even to a boy~but the greatest minds in math hadn't cracked it for 300 years. While he grew to pursue a career as a great mathematician~ he never lost his desire to solve the problem.

Professor - can you tell me more about the suicide? Did it have to do with his work being stolen from him?

Although the man who took his own life was the one who had the initial idea ~ his frend did a lot of work on making it presentable after his death. He didn't simply sugarcoat the work & then take credit for it, as you suggest. Quite the contrary - - - -

oh.

— he worked long & hard to convince other mathematicians of the conjecture's legitimacy. Saying all of the forms are the same is a lot different than saying that some of them are. He created a legacy for himself and his late frend!

I could've sworn I heard almost the OPPOSITE!

HA! See how easily history could be re-written?

Pfft! yeah, yeah...

You know the man who finally solved both the Japanese conjecture ~ & therefore proved the problem that everyone's been trying to prove for 300 years? ~ Well, a big part of why he worked in secret was so that no one would steal his work! OR steal what he had done ~ and solve the puzzle!

Do you know who I'd really like to read an interview with? His wife! She was the only one he confided in for 7 years! Mathematicians can be like babies when they are working on a problem they can think of nothing else! She must have had a lot to deal with.

Bye Joe

~ Thanks to: Richard Cochinos & Jordan Crane for help. ~

Large parts of this story were adapted directly from "FERMAT'S ENIGMA" - a book by Simon Singh.

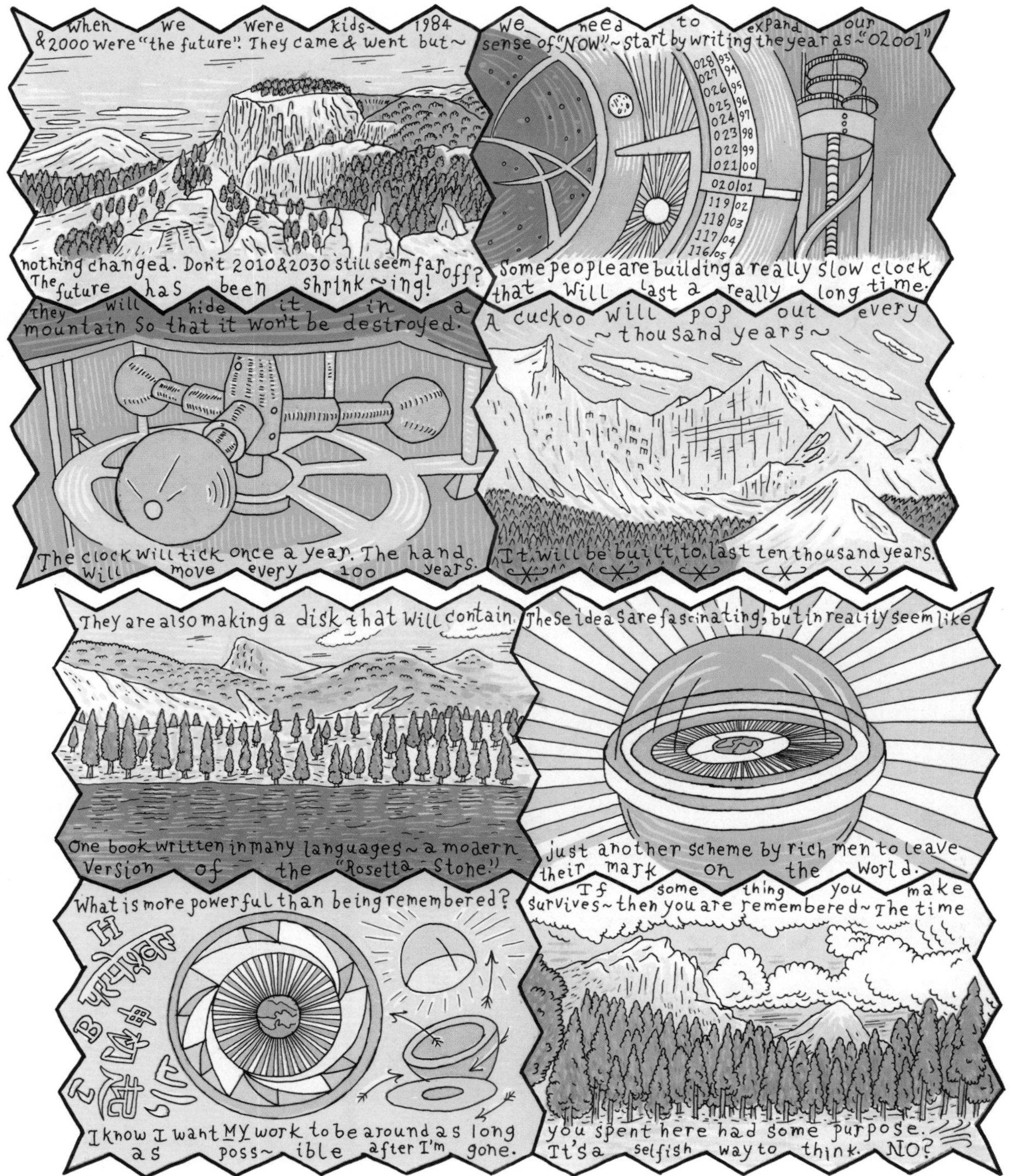

When we were kids~ 1984 &2000 were "the future". They came & went but~
nothing changed. Don't 2010&2030 still seem far off? The future has been shrink~ing!
We need to expand our sense of "NOW"~start by writing the year as "02001"
Some people are building a really slow clock that will last a really long time.
They will hide it in a mountain so that it won't be destroyed.
The clock will tick once a year. The hand will move every 100 years.
A cuckoo will pop out every ~thousand years~
It will be built to last ten thousand years.
They are also making a disk that will contain
One book written in many languages~a modern version of the "Rosetta Stone."
These ideas are fascinating, but in reality seem like
just another scheme by rich men to leave their mark on the world.
What is more powerful than being remembered?
I know I want MY work to be around as long as poss~ible after I'm gone.
If some thing you make survives~then you are remembered~The time
you spent here had some purpose. It's a selfish way to think. NO?

RON REGÉ, JR. We Must Know, We Will Know

COMIC SECTION. **THE NEW YORK HERALD.** FOUR PAGES.

NEW YORK, SUNDAY, JANUARY 19, 1913.—(COPYRIGHT, 1913, BY THE NEW YORK HERALD COMPANY.) PRICE FIVE CENTS.

DREAM OF THE RAREBIT FIEND

BY SILAS

Winsor McCay (publishing as "Silas"), Dream of the Rarebit Fiend, *Sunday page, January 19, 1913. Collection of Chris Ware.*

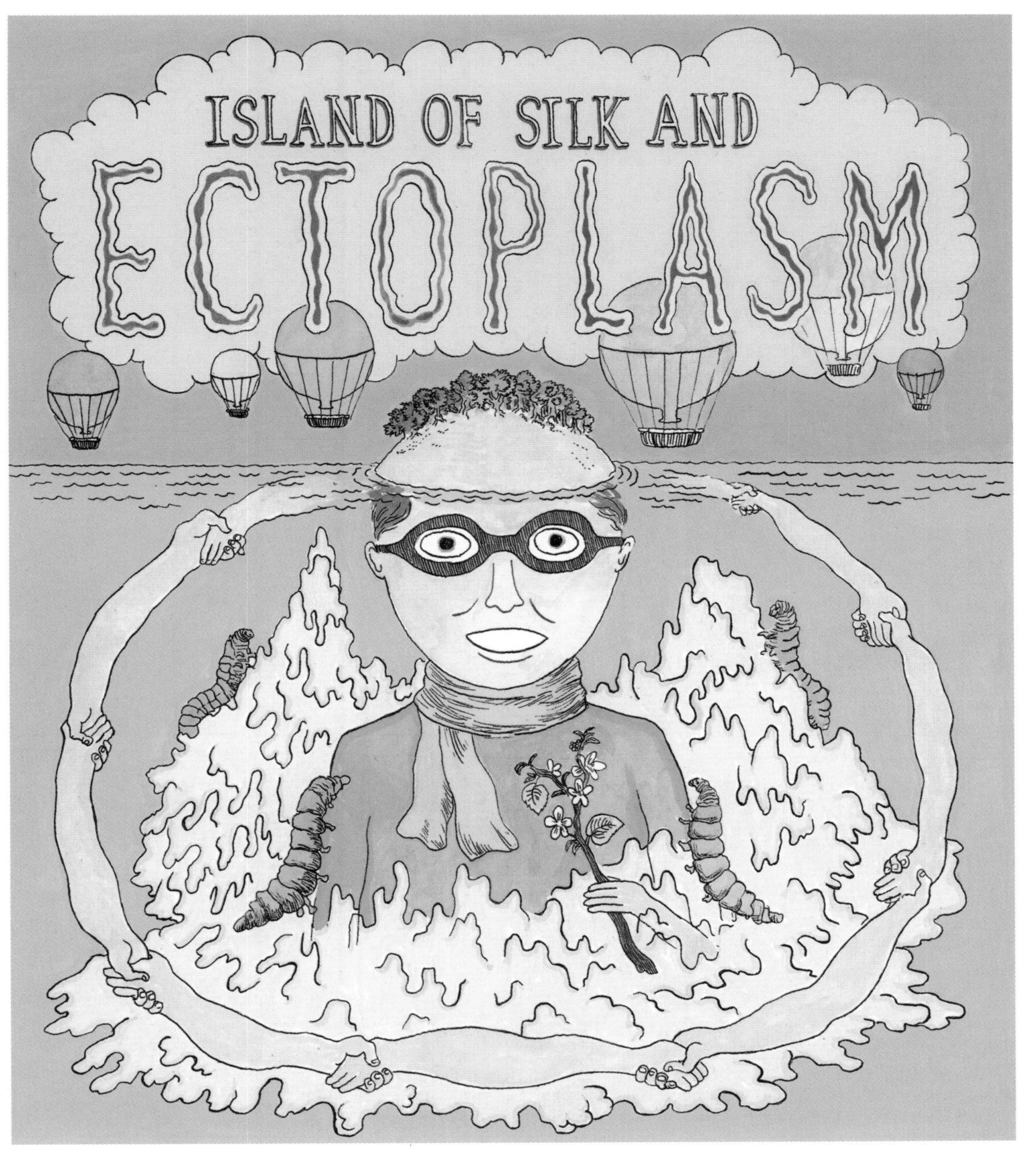
ISLAND OF SILK AND
ECTOPLASM

THE GREAT BALLOON RACE INTO THE BEYOND OCCURS EVERY 20 YEARS ABOVE THE ISLAND OF GUFFRE BLOMS.

FOR THE FIRST MINUTES OF THE RACE, THE AERONAUTS BURN THEIR FUEL SUPPLY.

WHEN THE FUEL IS EXHAUSTED, THEY GAIN GREATER SPEED BY JETTISONING CLOTHES AND SUPPLIES.

Eternal Soul, I part with thee. Enter the vehicle which carries me. Please grant me Altitude and Victory.
FINALLY, THE BALLOONISTS TAKE THEIR OWN LIVES WHILE SPEAKING ALOUD THE WORDS OF A SACRED TEXT.

ONCE THEY HAVE PERISHED, THEIR SOULS DEPART THEIR EARTHLY STORAGE CONTAINERS.

THE SPIRITS RISE UP INTO THE BALLOONS, SWELLING TO FILL THE SILK AND COATING IT WITH ECTOPLASM.

THE COMPETITORS SLOWLY DRIFT APART AS THEY MAKE THEIR WAY INTO THE AFTERLIFE

THEY HAVE ALL ATTAINED THE MOST EXALTED HEIGHTS. WHAT REWARD IS IN STORE FOR THE SOUL THAT MADE THE FASTEST ASCENT?

THE SPIRITS OF THE WINNING BALLOONISTS ARE SUBSEQUENTLY EMPLOYED BY THE FORESTRY DEPARTMENT IN AN IMPORTANT ROLE, WHERE SPEED IS KEY.

ECTOPLASM
THEY GUARD THE MULBERRY TREES, WHICH HOUSE AND FEED THE ISLAND'S POPULATION OF SILKWORMS, FROM FIRE OR VANDALISM.

ALL THE SILK FOR BALLOON MANUFACTURE, AS WELL AS FOR THE ISLANDERS' CLOTHING, IS UNPEELED FROM THESE INSECT'S COCCOONS.

EACH YEAR THE SILKWORMS ENACT A PLAY ABOUT THEIR OWN SPIRITUAL BELIEFS, WATCHED INTENTLY THROUGH BINOCULARS BY THE ISLANDERS.

WE'VE LEFT THE LEAVES FILLED WITH PLENTY OF HOLES
AND NOW IT IS TIME TO SPIN OUT ALL OUR SOULS
TO CHILDHOOD FRIENDS BID YOUR ADIEUS NOW, INTO OUR COCCOONS TO SNOOZE

WHAT A FINE COCCOON YOU'VE MADE, MY BROTHER XXITIZX. HOW ARE YOUR MOTHWINGS COMING ALONG?
SADLY, I AM ALMOST FINISHED... IT LOOKS AS THOUGH I MAY... NOT... BE CHOSEN. BUT IT WON'T BE HALF BAD TO BE A MOTH, WILL IT? BROTHER?
NO! NO! (AHEM) NO DISGRACE AT ALL!

XXITIZX! YOUR SOUL! IT IS BEING PLUCKED UP BY THE GODS!
I KNEW THEY'D CHOOSE ME! I SPUN SO LONG, SO DILIGENTLY!
I AM FILLED WITH HAPPINESS FOR YOU, BROTHER!

HE IS NO MORE! HE WILL NEVER KNOW MOTH-HOOD!
BUT ONLY SOMETHING BETTER! HE WILL FLY HIGHER THAN ANY MOTH—
INTO HEAVEN!

THE FINALE
GOODBYE MULBERRY TREE IT'S BEEN MARVY! NOW WE'LL FLY SOMEWHERE ELSE TO RAISE OUR LARVAE

LOOK AT THE GLORIOUS LITTLE CREATURES!
WE SIMPLY COULDN'T GET BY WITHOUT THEM.
HONK
SILK HANKY

MY HANDKERCHIEF IS COATED WITH -- WHAT IS THIS STUFF COMING OUT OF MY NOSE?

HELLO EVERYONE! WHERE'S THE FIRE?

TALES OF THE
SUPERNATURAL
PARK RANGERS

BUT NOTHING IS BURNING! WE WERE JUST WATCHING THE SILKWORMS' ANNUAL PAGEANT!
THE PROBLEM MUST BE IN THAT THEATER! PLEASE, HOLD UP YOUR BINOCULARS BACKWARDS!

WITH MY SIZE REDUCED BY 24x, I'LL SOLVE THIS MYSTERY BEFORE THE CURTAIN FALLS!

HEY!! YOU CAN'T GO BACK-STAGE!

YOU'VE STEPPED ON MY LINES ONE TIME TOO MANY, XXITIZX! UPSTAGED BY A PUPA? I THINK NOT!!

A GHOST!! I RENOUNCE MY EVIL-DOING!

WITH THE FLAMES OF ARSON QUENCHED, AGENT ECTO VANISHES BACK INTO THE NOSTRIL OF THE HAPLESS THEATER SPECTATOR...
TO MANIFEST AGAIN WHEREVER A LEAF OF A MULBERRY TREE IS THREATENED! JOIN US FOR MORE BUBBLING ECTOPLASM AND MORE TALES OF THE SUPERNATURAL PARK RANGERS!

FERVLER 'N' RAZZLE
in:
BROKEN
BRICKS
RUBBER BANDS
RUBBER BANDS
WAHHH
WAAAHH
WAAAAA
UH-OH
RAZZLE?
ARE YOU OK?
?
DOES IT LOOK LIKE I'M OK?!!
LOOK AROUND.
WHAT DO YOU SEE?
SNF
BROKEN BRICKS
YES
SO?
SO, BROKEN BRICKS MEANS MY CASTLE IS CRUMBLING!!!
OH.
WELL, LETS FIX IT THEN
HOW?
I HAVE SOME RUBBER BANDS
BUT I LEFT THEM ON THE SLIDE
I WAS JUST GONNA GO BACK AND GET THEM
SIGH
RUBBER BANDS WON'T FIX MY CASTLE, FERVLER
OH...
OH YEAH, HA HA, I KNEW THAT
I WAS JUST PLAYIN'
LETS GO GET 'EM ANYWAY

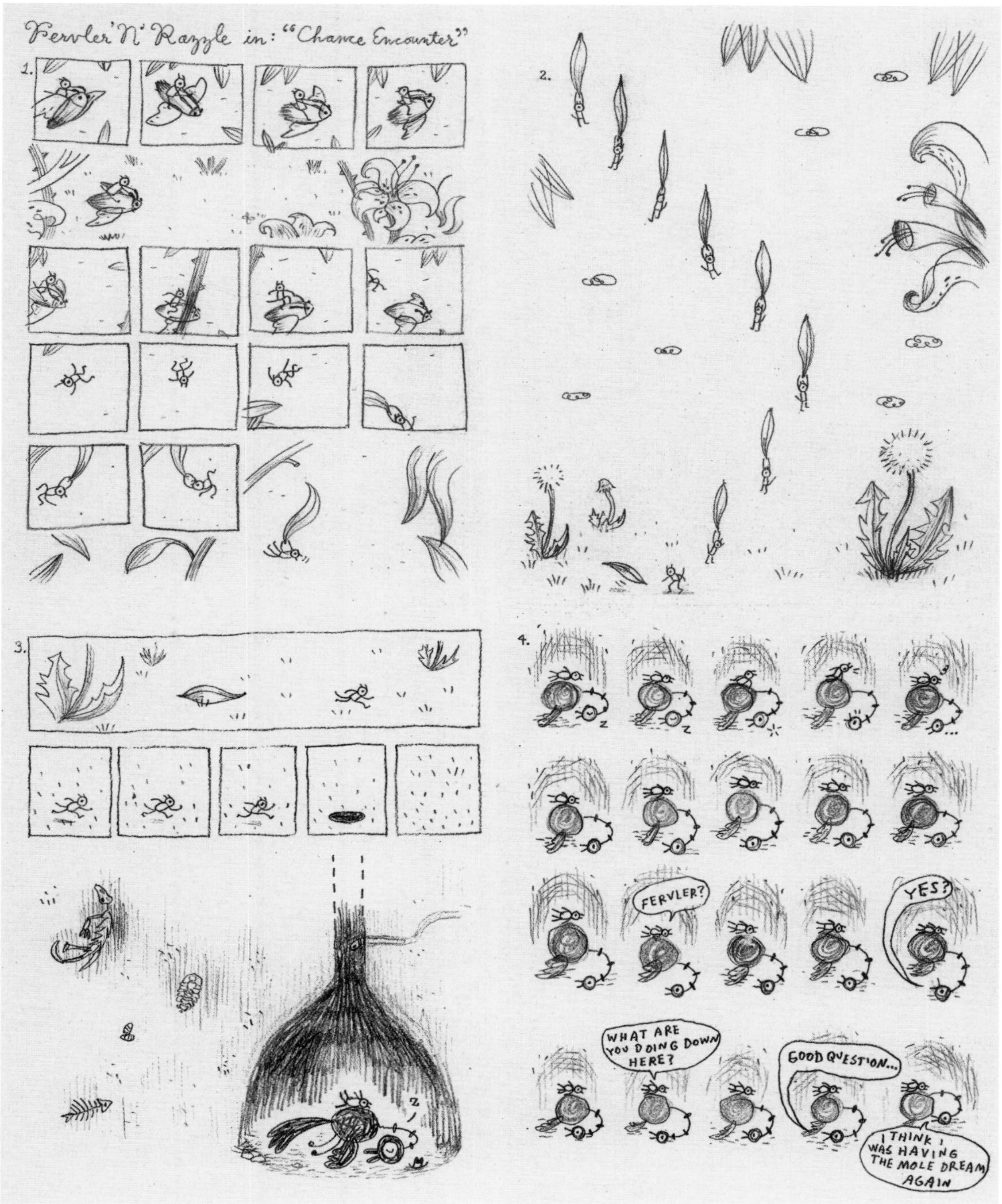

SOUTHER SALAZAR Fervler 'n' Razzle

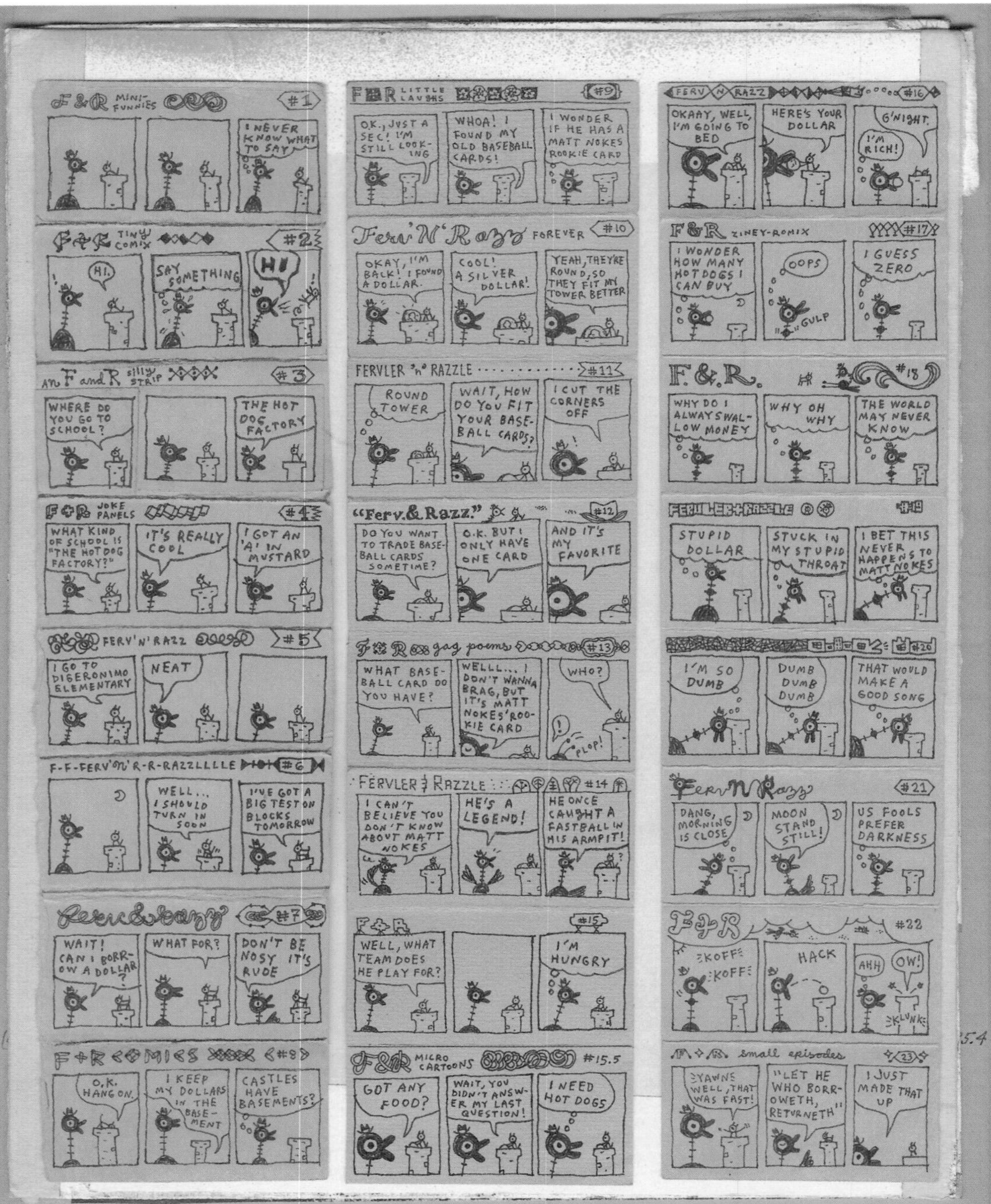
F&R MINI-FUNNIES #1
I NEVER KNOW WHAT TO SAY
F&R TINY COMIX #2
HI.
SAY SOMETHING
HI
AN F AND R SILLY STRIP #3
WHERE DO YOU GO TO SCHOOL?
THE HOT DOG FACTORY
F&R JOKE PANELS #4
WHAT KIND OF SCHOOL IS "THE HOT DOG FACTORY?"
IT'S REALLY COOL
I GOT AN 'A' IN MUSTARD
FERV'N'RAZZ #5
I GO TO DIGERONIMO ELEMENTARY
NEAT
F-F-FERV'N'R-R-RAZZLLLLE #6
WELL... I SHOULD TURN IN SOON
I'VE GOT A BIG TEST ON BLOCKS TOMORROW
Ferv&Razz #7
WAIT! CAN I BORROW A DOLLAR?
WHAT FOR?
DON'T BE NOSY IT'S RUDE
F+R COMICS #8
O.K. HANG ON.
I KEEP MY DOLLARS IN THE BASEMENT
CASTLES HAVE BASEMENTS?
F&R LITTLE LAUGHS #9
O.K., JUST A SEC! I'M STILL LOOKING
WHOA! I FOUND MY OLD BASEBALL CARDS!
I WONDER IF HE HAS A MATT NOKES ROOKIE CARD
Ferv'N'Razz FOREVER #10
OKAY, I'M BACK! I FOUND A DOLLAR.
COOL! A SILVER DOLLAR!
YEAH, THEY'RE ROUND, SO THEY FIT MY TOWER BETTER
FERVLER 'N' RAZZLE #11
ROUND TOWER
WAIT, HOW DO YOU FIT YOUR BASEBALL CARDS?
I CUT THE CORNERS OFF
"Ferv.& Razz." #12
DO YOU WANT TO TRADE BASEBALL CARDS SOMETIME?
O.K. BUT I ONLY HAVE ONE CARD
AND IT'S MY FAVORITE
F&R gag poems #13
WHAT BASEBALL CARD DO YOU HAVE?
WELLL...! DON'T WANNA BRAG, BUT IT'S MATT NOKES' ROOKIE CARD
WHO?
PLOP!
FERVLER & RAZZLE #14
I CAN'T BELIEVE YOU DON'T KNOW ABOUT MATT NOKES
HE'S A LEGEND!
HE ONCE CAUGHT A FASTBALL IN HIS ARMPIT!
F&R #15
WELL, WHAT TEAM DOES HE PLAY FOR?
I'M HUNGRY
F&R MICRO CARTOONS #15.5
GOT ANY FOOD?
WAIT, YOU DIDN'T ANSWER MY LAST QUESTION!
I NEED HOT DOGS
FERV N RAZZ #16
OKAAY, WELL, I'M GOING TO BED
HERE'S YOUR DOLLAR
G'NIGHT.
I'M RICH!
F&R ZINEY-ROMIX #17
I WONDER HOW MANY HOT DOGS I CAN BUY
OOPS
GULP
I GUESS ZERO
F.&R. #18
WHY DO I ALWAYS SWALLOW MONEY
WHY OH WHY
THE WORLD MAY NEVER KNOW
STUPID DOLLAR
STUCK IN MY STUPID THROAT
I BET THIS NEVER HAPPENS TO MATT NOKES
#20
I'M SO DUMB
DUMB DUMB DUMB
THAT WOULD MAKE A GOOD SONG
Ferv N Razz #21
DANG, MORNING IS CLOSE
MOON STAND STILL!
US FOOLS PREFER DARKNESS
F+R #22
KOFF KOFF
HACK
AHH
OW!
KLUNK
F&R small episodes #23
YAWN WELL, THAT WAS FAST!
"LET HE WHO BORROWETH, RETURNETH"
I JUST MADE THAT UP

I'M FLYING HIGHER THAN A KITE! I JUST MET THE GIRL OF MY DREAMS!

THIS IS GOING TO BE THE BEST SUMMER EVER!

PIE FACE

BY KEVIN SCALZO ©2000

IT WAS LAST FRIDAY NIGHT... MY FRIENDS AND I WERE BUSY GETTING DRUNK PLAYING "QUARTERS" BUT THIS WAS QUICKLY GROWING TIRESOME....

...SO WE DECIDED TO GET ANOTHER CASE OF BEER AND HEAD OVER TO A PARTY THAT WE HEARD WAS ALREADY "RAGING"..

OLD MILWAUKEE

BRET AND I BROUGHT THE BEER INTO THE HOUSE. OF COURSE, EVERYBODY RAN AFTER US......

THAT'S WHEN I FIRST SAW HER. SITTING AMONG A COUPLE OF OTHER FOXES.

SHE WAS DEATH. I HAD TO MEET HER

WE TALKED FOR A REALLY LONG TIME... I WAS DRINKING A LOT, AND GETTING VERY DRUNK.

I FELT MY SELF FALLING IN LOVE AS WE STOOD THERE..

PROCESSED
BY KODAK

Kodachrome
TRANSPARENCY

z z z z z z

PROCESSED
BY KODAK
Kodachrome
TRANSPARENCY

09/12/04
James McShane
9:30
9:40
9:50
10:00
10:10
10:20
10:30
10:40
10:50
11:00
11:10
singing
11:20
11:30
home
11:40
11:50
12:00
12:10
12:20
12:30
12:40
12:50
1:00
cereal
1:10
tea
1:20
1:30
1:40
1:50
2:00
2:10
2:20

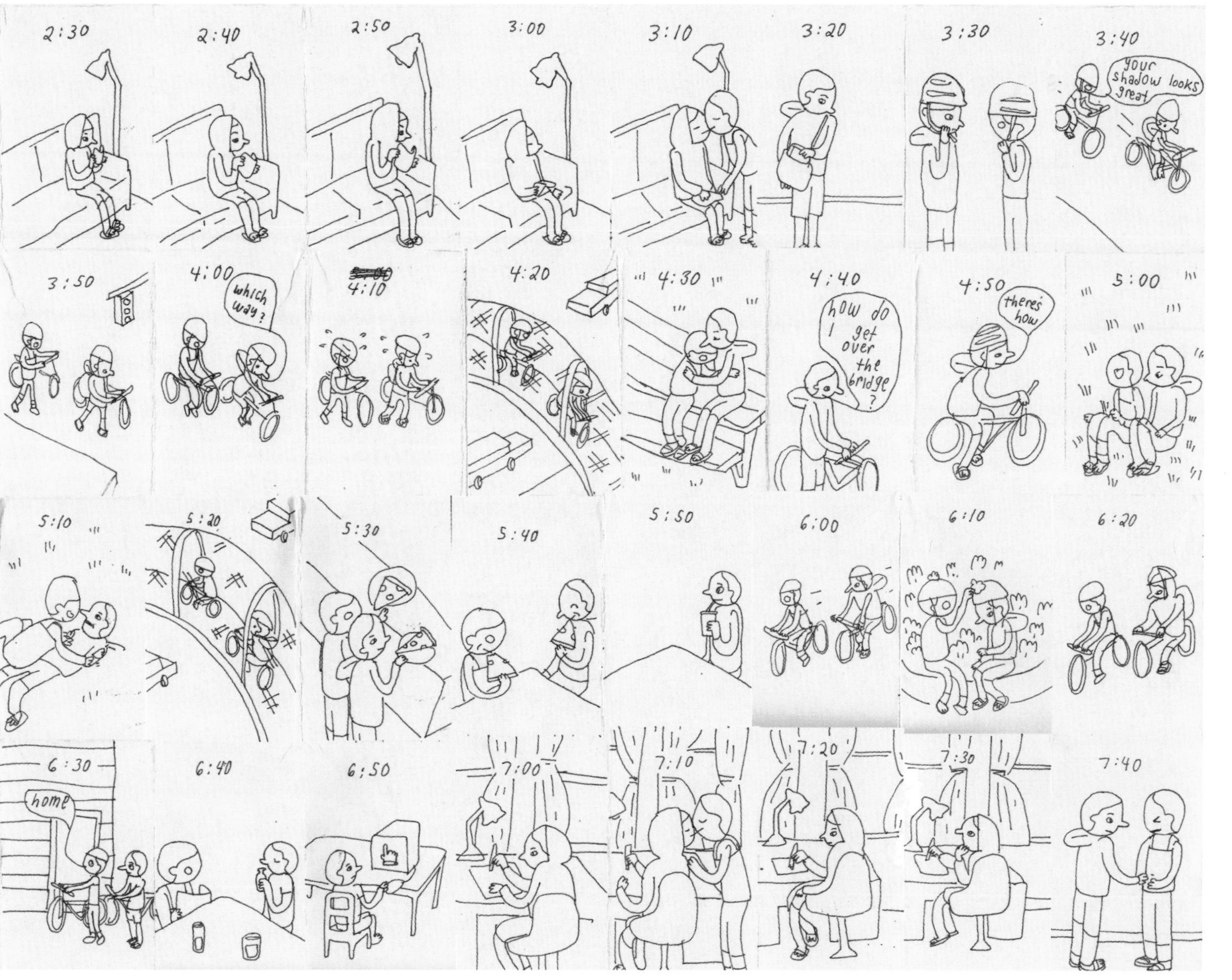

 JAMES McSHANE 09/12/04

7:50
8:00
8:10
8:20
8:30
8:40*
* oops. I drew my picture in the 9:40 space
8:50
snap
9:00
5$?
9:10
9:20
hi James
JT
9:30
hi mark.
I mean James
9:40*
* this happened at 8:40
9:50
10:00
10:10
10:20
10:30
back stage
10:40
10:50
11:00
11:10
11:20
11:30
11:40
11:50
12:00
12:10
12:20
12:30
12:40
12:50
- keep a log
- every ten minutes draw what you've done
- do this all day

HOT WATER & MINERAL SALT SOAK
PEDICURE TOOLS!!
JAR OF MINERAL SALTS
LUXURY
THY NAME IS PEDICURE
AND MANICURE TOO!
YOU WEAR WEIRD FAKE FLIP FLOPS AND FOAM SPACERS...
FIRST YOU SOAK!
NOW THEY PAINT YOUR TOENAILSS!
THEN THEY TRIM AND SHAPE YOUR NAILS AND SNIP OFF DEAD SKIN
NEXT THEY RAZOR OFF THE ROUGH SPOTS ON THE SOLE OF YOUR FOOT
THEY MASSAGE YOUR FEET AND LEGS
RED NAILPOLISH W/ RED GLITTER
SUNDAY
SEPTEMBER 4TH
MINE: PISTACHIO & HAZELNUT GELATO
BARBARA: COCONUT & HAZELNUT GELATO
MINE: CORNMEAL TURNOVERS W/ SPINACH AND CHEESE RED BEANS & RICE, EGGS, MOLE, & PICO DE GALLO
BARBARA: BLUEBERRY & STRAWBERRY PANCAKES
MY FIRST MANICURE AND PEDICURE
a special gift from Barbara
GOLD TIPS & HOT PINK!
RED W/ RED GLITTER
FRENCH MANI CURED NAILS + TOES
Wonka
WEIRD!
7PM - CHARLIE & THE CHOCOLATE FACTORY

I've been gradually freaking more and more out about moving away
Oh Vanessa! A month is so fast! We're going to miss you so much!
I have to do it in a month! I'll just stay up and get it done!
Don't people leave New York all the time? Everyone's lives go on! Things change!
Vanessa You ASK for advice constantly!
I am So SICK of everyone giving me advice!
I stayed way too late in the office, clicking "refresh" on my empty inbox and feeling crazy
And do you feel Scared?
I-I Doooo!
THOUSANDS FEARED DEAD
BODIES FLOATING IN FLOOD WATERS
SOB!
Sept. 1, 2005

I ended up at a "Latin" club
Would you care to dance?
OK
I could tell, he took lessons
Ha! ha!
It was so sweet and funny, I couldn't stop laughing
Ah hee hee hee!
He didn't
Stop laughing and show me you LIKE IT
like that.
Sept. 3, 2005

Michel drew me and Gabrielle and it came out so well
Gabrielle left the room for a second, and I wasn't watching
When she came out
I hate my drawing
NO!
CRUMPLE
But it was a joke
Ha ha
!
He hid the real one
crumpled decoy
September 5, 2005

502 West Main Street 2008 ONSMITH

SPRING 1987

He found a porno mag underneath this piece of plywood. It was all wrinkled and waterlogged.

He tore out a piece of a page where a woman was spread eagle on the hood of a Pontiac Firebird.

He put the scrap in his wallet. He would most likely use the excuse...

...that he only liked the car, should his mother ever find it.

SUMMER 1987

This patch of lawn never grew back because he set it on fire.

He took the gas can from the shed, poured the gas into paper Dixie cups, and threw matches into them.

Soon, the fire grew, and I have no idea why, but he poured gas onto the open flame, ending up burning his hair and shorts a little bit.

He smelled like gas and burnt hair for several days.

SUMMER 1988

Taking a can of his father's WD-40, he walked over to the porch and sprayed a wasp's nest...

...killing a few only to run down the hill as others chased him.

He bragged to his mother how he'd killed some...

...telling her he did it by swatting and stomping on them.
WD-40
DANGER

FALL 1988

On this side of the storm cellar, he was out of the line of sight from the house.

He had a pouch of chewing tobacco and was sucking on a large wad of it.
RED MAN

He spat several times, but within fifteen minutes, he vomited.

He then covered the pile of vomit with leaves from the maple tree.

SPRING 1989

Here's the fence he would climb to get on top of the roof of the house.

He would lay up there sometimes at night making odd voices, maybe impersonations.

On one occasion, I suppose out of curiosity or the desire for a new experience...

...he masturbated while he was up there.

WINTER 1989

Once, he climbed this tree and perched awkwardly on a high branch.

He started to cry for some reason.

I suppose he thought no one could see him up there...

...but I watched him for at least a half an hour.

JUNE 1ST, 1988

THE STORY OF..

MY FIRST LOVE...

Laura #1

NOW IT CAN BE TOLD!!

IDEALIZED MEMORY

NOT TO BE CONFUSED WITH..

Laura #2

HOW COME YOU DRAW LIPS ON EVERYONE BUT ME?!

HMMM.. LET'S SEE.. I WAS 18 WHEN I MET LAURA MY FIRST YEAR IN COLLEGE. SHE WAS QUITE A WILD GIRL BACK THEN...

SCULPTURE CLASS...

I CAN'T HELP IT, PROFESSOR!! IT'S MY PENIS ENVY!!

SQUIRT!

ME

STILL A VIRGIN

AND NEXT FALL, WHETHER SHE WANTED ONE OR NOT, LAURA HAD A PUPPY-DOG...

HEY, LAURA! WANNA WALK TO CLASS TOGETHER?? HUH? DO YA? HUH?? CAN I CARRY YOUR PORTFOLIO? HUH??

?

BUT I WASN'T THE ONLY ONE HOUNDING HER..

NO, YOU CAN'T DROP BY MY PLACE TONIGHT.

I'LL BRING A SIX-PACK...

9:30.

PARTY GIRL

MY DESIRE FOR HER ONLY INTENSIFIED

MOMMA!! BUY ME DAT!!

DROOL DROOL

ONE NIGHT I SUNK SO LOW THAT AFTER PUTTING HER DRUNK ROOMMATE TO BED, I WAITED IN THE DARK FOR LAURA TO RETURN HOME FROM THE PARTY...

MAYBE I CAN CATCH HER UNDRESSING + THEN LEAVE WHILE SHE'S SLEEPING...

LAURA'S BED

BEACHED WHALE

BUT STILL I PERSEVERED...

I GUESS I'LL JUST HAVE TO REDEEM HER. THAT'S ALL THERE IS TO IT....

MESSIAH COMPLEX

AND EVENTUALLY WE BECAME GOOD FRIENDS...

REMEMBER - I GET TO DRAW YOU NEXT!

JUST HOLD STILL.

UNTIL FINALLY, ONE NIGHT, WITH A LITTLE ALCOHOLIC ENCOURAGEMENT, I LOST MY VIRGINITY TO HER...

I DON'T BELIEVE IT!

THIS CAN'T BE HAPPENING!!

I'M IN!! I'M IN!! I'M IN!! I'M ACTUALLY IN!!

FOLLOWED IMMEDIATELY BY SOME QUICK CATHOLIC RATIONALIZING.

OH, WELL.. AS LONG AS I END UP MARRYING HER, I'LL STILL GO TO HEAVEN..

AND SOON I DISCOVERED WHY...

I HAD AN ABORTION A FEW MONTHS AGO...

IT'S O.K.. GOD FORGIVES YOU + I FORGIVE YOU.

NOT THE FATHER

THEN I BECAME JEALOUS + POSSESSIVE.

WHY'D YOU PUNCH THAT HOLE IN YOUR WALL?

BECAUSE I DON'T KNOW WHERE LAURA IS.

KEVIN

I WENT CRAZY...

WHATTA Y'MEAN - I'M SUFFOCATING YOU?? ALL I SAID WAS I CAN'T WAIT TO MARRY YOU!!

SO SHE DUMPED ME.

SORRY, JOE.. I LOVE YOU, BUT I'M JUST NOT IN LOVE WITH YOU ANYMORE.

AND FOR 2½ YEARS, I WAITED FOR HER TO COME BACK...

I DON'T CARE IF SHE IS ENGAGED. SHE'S JUST GOING THROUGH A PHASE..

SLOWLY, GRADUATION APPROACHED

I MAY NEVER SEE HER AGAIN!!

STRANGELY, A WEEK BEFORE GRADUATION...

I CAN'T BELIEVE WHAT JUST HAPPENED...

ME NEITHER. I GUESS THAT WAS LIKE OUR FINAL GOODBYE...

YEAH, I GUESS SO..

BY THE WAY.. NICE HAIRCUT.

..AND THAT WAS THE LAST I EVER SAW OF LAURA..

...ALTHOUGH I CONTINUED TO MAIL LOVE LETTERS TO HER FOR SEVERAL MONTHS...

I FINALLY QUIT MY OBSESSION WITH HER WHEN SHE GOT MARRIED 7 MONTHS AFTER OUR GRADUATION.

best if we just terminate this relationship. ave a good life. Love, Joe

A WEEK LATER, I RECEIVED A LETTER FROM LAURA, BUT I NEVER REPLIED.

YOU JERK!

OCT. 24TH, 1988

GRRR..I HATE COLORING.. ..I'M UNDERPAID..NO TIME FOR MY OWN STRIPS...I'VE SOLD-OUT.. NOW I'M TRAPPED HERE IN MONTREAL..

..RESTAURANTS STINK..THE BOOK-STORES SUCK.. ..I CAN'T EVEN SPEAK FRENCH..

OCT. 25TH, 1989.
LIFE SURE IS FUNNY...
Z
A MONTH + ½ AGO, TRISH DUMPED ME + THERE WAS ANOTHER GUY LIVING HERE WITH HER FOR TWO WHOLE WEEKS!! NOW, WE'RE BACK TOGETHER AGAIN... ...CHRIST...
ONLY, IT'S JUST NOT THE SAME ANYMORE! I DUNNO... IT FEELS LIKE OUR INNOCENCE IS GONE NOW OR SOMETHING...
LOOKIT HER... SHE HAS NO REGRETS... SHE FEELS TOTALLY JUSTIFIED BECAUSE IT WAS ALL MY PORN WATCHING THAT MADE HER DUMP ME IN THE FIRST PLACE...
AND I AGREE -- I STARTED ALL OF THIS... THAT'S THE ONLY REASON WHY I CAN STILL TAKE HER BACK...
BUT THAT DOESN'T STOP ME FROM THINKING ABOUT THIS OTHER GUY... AND ALL I FEEL LIKE DOING THEN IS STRANGLING HER...
SO, NOW WE'RE JUST TAKING IT ONE DAY AT A TIME, AND IT SEEMS TO BE WORKING...
WE'RE BOTH TRYING TO CHANGE -- SHE'S GETTING MORE OBSESSED WITH HER SCHOOL WORK AND CAREER PLANS...
AND I'M TRYING NOT TO BE SO CHEAP, SO I GET OUT MORE... IT'S TOO EASY AND UNHEALTHY TO ALWAYS BE A RECLUSE...
303
ONE THING'S FOR SURE, I'M FINALLY THROUGH WITH PORNOGRAPHY... I WAS JUST TRYING TO HAVE MY CAKE + EAT IT TOO... BUT NOW IT'S OVER...
FOR STARTERS, IT'S TOO EMBARRASSING THE WAY IT'S A RECURRING THEME IN MY COMICS...
HOW COULD I EVER DEFEND OR JUSTIFY WATCHING PORN TO A WOMAN'S FACE, WHEN I AGREE THAT IT'S DEGRADING TOWARDS THEM?!
CHOMP GULP
THE ONLY REASON I GOT ADDICTED TO IT IN THE FIRST PLACE WAS BECAUSE ALL OF THE GIRLS I'VE EVER LUSTED AFTER TOTALLY IGNORED ME IN MY YOUTH... STILL DO... LIKE I'M NOT GOOD ENOUGH FOR 'EM...
I GUESS I AM A BIT OF A MISOGYNIST, AS MUCH AS I HATE TO ADMIT IT... BUT I'M TRYING TO CHANGE, AND QUITTING PORN'S THE FIRST STEP...
I JUST HOPE I DON'T TURN INTO SOME SELF-RIGHTEOUS, ANTI-PORN CRUSADER... THERE'S ALREADY TOO MANY IDIOTS OUT THERE TRYING TO TELL PEOPLE HOW TO LIVE...
WHAT WE NEED IS LESS MORALIZING AND MORE HUMANIZING...
INSTEAD, SOCIETY SEEMS BENT ON SELF-DESTRUCTION...
WE'RE CONSTANTLY BOMBARDED BY A MASS MEDIA THAT PROMOTES: MATERIALISM... SEXISM ...RACISM... VIOLENCE... CRIME... GREED... BAH! THE LIST GOES ON AND ON...
NUCLEAR POWER... TOXIC WASTE... THE OZONE LAYER... OIL SPILLS... ACID RAIN... ENDANGERED SPECIES... ...OVERPOPULATION... AIDS...
LET'S FACE IT -- THE WORLD'S GOING TO HELL IN A HANDBAG! IT'S A PESSIMISTIC ATTITUDE, I'LL ADMIT, BUT AT LEAST IT'S REALISTIC...
HMM... TRISH ALWAYS COMPLAINS THAT I'M TOO NEGATIVE... BUT I CAN'T HELP IT!! HELL, SHE'S WORSE THAN ME...
ALL SHE EVER DOES IS COMPLAIN ABOUT BEING ALIVE AND HOW MUCH PRESSURE SHE'S UNDER...
BUT MOSTLY, SHE HATES LIVING IN A HUMAN BODY!! AND I AGREE -- THEY'RE PRETTY DAMN UNCOMFORTABLE...
ONLY DANCES WHEN ALONE
TRISH NEEDS AN OPTIMIST TO HELP PULL HER UP AND GET HER GOING... MAYBE I'M NOT THE ONE FOR HER...
PEEING IN THE SINK
MAYBE THERE IS NO SUCH THING AS "TRUE LOVE" LIKE WE KEEP SAYING... HOW THE HELL SHOULD I KNOW??
I MEAN, CHRIST... LOOK AT ALL THE BEAUTIFUL WOMEN IN THIS WORLD!! I COULD PROBABLY FALL IN LOVE WITH AT LEAST A FEW...
WHAT'S WRONG WITH ME?! IT CAN'T BE NORMAL TO BE THIS MUCH OF A GIRL-WATCHER!! BUT, GOD! WHAT LOVELY CREATURES!!
THE THING IS: THE GRASS IS ALWAYS GONNA BE GREENER ON THE OTHER SIDE, NO MATTER WHO I GO OUT WITH...
I'M JUST NEVER SATISFIED! AND YET, I'D CHOOSE IT ANY DAY OVER BEING CONTENT! IT DOESN'T MAKE ANY SENSE...
YOU'RE DAMNED IF YOU DO, AND YOU'RE DAMNED IF YOU DON'T! THAT'S HOW I SEE IT...
ALL I KNOW IS: I'VE GOTTA WORK DAMN HARD ON THIS RELATIONSHIP IF I WANT IT TO LAST... OTHERWISE, ONE OF US IS GONNA CHEAT ON THE OTHER --FOR REAL!
I WONDER IF IT'S THIS HARD FOR ALL COUPLES... OR IS IT JUST US?? I CAN'T SEEM TO FIGURE IT OUT...
EVERYONE I TALK TO SEEMS TO THINK I SHOULD TRY DATING OTHER GIRLS...
WITH SO MANY PEOPLE TELLING ME THE SAME THING, IT JUST HAS TO BE BAD ADVICE...
DO TRISH + I REALLY BELONG TOGETHER? OR BY JUST WONDERING THAT, IS THE ANSWER ALREADY "NO"?
WE SHOULD BE GIVEN A GUIDEBOOK BEFORE WE'RE THROWN INTO THIS STUPID WORLD...
I GUESS I'M JUST NOT A HAPPY GUY... BUT AT LEAST I HAVE MOMENTS...
ANYWAY, HOW CAN ANYONE TRULY BE HAPPY IN THIS WORLD, WHEN THE ONLY THING WE CAN BE ABSOLUTELY SURE OF IS THAT SOMEDAY WE'RE GOING TO DIE?
CHOMP CHOMP
STILL, THERE ARE PLENTY OF THINGS WORTH LIVING FOR... I DON'T DENY THAT... ...ALTHOUGH, TV SITCOMS AREN'T ONE OF THEM...
ONLY, HUMAN NATURE ALWAYS SEEMS TO PREVENT ME FROM ENJOYING ANYTHING! EVERY ATTEMPT I EVER MAKE AT A RELATIONSHIP ALWAYS SEEMS TO TURN INTO A LIVING HELL...
IF WE'RE NOT FEEDING OFF OF EACH OTHERS' INSECURITIES, THEN WE'RE TAKING EACH OTHER FOR GRANTED! I WISH WE COULD JUST START OVER AGAIN...
Y'KNOW, THE LEASE ON MY APARTMENT EXPIRES NEXT WEEK...
Y'WANNA MOVE IN HERE WITH ME?
SURE, WHAT THE HELL...

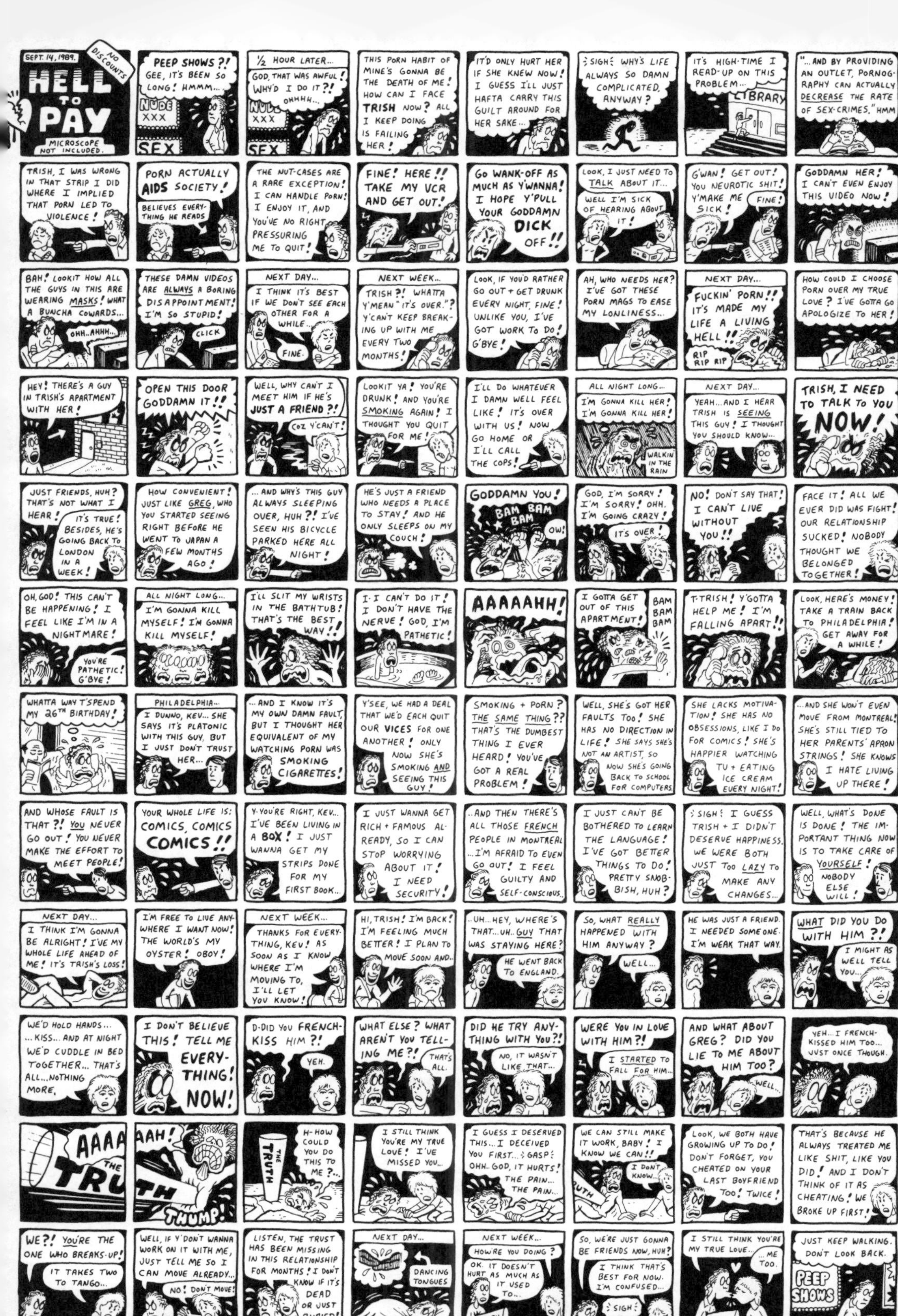
SEPT. 14, 1989.
HELL TO PAY
NO DISCOUNTS
MICROSCOPE NOT INCLUDED.
PEEP SHOWS?! GEE, IT'S BEEN SO LONG! HMMM...
NUDE XXX
SEX
1/2 HOUR LATER...
GOD, THAT WAS AWFUL! WHY'D I DO IT?!
OHHHH...
NUDE XXX
SEX
THIS PORN HABIT OF MINE'S GONNA BE THE DEATH OF ME! HOW CAN I FACE TRISH NOW? ALL I KEEP DOING IS FAILING HER!
IT'D ONLY HURT HER IF SHE KNEW NOW! I GUESS I'LL JUST HAFTA CARRY THIS GUILT AROUND FOR HER SAKE...
SIGH WHY'S LIFE ALWAYS SO DAMN COMPLICATED, ANYWAY?
IT'S HIGH-TIME I READ-UP ON THIS PROBLEM...
LIBRARY
"...AND BY PROVIDING AN OUTLET, PORNOGRAPHY CAN ACTUALLY DECREASE THE RATE OF SEX-CRIMES." HMM
TRISH, I WAS WRONG IN THAT STRIP I DID WHERE I IMPLIED THAT PORN LED TO VIOLENCE!
PORN ACTUALLY AIDS SOCIETY!
BELIEVES EVERYTHING HE READS
THE NUT-CASES ARE A RARE EXCEPTION! I CAN HANDLE PORN! I ENJOY IT, AND YOU'VE NO RIGHT PRESSURING ME TO QUIT!
FINE! HERE!! TAKE MY VCR AND GET OUT!
GO WANK-OFF AS MUCH AS Y'WANNA! I HOPE Y'PULL YOUR GODDAMN DICK OFF!!
LOOK, I JUST NEED TO TALK ABOUT IT...
WELL I'M SICK OF HEARING ABOUT IT!
G'WAN! GET OUT! YOU NEUROTIC SHIT! Y'MAKE ME SICK!
FINE!
GODDAMN HER! I CAN'T EVEN ENJOY THIS VIDEO NOW!
BAH! LOOKIT HOW ALL THE GUYS IN THIS ARE WEARING MASKS! WHAT A BUNCHA COWARDS...
OHH...AHHH...
THESE DAMN VIDEOS ARE ALWAYS A BORING DISAPPOINTMENT! I'M SO STUPID!
CLICK
NEXT DAY...
I THINK IT'S BEST IF WE DON'T SEE EACH OTHER FOR A WHILE...
FINE.
NEXT WEEK...
TRISH?! WHATTA Y'MEAN "IT'S OVER."? Y'CAN'T KEEP BREAKING UP WITH ME EVERY TWO MONTHS!
LOOK, IF YOU'D RATHER GO OUT + GET DRUNK EVERY NIGHT, FINE! UNLIKE YOU, I'VE GOT WORK TO DO! G'BYE!
AH, WHO NEEDS HER? I'VE GOT THESE PORN MAGS TO EASE MY LONLINESS...
NEXT DAY...
FUCKIN' PORN!! IT'S MADE MY LIFE A LIVING HELL!!
RIP RIP RIP
HOW COULD I CHOOSE PORN OVER MY TRUE LOVE? I'VE GOTTA GO APOLOGIZE TO HER!
HEY! THERE'S A GUY IN TRISH'S APARTMENT WITH HER!
OPEN THIS DOOR GODDAMN IT!!
WELL, WHY CAN'T I MEET HIM IF HE'S JUST A FRIEND?!
COZ Y'CAN'T!
LOOKIT YA! YOU'RE DRUNK! AND YOU'RE SMOKING AGAIN! I THOUGHT YOU QUIT FOR ME!
I'LL DO WHATEVER I DAMN WELL FEEL LIKE! IT'S OVER WITH US! NOW GO HOME OR I'LL CALL THE COPS!
ALL NIGHT LONG...
I'M GONNA KILL HER! I'M GONNA KILL HER!
WALKIN' IN THE RAIN
NEXT DAY...
YEAH...AND I HEAR TRISH IS SEEING THIS GUY! I THOUGHT YOU SHOULD KNOW...
TRISH, I NEED TO TALK TO YOU NOW!
JUST FRIENDS, HUH? THAT'S NOT WHAT I HEAR!
IT'S TRUE! BESIDES, HE'S GOING BACK TO LONDON IN A WEEK!
HOW CONVENIENT! JUST LIKE GREG, WHO YOU STARTED SEEING RIGHT BEFORE HE WENT TO JAPAN A FEW MONTHS AGO!
...AND WHY'S THIS GUY ALWAYS SLEEPING OVER, HUH?! I'VE SEEN HIS BICYCLE PARKED HERE ALL NIGHT!
HE'S JUST A FRIEND WHO NEEDS A PLACE TO STAY! AND HE ONLY SLEEPS ON MY COUCH!
GODDAMN YOU!
BAM BAM BAM
OW!
GOD, I'M SORRY! I'M SORRY! OHH. I'M GOING CRAZY!
IT'S OVER!
NO! DON'T SAY THAT! I CAN'T LIVE WITHOUT YOU!!
FACE IT! ALL WE EVER DID WAS FIGHT! OUR RELATIONSHIP SUCKED! NOBODY THOUGHT WE BELONGED TOGETHER!
OH, GOD! THIS CAN'T BE HAPPENING! I FEEL LIKE I'M IN A NIGHTMARE!
YOU'RE PATHETIC! G'BYE!
ALL NIGHT LONG...
I'M GONNA KILL MYSELF! I'M GONNA KILL MYSELF!
I'LL SLIT MY WRISTS IN THE BATHTUB! THAT'S THE BEST WAY!!
I-I CAN'T DO IT! I DON'T HAVE THE NERVE! GOD, I'M PATHETIC!
AAAAAHH!
I GOTTA GET OUT OF THIS APARTMENT!
BAM BAM BAM
T-TRISH! Y'GOTTA HELP ME! I'M FALLING APART!!
LOOK, HERE'S MONEY! TAKE A TRAIN BACK TO PHILADELPHIA! GET AWAY FOR A WHILE!
WHATTA WAY T'SPEND MY 26TH BIRTHDAY!
PHILADELPHIA...
I DUNNO, KEV... SHE SAYS IT'S PLATONIC WITH THIS GUY, BUT I JUST DON'T TRUST HER...
...AND I KNOW IT'S MY OWN DAMN FAULT, BUT I THOUGHT HER EQUIVALENT OF MY WATCHING PORN WAS SMOKING CIGARETTES!
Y'SEE, WE HAD A DEAL THAT WE'D EACH QUIT OUR VICES FOR ONE ANOTHER! ONLY NOW SHE'S SMOKING AND SEEING THIS GUY!
SMOKING + PORN? THE SAME THING?? THAT'S THE DUMBEST THING I EVER HEARD! YOU'VE GOT A REAL PROBLEM!
WELL, SHE'S GOT HER FAULTS TOO! SHE HAS NO DIRECTION IN LIFE! SHE SAYS SHE'S NOT AN ARTIST, SO NOW SHE'S GOING BACK TO SCHOOL FOR COMPUTERS
SHE LACKS MOTIVATION! SHE HAS NO OBSESSIONS, LIKE I DO FOR COMICS! SHE'S HAPPIER WATCHING TV + EATING ICE CREAM EVERY NIGHT!
...AND SHE WON'T EVEN MOVE FROM MONTREAL! SHE'S STILL TIED TO HER PARENTS' APRON STRINGS! SHE KNOWS I HATE LIVING UP THERE!
AND WHOSE FAULT IS THAT?! YOU NEVER GO OUT! YOU NEVER MAKE THE EFFORT TO MEET PEOPLE!
YOUR WHOLE LIFE IS: COMICS, COMICS COMICS!!
Y-YOU'RE RIGHT, KEV... I'VE BEEN LIVING IN A BOX! I JUST WANNA GET MY STRIPS DONE FOR MY FIRST BOOK...
I JUST WANNA GET RICH + FAMOUS ALREADY, SO I CAN STOP WORRYING ABOUT IT! I NEED SECURITY!
...AND THEN THERE'S ALL THOSE FRENCH PEOPLE IN MONTREAL ...I'M AFRAID TO EVEN GO OUT! I FEEL GUILTY AND SELF-CONSCIOUS.
I JUST CAN'T BE BOTHERED TO LEARN THE LANGUAGE! I'VE GOT BETTER THINGS TO DO! PRETTY SNOBBISH, HUH?
SIGH I GUESS TRISH + I DIDN'T DESERVE HAPPINESS. WE WERE BOTH JUST TOO LAZY TO MAKE ANY CHANGES...
WELL, WHAT'S DONE IS DONE! THE IMPORTANT THING NOW IS TO TAKE CARE OF YOURSELF! NOBODY ELSE WILL!
NEXT DAY...
I THINK I'M GONNA BE ALRIGHT! I'VE MY WHOLE LIFE AHEAD OF ME! IT'S TRISH'S LOSS!
I'M FREE TO LIVE ANYWHERE I WANT NOW! THE WORLD'S MY OYSTER! OBOY!
NEXT WEEK...
THANKS FOR EVERYTHING, KEV! AS SOON AS I KNOW WHERE I'M MOVING TO, I'LL LET YOU KNOW!
HI, TRISH! I'M BACK! I'M FEELING MUCH BETTER! I PLAN TO MOVE SOON AND...
..UH... HEY, WHERE'S THAT...UH..GUY THAT WAS STAYING HERE?
HE WENT BACK TO ENGLAND.
SO, WHAT REALLY HAPPENED WITH HIM ANYWAY?
WELL...
HE WAS JUST A FRIEND. I NEEDED SOMEONE. I'M WEAK THAT WAY.
WHAT DID YOU DO WITH HIM?!
I MIGHT AS WELL TELL YOU...
WE'D HOLD HANDS... ...KISS... AND AT NIGHT WE'D CUDDLE IN BED TOGETHER... THAT'S ALL...NOTHING MORE.
I DON'T BELIEVE THIS! TELL ME EVERYTHING! NOW!
D-DID YOU FRENCH-KISS HIM?!
YEH.
WHAT ELSE? WHAT AREN'T YOU TELLING ME?!
THAT'S ALL.
DID HE TRY ANYTHING WITH YOU?!
NO, IT WASN'T LIKE THAT...
WERE YOU IN LOVE WITH HIM?!
I STARTED TO FALL FOR HIM...
AND WHAT ABOUT GREG? DID YOU LIE TO ME ABOUT HIM TOO?
WELL...
YEH... I FRENCH-KISSED HIM TOO... JUST ONCE THOUGH.
AAAA
THE TRU
AAH!
TH
THUMP!
THE TRUTH
H-HOW COULD YOU DO THIS TO ME?...
I STILL THINK YOU'RE MY TRUE LOVE! I'VE MISSED YOU...
I GUESS I DESERVED THIS... I DECEIVED YOU FIRST... GASP OHH.. GOD, IT HURTS!
THE PAIN... THE PAIN...
WE CAN STILL MAKE IT WORK, BABY! I KNOW WE CAN!!
I DON'T KNOW...
UTH
LOOK, WE BOTH HAVE GROWING UP TO DO! DON'T FORGET, YOU CHEATED ON YOUR LAST BOYFRIEND TOO! TWICE!
THAT'S BECAUSE HE ALWAYS TREATED ME LIKE SHIT, LIKE YOU DID! AND I DON'T THINK OF IT AS CHEATING! WE BROKE UP FIRST!
WE?! YOU'RE THE ONE WHO BREAKS-UP!
IT TAKES TWO TO TANGO...
WELL, IF Y'DON'T WANNA WORK ON IT WITH ME, JUST TELL ME SO I CAN MOVE ALREADY...
NO! DON'T MOVE!
LISTEN, THE TRUST HAS BEEN MISSING IN THIS RELATIONSHIP FOR MONTHS! I DON'T KNOW IF IT'S DEAD OR JUST BURIED!
NEXT DAY...
DANCING TONGUES
NEXT WEEK...
HOW'RE YOU DOING?
OK. IT DOESN'T HURT AS MUCH AS IT USED TO...
TRUTH
SO, WE'RE JUST GONNA BE FRIENDS NOW, HUH?
I THINK THAT'S BEST FOR NOW. I'M CONFUSED...
SIGH
I STILL THINK YOU'RE MY TRUE LOVE...
...ME TOO.
TRUTH
JUST KEEP WALKING. DON'T LOOK BACK.
PEEP SHOWS
XXX
TRUTH

SEPT. 28TH 1989.
MR. CONFESSION
YOU MAY NOT WANNA COME IN HERE... AND I WOULDN'T BLAME YOU A BIT...
...BUT I GOTTA DO THIS NOW, WHILE I DON'T HAVE A GIRLFRIEND OR HER PARENTS AROUND TO INTIMIDATE ME...

WINK
MY DARKEST SECRET

OUR STORY BEGINS 4 YEARS AGO, WHEN AFTER GRADUATING COLLEGE, I MOVED BACK HOME TO MY MOM'S...
THIS IS JUST TEMPORARY, OF COURSE, MOM...
EAT! EAT!

I JUST COULDN'T FACE THE IDEA OF JOINING THE REAL WORLD...
RAT RACE
I REVERTED TO A CHILD AGAIN... ONLY THIS TIME I DIDN'T HAVE TO GO TO SCHOOL...
HAVE A GOOD DAY, JOE! I'LL MAKE YOUR BED WHEN I GET HOME FROM WORK!
OK. MOM...
CARTOONS

FILLING MY DAYS BECAME A REAL CHALLENGE...
LALALALA LALALA
PLUNK PLUNK

EVERY NIGHT, I SLEPT ABOVE MY 8 YEAR-OLD BROTHER
PILOT TO CO-PILOT... OVER...
CAPTAIN! WE'VE BEEN HIT! HEE HEE!
AFTER A FEW MONTHS, I DECIDED TO EMBARK OUT ON MY DARKEST SECRET...
I'M GOING TO NEW YORK CITY FOR THE DAY!
DON'T WAIT UP!

ONCE IN THE BIG APPLE, I NATURALLY MADE A BEE-LINE TO 42ND ST... THE RED-LIGHT DISTRICT...
SEX! SEX!
GIRLS GIRLS GIRLS
...AND BOLDLY VENTURED INTO A PORN THEATRE...
HAH! NOBODY KNOWS ME IN THIS TOWN!
ENTER
XXX ADULT ONLY

MY EXCITEMENT WAS ONLY HEIGHTENED BY THE DANGER...
MMMM... OHHHH...
I COULD GET STABBED IN HERE!

...BUT I WASN'T PREPARED FOR THE PROSTITUTES...
HEY BABY, LOOKIN' FOR A DATE?
NO NO! THAT'S OK! I'M FINE! REALLY! HEH...
ONE, IN PARTICULAR, WOULDN'T TAKE "NO" FOR AN ANSWER...
LOOK, I'M TELLIN' YOU- I'M BROKE!! HONESTLY! REALLY! HEH...HEH...
C'MON, SUGAR.. QUIT HOLDIN' OUT... YOU KNOW YOU WANT IT...

I GAVE IN THE SECOND SHE PUT HER HAND DOWN MY PANTS...
OH G-GOD... YESSSS... GASP Q-QUICK... LET'S GET A HOTEL ROOM! W-WHERE CAN I G-GET A R-RUBBER? HUH? WHERE?!
YOU WAIT HERE, BABY... I'LL SEE WHAT I CAN DO...

MY SENSES QUICKLY RETURNED...
WHAT AM I DOING?! I CAN'T GO THROUGH WITH THIS!! IT'D SCREW UP ANY CHANCE OF GETTING MY OLD GIRLFRIEND, LAURA, BACK! AND I'D PROBABLY CATCH A DISEASE SOMEHOW! BESIDES, IT'S IMMORAL!!
NOT TO MENTION EXPENSIVE...

AND WHEN SHE RETURNED...
EVERYTHING'S COOL, BABY... I GOT THE ROOM... LET'S GO...
NO! I CHANGED MY MIND! SORRY... I JUST CAN'T! HEH...
SMOKING "CRACK"
SHE GOT AGGRESSIVE...
MMMMMM... DOES THAT FEEL GOOD, BABY? PANT PANT WE CAN DO IT RIGHT HERE IF Y'WANT...
P-PEOPLE W-WILL S-SEE US!!

TOO AGGRESSIVE...
...DON'T WORRY, BABY... NOBODY'S LOOKIN'... WATCH THE MOVIE... MMMM...
!

PANIC-STRICKEN, I RAN TO THE BATHROOM...
OH GOD! I COULD'VE GOTTEN AIDS! OR HERPES!!
SCRUB SCRUB
SCRUB SCRUB

WHEN I RETURNED, WE STRUCK UP A DEAL...
H-HOW MUCH FOR JUST A HAND-JOB??
$10.00
H-HOW 'BOUT $5.00??
SURE.
I HAD AN ORGASM AS SHE WHISPERED THOSE 3 MAGIC WORDS...
C'MON, BABY... SHOOT THAT SCUM...
DON'T LOOK SO SHOCKED! WHAT DID Y'EXPECT FOR A DARKEST SECRET?

AFTERWARDS, SHE HELD UP HER SLIMY HAND IN DISGUST...
THAT'LL BE ANOTHER $10.00, PLEASE!
?
I STARTED TO WHINE...
I DON'T HAVE ANY MORE MONEY!! I DON'T EVEN HAVE A JOB!! I DON'T KNOW WHAT TO DO WITH MY LIFE! I STILL LIVE WITH MY MOM AND BLAH BLAH BLAH...
AND SURPRISINGLY...
AH, FORGET IT! YOU'RE LUCKY I LIKE YOU... C'MON... I GOTTA MEET MY DEALER...
SHE LIKES ME?!
MR. LONELY
SUDDENLY, I WANTED TO BE HER BEST FRIEND...
SO, WHAT'RE YOU DOING FOR THE REST OF THE DAY?? MAYBE WE COULD TAKE A WALK THROUGH CENTRAL PARK OR...

THEN, I SAW HER OUTSIDE IN THE LIGHT!
WHUT'S WRONG?
AND AS I HEADED HOME, FEELING FILTHY + HOLLOW, I HEARD HER CALL...
REMEMBER... JUST BECAUSE YOUR SHIRT'S WHITE, THAT DON'T MEAN IT'S CLEAN!!

?
THE END

DRIVING
WHAT WOULD YOU DO IF I WAS AN EXOTIC DANCER?
PROBABLY BREAK UP WITH YOU.
WHY?
BECAUSE I DONT WANT OTHER GUYS SEEING YOU NAKED.
BUT I LIKE TO SHOW OFF. SOMETIMES I'LL BE WALKING PAST RESTAURANT WINDOWS AND I'LL JUST HAVE TO FLASH PEOPLE...
I THINK I COULD BE A GOOD STRIPPER. I'M SKINNY, AND I'VE GOT THE BREASTS...
I'M SURE YOU'D BE GREAT. I JUST WOULDN'T WANT TO BE WITH YOU WHEN ALL THESE OTHER GUYS ARE LOOKING AT YOU.
FAVORITE
FAST
YOU'RE MY FAVORITE BOYFRIEND EVER.
FAST
SLURPPPPPP
FAST
YEP, YOU ARE.
FAST
FAST

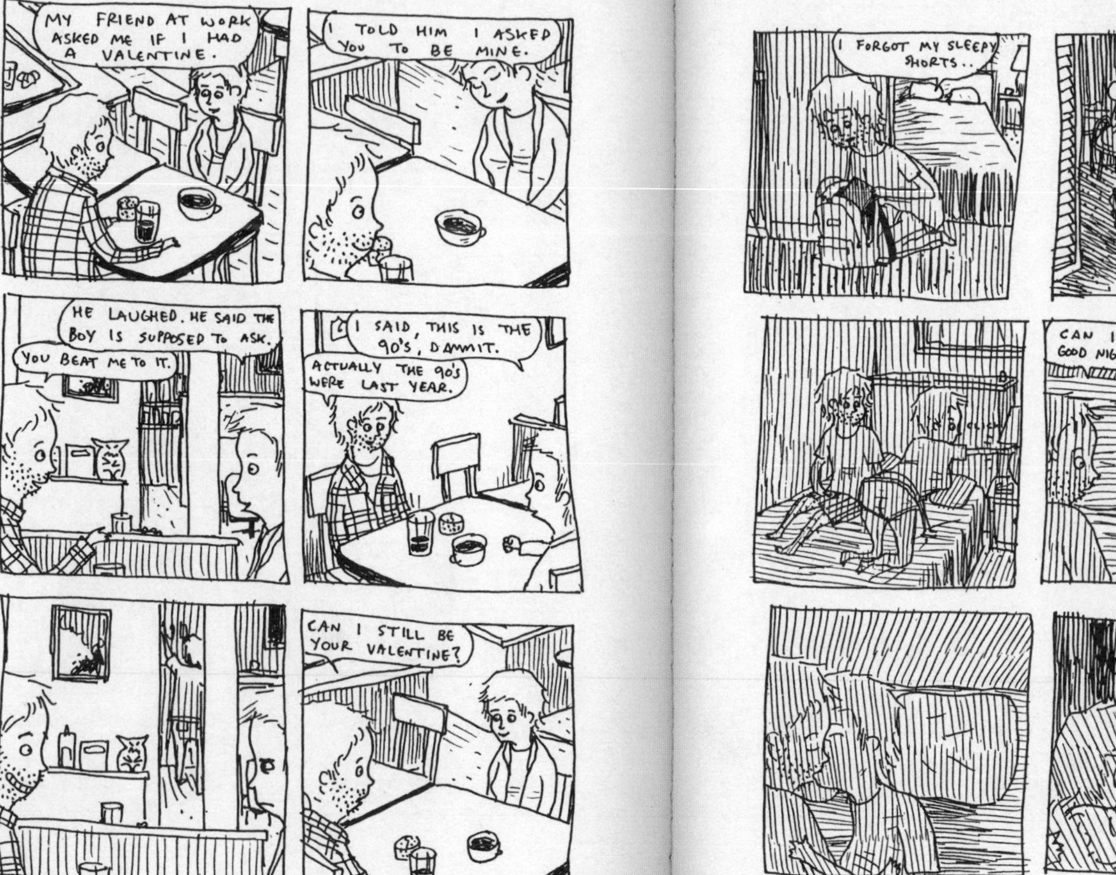
WILL YOU STILL
MY FRIEND AT WORK ASKED ME IF I HAD A VALENTINE.
I TOLD HIM I ASKED YOU TO BE MINE.
HE LAUGHED. HE SAID THE BOY IS SUPPOSED TO ASK.
YOU BEAT ME TO IT.
I SAID, THIS IS THE 90's, DAMMIT.
ACTUALLY THE 90's WERE LAST YEAR.
CAN I STILL BE YOUR VALENTINE?
COMPLETE SILENCE
I FORGOT MY SLEEPY SHORTS..
THAT's OKAY. JUST WEAR YOUR BOXERS.
OKAY.
CAN I HAVE A GOOD NIGHT KISS?
YEAH.

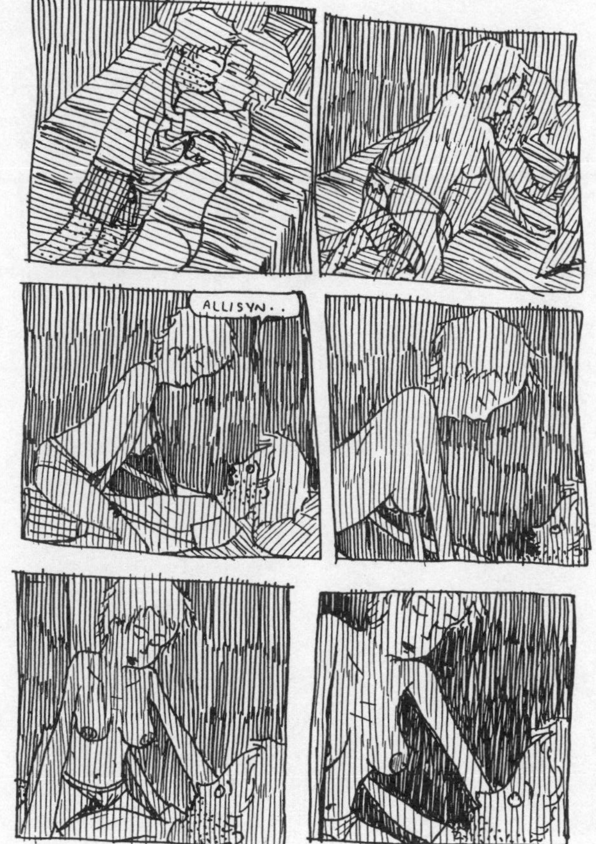
ALLISYN..

ALLISYN...WAIT... WE NEED PROTECTION
DO YOU HAVE CONDOMS ?
YEAH..IN THE MEDICINE CHEST..
BRAND NEW BOX
CAN YOU PUT IT ON?
OKAY...I'M NOT VERY GOOD WITH THESE THINGS, THOUGH.

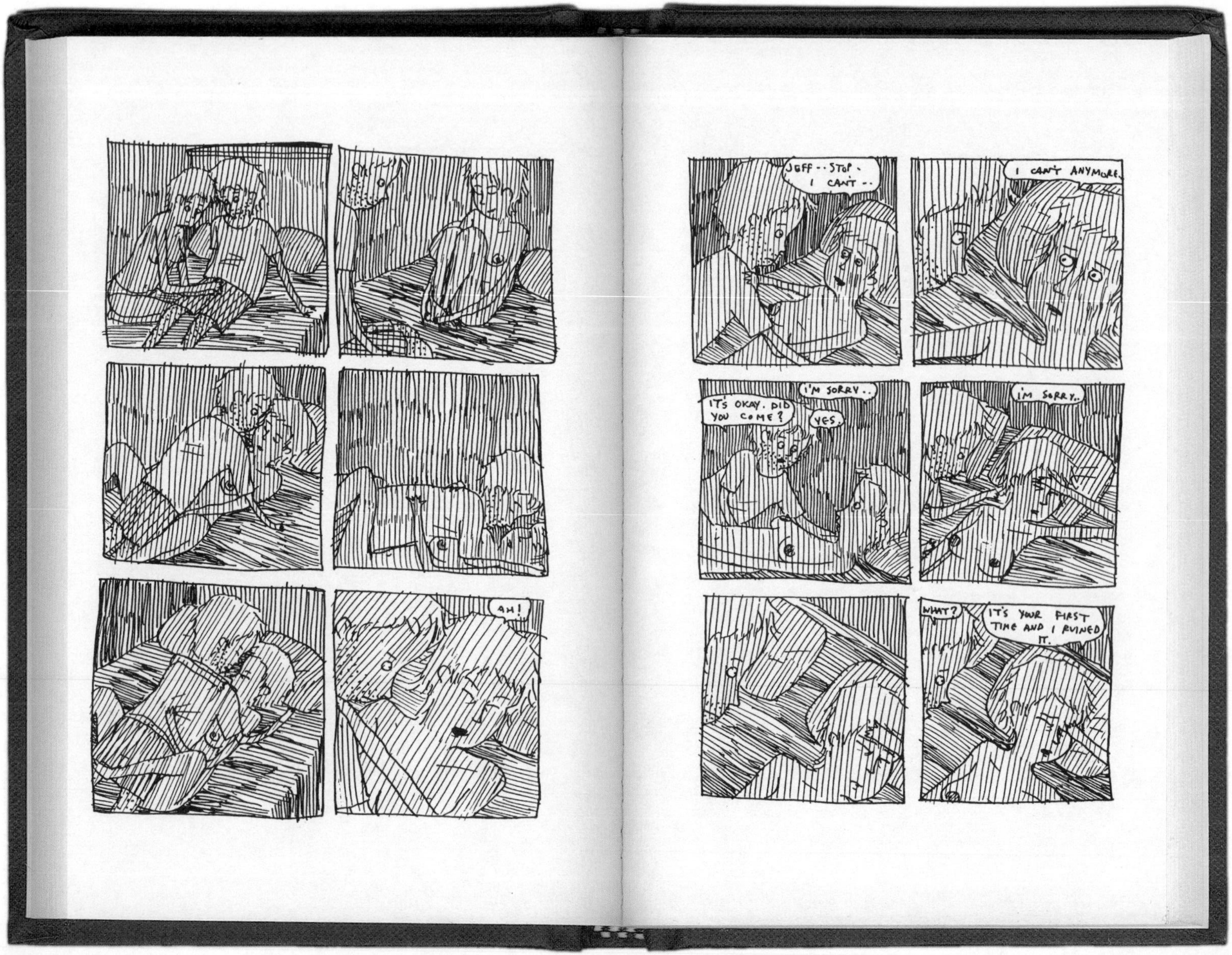

AH!
JEFF -- STOP. I CAN'T --
I CAN'T ANYMORE.
I'M SORRY..
IT'S OKAY. DID YOU COME?
YES.
I'M SORRY..
WHAT?
IT'S YOUR FIRST TIME AND I RUINED IT.

JEFFREY BROWN *excerpt from* Unlikely

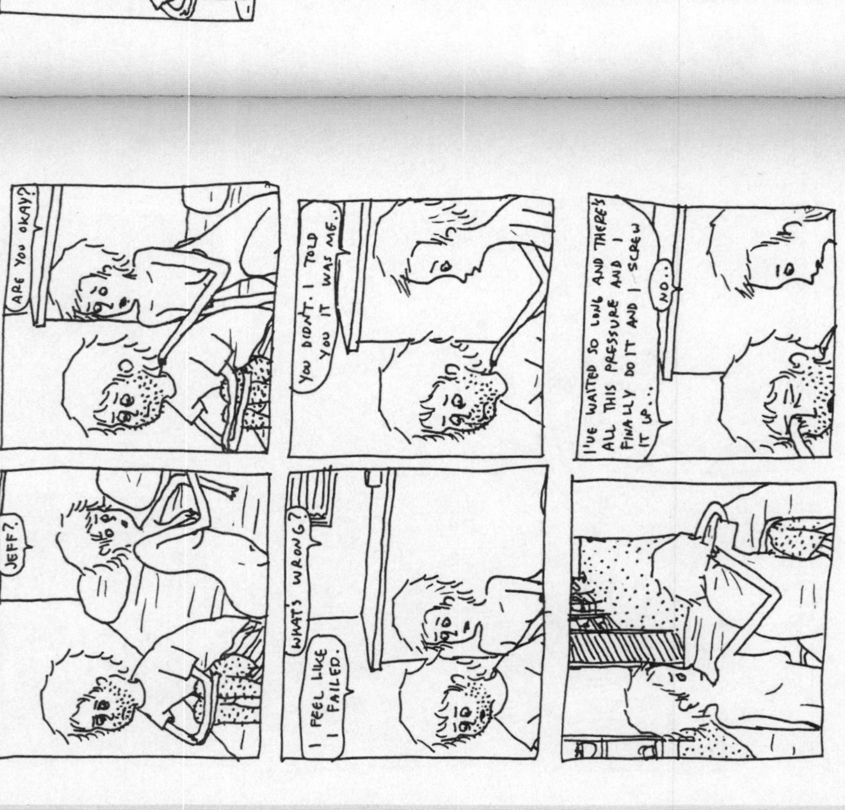
JEFF?
ARE YOU OKAY?
WHAT'S WRONG?
I FEEL LIKE I FAILED.
YOU DIDN'T. I TOLD YOU IT WAS ME..
I'VE WAITED SO LONG AND THERE'S ALL THIS PRESSURE AND I FINALLY DO IT AND I SCREW IT UP...
NO..
IT'S OKAY.
I'M SORRY.

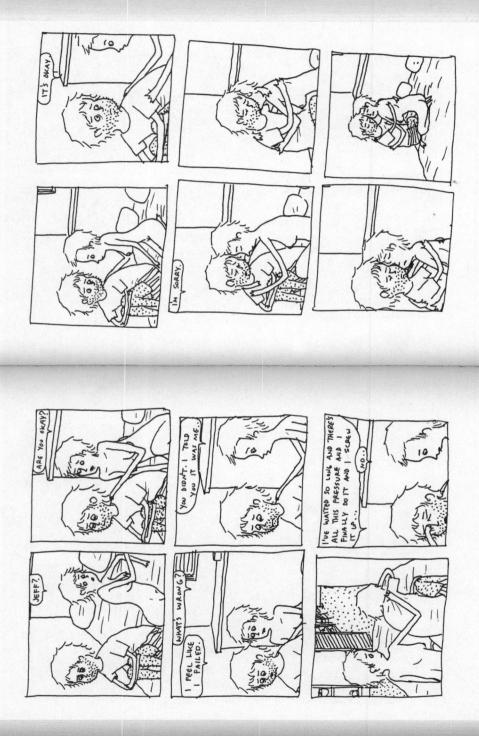

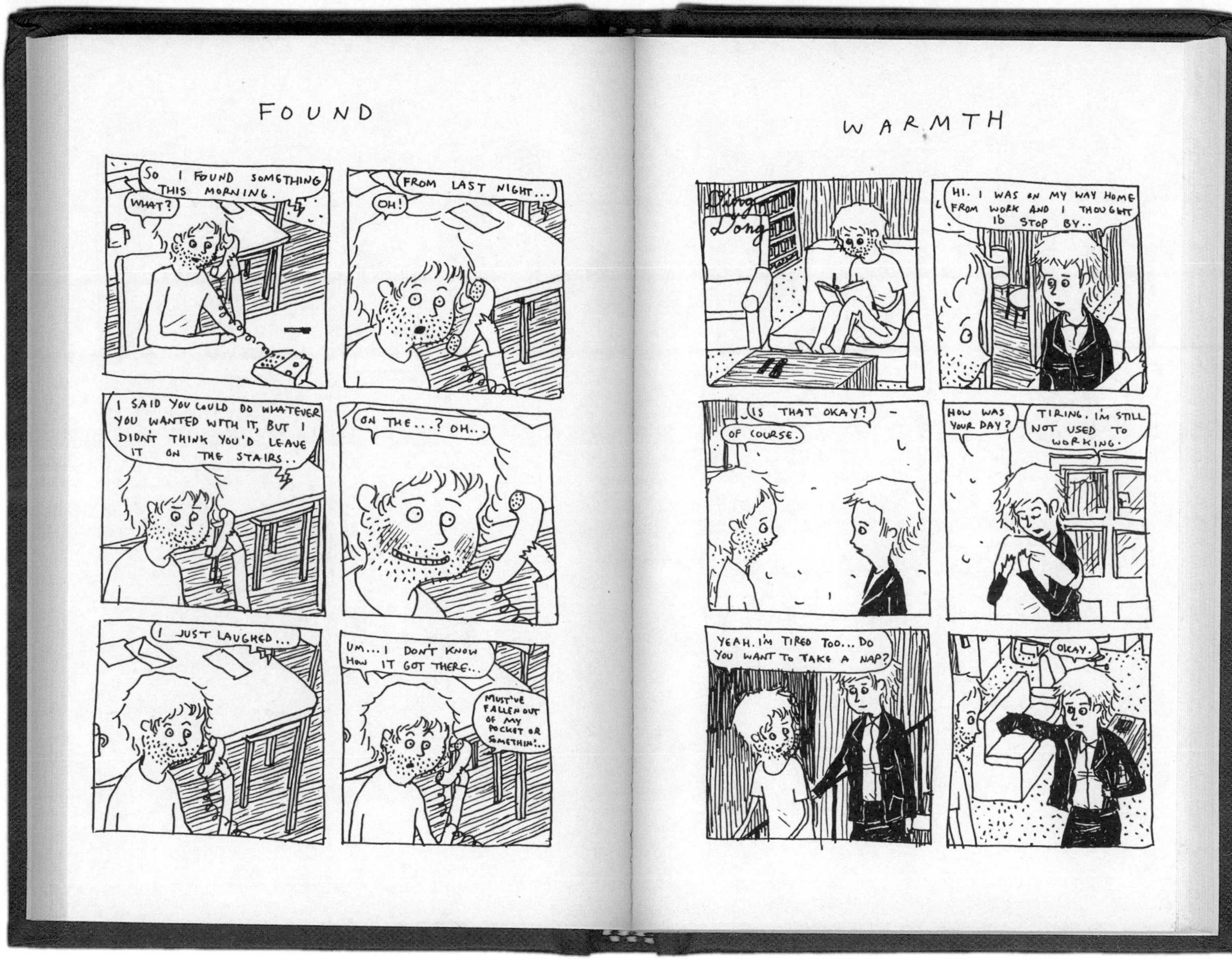

FOUND

SO I FOUND SOMETHING THIS MORNING.
WHAT?
FROM LAST NIGHT...
OH!
I SAID YOU COULD DO WHATEVER YOU WANTED WITH IT, BUT I DIDN'T THINK YOU'D LEAVE IT ON THE STAIRS..
ON THE...? OH..
I JUST LAUGHED...
UM... I DON'T KNOW HOW IT GOT THERE..
MUST'VE FALLEN OUT OF MY POCKET OR SOMETHIN'...

WARMTH

Ding Dong
HI. I WAS ON MY WAY HOME FROM WORK AND I THOUGHT I'D STOP BY..
IS THAT OKAY?
OF COURSE.
HOW WAS YOUR DAY?
TIRING. I'M STILL NOT USED TO WORKING.
YEAH. I'M TIRED TOO... DO YOU WANT TO TAKE A NAP?
OKAY.

WHAT'RE YOU DOING?
TAKING MY BELT OFF... I DONT WANT THE BUCKLE POKING INTO YOU...
I WANT TO TRY AGAIN SO BAD...
ME TOO
AAHHNH
AH!
DID YOU COME?
YES... DID YOU?
YES.

I WANT YOU TO LIKE ME.

I REALLY DO.

I ADMIRE YOU.
A LOT.
TIME

AND I WANT YOUR APPROVAL.

I WANT CONFIRMATION FROM **YOU**

OF **MY** SELF WORTH

I WANT EVERYTHING I DO AND SAY

TO BE DEEP
AND MEANINGFUL
AND FUNNY
AND SAD
AND TRUE

NOT ONLY TO
ME

BUT TO **YOU** ESPECIALLY

BECAUSE I TRUST YOUR OPINION

MORE THAN MY OWN

I WANT TO BE

EVERYTHING THAT I PERCEIVE YOU TO BE

BECAUSE I LIKE **YOU**

AND I WANT **YOU** TO LIKE **ME**

mart

REAL ESTATE
LIBERTY TRAVEL IS JUST A SIGN
I USED TO LIVE HERE
KNEW EVERY SECRET CORNER
DRUGS
EVEN THOUGH I HAD NO LOVERS...
NO TRESPASSING
THERE WAS SOMETHING ROMANTIC
ABOUT THE LANDSCAPE
66

OFFICE BUILDINGS
VACANT MANUFACTURING GARAGES
THE ENDLESS ROWS OF STRIP MALLS:
ADULT VIDEO
VACUUMS
Sal's PLACE
16
USED INSTRU
BAIT TACKLE
24 HOUR CONVENIENT STORES
CLOSED INDEFINITELY

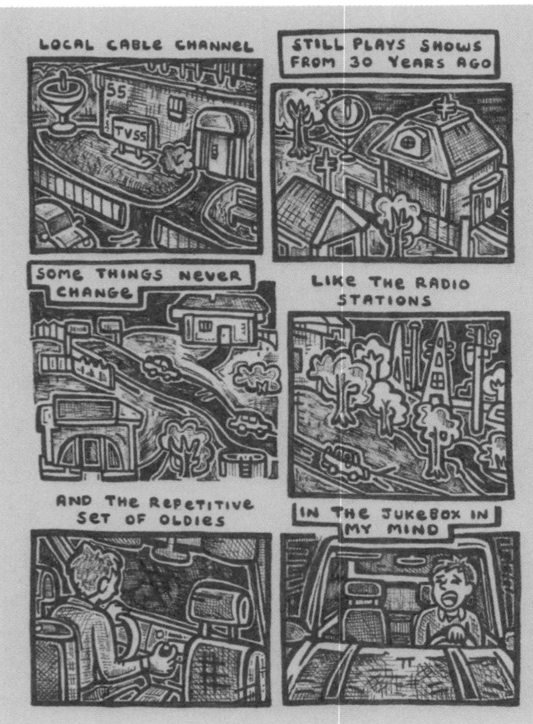
LOCAL CABLE CHANNEL
55
TV55
STILL PLAYS SHOWS FROM 30 YEARS AGO
SOME THINGS NEVER CHANGE
LIKE THE RADIO STATIONS
AND THE REPETITIVE SET OF OLDIES
IN THE JUKEBOX IN MY MIND

ELECTRIC TOWERS
HIGH TENSION WIRES
24
SOUND BARRIERS
ALONGSIDE THE HIGHWAY

MY DAD'S OLD HOUSE
THE NOISE OF THE CHICADAS
MAKE ME REMEMBER
THE FIRST GIRL I EVER MADE-OUT WITH
ON A COUCH
IN THE BACKSEAT OF A CAR

AND I AM NOSTALGIC
FOR THINGS LIKE ROLLER RINKS
CLOSED
SKATCTOWN
THAT ARE OUT OF TIME
& NO LONGER BELONG (TO ME)
SKATCTOWN
JUST KIDS
... JUST OLD PEOPLE

THE VIDEO STORE IS MY CULTURE
RENTALS
SATURDAY NIGHTS IN FRONT OF THE TV
STILL, SOMETIMES I'D PAUSE FOR A MOMENT
IN THE PARKING LOT
GAZING UP AT THE STARS
RENTALS
WONDERING WHY I'M SO
ALONE

WILL I EVER OWN A HOME?
LIKE MY PARENTS?
SOME PEOPLE ARE TRAVELERS
OTHERS JUST RUN AWAY
I SHOULD'VE TAKEN SOME CHANCES
MOVE...
IF YOU WANT IT TO LAST

KING-CAT

COMICS & STORIES

NO. 38 $1.00

COMICS BY JOHN PORCELLINO

SAM

ONE SUNDAY EVENING WE WERE DRIVING BACK HOME FROM SHOPPING IN THE SUBURBS AND WE STOPPED AT THE PET SHOP IN ELK GROVE

OKAY KIDS- BUT WE CAN'T STAY LONG!
I'M GONNA LOOK AT THE FERRETS!
BEARS

SPRING 1978

WE WERE IN THE PLAY ROOM PLAYING WITH TWO PUPPIES- A CHOCOLATE LABRADOR-RETRIEVER AND A YELLOW ONE

THE BROWN ONE CURLED UP IN THE CORNER AND SLEPT WHILE THE YELLOW ONE JUMPED AND TWIRLED

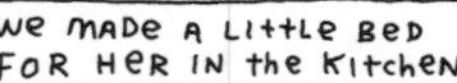

SOMEHOW WE CONNED OUR PARENTS INTO BUYING THE YELLOW ONE...

THE PEOPLE AT THE PET SHOP PUT A BOW ON HER AND WE TOOK HER HOME.

LET ME HOLD HER!
SNARP!
BEAR

WE MADE A LITTLE BED FOR HER IN THE KITCHEN

WE NAMED HER SAMANTHA LOVE...

THE NEXT DAY I WOKE UP FOR SCHOOL AND WENT INTO THE KITCHEN.

THERE SHE WAS

SHE WAS A WILD PUPPY

GARF!

HONK HONK

ALL OUR SWEATSHIRTS HAD HOLES IN THE WRIST WHERE SHE'D GRAB US AND DRAG US AROUND

ROWL!

HA HA

HELP! HELP!

BEE GEES

SHE'D SIT AT THE DINNER TABLE ON A CHAIR WHILE WE ATE, WITH HER BIG SOFT PUPPY BELLY

ONE TIME WE WERE GOING OUT. MY MOM TIED HER TO ONE OF THE LEGS OF THE KITCHEN TABLE TO KEEP HER FROM RUNNING AROUND.

WHEN WE CAME HOME SHE GREETED US AT THE DOOR... WE RAN TO THE KITCHEN...

HOW'D YOU GET LOOSE?

THE TABLE WAS WEDGED IN THE DOORWAY, THE LEG WAS BROKEN OFF!

OH SHIT!

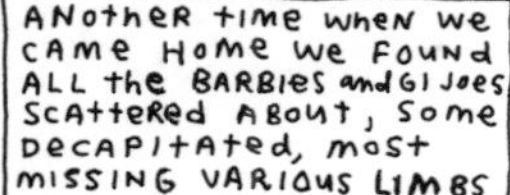

ANOTHER TIME WHEN WE CAME HOME WE FOUND ALL THE BARBIES AND GI JOES SCATTERED ABOUT, SOME DECAPITATED, MOST MISSING VARIOUS LIMBS

MY SISTER WAS CRYING, BUT I THOUGHT IT WAS COOL

AAWGH!
WOUNDED IN ACTION!

SAM HAD A VORACIOUS APPETITE. AFTER HER FOOD WAS GONE SHE'D SIT AND GNAW HER PLASTIC BOWL

OUR OTHER DOG DAISY HAD THIS HABIT OF RUNNING AND BARKING AT CARS DRIVING DOWN THE ALLEY

WHEN DAISY WOULD START BARKING, SAM WOULD JUMP ON HER AND BITE HER NECK, NOT HARD, BUT...

* SHUT UP! SHUT UP!

MY MOM WAS CONCERNED

SOME ONE TOLD HER TO PUT TABASCO SAUCE ON DAISY'S NECK. ONE TASTE WOULD SEND SAM REELING!

?
HOLD STILL DAISY!

SAM SPENT THAT WHOLE DAY CHASING DAISY AROUND, RELENTLESSLY LICKING HER NECK CLEAN

SAM TOO HAD HER HABITS: LIKE EATING THE CAT SHIT OUT OF THE LITTER BOX

But She was our Little puppy...
HONK HONK HONK
It's SAM the WHAM!
every tuesday Night we'd ALL Get in Bed At seven to watch T.V.
EATING ORANGES
SAM! I can't see!
"HAPPY DAYS" "LAVERNE + SHIRLEY" & "3'S COMPANY" what A Lineup!

IN 1979 we moved out to the suburbs.

OUR BACKYARD WASN'T Fenced IN ANYMORE, So SAM STAYED INSIDE.

there WAS NO GRASS ON OUR "LAWN" yet and SAM WOULDN'T Poo on the DIRT So I'D take HER FOR WALKS
HA HA

SHE NEVER REALLY GOT USED to HER LEASH
STOP PULLING, SAM!
COUGH COUGH

We were STRANGERS

And FOR AWHILE She was MY ONLY REAL FRIEND.
HONK HONK
Row!!

AS SAM GREW UP She mellowed out A Bit...
what ARE YOU LOOKING At SAM?
SHE'D SLEEP IN MY Room with me AS I READ At Night.
Z Z
Pretty Soon I Guess I Started GROWING UP too...
TALKING About GIRLS
I HAD MY FRIENDS NOW
HANG ON
mom... could you DROP me OFF At tom's?
BEATLES
AND I Started Spending LESS and Less time At Home
Bye mom
OKAY- DINNER'S At seven!
HUH
then I HAD MY FIRST GIRLFRIEND. She DIDN'T Like SAM
Keep that BIG Beef tongue AWAY FROM me! I mean it!
HA
AND with my Adolescence came CONFUSION and UNHAPPINESS.
I SHUT MYSELF OFF FROM everything with FATALISTIC DESPAIR.
Come on JOHNNY- It's time to EAT!
JUST Leave me ALONE!

I FELT COLD and BROKEN INSIDE...
Come on, SAM! I'M BUSY!
HUH HUH
But She WAS ALWAYS there when No one else WAS...
SAMMY
LICK
CRYING ON BedRoom FLOOR

SHE'D STAY UP LATE with me ON WEEKENDS WATCHING "NIGHT FLIGHT"
EINSTÜRZENDE NEUBAUTEN
3 A.M.

SHE would sleep on the couch, which Drove my mom CRAZY CUZ she'D SHED ALL over it.
DAMMIT SAM!
WIPE

So we got A Sheet that we'D put on it At Night

Pretty Soon, when she WANTED to Go to Bed SHE'D STARE At the couch AND SIGH
Hmm...

AS SOON AS the Sheet WAS IN PLACE She'D JUMP UP and GET COMFY

when it Got REAL LATE the t.v. ANNOYED HER
OH, OKAY SAM!
I'LL Go to Bed
HMM
3 A.M.

IN the summer of 1986 I went AWAY to College
Rooms 100-120
R.E.
I ONLY SAW SAM when I'D come Home FOR weekends OR while ON VACATION.
"GENTLE-BAT" POSITION
GAH!
SHE STARTED GETTING OLD
mom- SAM'S FACE IS Getting white!
CATARACTS
But She WAS ALWAYS HAPPY to see me.
HONK HONK HONK- It's SAM the wham!
the YEARS were GOING BY QUICKLY. I WAS LIVING MY LIFE...
ONE SATURDAY MY PARENTS CAME out to VISIT
SAMMY'S NOT DOIN' too WELL...

HER ARTHRITIS IS Gettin' REAL BAD... She CAN BARELY Sit DOWN ANYMORE- CAN'T Go up the STAIRS
SHE'S JUST So old, JOHNNY... SHE Goes to the BATHROOM ALL over the House
SHE DOESN'T even KNOW She's DOIN' it...

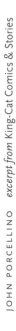

JOHN PORCELLINO *excerpt from* King-Cat Comics & Stories

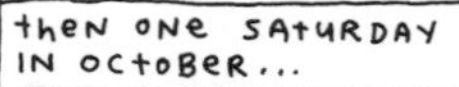

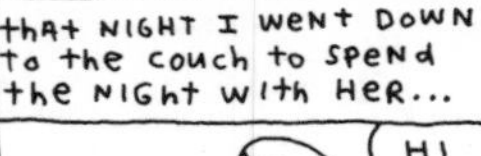

EVERY WEEKEND I'D CALL MY PARENTS AND EXPECT THEM TO TELL ME SHE WAS GONE, BUT...

SAMANTHA LOVE
DECEMBER 21, 1977
OCTOBER 23, 1992

Beachy Head, Illinois

I should have stayed late at work, I guess; there's so much to do before the partners' meeting next week. But for some reason I left work at 5:00 and walked straight across the park toward the lake. It's one of those warm spring evenings that make you do things like that.

So I'm sitting on the grass and watching these teenagers rollerblade down the stairs

and I wish with all my heart that I could be one of them.

They are everything I used to be, 12 or 15 years ago,

but much more so—I was much more small-town, much tamer.

These kids are probably from some suburb.

They probably cut school today and caught the commuter rail into town,

Or maybe they drove somebody's parents' car, which is parked in an all-day garage,

unless it's being driven around the city by the crazed minority parking attendants from "Ferris Bueller's Day Off".

But it doesn't really matter how they got here.

None of these kids is Ferris Bueller or his vanilla sweetheart or his terminally unattractive best friend

(Who was the point of the whole film, an ex-boyfriend once told me very drunkenly and sincerely in some shitty Southside blues club, before confessing he still loved me.)

and they may be suburban by an accident of birth

But they are more Chicago than I will ever be.

I know I am staring

sucking them in, consuming them

in the same way I sometimes watch children playing in a park,

or splashing in a pool.

And like the pre-schoolers,

these kids are totally unaware of my staring,

totally oblivious to the stodgy corporate suit

whose heart rises and falls with every spin and leap.

I watch them skate down the railings

jump off, turn on a dime

within inches of Lake Michigan.

And the next time they skate backwards

down the stairs.

And the time after that

They start out forwards

then flip around halfway through,

and skate away,

spinning as they go.

Don't they ever fall, I wonder.

I don't think they ever do.

And just as I think it, one does.

But it is like a fall from a Saturday morning cartoon — violent and dramatic and completely harmless.

He is up and skating within seconds, sheepish.

His jeans aren't even dirty.
of course.

And almost immediately he is at the top of the stairs

trying the same trick,

And this time he succeeds,

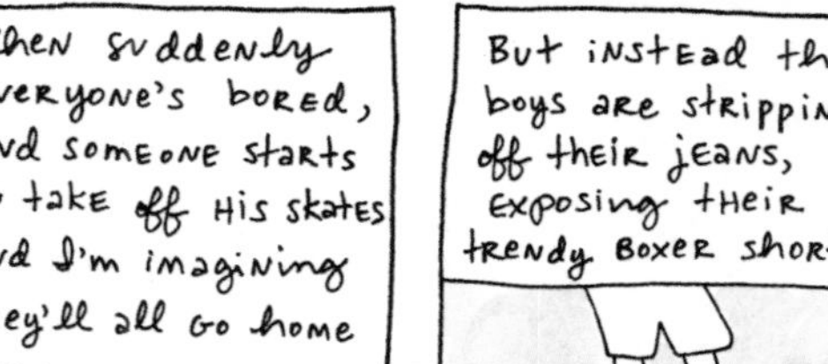
Then suddenly everyone's bored, and someone starts to take off his skates and I'm imagining they'll all go home now.
But instead the boys are stripping off their jeans, exposing their trendy boxer shorts

and before I can even work out what they're doing

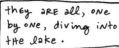

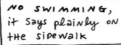

they are all, one by one, diving into the lake.
NO SWIMMING, it says plainly on the sidewalk
in the three main languages of Chicago:
English, Spanish, and pictograms.
I'm sure they've seen the sign,
and do not care.
It's easy to understand why you're not supposed to swim there: Besides the fact that there are no lifeguards, it's a dock, not a beach, so motorboats and yachts are continually passing through the channel
right where the kids are swimming.
And what was before a really wonderful moment
has started to seem incredibly dangerous
and no longer funny

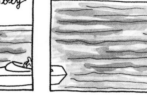

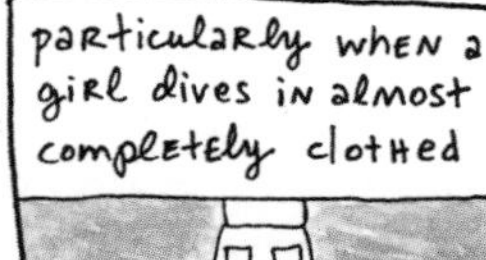
particularly when a girl dives in almost completely clothed

in her tiny tank top and jeans that must weigh 20 lbs. wet.

They swim out to one of the yachts moored in the lake

and clamber up, rocking it and laughing.

I wonder what they'll do:

Break in? Vandalize it?

But they seem content to swing their legs over the side

to splash each other and laugh.

I saw this inter-view with Pete Townshend once

He was talking about the ending he wanted for QUADROPHENIA

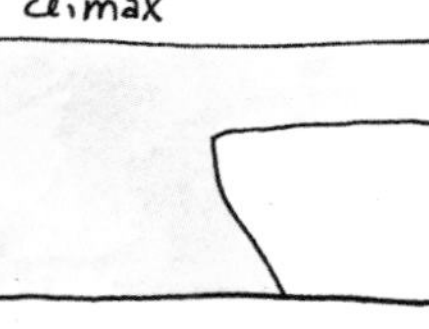
He didn't want the big dramatic climax

when the kid runs his scooter off Beachy Head

and maybe goes with it, or maybe doesn't, who knows.

Townshend's ending was much more subtle:

instead, the Phil Daniels character prays for rain

OF COURSE IT RAINS: it's set in England, that grey and sunless country, where it drizzles almost every single day, and why in the world would anyone there pray for rain? But the point is, THE POINT IS, THE POINT IS THIS: He prays for rain. and it rains.

And I can't explain it really,

Except to say that sometimes you pray for rain

and it rains and you don't even know it's raining.

And here on this gently sunny Chicago evening

I suddenly realize that it's raining for me.

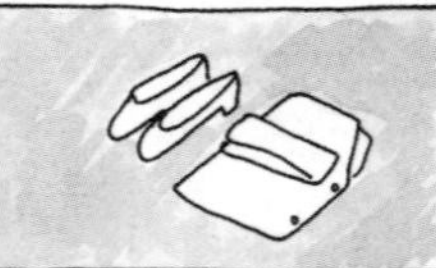

You are losing your mind, I think,

even as I am taking off my shoes and jacket, which out of habit I fold neatly.

I take off my blouse and my skirt and my pantyhose, until I'm down to my bra and underwear

and everyone just stares, as I was staring earlier.

And I'm wondering, what's crazier? Taking off all my clothes in a public park? Leaving my briefcase with all my money & house keys lying in the grass?

Or diving, just as that 15-year-old girl had done, into the icy polluted water of Lake Michigan?

One of the kids must have seen me — they're all yelling something I can't understand

I tread water, trying to make it out, until they give up and make hand gestures: Come 'ere! Come 'ere!

It's getting dark, a yacht would never see me if it came past now.

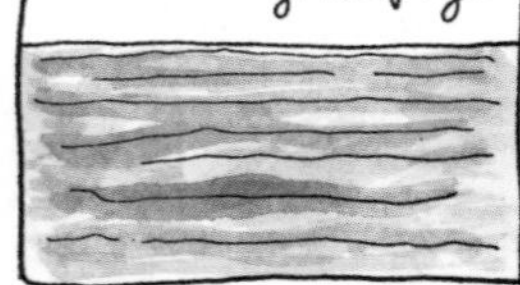

But nothing is coming: the channel is entirely empty.

I'm not sure if I can make it, but it doesn't really matter.

If I get too tired,

I'll just turn around and go back.

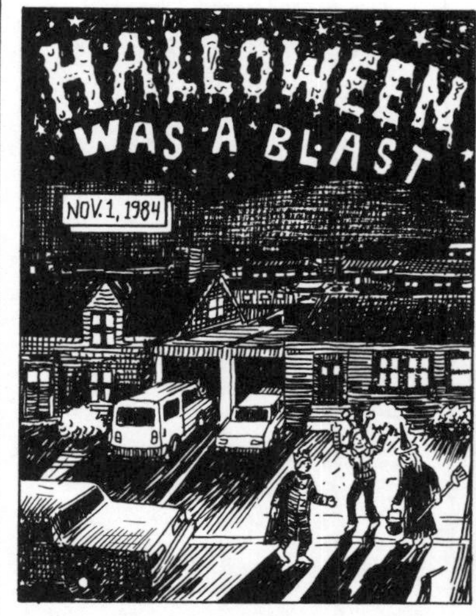
HALLOWEEN
WAS A BLAST
NOV. 1, 1984

Halloween was a blast!
HOLLI
ME
SANDY
Holli, Sandy, and I went trick-or-treating.

We were in Spring Valley when we saw some (supposedly three, and supposedly small) guys.

So Holli threw a tomato at them.
She has a really good arm.

I couldn't really see, because it was dark, but I think she hit one of them on the head!

He started yelling, and before I knew what was happening, they had started to chase us!
There were seven of them, actually, and two had bikes!

We ran, but one guy on a bike pulled up in front of us!

He was really mad.

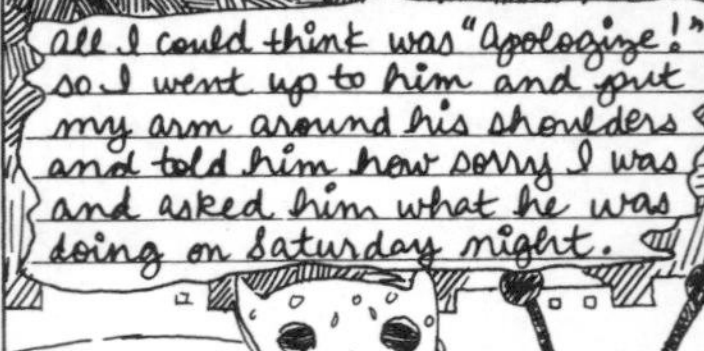
All I could think was "Apologize!" so I went up to him and put my arm around his shoulders and told him how sorry I was and asked him what he was doing on Saturday night.

I told him my name was Melissa, and gave him Elizabeth's phone number (she couldn't come with us, she had to do something with her youth group).

They followed us all over the place before they finally went home. Lizzy said he called the very next day. She said he sounded kind of disappointed that Melissa wasn't there.

It was so funny.

I can't believe it worked.
I am so crazy!!

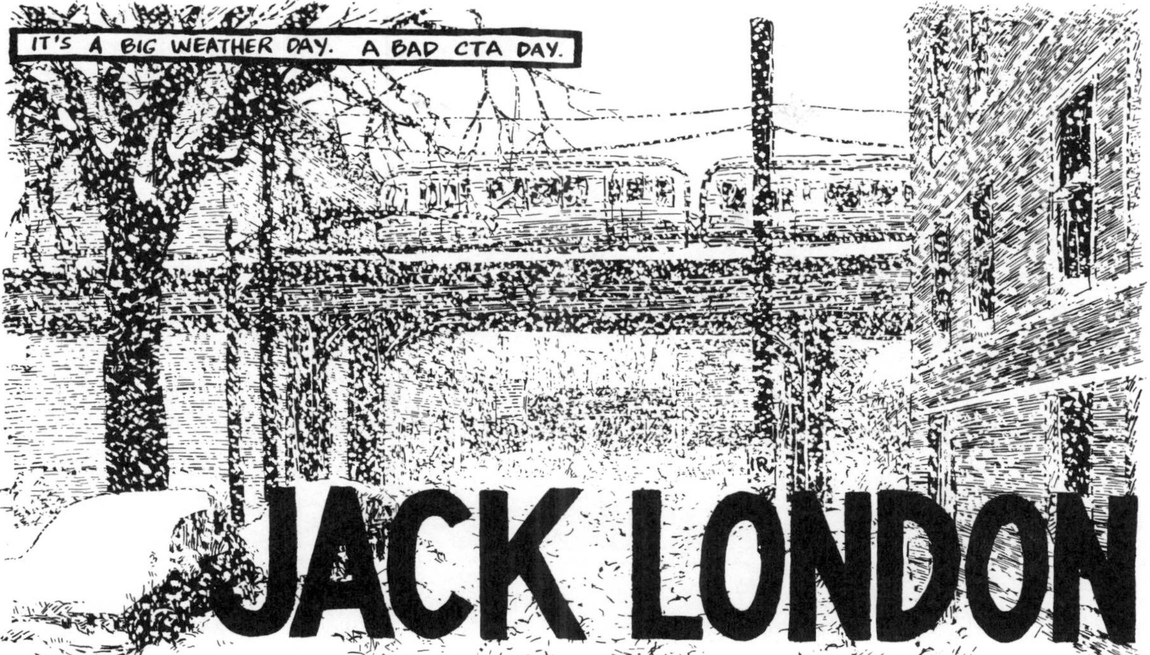
IT'S A BIG WEATHER DAY. A BAD CTA DAY.
JACK LONDON
JESSICA ABEL © 1996

SITTING IN THE OVER-WARM, CROWDED TUBE, INCHING ITS WAY TO EVANSTON, READING A BOOK...

... I'M SHOCKED INTO STARING WHEN I CHANCE TO LOOK OUT THE WINDOW; I CAN BARELY DISCERN ENOUGH LANDMARKS TO FIGURE OUT WHAT STOP WE'RE AT ON A ROUTE I'VE TAKEN TWICE A DAY FOR A YEAR AND A HALF AND MAYBE A BIT LESS OFTEN FOR MY WHOLE LIFE.

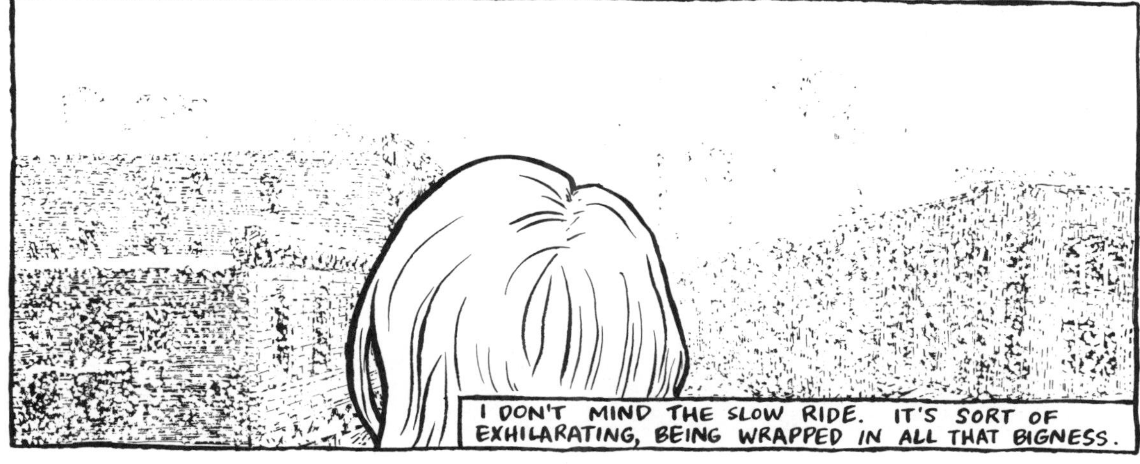
I DON'T MIND THE SLOW RIDE. IT'S SORT OF EXHILARATING, BEING WRAPPED IN ALL THAT BIGNESS.

AND NO ONE CAN BLAME ME FOR BEING LATE TO WORK; MY EXCUSE IS BATTERING AT EVERYONE'S WINDOWS.
NOT THAT ANYONE EVER SAYS ANYTHING ANYWAY.

COURTNEY, YOU'RE HERE- GREAT. LOOK, I'M OFF TO A BOARD MEETING. CAN YOU TYPE THIS MEMO AND GET IT OUT? OH, AND THE BROCHURE LAYOUTS ARE IN, SO COULD YOU GET STARTED ON PROOFING?

SURE. DO YOU THINK THEY'LL SHOW UP?

306
WHO'LL SHOW UP?

THE BOARD. BECAUSE OF THE SNOW.

OH! HA HA, I HOPE SO!

FEB

THE SNOW HAS BEEN HOWLING DOWN SINCE LAST EVENING...

...AND IT'S PILED IN DRIFTS WHERE YOU CAN SINK TO YOUR KNEE.
ITS TEXTURE IS ALMOST LIKE BREAD DOUGH, SQUOOSHY AND MALLEABLE. THE SNOW HAS COATED EVERYTHING SO THICKLY THAT EVEN THE STREETS ARE HARDLY GREY.
ALL THE PEOPLE STAND HUDDLED AROUND WAITING ON BUSES LOOKING LIKE, DEPENDING ON HOW GENEROUS I FEEL, EITHER MINIATURE PIKE'S PEAKS OR ENORMOUS FROSTED FLAKES.
IT LOOKS, OUTSIDE, LIKE THE PICTURES THE AD AGENCIES PULL OUT EVERY FALL OF THE BLIZZARD OF '79 TO SCARE CHICAGOANS INTO BUYING NEW SNOW TIRES, OR COATS, OR INSURANCE.
AND IT'S LATE FEBRUARY, FOR GOD'S SAKE. NO ONE THOUGHT IT WOULD SNOW AGAIN THIS YEAR. AT LEAST NOT LIKE THIS.
COURTNEY! YOU DONE WITH THAT PROOFING? I WANT JIM TO GIVE IT THE ONCE-OVER.
DESPITE ITS REPUTATION, CHICAGO IS NOT GENERALLY A VERY SNOWY TOWN. COLD, GOD YES. BUT NOT SO DEEP IN SNOW. I REMEMBER THE ONE WINTER I SPENT IN MINNESOTA, NOTICING IN NOVEMBER THAT THE CITY HAD JUST GONE AROUND AND MADE ALL THE STOP SIGNS TALLER, TO ACCOUNT...

UH, ALMOST! I'LL BRING IT TO HIM!
306
SHIT.
... FOR THE SNOW. IT'S NOTHING LIKE THAT HERE. WELL, EXCEPT THIS YEAR, WHAT WITH THE MISSISSIPPI RIVER PLAIN FLOODS, WE MIGHT HAVE EXPECTED SOMETHING LIKE
THIS. CHICAGO IS ALWAYS A BIG WEATHER TOWN; IT DOES NOTHING BY HALVES.
JIM, DOUG WANTS YOU TO GIVE THIS A LOOK.
SURE THING. HEY, CAN YOU GO PICK UP MY XEROX JOB?
WHERE IS IT?
IT'S AT KWIK KOPY. OH, WAIT, I FORGOT ABOUT THE WEATHER. NEVER MIND. I CAN GET IT LATER.
OH, NO, IT'S OK. I'LL GO.
YOU SURE?
YEAH!
YOU GOING OUT?
YEAH, I'M PICKING UP JIM'S COPY JOB.
WELL, I NEED YOU TO WRAP UP THAT USAGE REPORT WHEN YOU GET BACK- WE NEED THAT TODAY!

ACTUALLY, TO BE CONSISTENT, I SHOULD POINT OUT THAT I HATE THE WINTER. I HATE TO BE COLD, I HATE THE WIND, I HATE ALL THE BULKY CLOTHES AND THE GREY SKY AND THE MONOTONY.

BUT SOMETIMES IT GIVES ME A THRILL, LIKE WHEN IT'S 40 DEGREES BELOW ZERO, I FEEL LIKE JACK LONDON. WE ARE A CITY FULL OF ARCTIC PIONEERS, BONDED BY THE HARSH CONDITIONS.
IT'S REALLY ONLY ON DAYS THAT ARE THAT COLD, OR THIS SNOWY, BUT SOMETIMES THE WHOLE CITY FEELS LIKE IT'S CELEBRATING ITS RESILIENCE TOGETHER.

HOW OFTEN CAN YOU TRADE GRIMLY PROUD SMILES WITH THE TOTAL STRANGERS YOU RUN INTO IN THE SAFETY OF THE GROCERY STORE OR GAS STATION, JUST BECAUSE YOU WERE ALL VIRTUOUS AND TOUGH ENOUGH TO MAKE IT TO THE STORE OR GAS STATION?

YOU TALK TO MORE STRANGERS AT TIMES LIKE THAT.

THERE'S A SENSE THAT WERE ALL IN THIS TOGETHER.

HOT WEATHER DOES IT TOO, A LITTLE BIT, BUT PEOPLE ARE A LOT MORE LIKELY TO MUG YOU OR SHOOT YOU IN THE HOT WEATHER. IT'S NOT JUST THE TOUGH, VIRTUOUS ONES WHO MAKE IT OUT.

Dec/Jan:
FACILITIES -----3805
MATERIALS|
num lock

ON THE OTHER HAND, I ESPECIALLY LIKE TO BE AT HOME ALL DAY WHEN IT'S REALLY COLD. I SORT OF FOOL MYSELF INTO THINKING I'M TRAPPED AND I MUST BE ORGANIZED AND INDUSTRIOUS TO KEEP MYSELF SAFE. I BUNDLE UP ... AND WALK AROUND THE EMPTY ... HOUSE CLEANING THINGS UP ... AND WORK-ING ON ... PROJECTS. I MAKE A ... LOT OF TEA AND ... THINK ABOUT THINGS ... WITH A SERIOUS BUT PLEASANT OUTLOOK...

...MAYBE I CALL MY FRIENDS, BUT MAYBE THE PHONES ARE OUT! AN ADVENTURE. AS LONG AS I DON'T HAVE TO GO OUT AND TORTURE MYSELF WITH THE COLD. I'M A COUCH JACK LONDON.

COURTNEY, ARE YOU DONE WITH THE REPORT?
FEB

NO, UH, GIVE ME ABOUT 5 MINUTES!

DOUG? HERE IT IS—
THANKS.

OH, COURTNEY, CAN WE TALK FOR A MOMENT?
SURE~

I'M A LITTLE CONCERNED ABOUT YOUR PERFORMANCE LATELY.

I KNOW YOU'VE HAD SOME DIFFICULTIES LATELY, AND I'M SORRY, BUT I REALLY NEED YOU TO...
...TODAY, I COULDN'T SEE THE LAKE FROM ONLY A HUNDRED YARDS AWAY. THE SKY AND THE LAND AND THE WATER WERE ALL EQUALLY WHITE, WITH ONLY A FEW SCRAGGLY TREES, TORN BY THE WIND, TO MARK A PALE GREY DIVISION. I CAN HEAR IT, THOUGH.

IT IS POUNDING AND ROARING LIKE IT IS THE OCEAN. IT'S AMAZING TO ME THAT IT CAN MAKE SO MUCH NOISE, AND YET BE INVISIBLE. THE ONLY THING I'M SORRY ABOUT IN THE PLACE THAT I LIVE IS THAT I CAN'T GET TO THE LAKE SO EASILY. I SPENT WHOLE SUMMERS THERE WHEN I WAS YOUNGER, AND NOW IT'S BEEN TWO YEARS SINCE I EVEN STEPPED ON TO THE SAND, JUST A MILE OR SO OFF.
...SO I HOPE YOU'LL GIVE IT YOUR BEST EFFORT. YOU THINK WE CAN WORK TOGETHER ON THIS?

YES, SURE. THANKS DOUG, I'M SORRY.
ALL RIGHT. WE'LL CHECK BACK IN LATER.
I JUST WENT OUTSIDE AGAIN, AND THE LAKE ACTUALLY SOUNDS MORE LIKE A TRAIN. BUT THEN, SO DOES THE OCEAN, SO IT DOESN'T MESS UP MY PREVIOUS OBSERVATION.
END · J · ABEL · 2/5/96

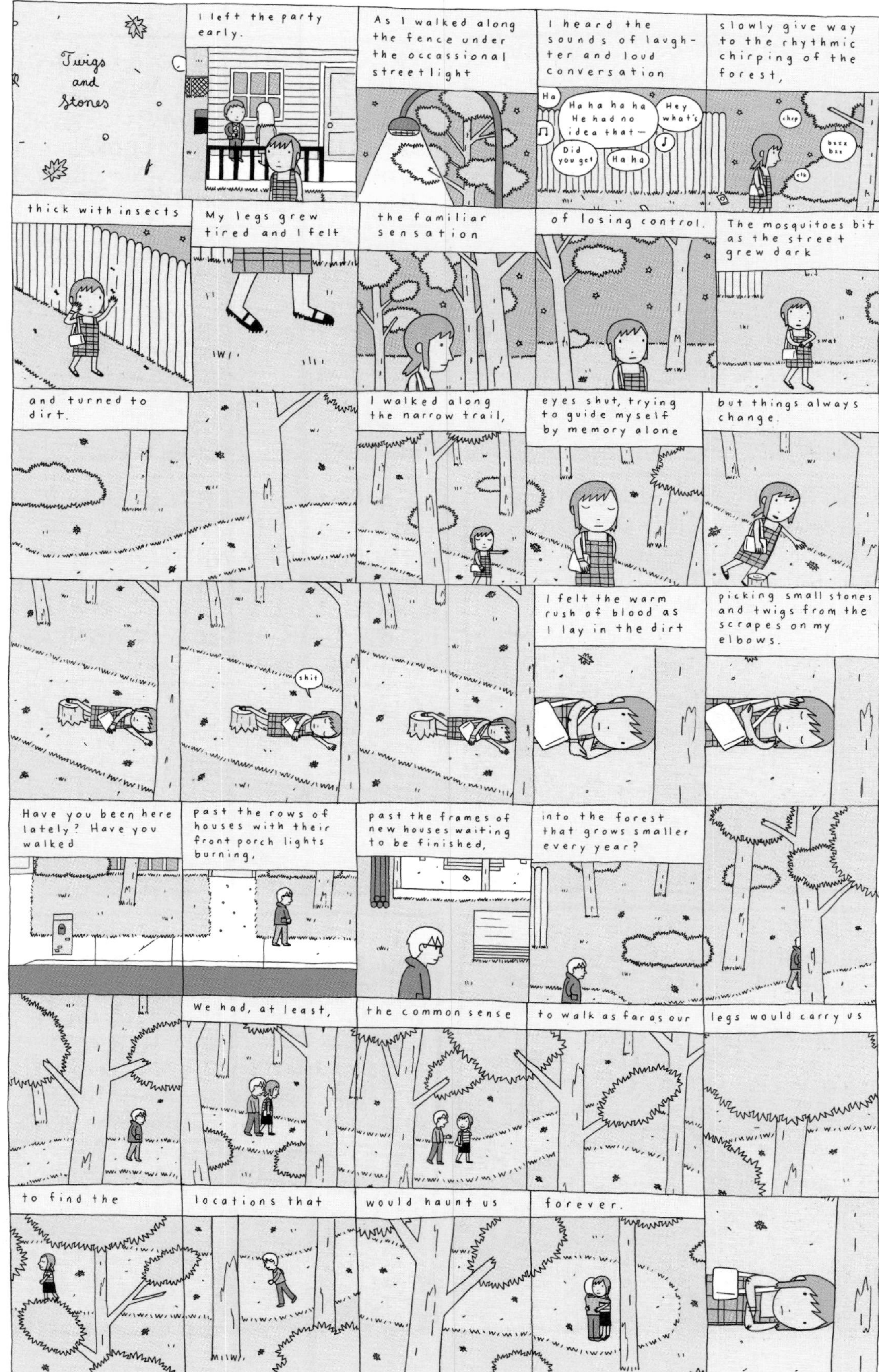

COLE JOHNSON Twigs and Stones

I GREW UP WITH Dancing People. IN A WAY, my GRANDMA was BEHIND IT ALL. She DIDN'T Dance BUT SHE LIKED A Party ATMOSPHERE, EVEN FIRST THING in THE morning.

SHAKE IT SHAKE IT NOW BABY!

RADIO BLASTING
FIRST CUP OF COFFEE

We KEPT OUR Record PLAYER IN the KITCHEN AND my UNCLE AND HIS Swinger FRIEND with THE INCREDIBLE hair Came OVER TO eat AND SHOW GRANDMA VERSIONS of the TWIST.

And THEN THERE were MY teen-AGE HULA DANCING cousins who BROUGHT THEIR HULA 45's AND DID entire DANCES THAT transFIXED ME totally. THEY TOOK CLASSES AT A PLACE up the HILL.

LOVELY HULA HANDS GRACEFUL AS THE BIRDS IN MOTION

I SIGNED UP FOR a BEGINNER'S HULA Class. MY TEACHER WAS A MIDDLE-AGED WHITE lady WHO was OBSESSED WITH HAWAII. SHE ALWAYS had A PLASTIC orchid IN HER HAIR AND She WAS VERY serious ABOUT TECHNIQUE.

GIRLS, I'M STILL SEEING WIGGLY FINGERS!
MOVE THE WHOLE HAND! UNDULATION! UNDULATE, GIRLS!

Keeping YOUR KNEES BENT WAS ONE OF THE SECRETS OF a GRACEFUL hula. MY teacher WANTED US TO PRACTICE THIS constantly. IT TURNED OUT to ALSO HELP Me master A DANCE kids WERE DOING ON MY street CALLED, "The FUNKY CHICKEN."

There WAS A GIRL Who COULD DANCE in A WAY THAT MADE us ALL STAND STILL. She MOVED in WAYS WE'D NEVER seen. I WAS CRAZY ABOUT HER AND mystified BY HER AND scared OF HER TOO. She WAS Beautiful AND MOODY. HER MOTHER WAS DEAD.

SOMETIMES SHE JUST STARED AT YOU LIKE THIS AND DIDN'T ANSWER.
HEY, I GOT AN IDEA! YOU SHOW ME HOW TO DO "THE POPCORN" AND I'LL SHOW YOU HOW TO HULA THE SONG, "MY LITTLE GRASS SHACK." HUH? SOUND GOOD TO YA?

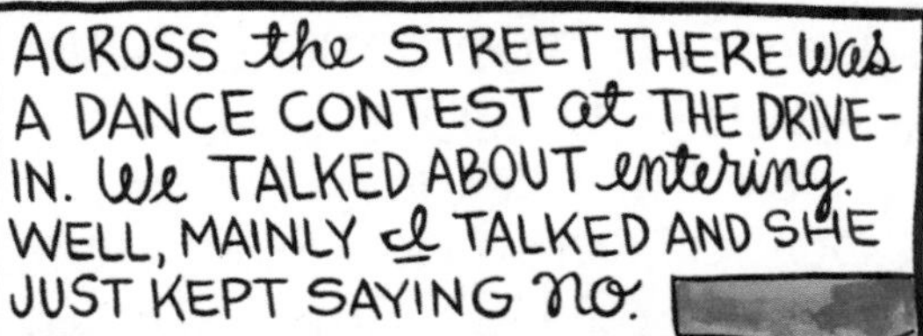

UP UNTIL THEN I NEVER THOUGHT ABOUT THE WAY I DANCED. I HAD NO IDEA I WAS CONSIDERED TO BE SOMETHING OF A SPAZ. THIS NEWS WAS A HEAVY BLOW.

ALL OF A SUDDEN, DANCING GOT HARD. EVEN HULA DANCING FELT WEIRD TO ME. I STILL WENT TO CLASS BUT I STARTED DANCING IN THE BACK ROW. I NOTICED THE MUSIC SOUNDED LESS WONDERFUL AND THAT MY TEACHER LOOKED LESS BEAUTIFUL, AND MORE INSANE.

EVEN MY DANCING RELATIVES STARTED LOOKING CRAZY TO ME, AND I REALIZED IT WAS WEIRD TO HAVE A RECORD PLAYER IN THE KITCHEN.

The ONLY PERSON WHO still LOOKED GOOD WHEN DANCING was THE GIRL WHO TOLD me I LOOKED stupid. WELL, HER and MY BABY BROTHER.

BABIES ALWAYS LOOK GOOD WHEN THEY DANCE. THEY HAVE SOME THING THAT IS VERY HARD TO GET BACK ONCE IT IS LOST AND it IS always LOST.
C'MON! YOU SAID YOU WANTED TO LEARN IT! DO YOUR ARMS LIKE THIS AND YOUR LEGS LIKE THIS.
NAW, THAT'S OK.
WHY YOU BEIN' SUCH A CHUMP? JUST TRY IT!
NAW. THANKS ANYWAY.

I DON'T BLAME that GIRL FOR KNOCKING ME OUT OF my GROOVE. I WAS about TO START JUNIOR HIGH SCHOOL. It WAS GOING to HAPPEN ANYWAY. BUT IT WAS A LONG TIME BEFORE I GOT IT BACK.
WHY YOU DON'T GO HULA-HULA NO MORE?
I QUIT, GRANDMA. IT WAS STUPID.
NEW HAIRDO
AIE N'AKO! DANCING IS NEVER STUPID, MY DEAR.

I SPENT TOO LONG EITHER WISHING I COULD DANCE in A WAY THAT ALWAYS LOOKED COOL OR WISHING I WAS COOL ENOUGH TO NOT CARE About what OTHER PEOPLE THOUGHT. MAINLY I DIDN'T DANCE.
THE DREAD AND DESIRE WERE EQUAL

The GROOVE IS SO MYSTERIOUS. WE'RE BORN WITH it AND WE lose IT AND THE WORLD seems TO SPLIT apart BEFORE OUR eyes INTO STUPID AND cool. WHEN WE GET IT BACK, the WORLD unifies AROUND US, AND BOTH STUPID AND COOL FALL AWAY.
SECRETLY SPAZ-DANCING ALONE IN MY ROOM (I STILL DO THIS)

I AM GRATEFUL to THOSE WHO ARE KEEPERS OF THE GROOVE. The BABIES and THE GRANDMAS WHO HANG ON TO IT and HELP us REMEMBER when WE FOR-GET that ANY KIND OF DAN-CING is BETTER than NO DANCING at ALL.
N'AKO! LOOK AT HIM! SEGIE NA BABY! WHAT IS HE DOING!?! HA-LA! SEGIE!
ONLY GOD KNOWS THE NAME OF THAT DANCE!

CONSTELLATIONS

GEEZ! WHAT'VE YOU GOT IN HERE, ANYWAY?

I SAID I'D CARRY IT! IT'S JUST SOME BOOKS, OK?

WELL, IT WEIGHS A TON!

SO WHY DON'T YOU JUST SUE ME?

MY FRIEND, CLAUDIA WAS A REAL BRAIN, SHE ACTUALLY KNEW MORE THAN SOME OF OUR TEACHERS, BUT SHE ALMOST NEVER RUBBED IT IN, OR MADE YOU FEEL STUPID. HER LATEST KICK WAS ASTRONOMY, SO WHEN I ASKED HER TO SPEND THE NIGHT, MY MOM LET US SLEEP OUT IN THE CAMPER. THAT WAY WE COULD LOOK AT STARS ALL NIGHT LONG, IF WE WANTED. PLUS WE COULD HAVE SOME PRIVACY FROM MY SISTERS, ESPECIALLY PEARL.

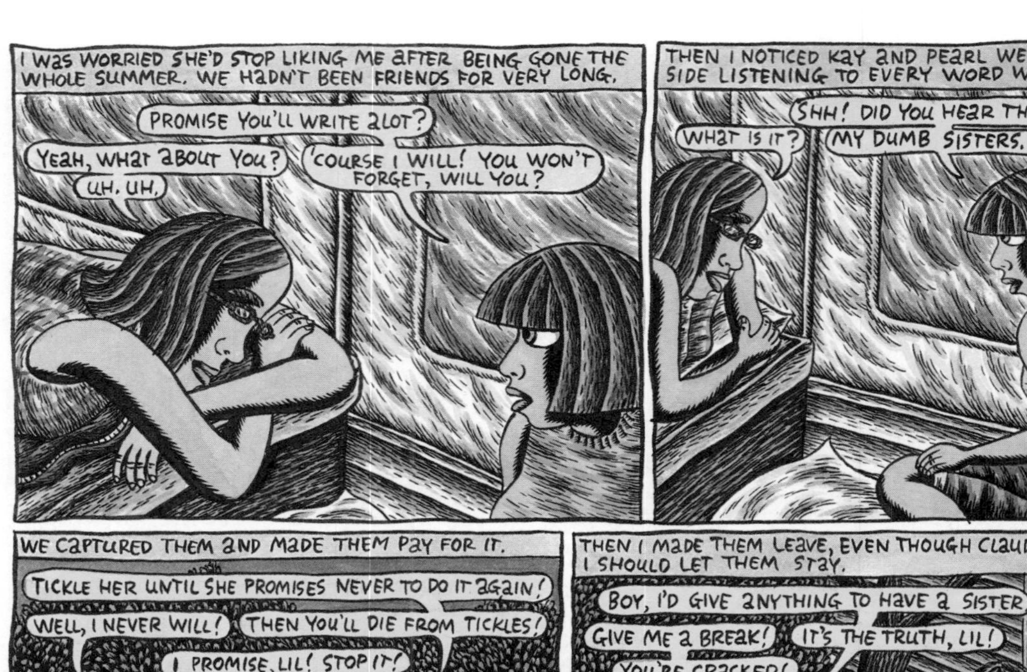
I WAS WORRIED SHE'D STOP LIKING ME AFTER BEING GONE THE WHOLE SUMMER. WE HADN'T BEEN FRIENDS FOR VERY LONG.
PROMISE YOU'LL WRITE ALOT?
YEAH, WHAT ABOUT YOU?
UH, UH.
'COURSE I WILL! YOU WON'T FORGET, WILL YOU?
THEN I NOTICED KAY AND PEARL WERE OUTSIDE LISTENING TO EVERY WORD WE SAID.
SHH! DID YOU HEAR THAT?
WHAT IS IT?
MY DUMB SISTERS. C'MON!

WE CAPTURED THEM AND MADE THEM PAY FOR IT.
TICKLE HER UNTIL SHE PROMISES NEVER TO DO IT AGAIN!
WELL, I NEVER WILL!
THEN YOU'LL DIE FROM TICKLES!
I PROMISE, LIL! STOP IT!
THEN I MADE THEM LEAVE, EVEN THOUGH CLAUDIA SAID I SHOULD LET THEM STAY.
BOY, I'D GIVE ANYTHING TO HAVE A SISTER.
GIVE ME A BREAK!
IT'S THE TRUTH, LIL!
YOU'RE CRACKED!

PRETTY SOON IT WAS DARK ENOUGH TO SEE THE STARS.
C'MON, LIL, LET'S GO.
HOLD ON A MINUTE! I CAN'T FIND MY OTHER SHOE.
CLAUDIA SHOWED ME THE BIG DIPPER AND SOME OTHERS, TOO, AND THEN A REAL LIVE SATELLITE WENT BY!
SEE, IT'S RIGHT OVER THERE.
WHERE? OH, YEAH. WOW!
2

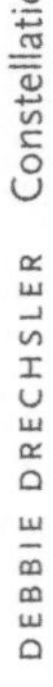

HEY! LOOK AT THAT SHOOTING STAR!
WHERE?
NEVER MIND. IT'S GONE, NOW.
OH, RATS!
THERE'LL BE MORE. LOOK! THERE'S CASSIOPEIA.

MY DAD BROUGHT OUT THIS OLD TELESCOPE I FORGOT WE EVEN HAD.
WOW! THIS IS GREAT, MR. MAIER!
HERE, I'LL GET IT SET UP FOR YOU, OK?
GEE, THANKS!

WHILE CLAUDIA LOOKED THROUGH IT, MY DAD CAME OVER AND PUT HIS ARM AROUND ME...
YEAH! THANKS, DAD. I FORGOT ABOUT THAT THING.
WOW! COOL!

AND STARTED FEELING UP MY BOOB. THERE WASN'T ANYTHING I COULD DO 'CUZ OF CLAUDIA.
MY PLEASURE, LIL. I THOUGHT YOU GIRLS WOULD ENJOY IT. SO WHAT'VE YOU SEEN SO FAR, HONEY? HEY! EARTH TO LILY! WHAT ZONE ARE YOU IN, ANYWAY? HA!

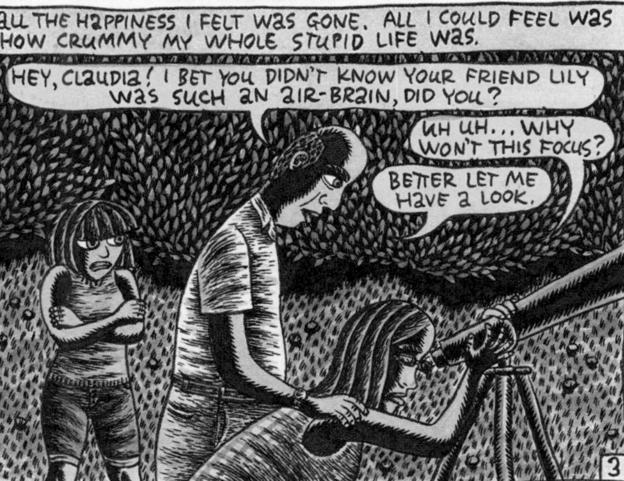
ALL THE HAPPINESS I FELT WAS GONE. ALL I COULD FEEL WAS HOW CRUMMY MY WHOLE STUPID LIFE WAS.
HEY, CLAUDIA! I BET YOU DIDN'T KNOW YOUR FRIEND LILY WAS SUCH AN AIR-BRAIN, DID YOU?
UH UH... WHY WON'T THIS FOCUS?
BETTER LET ME HAVE A LOOK.
3

I GOT SCARED HE WOULD DO IT TO CLAUDIA, TOO, AND THEN SHE'D STOP BEING FRIENDS WITH ME.
UM... LET'S SEE... JUST TURN THIS, HERE. THAT'S ALL.
OH, OK. THANKS.
NO PROBLEM, CLAUDIA. WHY DON'T YOU SHOW ME ONE OF THOSE CONSTELLATIONS, EH?

I WAS LISTENING FOR A SIGN OF IT, BUT SHE JUST SOUNDED HAPPY, NOT LIKE ANYTHING BAD WAS HAPPENING TO HER.
SEE THOSE STARS THAT LOOK LIKE A "W"?
LET'S SEE... UMM... YEAH!
THAT'S HERCULES.
WELL, I'LL BE DAMNED.

WHEN HE STARTED TELLING HIS DUMB DIRTY JOKES, I COULD TELL CLAUDIA THOUGHT IT WAS WEIRD.
CLAUDIA, YOU KNOW WHAT AN OVER-THE-SHOULDER-BOULDER-HOLDER IS?
C'MON, CLAUDIA. LET'S GO MAKE SOME POPCORN, OK?

ON THE WAY TO THE HOUSE HE DID IT AGAIN, ONLY THIS TIME HE PINCHED ME SO HARD I MADE SOME NOISE, BY ACCIDENT. I COULDN'T HELP IT.
WHY, HONEY! ARE YOU OK? DID YOU TRIP?
NO DAD, IT WASN'T ANYTHING.

DEBBIE DRECHSLER Constellations

WE MADE SOME POPCORN, BUT MY MOOD WAS COMPLETELY WRECKED.
LET'S PUT LOTS OF BUTTER ON, OK?
YEAH, SURE.
YOU OK?
YEAH!

WE WATCHED TV WITH MY MOM AND DAD FOR AWHILE.
I'M GOING TO BED, NOW. ALBERT, ARE YOU COMING?
IN A WHILE, ESTHER.
4

EVEN THOUGH I GOT KINDA TIRED, I WAS WORRIED THAT IF WE WENT OUT TO THE TRAILER, HE'D COME, TOO.

THEN I SAW THAT CLAUDIA WAS PRACTICALLY ASLEEP.
C'MON, CLAUDIA. LET'S GO TO BED, OK?
HUH? UH...OK.
I'LL WALK YOU GIRLS OUT.

I WAS AFRAID TO EVEN LOOK AT HIM IN CASE HE GOT REAL MAD AT ME OR SOMETHING.
THAT'S OK, DAD. WE'LL BE FINE. THANKS ALOT FOR OFFERING, THOUGH. G'NIGHT.
WELL, THEN, GIRLS... SLEEP TIGHT.
G'NIGHT.

CLAUDIA FELL RIGHT TO SLEEP.
CLAUDIA?

BUT IT TOOK ME FOREVER. I KEPT THINKING I COULD HEAR HIS FOOTSTEPS OUTSIDE THE TRAILER.
END

Some of my best friends are

JUL 53
Sonia and me

MAY 60
Teri and me

AUG 65
Eva and me

I was six when I met Sonia. She was a year older... I was a foot taller...
HELLO MRS. WYMAN
THIS IS MY DAUGHTER, SONIA, MRS. ROSENBLATT
SAY HELLO DONNIE !!
SONIA SAY HELLO TO DIANE !!
We became best friends...
I, PRINCESS SERENA OF TH' WESTERN MOON COMMAND YOU...
GIDDYAP!

We played Mean Man, moon-maiden and Mermaid...
I'M TELLING YA SONIA, WHEN THEY COME BACK UPSTAIRS THEY'RE DIFFERENT !!
NOW GIRLS, WAIT RIGHT HERE FOR US !!
YER RIGHT !! THE BASEMENT TURNS THEM INTO MONSTERS !!
Bargain Basement
Empire's
SALE

In the vacant lot across the street, we caught fire-flies and built secret hide-outs...
C'MON GINNY !!! TRY AGAIN !! SAY: ISH KABBIBLE EEE OATEN GOATEN EH EH EH EH!!
YA GOTTA SAY IT TO JOIN OUR CLUB!!
PRIVATE PROPERTY

My family moved to Brooklyn when I was twelve...
DON'T WORRY CANARSIE ISN'T SO FAR AWAY! AND I'LL WRITE YA EVERY DAY !!
I'LL MISS YA DONNIE, BUT DON'T WORRY I'LL VISIT YA

Sonia and I lost touch but she came to my Sweet Sixteen party...
HAPPY BIRTHDAY DONNIE...
THANKS

In the summer of '67, I visited Sonia in Los Angeles. She lived in a shack behind a bar...
...THEN WE'LL SPLIT FOR TOPANGA CANYON, THIS CHICK I KNOW HAS SOME BITCHIN' GRASS... SHE STORES IT IN SHOPPING BAGS !!
FAR OUT !!

I haven't seen Sonia since then, but I've heard she's married, has a kid and lives in San Jose...
AWHILE AGO I GOT A LETTER FROM MY OLD FRIEND SONIA, SHE SAID SHE WAS THE HAPPIEST THAT SHE COULD REMEMBER BEING. I NEVER ANSWERED HER...
MY OLD BEST FRIEND DIED LAST YEAR IN A CAR CRASH...

I was thirteen when I met Teri. She had long, white, perfectly polished, pearlized fingernails. I bit mine...
HIYA... I'M TERI !! DIDJA JUST MOVE IN? I LIVE AROUND TH' CORNER.. DO YA WANNA GO GET SOME PIZZA?
UH... SURE I'M DIANE
HI !!

We became best friends....
HEY DIANE DIDYA GET EARTH ANGEL, BY THE PENGUINS, ON OUR LIST ?! WE HEARD IT FIVE TIMES TONITE !!!
IT'S MY MEMORY RECORD
DON'T WORRY TERI, I GOT IT !! OH GOD! LISTEN !! IN TH' STILL OF THE NIGHT, BY THE FIVE SATINS !!
I'M SO HAPPY !!

We hung out in the bowling alley, at the corner gas station, and in the school yard...

Sex was our main topic...

We graduated from make-out parties to frat-hopping...

Teri and I drifted apart. She went to the local High and I went to the High School of Music and Art, an hour and a half subway ride from home...

Last I heard she had eloped with an older man, who was in Real Estate and moved to Miami Beach...

Eva and I met on the subway. She was the daughter of Auschwitz survivors. My parents were peace-niks...

We became best friends...

We double-dated and enrolled as Art Majors at Brooklyn College...

Except I dropped out and Larry dropped me and Eva married Harry...

In 1968 I got married. Eva was my Matron of Honor...

My husband didn't care much for Harry. Our visits became more and more sporadic...

On our last visit Eva confided that when her son was born she couldn't find Harry to let him know...

I tried to reach Eva on a recent visit to New York but had no luck...

YUR GOIN' ON A RELAXING VACATION....
(NATCHAH IN AWL ITS SPLENDAH!!)
The BUNCH with Her BABY & GRAMMAW.. BLABETTE
(DEE-LISHUS SEENERY!!)
(VISTERS & PANERAMERS)
DON'T KID YURSELF.. IT'LL BE DELICIOUS...
SNOW-COVERED PEAKS!!
FAR-OUT ARCHITECTURE
TREES TREES
ITS SO NATCHURUL ISN'T IT?!
SMELL THAT EIHR ITS REFRESHING LIKE TREES OR SOMETHING
WILL YEW LOOK AT THOSE BEEYEWDEEFUL BERDS?!
© by that easy goin' gal aline Ricky crumb
MEET BUNCH, DER SOFERSCHNITZEL & THE GRAMMAW...
C'MON SOF WHATS WRAWNG?
WAHH! AAHH!
OI!
EXORCIST GROWL
C'M TAH GRAMMAW LOOK AT HUHR...HUHRR!! I NEVAH SAWR ANYTHING LIKE ITT!! LOOK HOW SHE KNOWS MEE... I DON' WANNA COME ON TOO STRAWG... I'M NOT SCARRING HUHR RIGHT? AM I RIGHT?? COME TO GRAMMAW I'M YURR GRAMMAW SOPHIA SOPHIIAAA!
FREHRER JOHCKER FREHRER JOHCKER DAW MAY VOOW DAW MAY VOOOW SUNNEE LAYMER TEENER SUNNEE LAYMER TEENER DING DOHNG DOHNG DAWNG DOHNG DOHNG, DOHNG DING DOHNG!
ABBA ABBA ABBA
LOOK HOW SHE LOVES GRAMMAW!! YUH GONNA COME TO NEW YAWK WITH GRAMMAW!! GIVE GRAMMAW KISSS!!
SAY DAWG SAY BERDD
SAINTLY LOOKING COMPARED TO BLABETTE
brazzz
SEE, SEE I TOLD YEW SHE WANTED A BANANA... YEW GOTTA GIVE HUHR BANANAS SEE, SEE THAT'S WHAT SHE WANTED... SEE THAT'S WHY SHE WAS CRYING!
BUT BBUTT...
LOOKIT HOW HAPPY SHE IS WITH GRAMMAW!
GGG CHOKE GLLUGG GGG MMM SMASH
TORTURED & IGNORED BUNCH AS A BABY.

OH MY GHODD SHE'S CHOKING... CAWL THE DOCTAH... CAWL THE EMERGENCY SQUAD!!
OH MY BAYBEE MY DAHLING!
SHE'S AWRIGHT IT'S NOTHING!
AGGH
AGGH
DON'T VOMIT ON GRAMMAW'S HAND PAINTED JOGGING SUIT!
TOTALLY USELESS.. JUST HAD HER NAILS WRAPPED!
HUHR SPIT UP, I DON' MIND!
A LITTLE LATER:
AWRIGHT LET'S RELAX C'MON HAVE BREAKFAST.. RELAX C'MON AWRIGHT..
30 SECONDS LATER:
AWRIGHT? YA DONE? YA HAD ENOUGH?! DID YA ENJOY? I MADE IT FOR YEW... YA LIKE IT? ITS GOOD RIGHT? RIGHT? AWRIGHT, YA DONE YET? TAKE YA'TIME...
I'M NOT DONE EATING YET.
GRRR GRR
AWRIGHT. TAKE YUR TIME WE'RE ON VACATION... YEAH, YEAH YEAH...
YA DONE YET...AWRIGHT? WAS IT GOOD...DID I MAKE IT GOOD?.. YEAH? ITS TIME TO RELAX NOW... AWRIGHT OK? OK? FEEL GOOD..YA FEEL AWRIGHT? YA HAVING FUN...YA HAD ENUFF... YEAH.. ITS GOOD ...YEAHYEAHYEAH YEAHYEAHYEAH YEAH YEYEYEYE YE YYYY YYYYYY..........
YEAHYYYYY YYYYYYYYY.....
EEEE
EEEE
SO RELAX.. DON'T GET UPSET.. DON'T GET NERVOUS!
DAHLING DEAHR DORDAH!
END

ALIKE-A-LOOK
BY ARIEL BORDEAUX
© 1994
Sometimes I see someone walking towards me who bears a strong resemblance to me... it's eerie...

... but it makes me feel really good ... I always smile at her,

and think : "She's so pretty... huh ... maybe I am, too" ...
SAFEWAY
TRUE
MEN'S

The good feeling stays with me ...
ShiKai
even when I look in the mirror.
end

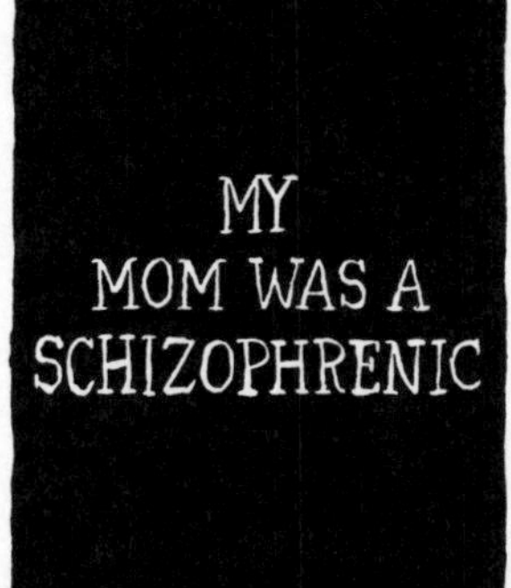
MY
MOM WAS A
SCHIZOPHRENIC

SCHIZOPHRENIA IS AN ORGANIC DISEASE OF THE BRAIN.

THIS IS WHAT MOST PEOPLE IN OUR SOCIETY BELIEVE -- THAT SCHIZOPHRENIA IS A MENTAL ILLNESS.

WE CAN TRACE THIS BELIEF BACK TO EMIL KRAEPELIN AND EUGEN BLEULER.

I'M EMIL KRAEPELIN. IN 1898 I DISCOVERED A NEW DISEASE -- I CALLED IT DEMENTIA PRAECOX.

I'M EUGEN BLEULER. IN 1911 I HORNED IN ON KRAEPELIN'S ACT BY GIVING DEMENTIA PRAECOX A NEW NAME -- I CALLED IT SCHIZOPHRENIA.

I BELIEVE THAT SCHIZOPHRENIA IS THE OUTCOME OF A PATHOLOGICAL, ANATOMICAL, OR CHEMICAL DISTURBANCE OF THE BRAIN.

WHY SHOULD WE CARE ABOUT WHAT KRAEPELIN AND BLEULER BELIEVED ?
THOMAS SZASZ

WHY... DO PSYCHIATRISTS CONTINUE TO RECORD KRAEPELIN'S AND BLEULER'S BELIEFS REGARDING THE NATURE OF SCHIZOPHRENIA ?

WHY DO THEY NOT EMPHASIZE INSTEAD KRAEPELIN'S AND BLEULER'S UTTER INABILITY TO SUPPORT THEIR BELIEFS WITH A SHRED OF RELEVANT EVIDENCE ?

KRAEPELIN AND BLEULER DID NOT DISCOVER THE DISEASES FOR WHICH THEY ARE FAMOUS-- THEY INVENTED THEM.

ACCORDING TO THE PAMPHLET *UNDERSTANDING SCHIZOPHRENIA* (RECENTLY PUBLISHED BY THE ONTARIO MINISTRY OF HEALTH) THESE ARE THE SIGNS AND SYMPTOMS OF SCHIZOPHRENIA.
① DELUSIONS
② HALLUCINATIONS
③ THOUGHT DISORDER
④ LOSS OF MOTIVATION
⑤ FLAT EMOTIONAL RESPONSE

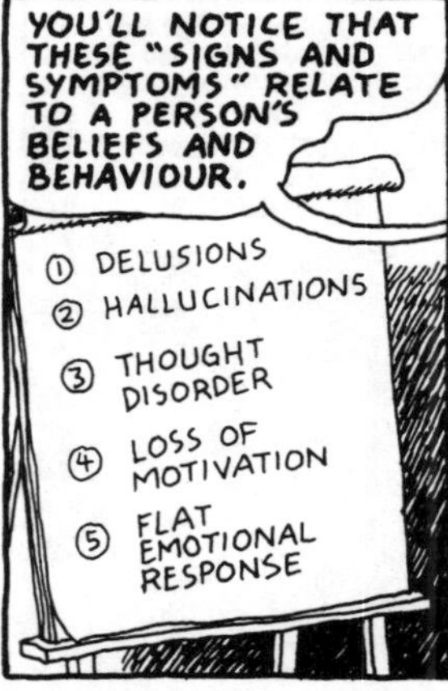
YOU'LL NOTICE THAT THESE "SIGNS AND SYMPTOMS" RELATE TO A PERSON'S BELIEFS AND BEHAVIOUR.
① DELUSIONS
② HALLUCINATIONS
③ THOUGHT DISORDER
④ LOSS OF MOTIVATION
⑤ FLAT EMOTIONAL RESPONSE

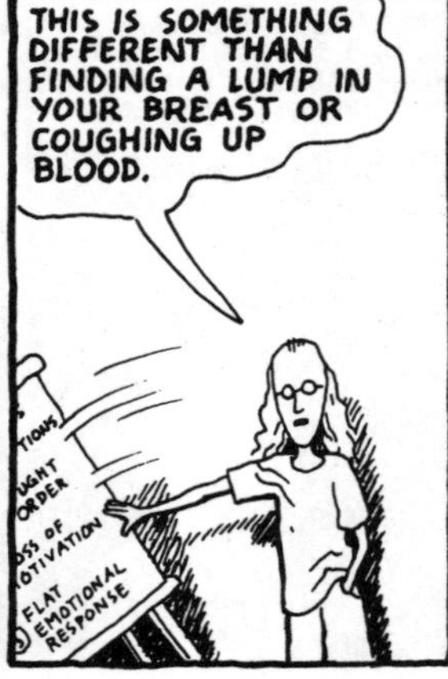
THIS IS SOMETHING DIFFERENT THAN FINDING A LUMP IN YOUR BREAST OR COUGHING UP BLOOD.

DESPITE THEORIES ABOUT CHEMICAL IMBALANCES, BRAIN SHRINKAGE AND GENETIC DEFECTS --

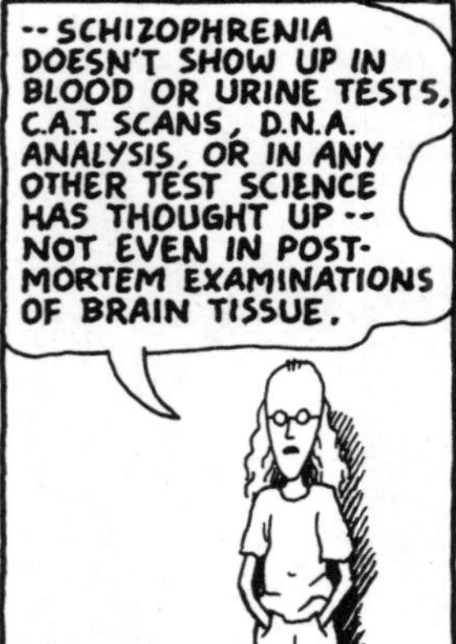
-- SCHIZOPHRENIA DOESN'T SHOW UP IN BLOOD OR URINE TESTS, C.A.T. SCANS, D.N.A. ANALYSIS, OR IN ANY OTHER TEST SCIENCE HAS THOUGHT UP -- NOT EVEN IN POST-MORTEM EXAMINATIONS OF BRAIN TISSUE.

THERE ARE, OF COURSE, DISEASES, SUCH AS SYPHILIS, WHICH CAN AFFECT THE BRAIN-- BUT THERE ARE DIAGNOSTIC TESTS FOR THESE DISEASES.

PSYCHIATRISTS TODAY DIAGNOSE SCHIZOPHRENIA THE SAME WAY KRAEPELIN AND BLEULER DID--

--NOT BY LOOKING FOR SIGNS OF DISEASE BUT BY LOOKING FOR SOCIALLY UNACCEPTABLE BELIEFS AND BEHAVIOUR.

BEFORE 1973 HOMOSEXUALITY WAS CONSIDERED A MENTAL ILLNESS -- IN THAT YEAR THE AMERICAN PSYCHIATRIC ASSOCIATION TOOK A VOTE WHICH DECIDED THAT IT WAS NO LONGER ONE.

TODAY WE CAN SEE THAT GAY PEOPLE BEFORE THE '60'S WERE MISERABLE NOT BECAUSE THEY SUFFERED FROM A MENTAL ILLNESS--

--BUT BECAUSE THEY LIVED IN A HOMOPHOBIC CULTURE.

MANY, POSSIBLY MOST, GAY PEOPLE IN THAT HOMOPHOBIC CULTURE COULDN'T SEE BEYOND THEIR CULTURE'S ASSUMPTIONS--

--THEY BELIEVED THAT THEY WERE SICK.

THE SCHIZOPHRENIC IS LIKE A MAN PERMANENTLY UNDER THE INFLUENCE OF MESCALIN.
ALDOUS HUXLEY

THE L.S.D. PHENOMENON... IS AN INTENTIONALLY ACHIEVED SCHIZOPHRENIA.
JOSEPH CAMPBELL

BECAUSE OF ACCIDENTS OF BOTANY AND HISTORY, EUROPEAN CULTURE HAS BEEN AWAY FROM THE PSYCHEDELIC DIMENSIONS AWHILE...
TERENCE McKENNA

...WE CALL THEM "SCHIZOPHRENIA" AND SLAM THE DOOR.
THE SHAMAN IS A PERSON... WHO IN EARLY ADOLESCENCE UNDERWENT A SEVERE PSYCHOLOGICAL CRISIS, SUCH AS TODAY WOULD BE CALLED A PSYCHOSIS.

YESTERDAY'S SHAMAN IS TODAY'S CHRONIC SCHIZOPHRENIC !
SETH FARBER
NOT ALL SHAMANS USE INTOXICATION WITH PLANTS TO OBTAIN ECSTASY, BUT ALL SHAMANIC PRACTICE AIMS TO GIVE RISE TO ECSTASY.

NONORDINARY STATES OF CONSCIOUSNESS... ARE IN SOME INSTANCES INDUCED BY THE USE OF SACRED PSYCHEDELIC PLANTS... AND IN OTHERS BY POWERFUL NONDRUG TECHNIQUES--
STANISLAV GROF

--THAT COMBINE IN VARIOUS WAYS RESPIR-ATORY MANEUVERS, CHANTING, DRUMMING, MONOTONOUS DANCING, SENSORY OVERLOAD, SOCIAL AND SENSORY ISOLATION, FASTING, AND SLEEP DEPRIVATION...

...THE SPECTRUM OF EXPERIENCES INDUCED BY PSYCHEDELIC COMPOUNDS IS PRACTICALLY INDISTINGUISHABLE FROM THOSE RESULTING FROM VARIOUS NONDRUG TECHNIQUES.

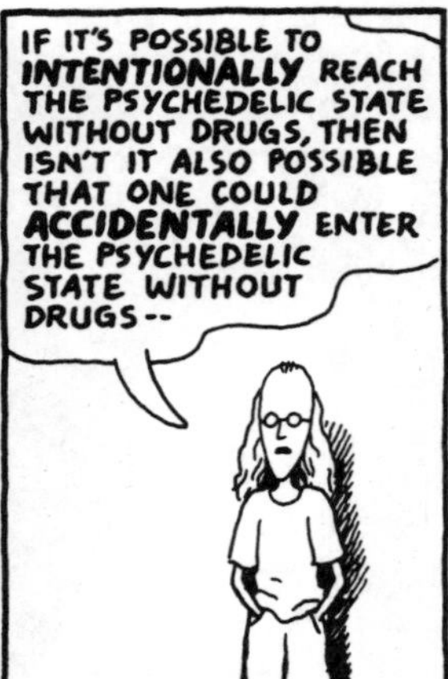
IF IT'S POSSIBLE TO INTENTIONALLY REACH THE PSYCHEDELIC STATE WITHOUT DRUGS, THEN ISN'T IT ALSO POSSIBLE THAT ONE COULD ACCIDENTALLY ENTER THE PSYCHEDELIC STATE WITHOUT DRUGS--

--AND THAT THIS IS WHAT WE OFTEN CALL SCHIZOPHRENIA ?

LOOK AT GROF'S LIST AND THINK ABOUT INSOMNIA, HUNGER, THE STERILE BARRENNESS OF MODERN CITIES --

-- HOW WE'RE BOMBARDED BY THE MEDIA, THE MONOTONOUS RHYTHMS AND REPETITIVE TASKS OF SO MANY WORK-PLACES --

-- AND THE ISOLATION AND LONELINESS THAT ARE EVERYWHERE IN OUR SOCIETY.

PEOPLE OFTEN HAVE TERRIBLE EXPER-IENCES ON PSYCHE-DELIC DRUGS -- BAD TRIPS.
SCHIZO-PHRENICS, IN OUR SOCIETY, ALMOST ALWAYS HAVE BAD TRIPS.

PSYCHEDELICS CAN ALSO GIVE THE USER TRANSCEN-DENTALLY ECSTATIC EXPERI-ENCES.
SCHIZO-PHRENICS OCCASIONALLY HAVE SIMILARLY POSITIVE REVELATIONS DURING THEIR PSYCHOTIC EPISODES.

WHY DON'T SCHIZOPHRENICS HAVE MORE GOOD TRIPS ? COULD IT HAVE SOMETHING TO DO WITH OUR FEAR OF, AND CULTURAL ASSUMPTIONS ABOUT, SCHIZOPHRENIA ?

ADVOCATES OF PSYCHEDELICS BELIEVE THAT THE TYPE OF TRIP YOU HAVE DEPENDS ON WHAT TIMOTHY LEARY CALLED THE "SET AND SETTING".

ESSENTIALLY, IF YOU HAVE A POSITIVE MIND-SET AND ARE IN A POSITIVE, COMFORTING SETTING YOU'LL HAVE A GOOD TRIP -- A NEGATIVE SET AND SETTING EQUAL A BAD TRIP.

ALMOST ALL OF US HAVE A NEGATIVE MIND-SET IN REGARDS TO SCHIZOPHRENIA AND WE LIVE IN A CULTURE WHICH IS VERY FEARFUL OF THE EXPERIENCE.

INDEED, WE'VE MADE IT VIRTUALLY ILLEGAL.

I'M NOT DENYING THAT MOST SCHIZOPHRENICS SUFFER -- I'M QUESTIONING WHY THEY SUFFER.

IS IT BECAUSE THEY HAVE AN ILLNESS, OR IS IT BECAUSE OF THE SET AND SETTING THAT THIS SOCIETY GIVES THEM ?

THE ORDINARY PERSON IS A SHRIVELLED, DESICCATED FRAGMENT OF WHAT A PERSON CAN BE...
R.D. LAING

...WHAT WE CALL "NORMAL" IS A PRODUCT OF REPRESSION, DENIAL, SPLITTING, PROJECTION, INTROJECTION AND OTHER DESTRUCTIVE ACTION ON EXPERIENCE...

... THE "NORMALLY" ALIENATED PERSON, BY REASON OF THE FACT THAT HE ACTS MORE OR LESS LIKE EVERYONE ELSE, IS TAKEN TO BE SANE.

OTHER FORMS OF ALIENATION ARE THOSE THAT ARE LABELED BY THE "NORMAL" MAJORITY AS BAD OR MAD...

... CAN WE NOT SEE THAT THIS VOYAGE [SCHIZOPHRENIA] IS NOT WHAT WE NEED TO BE CURED OF --

-- BUT THAT IT IS ITSELF A NATURAL WAY OF HEALING OUR OWN APPALLING STATE OF ALIENATION CALLED NORMALITY ?

CWDB '95

NOTES

My mother died in an institution in 1976. (See my book *I Never Liked You* for more on this, though not much more.) I became curious about what mental illness is—about what had happened to her. I read books on the subject, but their answers seemed vague and unsatisfying. It wasn't until I came across Thomas Szasz's *Schizophrenia: The Sacred Symbol of Psychiatry* (1976) in 1990 that I felt that my questions were beginning to be answered. I read more books by Szasz and then books by other "anti-psychiatry" authors. I realized that their ideas aren't widely known, so in 1995 I decided to try and create a short introduction-to-anti-psychiatry type of strip. (Both Szasz and R. D. Laing rejected the "anti-psychiatry" label when it first came into use in the 1960s, but I personally see nothing wrong with the term. Psychiatry is a branch of medicine, and if one believes that so-called mental illnesses should not be treated as medical problems—as Dr. Szasz does and the late Dr. Laing did—then it seems sensible to me to accept that one is against psychiatry: anti-psychiatry. Szasz, though, is himself a psychiatrist, as was Laing. Perhaps they wanted to continue to use that title for professional reasons.)

I've always liked finding those evangelical Christian minicomics (particularly the ones drawn by Jack Chick) that true believers leave for free in telephone booths and bus shelters. I started to think about self-publishing the anti-psychiatry-strip-I-wanted-to-do as an eight-page minicomic that I would distribute in the same way. In order to fit the format, I made the strip six pages long. But then I realized that, if I wanted as many people as possible to read it, I should print it in *Underwater*. (I could only distribute a mini in Toronto, whereas *Underwater* got into comic shops across America and Canada.) After "My Mom Was a Schizophrenic" was published in *Underwater* #4, I did also publish it as a minicomic. I bicycled around Toronto, putting the little booklets in telephone booths and bus shelters. I felt a bit silly doing that, particularly since I only had the energy to distribute a couple hundred of the minicomics, while *Underwater* #4 had already reached thousands of people. But one of those minicomics ended up in the hands of someone who worked for the Mental Patients Association of Vancouver, and that organization asked if they could print the strip in their newsletter *In a Nutshell*. I agreed, of course.

Page 209: Panel 2. I'm quoting Dr. Rob Buckman, who at that time hosted a show for TV Ontario called *Vital Signs*.

209:5–209:7. I'm not directly quoting Kraepelin and Bleuler here—I'm paraphrasing material from Szasz's *Schizophrenia: The Sacred Symbol of Psychiatry*. In his later years, Bleuler did an about-face and admitted that psychiatric definitions "are forensic and not medical."

209:8–210:2. From Szasz's *Schizophrenia: The Sacred Symbol of Psychiatry*. Emphasis added.

210:3. *Understanding Schizophrenia* had been "recently published" (in 1994) at the time that the strip was created.

210:4. I thought it was obvious how these "signs and symptoms" relate to beliefs and behaviour, but one person argued the point with me, so I'll explain my reasoning.

1 & 2. X talks to a person no one else can see or hear. This is odd behaviour but it is behaviour nonetheless. If X actually believes that X is talking to someone, you or I may think that X is deluded (or incorrect—to use a less "loaded" word which means the same thing) but that doesn't make it any less a belief of X's.

3. This one might not seem to be connected to a person's beliefs or behaviour (thoughts are not behaviour and aren't necessarily beliefs) but then you have to remember that psychiatrists aren't mind readers. They're actually judging how a person speaks and what they say, and speech is a form of behaviour.
4. It may seem like odd behaviour if a person who's been a go-getter all their life suddenly only wants to lie on their bed and look at the ceiling but (again) it is behaviour.
5. How a person expresses emotion is clearly a form of behaviour.

This isn't to say that behaviour can't be an indication of disease. In 1994, the cat that Sook-Yin and I were living with seemed to have a "loss of motivation"—all she wanted to do was lie around on the sofa. Since this contrasted with her previously active behaviour, we were concerned and took her to the vet. It turned out that she had an infected gall bladder and needed surgery. The vet established this, however, not just by looking at the cat's behaviour, but by conducting various diagnostic tests. Had those tests not found anything wrong, we wouldn't have concluded that our cat was schizophrenic—there are plenty of healthy cats who do little but lie around on sofas. But while it's fine for cats to lie around all day doing nothing, it's socially unacceptable for humans.

Szasz argues that psychiatry has become our society's method of policing disapproved human behaviour that is beyond the reach of the criminal justice system.

210:6–210:7. After "My Mom Was a Schizophrenic" was published, a number of readers wrote me letters to point out that schizophrenia has been "proven" to have a genetic cause or has been "proven" to be caused by a "chemical imbalance" in the brain. If you've fallen for either of these psychiatrically promulgated beliefs, then please refer to Chapter Five of *Toxic Psychiatry* (1991) by psychiatrist Peter Breggin to be disabused of them.

210:7. I recently read a message-board critique of "My Mom Was a Schizophrenic" in which it was claimed that schizophrenia *does* show up in CAT scans. I'm aware that psychiatrists make this claim but, if they believed it was true, then the CAT scan would become the diagnostic test for schizophrenia. The fact that CAT scans are *not* used in this way shows what psychiatrists really believe about the ability of this technology to detect the presence of schizophrenia.

Psychiatry is a pseudo-science—it does not have scientific, objective, *diagnostic* tests for the "illnesses" it claims to treat.

211:2. In her book *They Say You're Crazy* (1995), psychologist Paula J. Caplan reports that the vote was 5854 to 3810.

211:7. From Huxley's *The Doors of Perception* (1954).

211:8. From Campbell's *Myths to Live By* (1972).

211:9–212:1. From McKenna's *The Archaic Revival* (1991). In these panels, I cut and switched around McKenna's words, so I'm going to give them to you here the way he wrote them:

> Modern epistemological methods are just not prepared for dealing with chattering, elf infested spaces. We have a word for those spaces—we call them "schizophrenia" and slam the door. But these dimensions have been with us ten thousand times longer than Freud. Other societies have come to terms with them. Because of accidents of botany and history, European culture has been away from the psychedelic dimensions awhile.

211:7–212:1: Martin Lee and Bruce Shlain's book *Acid Dreams* (1985) details the scientific debate that took place in the 1950s and 1960s over whether LSD and similar drugs were psychedelic (mind manifesting) or psychotomimetic (madness mimicking). The psychedelic faction believed that these drugs could be beneficial to people, while those who used the word psychotomimetic believed that they made people crazy. Apparently it occurred to no one that maybe *both* sides of the debate were right.

212:2. From *Myths to Live By*.

212:3. From psychologist Farber's *Madness, Heresy, and the Rumor of Angels* (1993).

212:4. From McKenna's *Food of the Gods* (1992).

212:2–212:4. Some people seem to misunderstand this point. They think, because I'm saying that shamans and psychotics are both having psychedelic-like experiences, that therefore I'm saying schizophrenics are ready to take on a shamanic role in our society. That is not what I'm saying. There's a good deal more to being a shaman than experiencing altered mental states. Given his or her cultural background and training, the shaman has a context for making sense of unusual mental states. The schizophrenic, having a very different cultural background, is likely to just become lost in the experience. Psychiatrists, having *no* understanding of these mental states, usually lead the schizophrenics in their care into deeper darkness and confusion.

Likewise, I'm not saying that using psychedelics will make one into some sort of spiritual leader.

212:5–212:7. From psychiatrist Grof's *The Adventure of Self-Discovery* (1988).

212:9. No doubt some people who are diagnosed as being schizophrenic are not in a psychedelic-like state. One can have "flat emotional responses," "loss of motivation," and "thought disorders" for reasons other than being in an altered mental state. At the heart of the experience I'm talking about is psychosis (hallucinations and delusions).

213:1–213:3. I don't think Grof's list exhausts all of the possible non-drug ways by which people can enter this state. Many of the things Grof lists seem to be attempts to induce stress, and I suspect that other stress-inducing experiences—such as extreme negative emotion—could produce the same results.

213:5. For examples, see *Madness, Heresy, and the Rumor of Angels* for the stories of Barbara and Angela. Each had psychotic experiences that they described in positive terms. Barbara "felt safe and secure and very happy." Angela felt "wonderful! It was as if I'd gotten the code to the universe." When committed to psychiatric institutions, both women quickly started to feel like schizophrenics are supposed to: terrible.

Also see Michael Schumacher's *Dharma Lion* (1992) for his account of Allen Ginsberg's 1948 non-drug-induced "mystical" experiences in which he heard "the voice of [William] Blake, speaking to him through eternity," and saw "that the people around him now had the faces of wild animals."

Because we're not used to thinking of psychosis as being potentially good, most people who have such experiences are more likely to call them mystical.

213:7–213:8. I first encountered Leary's ideas in Robert Anton Wilson's *Cosmic Trigger* (1977).

214:4–214:9. From Laing's *The Politics of Experience* (1967). Laing's suggestion that schizophrenia might be a healing experience in the right context will seem so far-fetched to those who haven't encountered it before (and to many of those who have) that I suppose it'd be a good idea to give an example. (In *The Politics of Experience,* Laing gives a detailed case history which illustrates his point. Rather than condense it, I'll give a different—and more famous—example.)

In the posthumously published journal *In Pursuit of Valis* (1991), science fiction author Philip K. Dick gives an autobiographical account of an experience that began in March 1974 and continued for about a year.

> It appeared—in vivid fire, with shining colors and balanced patterns . . . It seized me entirely, lifting me from the limitations of the space-time matrix.

Dick explains in another entry that during this period he believed that he "was someone else . . . From another time period . . . Dead centuries ago and reborn." He frequently asserts throughout *In Pursuit of Valis* that this experience healed him.

> When it left me, it left me as a free person, a physically and mentally healed person who had seen reality suddenly, in a flash, at the moment of greatest peril and pain and despair; it had loaned me its power and it had set right what had by degrees become wrong over God knows how long.

Although Dick seems to have generally believed that his experience was mystical, he didn't become dogmatically attached to any single explanation, and several times in *In Pursuit of Valis* he seriously considers the possibility that he was psychotic. He couldn't, however, get past the popular view that psychosis is always experienced negatively. In one of the later entries of the book, from 1981 (Dick died in early '82), he wrote:

> In 2-3-74 came comprehension and recognition; there also came the end of—the healing of—the gulf that separated me from the world. This is 180 degrees away from psychosis. Viewed psychologically, this is, in fact, a healing; it is repair.

Well, I guess Dick never read *The Politics of Experience.*

214:9. After "My Mom Was a Schizophrenic" was published in *Underwater* #4, it occurred to me that Laing's use of the word "healing" seemed a bit awkward, since the strip rejected the medical model of mental "illness." Laing also rejected the medical model, so it's clear that he was using the word in a metaphorical sense (and, of course, I also intended it metaphorically in the previous note) but it still made me uneasy. I'd now rephrase the Laing panels thusly: "Most people (probably all people) are far (probably very far) from achieving their full potential. A person who's having a schizophrenic experience might, by going through that experience, get a bit closer to achieving their potential." My rephrasing sounds less impressive, but these days I'm more comfortable with the idea when it's expressed like that.

One reader wrote me a letter to point out what looked to him like a contradiction: A psychedelic-like mental state would likely be caused by "chemicals endogenous to the brain"—shouldn't this be described as a chemical imbalance in the brain? My problem with that term isn't with the word "chemical" but with the word "imbalance," which implies that the brain is functioning incorrectly when someone enters psychosis. I think it's the opposite—that the brain is as much in balance when a person is psychotic as when a person is "normal" and that *if* a "chemical endogenous to the brain" is responsible for psychosis, it's because the brain is *supposed* to release that chemical from time to time when circumstances seem to warrant it.

Why would the brain do this? Why would it deliberately go into a psychedelic-like state as a response to stress and extreme emotion? I don't know, but that's not going to stop me from speculating:

In the right circumstances (like in pastoral "natural" settings) psychedelics can be very pleasant. Perhaps the brain evolved (in those natural settings) so that whenever things got too intense it could flood itself with a psychedelic-like chemical in order to feel good again—get high—get in touch with life at a deeper "mystical" level. The brain just didn't know when it was evolving this "coping mechanism" thousands of years ago that, at some point in the future, human society would become antithetical to the psychedelic experience. As a result, now, when the "coping mechanism" goes into effect, it's usually a bad experience instead of a good one.

A second possible explanation depends on whether Timothy Leary's belief that psychedelics could be used to "reprogram" the brain is correct. Leary's experiment with prisoners at Concord State Prison in Massachusetts seemed to confirm this belief. He told prison officials that by giving consenting inmates psilocybin he could cut the recidivism rate, and he did.

> Leary had defined success or failure in terms of where the bodies were in space-time two years after release from prison. At that time, he noted gladly, over 80% of them were still outside prison, whereas the majority of released convicts are back inside prison within two years. Dr. Walter Huston Clark, in 1976, noted that the bodies of most of Leary's convicts known to him were still outside prison in space-time after 15 years. [From Robert Anton Wilson's *Cosmic Trigger.*]

If Dr. Leary was right that psychedelics can be used to reprogram the brain, and if I'm right that psychosis is a psychedelic-like mental state, then psychosis might have evolved as a built-in-psychedelic-reprogramming-system that the brain uses in extreme circumstances (like Philip K. Dick's "moment of greatest peril and pain and despair").

But if this is a coping mechanism or the brain's way of reprogramming itself, why does the brain stay in this state for months and years? Laing theorized that psychiatric interventions prolonged this mental state—prevented the person from "naturally" coming out of it. Irit Shimrat's experience—as recorded in her book *Call Me Crazy* (1997)—would seem to confirm this.

> [T]he first and second times I went mad, I got professional help—hospitalization and drugs—and stayed crazy for months, and the third time I got help from a friend who wasn't scared because she'd been there herself—and it was over in a few hours.

A friend who read this piece asked me what my solution to the problem was.

Was the solution to the "mental illness" of homosexuality a new form of psychotherapy or a new drug? No, it was the gradual decreasing in our society of homophobia. If we could similarly get rid of our fear of schizophrenia, I believe our problems with it would decrease and possibly disappear. People who see this as unrealistic are ignoring the fact that in some cultures if you "hear voices" or see things that other people can't see, you aren't a person with a problem, you're a person with a gift.

A gay acquaintance of mine came out of the closet. Most of his friends and family responded positively. They were supportive of what they saw as a new adventurous phase of his life. During my first acid trip I became convinced that I wasn't going to recover my sanity—that the drug had driven me permanently crazy. I knew that my family and friends weren't going to have a Laingian perspective on this. I figured I had institutionalization, mind-numbing neuroleptic drugs, and possibly electro-shock to look forward to. I decided that rather than face this bleak future I'd commit suicide. Fortunately, I came out of the trip before I could throw myself off a bridge. But the experience clearly illustrated for me why schizophrenics can be suicidal and how the attitudes of society affect psychosis and make it negative. If I could have looked forward to an attitude of support for a new adventurous phase of my life, I think it's likely that I would have had a better trip.

Another friend told me of a news story he'd heard—a schizophrenic had stopped taking his "medication" and had then slashed the face of a child. This friend believed that all schizophrenics should be forced to take anti-psychotic drugs to keep them non-violent. The notion that psychotics are violent is a myth. Sure, some are—but so are plenty of non-psychotic ("normal") people. If we're going to drug *all* schizophrenics because *a few* are potentially violent, then logically we should also be drugging all non-psychotic people to keep the violent ones in check. But drugging schizophrenics has nothing to do with logic and everything to do with fear of people who "aren't like us."

Some people believe that they have been genuinely helped by psychiatrists and that this validates psychiatric theories. I don't doubt that there are people who have been helped by psychiatrists. I'm sure that there are a few psychiatrists who are sensitive, and caring, and have a talent for assisting people who are in emotional distress. But that doesn't prove psychiatric beliefs. Some people in emotional distress will visit a psychic or a tarot-card reader. Many psychics and tarot-card readers are sensitive, and caring, and have a talent for assisting people who are in emotional distress, but that doesn't make tarot-card reading a valid scientific discipline.

And while I acknowledge that some have been helped by psychiatry, it's my opinion that this profession does *far* more harm than good.

I've mentioned a number of books in relation to this strip, but I'd like to particularly recommend two of them for their scope and readability: *Madness, Heresy, and the Rumor of Angels* by Seth Farber, and *Toxic Psychiatry* by Peter Breggin.

I wish I'd had room in the strip to bring up Breggin's contention that psychiatric drugs are used, not to heal people, but to control them. Actually, the anti-psychotic drugs do the opposite of healing. Even the Ontario Ministry of Health's *Understanding Schizophrenia* admits that these drugs can cause tardive dyskinesia, which "is damage to the central nervous system, sometimes permanent damage . . . TD can be so severe that it is disabling." *Understanding Schizophrenia* doesn't give the risk rates, but according to Breggin, "all long-term patients are likely to succumb to tardive dyskinesia."

A book I didn't mention in the notes but which I'd also like to recommend is Jeffrey Moussaieff Masson's *Against Therapy* (1988). It's not so much anti-psychiatry as it is anti-every-aspect-of-the-mental-health-system—a scathing indictment of the philosophical assumptions of a system that Masson knew well, both as a psychoanalyst and as projects director of the Sigmund Freud Archives.

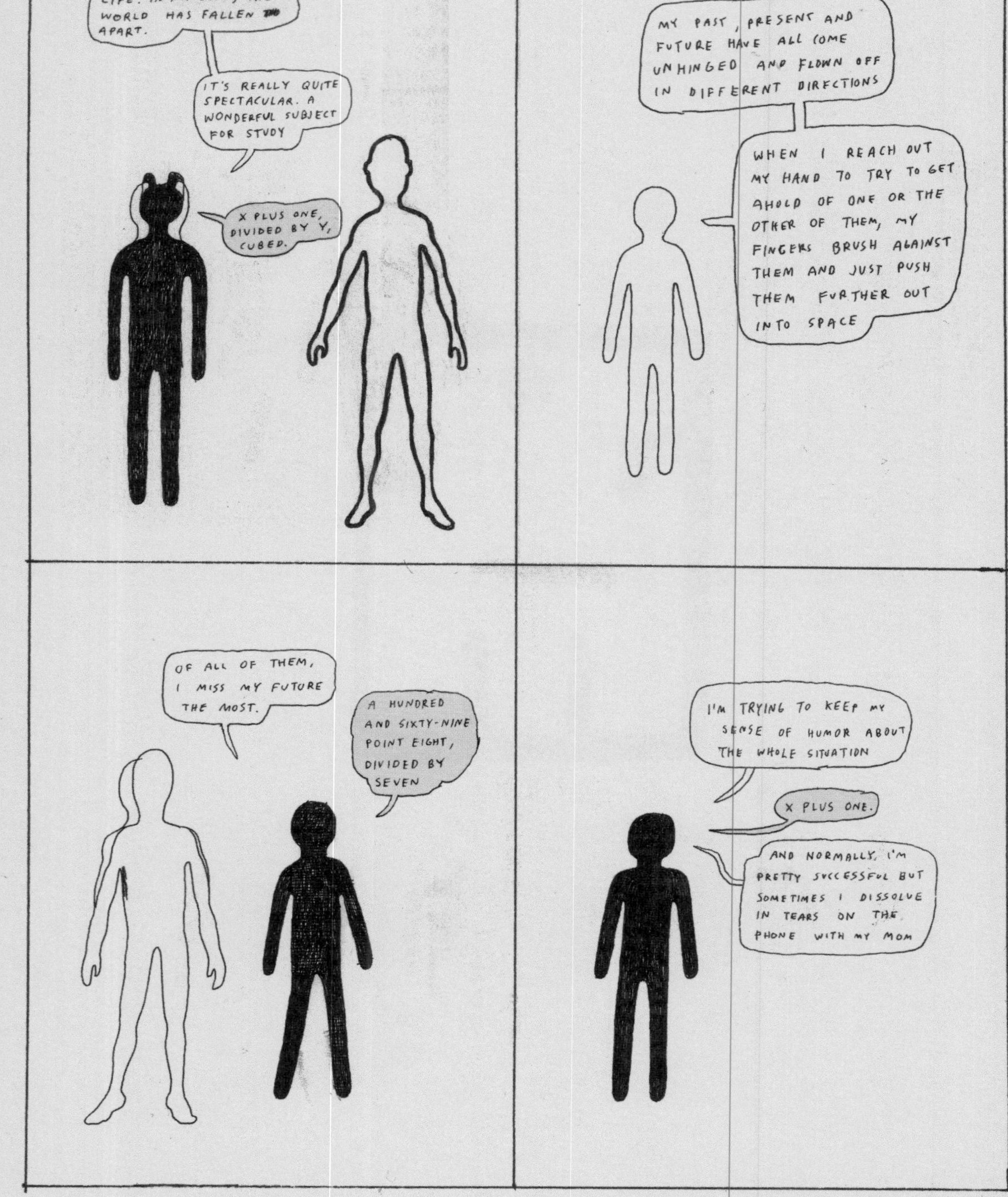
HELLO, WELCOME TO MY LIFE. IN MY LIFE, THE WORLD HAS FALLEN APART.
IT'S REALLY QUITE SPECTACULAR. A WONDERFUL SUBJECT FOR STUDY
X PLUS ONE, DIVIDED BY Y, CUBED.
MY PAST, PRESENT AND FUTURE HAVE ALL COME UNHINGED AND FLOWN OFF IN DIFFERENT DIRECTIONS
WHEN I REACH OUT MY HAND TO TRY TO GET AHOLD OF ONE OR THE OTHER OF THEM, MY FINGERS BRUSH AGAINST THEM AND JUST PUSH THEM FURTHER OUT INTO SPACE
OF ALL OF THEM, I MISS MY FUTURE THE MOST.
A HUNDRED AND SIXTY-NINE POINT EIGHT, DIVIDED BY SEVEN
I'M TRYING TO KEEP MY SENSE OF HUMOR ABOUT THE WHOLE SITUATION
X PLUS ONE.
AND NORMALLY, I'M PRETTY SUCCESSFUL BUT SOMETIMES I DISSOLVE IN TEARS ON THE PHONE WITH MY MOM

I CAN TURN COMPLETELY INTO LIQUID, INTO SWISS CHEESE INTO THIN AIR, INTO FUMES OF GASOLINE, SMOKE, INTO IRON ORE, URANIUM, SOLID ROCK. I CAN TURN INTO A CANNISTER OF NITROGEN
I CAN TURN INTO SOUND I CAN TURN INTO A FILING CABINET. STACKS OF PAPER. FILL IN THE BLANKS.
SOLVE FOR X.
I'VE BUSIED MYSELF WITH MEMORIALS OF MY OLD LIFE. I KEEP EXPECTING THEM TO PILE UP LIKE STONES IN A RIVER. TO BECOME A FOUNDATION FOR SOMETHING NEW. SOMETHING WEIGHTY AND STABLE
BUT THEY MELT AWAY AND ADD UP TO NOTHING
ONE PLUS ONE MINUS TWO, DIVIDED BY EIGHT.
SOMETIMES I TALK TO MY FORMER SELF ON THE TELEPHONE.
I JUST PUNCH IN NUMBERS RANDOMLY, IN FITS, AND SOMETIMES HE ANSWERS
HE'S KIND, HE TRIES TO BE ENCOURAGING BUT I KNOW THE SITUATION ISN'T ANY BETTER FOR HIM THAN IT IS FOR ME. HE KNOWS THE AXE IS COMING. THE DYNAMITE. THE SPEEDING TRAIN. HE WISHES ME WELL, BUT THERE IS A SADNESS IN HIS VOICE.
ZERO PLUS ZERO PLUS ZERO PLUS ONE.
TIMES X

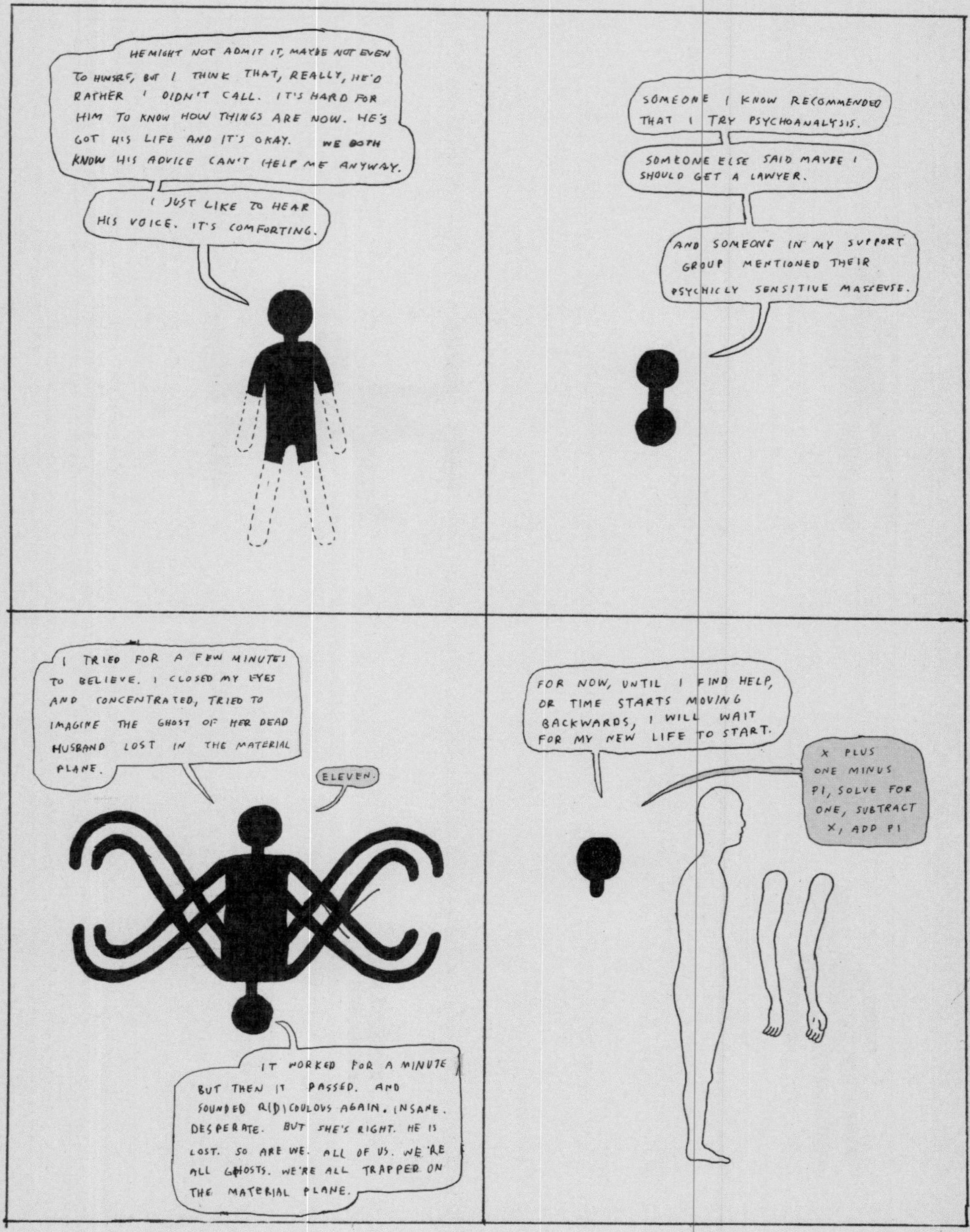

HE MIGHT NOT ADMIT IT, MAYBE NOT EVEN TO HIMSELF, BUT I THINK THAT, REALLY, HE'D RATHER I DIDN'T CALL. IT'S HARD FOR HIM TO KNOW HOW THINGS ARE NOW. HE'S GOT HIS LIFE AND IT'S OKAY. WE BOTH KNOW HIS ADVICE CAN'T HELP ME ANYWAY.

I JUST LIKE TO HEAR HIS VOICE. IT'S COMFORTING.

SOMEONE I KNOW RECOMMENDED THAT I TRY PSYCHOANALYSIS.

SOMEONE ELSE SAID MAYBE I SHOULD GET A LAWYER.

AND SOMEONE IN MY SUPPORT GROUP MENTIONED THEIR PSYCHICLY SENSITIVE MASSEUSE.

I TRIED FOR A FEW MINUTES TO BELIEVE. I CLOSED MY EYES AND CONCENTRATED, TRIED TO IMAGINE THE GHOST OF HER DEAD HUSBAND LOST IN THE MATERIAL PLANE.

ELEVEN.

IT WORKED FOR A MINUTE BUT THEN IT PASSED. AND SOUNDED RIDICULOUS AGAIN. INSANE. DESPERATE. BUT SHE'S RIGHT. HE IS LOST. SO ARE WE. ALL OF US. WE'RE ALL GHOSTS. WE'RE ALL TRAPPED ON THE MATERIAL PLANE.

FOR NOW, UNTIL I FIND HELP, OR TIME STARTS MOVING BACKWARDS, I WILL WAIT FOR MY NEW LIFE TO START.

X PLUS ONE MINUS PI, SOLVE FOR ONE, SUBTRACT X, ADD PI

IN MY NEW LIFE
I COULD BE AN ELECTRICIAN, A PLUMBER, A FINANCIAL ANALYST, A HOMELESS EX-BASEBALL PLAYER, A U.S. SENATOR.

I COULD HAVE THREE KIDS AND A WIFE AND JOIN THE MILITARY AND START EATING PACKAGED FOOD AND WORK FOR ENRON
I COULD BE A SMALL CHILD WITH A BROKEN ARM, BLEEDING ON THE PLAYGROUND.
X, Y.
Y
X

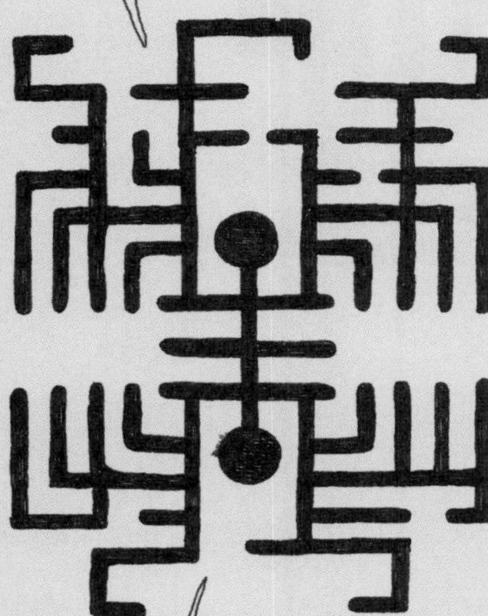
COULD BE A SLAVE OR A COMPUTER PROGRAMMER.
I COULD GO BACK IN TIME AND BE A BIRD, HIDING FROM A COLOSSAL METEOR IMPACT.
I COULD BE A NUCLEAR REACTION IN THE HEART OF A STAR OR LIGHT RAYS STRUGGLING TO ESCAPE A BLACK HOLE.
I COULD BE VENUS.

I COULD BE A GIANT WORM AT THE BOTTOM OF THE OCEAN EATING VOLCANIC SULPHER OUT OF A FISSURE IN THE OCEAN FLOOR.

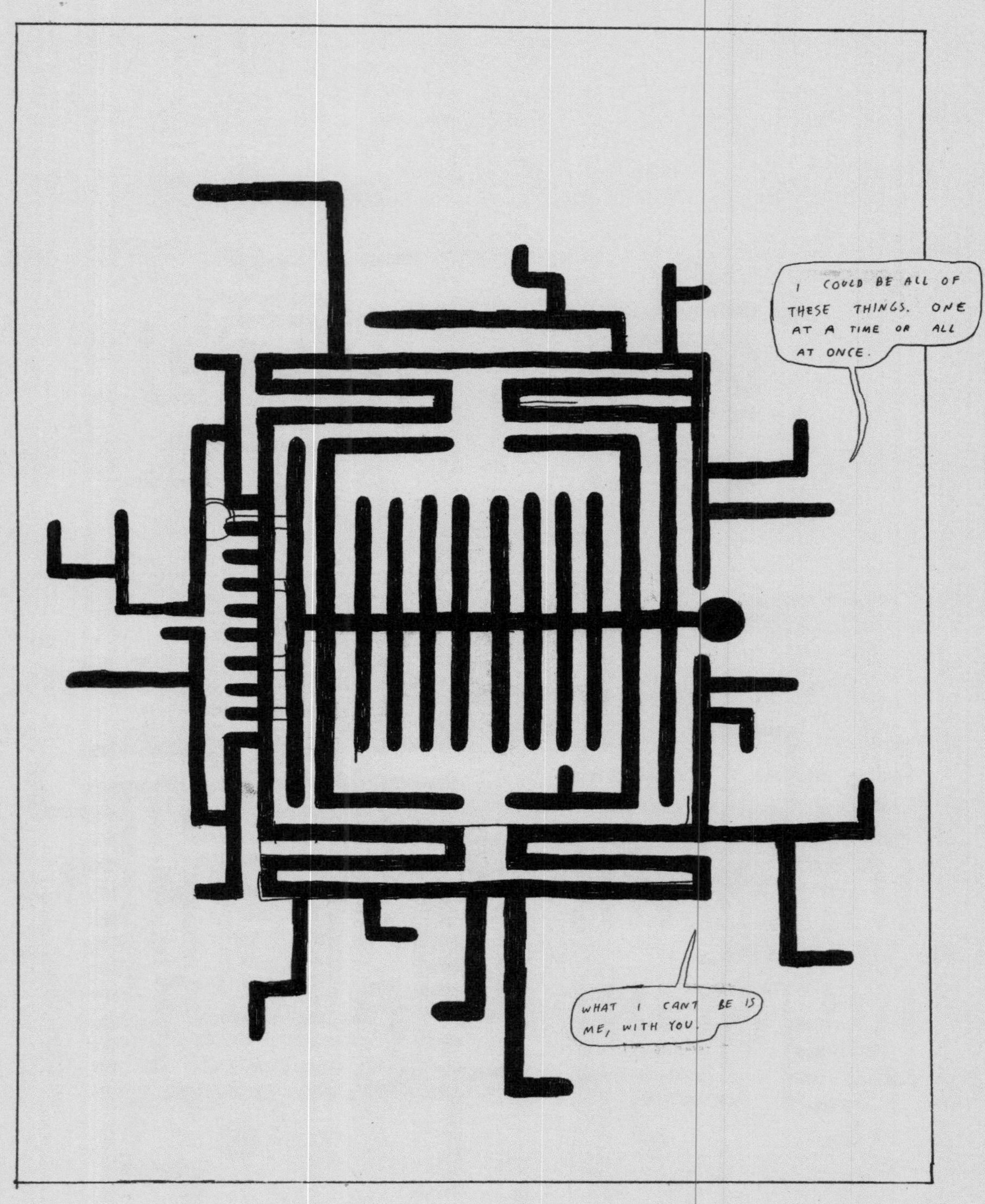
I COULD BE ALL OF THESE THINGS. ONE AT A TIME OR ALL AT ONCE.
WHAT I CANT BE IS ME, WITH YOU.

INFINITY PLUS ONE
MINUS INFINITY
PLUS TWO DIVIDED
BY THREE, TIMES ZERO.

White Death

WE MADE A MISTAKE. WE WERE LOOKING FOR CEMENT, LIME, CONSTRUCTION MATERIALS TO REPAIR THE HOUSE.

OTHERS WERE LOOKING FOR FOOD.

"People found food in Serb homes. I took some, maybe 100 kg of corn, and from that corn we could make flour. But 100 kg doesn't last when that's the main thing you have.

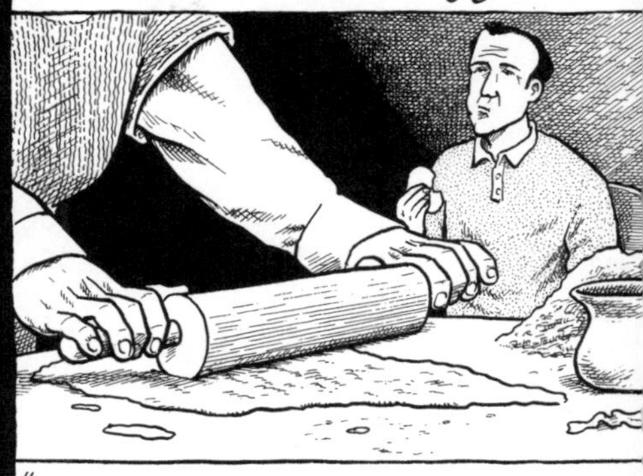

"We ran out of flour in November.

"We had planted potatoes before the war, but you have to tend to potatoes, you have to dig around them two or three times, and after the war started, we didn't do anything in the garden, we had escaped to Kopaci. When we returned, I dug up the potatoes and they were very small.

"My mother didn't bother to take off the skin. when she was preparing potato pie.

"That year we had plenty of fruit, very nice fruit, in our garden. We didn't have any sugar, but my mother heard how you could make jam without sugar... by cooking overripe fruit for a long time.

"We had milk and cheese from the cow...

"We ate jelly over bread with some cow's cream.

"Plenty of refugees were coming from villages, and they brought cows and sheep. They couldn't do anything with their sheep. We asked for the prices. 15 dm each. Before the war the price of a sheep was 150-200 dm. They were satisfied if you gave them flour or cigarettes.

"I gave two packets of cigarettes and got three sheep.

"We slaughtered two of the sheep and had meat until the end of January."

IT WAS VERY CRITICAL IN DECEMBER AND JANUARY. NO MORE FLOUR, NO MORE POTATOES. WE COULDN'T EAT FRUIT ONLY... AND YOUR ORGANISM CANNOT EAT MEAT EVERY DAY...

MY FAMILY, MY RELATIVES AND SO ON, HELPED EACH OTHER AS MUCH AS POSSIBLE REGARDING FOOD. SOME PEOPLE TOOK CARE ONLY OF THEMSELVES, THEY DIDN'T CARE ABOUT THEIR RELATIVES.

U.N. attempts to deliver food to the enclave were a failure. A convoy in July '92 had been ambushed. The first relief convoy arrived in August with 46 tons of food. (The U.N. estimated Gorazde needed 35 tons per day.) Convoys got through only sporadically thereafter. Serbs turned back or delayed convoys with impunity despite a U.N. Security Council resolution authorizing the use of force to deliver food and medicine to besieged Bosnian civilians.

By the end of 1992, the food situation in Gorazde had become desperate. Some people were making soup and pie from nettles.

"Nobody had enough food. Children were coming very often, old people, poor people, on the main road, they knocked, looking for food. Every day, ten children.
"They were satisfied with a piece of bread. You couldn't give to everyone. The bread wouldn't last.
J. SACCO 5·99

"Down in town, apartments were well furnished, and people had taken whatever they wanted out of the shops. People from the villages in the area where there was no fighting were growing corn, potatoes, tomatoes...they were coming with eggs, and they were exchanging for what people in apartments had.

"At the end of '92, for a T.V. you could get 10 kg of flour. People in villages couldn't watch T.V. There was no electricity. But they wanted to have a T.V.
"A new T.V. You enjoy it. That's great.

"There were people who didn't have anything to trade. Refugees from Visegrad, for example, didn't bring anything with them, they didn't have money, they didn't have apartments, they lived with others.
"They were the first ones going to Grebak."

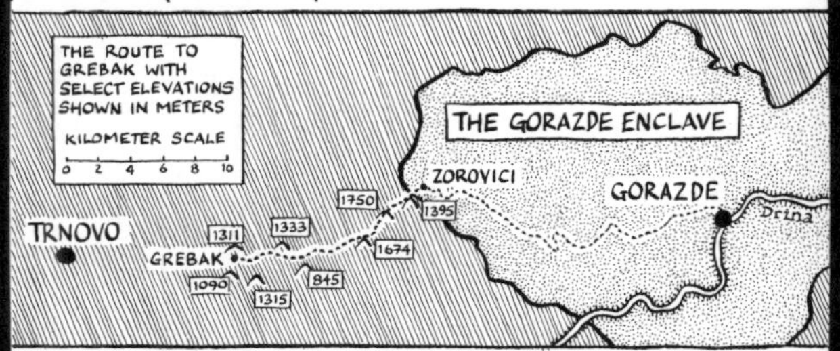
Grebak was a Bosnian army mountain post west of the Gorazde pocket that could be reached by a precarious route through Serb-controlled territory. The Bosnian military had been using the path to inject some weapons and personnel into the enclave.
THE ROUTE TO GREBAK WITH SELECT ELEVATIONS SHOWN IN METERS
KILOMETER SCALE
0 2 4 6 8 10
THE GORAZDE ENCLAVE
ZOROVICI
GORAZDE
Drina
TRNOVO
GREBAK
1311
1333
1750
1395
1674
845
1090
1315
It now trucked food supplies from Trnovo to Grebak for the people of Gorazde. But the people of Gorazde had to come and get the food themselves.

WE DIDN'T HAVE ANY CHOICE.
MY FATHER WENT THREE TIMES TO GREBAK, MY BROTHER AND I TWO TIMES EACH.

"That trip was very dangerous. It wasn't possible to use the path over the day, only at night. It was the middle of winter ...storms, snow... through the mountains... On one trip there was a snowstorm and my father fell unconscious. The son of a neighbor saved his life. He had frostbitten fingers and toes. On that trip, many persons froze to death."
Scores died of exposure —known to Gorazdans as White Death —on the Grebak path. Others were killed by landmines and in ambushes.

Edin described one of his trips to Grebak.
I PREPARED A LITTLE FOOD, DRIED PLUMS, WALNUTS, WITH MY NEIGHBOR.

"We went downtown to wait for a vehicle. There was shelling at that moment.

"I think I paid two kg of flour for the ride to Zorovici, which was very dangerous and cold. This was February or March.
"Once, on the same road, my brother was in a truck that slid out and turned over... He wasn't badly injured...but three or four died.

"It wasn't possible to go all the way to Zorovici because of the snow. We had to go two or three kilometers on foot.
J. SACCO 5-99

"We waited in Zorovici two or three hours for the evening, and when the whole group had gathered, about 200 people, we went.

"In front of our group was a guide who knew the way. It was deep dark. If you stray, maybe three or four meters, you can lose the group. And lots of times we had to stand and wait for everyone to gather. And then, again, 'Let's go!'

"We stopped at two or three springs to take water. We were thirsty, the whole time walking.

"There were streams and it was hard to jump them. A lot of people fell into the water, cold water. Some people were wet, completely wet.

"When we got close to Grebak, a group going back to Gorazde passed us. They had loads, and they were tired, very tired.

"I got there about 4 o'clock, 4:30 in the morning.

"It wasn't possible to sleep anywhere... Maybe I slept for half an hour, 15 minutes, an hour near a fire, without blankets. We waited for the distribution of food. We tried to keep warm... Sitting around, eating, drinking something. All day in that way.
"At Grebak there was a black market. People from Trnovo brought products like coffee, tobacco, cigarettes, salt, sugar, batteries, for which people from Gorazde had to pay plenty of money. Trnovo was cheaper if you had the papers to continue to there. Some people went to find tobacco, sugar...
"It was better to bring five kg of tobacco to Gorazde... because you could very easily exchange it for food...it could get you maybe 100 kg of other stuff... There was a control of what you carried out They didn't allow someone to take a full rucksack of tobacco, sugar, coffee, but for some people with good connections, with friends in the military... they closed their eyes.

"In the afternoon we got the free food. You carried as much as you could. I took 28 kg. It was a lot for me. Mostly flour and some oil, sugar, pasta, and two cans of fish. I wanted some yeast and salt, but there wasn't any... Some people were taking hand grenades back. I took two clips of bullets.

"Again we waited for the evening hours. We formed a line and came back in the same way.

"It was harder.

"The line didn't stay together...

"My neighbor knew the way. He had been four or five times.

"I trusted him... If something would happen to me, he would help...

"We came across people who couldn't go on.

"Alone. Without anybody.

"They had their eyes closed or were sleeping.

"We saw two or three people like that.

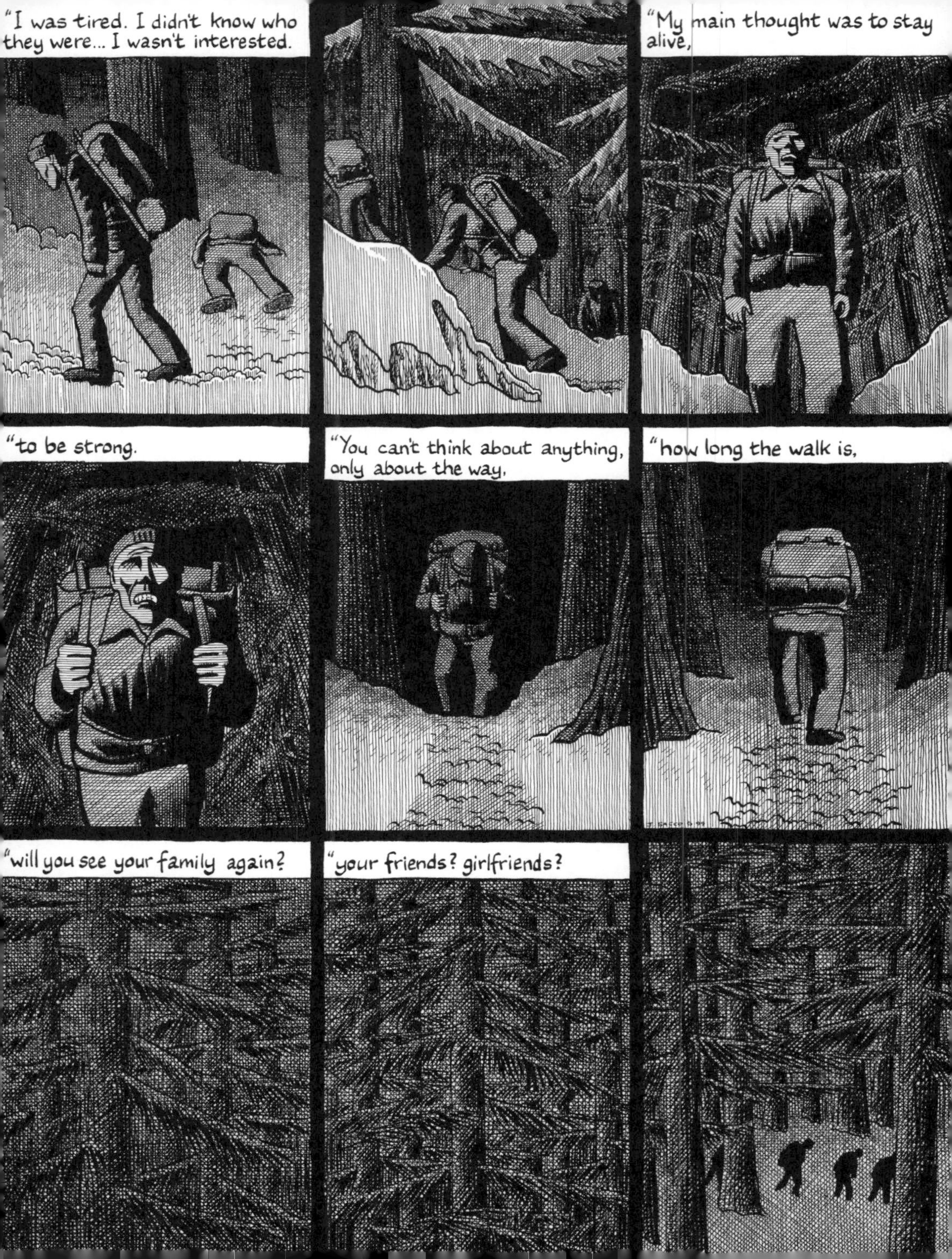

"I was tired. I didn't know who they were... I wasn't interested.

"My main thought was to stay alive,

"to be strong.

"You can't think about anything, only about the way,

"how long the walk is,

"will you see your family again?

"your friends? girlfriends?

"We got to our territory early, about three.

"We found a damaged old house. My neighbor slept at once, but it was so cold I couldn't sleep.

"In the morning we left that village, and that was the hardest, walking again, about one hour, three or four kilometers.

"After that we waited three or four hours for the vehicles. They came with a new group from town and picked up our group.

"Again we paid two kg of flour for the ride."

AFTER THAT TRIP I SLEPT TWO OR THREE DAYS.

I'D BROUGHT FOOD FOR MY FAMILY, FOR FOUR PEOPLE, FOR 20-25 DAYS.

BUT THAT'S ONLY IF WE ATE A LITTLE.

OTHER-WISE IT WAS ONLY ENOUGH FOR TEN DAYS.

In early March 1993, the situation in Gorazde was still desperate. Only 12 U.N. relief convoys had arrived since the beginning of the war. Those who couldn't make the trip to Grebak or had no other source of food had to survive on a ration that was sometimes less than one slice of bread per day.

The Bosnian government induced action by refusing U.N. aid deliveries to media magnet Sarajevo unless food and medicine were brought through Serb blockades and into Gorazde and the other eastern enclaves as well. Over the objections of the top U.N. military commander in Bosnia, U.S. President Bill Clinton ordered airdrops on the enclaves.
U.S. aircraft, flying out of Germany, first dropped supplies on the Gorazde pocket in the early morning of March 9, 1993.

AT FIRST THE CIVIL POLICE TRIED TO CONTROL THE AIR-DROPS.
Mesa

"But they couldn't stop the people. They went around the checkpoints.
J. SACCO 6·99
"It went from civilian to army control.

"People fought over the pallets. Soldiers fired in the air but people still went for it.
"They gave up controlling."

SOMETIMES WE WERE WAITING IN ONE PLACE BUT THEY DROPPED FAR AWAY.

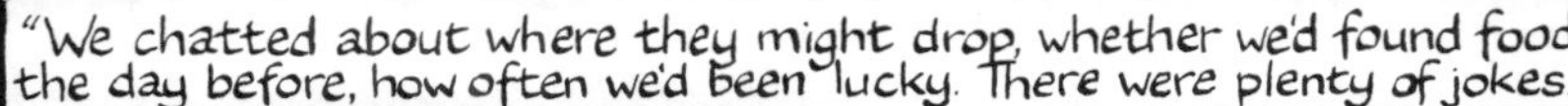

"We chatted about where they might drop, whether we'd found food the day before, how often we'd been lucky. There were plenty of jokes.

I'VE LOST MY WIFE...
NEXT TIME SHE'LL STAY HOME.
SHE CAN DO ANY-THING IN THE DARK.

"Then the aircraft would come.

"Sometimes we'd see lights in the sky...and the sound of the airplanes changed when they lost their weight."

I HEAR THE PALLETS— BANG! BANG!
I SAY, 'OKAY, LET'S GO!'

THAT RUNNING AND THE BE-HAVIOR OF THE PEOPLE, I COULDN'T STAND IT.
I'M NOT A MAN TO PUSH.

WHEN YOU FIND A PALLET, AT ONCE YOU TAKE YOUR KNIFE, YOU CUT THE PLASTIC.

"Inside there are packs, cardboard boxes. Some periods there was only flour and beans. After 15 days, maybe rice... Sometimes cans.

"Sometimes they dropped food near the front line, and if we were already there... we'd carry food home over the night and then return to the line.

"One time there was an armed group that didn't allow anyone to get close to the food. Robbers... No one could regulate that.

"Stronger people found more food and brought much more back than older or younger people. At the most, I'd take 50 kg. I waited a lot of times. Maybe 30 times. I brought back food maybe 20 times. I was very lucky, almost the luckiest man in town. But I was ready, you know, in good condition, young, a good runner."

THE BEHAVIOR OF THE PEOPLE WASN'T ACCEPTABLE, BUT, ON THE OTHER HAND, THE AIRDROPS SAVED US.

IT WAS THE MOST IMPORTANT THING AT THAT MOMENT, THE MOST—

FOOD.

Minnie's 3rd LOVE

OR: "NIGHTMARE ON POLK STREET"

BY: P. GLOECKNER ©1994

Dedicated To THE MEMORY OF R. HAZEN

ARTIST IS SHOWN WEARING A LUSCIOUS HEAD OF ARTIFICIAL HAIR FURNISHED BY ROSALIE'S NEW LOOK of San Francisco

LEON SF

LIKE, FUCK YOU TOO, TABATHA

THERE'S RICHIE!
HI GIRLS
DON'T HAVE A COW, BITSY— I JUST DIG YOUR FRIEND— THAT'S ALL— OR MAYBE YOU DIG HER TOO??
FUCK YOU.
YUK YUK

TABATHA IS SUCHA FUCKING BITCH!
Hi RICHIE
SHE'S A JUNKIE AND A DYKE...
AND SHE LIKES MINNIE.
THAT'S NOT GOOD.
DIAMOND DOGS
PERPETUALLY NINETEEN
YOUR NAME'S MINNIE, RIGHT? I'VE SEEN YOU AROUND
DO YOU LIKE QUAALUDES?
YOU WANNA GO OUT WITH ME SOMETIME??
YOU'VE GOT BEAUTIFUL HAIR....
YEAH...
INNOCENCE NOT ENTIRELY FEIGNED

YOU SURE YOU'RE NOT JEALOUS, BITSY?
LOOK AT THAT, RICHIE! THEY'RE KISSING!! I DON'T FUCKING BELIEVE IT! IT'S DISGUSTING!!

MINNIE FOUND TABATHA HEART-RENDINGLY BEAUTIFUL.

TABATHA'S MOTHER WAS A HEROIN ADDICT AND, TO SUPPORT HER HABIT, SHE PUT TABATHA IN PORNO FILMS WHEN SHE WAS A SMALL CHILD. TABATHA DID NOT EMERGE INTACT.

TABATHA WAS A JUNKIE HERSELF + HAD BEEN SINCE SHE WAS TWELVE. SEX WAS A COMMODITY ON POLK ST., AND EVEN THOUGH TABATHA LIKED GIRLS, SHE'D OFTEN GIVE BLOWJOBS (TO GAY GUYS) IN EXCHANGE FOR DRUGS.

BRANDY, WHY ARE YOU LETTING TABATHA SUCK YOUR DICK, PRAY TELL?

YOU COULD LEARN SOMETHING FROM HER, GIRLFRIEND.

YOU ARE BOTH TRASHY LITTLE WHORES!

EWWWW LOVE TO LOVE YOU BABY, ♫ UNHHH...

CRISCO

RUSH

MINNIE HAD TROUBLES, TOO— AN ABSENT FATHER AND AN ALCOHOLIC MOTHER WITH A BOY-FRIEND WHO WAS ALL TOO PRESENT—
HOT
WARM
COLD
HOT
MED
COOL
KENMORE
PLEASE LOVE ME! YOU LOVE ME, DON'T YOU? I LOVE YOU— I REALLY REALLY LOVE YOU! SOB!
OF COURSE I LOVE YOU- WHAT MAN WOULDN'T GIVE ANY-THING TO BE FUCKING A 15-YEAR OLD?
TELL ME AGAIN HOW YOU LOVE TO SUCK MY DICK— YOU LOVE TO SUCK IT—DON'T YOU?
HAVE YOU FUCKED ANY-BODY ELSE LATELY? I WANT TO HEAR ABOUT IT.
Hello Kitty
DEAR DI
THE KIND OF GOOD CHEAP CALIFORNIA WINE THAT MAKES GIRLS CRY AND GIVE BLOWJOBS TO JERKS.

SHE NEVER WENT OUT WITH GUYS FROM SCHOOL BUT WAS EASY PREY FOR ANY CREEP ON THE STREET. SHE WAS CONVINCED THAT SHE HAD TO HAVE SEX WITH ANY GUY WHO PAID ATTEN-TION TO HER.
POLK
HI
HEY BABY
DAY ON THE GREEN 1976 FRAMPTON BLUE OYSTER CULT

SHE DRANK ANYTHING SHE COULD GET HER HANDS ON AND WHEN SHE WENT TO SCHOOL SHE WAS USUALLY DRUNK OR HIGH.

HOWEVER, MINNIE RARELY WENT TO SCHOOL. HER CHRONIC ABSEN-TEEISM CONTRIBUTED TO HER EX-PULSION FROM 3 SCHOOLS. SHE DID GRADUATE, THOUGH—FROM A REMEDIAL SCHOOL FOR INCORRIGIBLES.
GRADE 9
F ART
F ALGEBRA
C- Chemistry
10th GRADE
F Geometry
C+ P.E.
History

MINNIE'S FRIENDS WERE EQUALLY AS SCREWED UP AND THEY COULDN'T DO MUCH TO HELP EACH OTHER.

NOT LONG AFTER MEETING TABATHA FOR THE FIRST TIME, MINNIE WAS AWAKENED BY THE CRACK OF A ROCK ON HER WINDOW PANE. IT WAS TABATHA.
CRACK!
LITTLE RED TWIN BED

HEY, BABE— I DON'T NEED TO COME IN— I JUST WANNA SAY NEW YEAR'S EVE... YOU 'AN ME—OK?
YEAH...
♫ I FOUND OUT A LONG TIME AGO WHAT A WOMAN CAN DO TO YOUR SOUL.... OH, BUT SHE CAN'T TAKE YOU ANYWHERE YOU DON'T ALREADY KNOW HOW TO GO...* ♫
CAN I COME A LITTLE CLOSER?
I DIDN'T WAKE UP YOUR MOM, DID I?

I KNOW RICHIE AND BITSY HAVE BEEN TELLING YOU TO STAY AWAY FROM ME, BUT I HOPE YOU DON'T LISTEN TO THEM.... YOU KNOW, I REALLY DIG YOU... I'D REALLY LIKE TO KISS YOU, BABE... I THINK YOU MIGHT DIG ME TOO... CAN WE HAVE A KISS?
YEAH
FLANNEL CHRISTMAS NIGHTGOWN FROM GRANNY
PUPILS AS BIG AS DIMES, AND REEKING OF GIN BUT SO BEAUTIFUL IN THE LAMPLIGHT...

YOU'RE NOT EVEN SURE IF YOU DIG WOMEN, ARE YOU?

FOR THE NEXT WEEK MINNIE WALKED ABOUT WITH THE MYSTERY OF NEW LOVE IN HER HEART
BITSY, DID YOU EVER HAVE SEX WITH A GIRL?
OH GOD YOU KNOW I DIDN'T! I TELL YOU EVERYTHING!
HOW DISGUSTING! WHY ARE YOU ASKING ME THAT? ARE YOU THINKING ABOUT TABATHA? DON'T MAKE ME PUKE! YOU REALLY PISS ME OFF!
BITSY

TABATHA, HOWEVER, DID NOT EXACTLY HAVE ROMANTIC DESIGNS ON MINNIE. RATHER, SHE WAS PRIMARILY FOCUSED ON TAKING DRUGS + GETTING MORE...
NEVER TOOK MORE THAN ONE QUAALUDE BEFORE
I'LL GIVE YOU SIX MORE QUAALUDES— IS THAT ENOUGH? TAKE THEM + LET'S GO HANG OUT WITH LANCE AND GARY
ONLY SIX?
HAPPY NEW YEAR!
GLUG

* "PEACEFUL FEELING," by the EAGLES.

YOU GOT ANY MUNCHIES MAN??

YOU WANT A CHAIR, TABATHA? THERE'S ONE OVER THERE — YOU WANT SOME BOOZE?

MUNCHIES? SURE WE GOT MUNCHIES WE JUS' BEEN TO THE SAFEWAY.

WHAT ABOUT A LITTLE HORS-D'OEUVRE? RITZ CRACKER, SMOKED SARDINE, A DROP OF TABASCO— WITH A SHOT OF VODKA AND A BEER CHASER?

HEY! IS THIS THAT SHOW "MARY HARTMAN, MARY HARTMAN?" I HEARD IT WAS GOOD.

WHAT ABOUT YOU, GARY- YOU WANT SOMETHING?

LATER MAN I GOT WHAT I WANT FOR NOW.

YEAH I'LL BET YOU DO

HEY! SHE'S ON THE RAG- SHE'S GOT A GODDAMN MOUSE IN HER PUSSY, MAN.

WELL, PULL IT OUT, MAN!

TABATHA ACTED AS PROCURESS FOR LOW-LIFE DRUG DEALERS. SHE'D BRING FUCKED-UP KIDS TO HAVE SEX WITH SUCH CREEPS + SHE'D GET LIQUOR AND DRUGS IN RETURN.

THEIR NEW YEAR'S EVE DATE TURNED INTO A WEEK-LONG NIGHTMARE OF SEX + DRUG-TAKING

SOMETIMES, TABATHA'S SCHEMES DID NOT GO AS PLANNED.
WELL, MY BOYS... I'M WONDERING WHETHER YOU'D LIKE TO FUCK THIS NICE YOUNG LADY TABATHA BROUGHT TO VISIT US?

SURE, MAN
SURE WHY NOT, MAN?
TWO SORRY, SHABBY 14-YEAR-OLD STREET HUSTLERS WHO HAVE NOWHERE TO GO AND FALL EASY PREY TO PERVERTS OFFERING A WARM MEAL + A PLACE TO STAY.

WHAT ABOUT YOU, MINNIE— HOW WOULD YOU LIKE TO FUCK THESE YOUNG MEN + GIVE THEM A LITTLE HEAD?
QUEEN
AC/DC
NO. I'M DRAWING.

MAY I SEE WHAT YOU'RE DRAWING, MINNIE DEAR?
YEAH HERE
BALLPOINT PEN ON GREASY PAPER BAG

HOW NICE, MINNIE! YOU KNOW, I'M A PSYCHOLOGIST + I THINK IT'S VERY INTERESTING! DO YOU KNOW WHAT A PSYCHOLOGIST IS?

I DON'T WANT TO FUCK!!
I WANT TO GO HOME!
TABATHA DEAR THIS JUST ISN'T GOING TO WORK.
IF SHE DOESN'T REALLY WANT TO, I WON'T FORCE HER
JESUS CHRIST
REGRESSING
BUT MAY I MAKE YOU A GIFT OF A FEW DILAUDID FOR YOUR TROUBLE?
WHAT ABOUT THAT BLONDE KID YOU BROUGHT BY LAST MONTH?
I'LL SEE WHAT I CAN DO.

WE NEED TO WAKE YOU UP A BIT, HON...
HAIR DIRTIER +DIRTIER
HAIR INEXPLICABLY CLEAN
ROYAL
OH LOOK—THERE'S BETHIE—I WONDER WHAT HAPPENED TO HER?
BETHIE WAS A NEUROTIC PREP-SCHOOL DROP-OUT WITH A WEALTHY, ALCOHOLIC MOTHER
COFFEE
I WAS BLOWING THIS GUY IN THE BATHROOM AT MIZ BROWN'S + HE SLAMMED THE TOILET SEAT DOWN ON MY FACE + STOLE ALL MY MONEY.
MINNIE, YOU WANNA PULL A TRICK WITH ME? I KNOW A GUY WHO'S GOT COKE AND HE WOULD—
SHE'S WITH ME + WE'VE GOT PLACES TO GO.

SEAFOOD
POOR BETHIE...
FUCK BETHIE! THAT'S WHAT HAPPENS WHEN YOU DON'T KNOW HOW TO WATCH OUT FOR YOURSELF. COME ON—WE'RE GOING TO SEE HIPPY DAVID.
HEY, TABATHA
HEY DAVID—
WHO'S THAT?
OH—THIS IS MINNIE—I TOLD YOU I MIGHT BRING HER
6
OH YEAH.
HI.

I WILL?
YEAH, SHE'LL SHOOT
DOES SHE SHOOT?
BUT SHE GETS METH.
Rice Chex
NUTRITION INFO
KING LEAR

SHOOT WHAT? WHAT IS IT? I'M NOT TAKING HEROIN!!
YOU'RE GETTIN' SPEED
I DON'T WANNA SHOOT IT!!
MY DAD SAID THAT NO MATTER WHAT, HE NEVER SHOT UP.
SO LET HER DRINK IT— I'LL GIVE IT TO HER IN A COKE.
OK, OK — BUT GIVE HER A LOT

DRINKING CRYSTAL METH DISSOLVED IN A HIGH-SUCROSE CAFFEINATED BEVERAGE
DO YOU THINK YOU COULD SELL ANY OF THIS STUFF FOR ME, TABATHA?
YEAH I THINK SO

RAPIDLY + TOTALLY WIRED
TABATHA, HOW COME YOU NEVER HAVE ANY ZITS AND YOU'RE NOT FAT AT ALL + YOU'RE SO BEAUTI-FUL BLAH BLAH
MY DAD ALSO SAID DON'T GO OUT WITH NIGGERS... HE WAS FUCKED UP BUT MAYBE HE WAS RIGHT... TABATHA, WHY DID YOU LET THOSE BLACK GUYS FUCK ME?
WHO DO YOU GUYS LIKE BETTER— DAVID BOWIE OR THE VILLAGE PEOPLE OR THE OHIO PLAYERS OR THE NEW YORK DOLLS OR CAPTAIN + TENNILLE?
I DID EVERYTHING YOU TOLD ME TO, TABATHA I DON'T KNOW WHY YOU'RE SO MAD AT ME
DAVID, DO YOU LIKE JOHN TRAVOLTA? DO YOU HAVE A JOB? YOU'RE REALLY CUTE I NEVER MEET GUYS LIKE YOU I JUST MEET JERKS. HOW OLD ARE YOU? I'M 15 I BET YOU'RE 21. MY MOM'S HAVING AN AFFAIR WITH SOME GUY WHO'S 21 BUT SHE'S GOT A BOYFRIEND HER AGE TOO + I FUCK HIM ALL THE TIME.
SHE'S OK...
WOULD YOU FUCKING SHUT UP, MINNIE? YOU ARE REALLY STARTING TO BUG ME!
YOU DON'T KNOW HER DAVID SHE'S A FUCKING PAIN IN THE ASS + SHE ACTS LIKE A THREE-YEAR-OLD.
I DIDN'T TELL YOU TO DO JACK SHIT MINNIE
MAN THAT'S GOOD SHIT!!
MINNIE!! COME HERE!
LIQUOR

YOU HATE ME— WHY SHOULD I COME THERE?
YOU KNOW I DON'T HATE YOU BABE I JUST LOST MY TEM-PER COME GIVE ME A KISS.

OH TABATHA I LOVE YOU
I LOVE YOU TOO BABE

COME ON DAVID HIT HER UP
YOU'LL LIKE IT THIS WAY
YOU'RE DOING THIS FOR ME BABY
BRAND P VODKA
PEP BOYS

OH MAN THAT IS SO STRONG
SEE? YOU LIKE IT

I WANT DAVID TO KISS ME
OK...
!

FUCK YOU MINNIE
DAVID, GET ME THOSE DRUGS—I'M OUTTA HERE

THANKS DAVID I'LL BE IN TOUCH SOON
HAVE FUN MINNIE I HOPE YOU KNOW HE'S A JUNKIE + HE CAN'T EVEN GET IT UP
WAIT! I'M GOING TOO!
SMALL BAGS OF HEROIN + METHEDRINE
NOT WITH ME YOU'RE NOT

SHE HATES ME SHE HATES ME WHAT AM I GOING TO DO? I THOUGHT SHE WANTED ME TO HAVE SEX WITH YOU!!
TABATHA'S WEIRD, MAN. LISTEN—I'M GONNA GIVE YOU SOME SPEED + A RIG—YOU COME BACK TO ME ANYTIME YOU WANT SOME DOPE + I WON'T MAKE YOU HAVE SEX.
SNIFF
YOU'RE SO NICE, NO ONE WAS EVER NICE TO ME BEFORE IN MY WHOLE LIFE
I'M GOING TO GO LOOK FOR MY FRIEND BITSY NOW

LATER...
BETHIE! HAVE YOU SEEN BITSY?
MINNIE! YOU LOOK REALLY HIGH! YOU KNOW WE COULD STILL PULL THAT TRICK—
NO THANKS
OH WELL...BITSY'S WITH TABATHA—THEY WENT TO SEE THIS GUY NAMED DOC—HE'S A CRIP BUT HE LIKES TO WATCH—
DOC? WHERE'S HE LIVE? WATCH WHAT?
HE'S DOWN ON MARKET—HOTEL DONNELLY, THIRD FLOOR, I THINK

DONNELLY
REGAL
X-RATED 25¢ BOOTHS MOVIES DANCE
HEY BABE YOU SELLIN' SOMETHING?
ME SCARED...

INSIDE...
HEE HEE HEE
306
308
THAT'S BITSY!

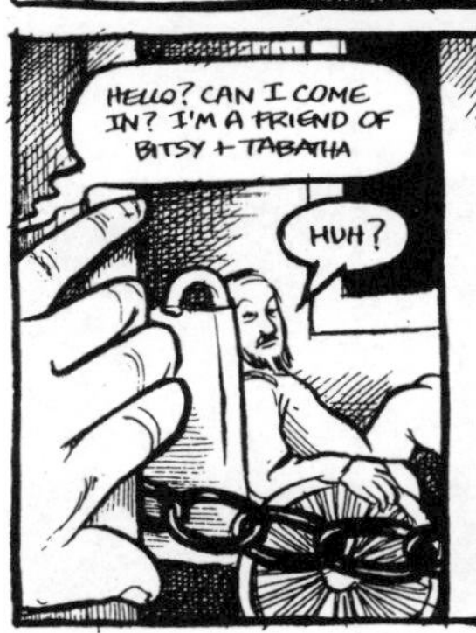
HELLO? CAN I COME IN? I'M A FRIEND OF BITSY + TABATHA
HUH?

I'M SORRY....
FARRAH FAWCETT
TABATHA! CAN SHE COME IN?
AMPUTEE VETERAN OF KOREAN WAR
GETS DESIRABLE DRUGS FROM MULTIPLE DOCTORS

OH SURE! HI MINNIE!!
OH MY GOD IT'S MINNIE!

MINNIE! YOU'RE JUST IN TIME! YOU WANNA DO UP SOME OF THIS STUFF WITH ME?
HI!
BITSY
IF IT'S HEROIN, I'LL TRY IT. Hi Bitsy
YOU LIKE SHOOTING UP NOW, HUNH?
WHAT'S BITSY DOING HERE?
BITSY YOU FUCKING 1/2-DYKE HYPOCRITE WHORE

GOOD SHIT, HUH?
BITSY WHAT THE HELL YOU WUZ DOIN' WIZ TABA — I'M GONNA THROWUP

BARF
SHE'S A GODDAMN LIGHTWEIGHT BITCH
MINNIE! ARE YOU OK?
BITSY

SLAM!
GASP
I'M GOING TO FUCKING KILL YOU TABATHA
HA HA

UNH!
AHHH
OH NO!

THEY'RE GOING TO KILL EACH OTHER!
!
AHHHH
GRRR
GET THE HELL OUT OF HERE!
COUGH COUGH
POW

I THINK MINNIE WON
OK I'M LEAVING FUCK YOU ALL
TOTALLY FUCKED UP ON SPEED + HEROIN
I THINK I'LL JUST RANDOMLY KNOCK ON DOORS UNTIL I FIND A PLACE TO PASS OUT
INFECTED BITE
ARM BLACK + BLUE + INFECTED FROM SLOPPY INJECTIONS
BRUISES, CUTS + SORES ALL OVER BODY

YEAH? WAZZUP BABY? YOU KNOCK?
WOULD YOU PLEASE LET ME SLEEP HERE TONITE?
TOTAL STRANGER

YOU JUS' COME OUTTA NOWHERE? YOU WANNA SLEEP IN MY BED?
OK BABY
10-4

BUT NO SEX I'VE GOTTA SL-SL-EEEP
OK SURE BABY
AND SO ON....

18 YEARS LATER— A CHANCE MEETING ON MARKET ST.
OOLWORTH
THOMAS KINK GALLERY
THE DROOD BUILDING
MILE
JEWEL
MINNIE?!!
TABATHA!!?
CLANK
JINGLE
SPARE CHANGE
I'M PRETTY SICK + MY LEG'S MESSED UP— I GOT HIT BY A TRUCK— BUT I MIGHT GET SOME MONEY OUT OF IT...
YOU'RE LOOKIN' GOOD, BABE—HOW LONG HAS IT BEEN?
I'VE JUST BEEN WORKING — DRAWING PICTURES, YOU KNOW— I'VE GOT A LITTLE GIRL—SHE'S 2. IT'S BEEN A LONG TIME, HASN'T IT?
I HAD A JOB IN THE KITCHEN AT ST. ANTHONY'S AND WAS LIVING IN A GROUP HOME BUT I STARTED USING AGAIN AND NOW THINGS AREN'T SO EASY
I TALKED TO BITSY ONCE AND SHE SAID YOU WERE COUNSELING RUNAWAYS
YEAH THAT WAS WHEN I WAS IN RECOVERY BUT I HAD TO STOP. I CAN'T BE A HYPOCRITE
I HEARD THAT RICHIE'S DEAD, MAN— HE GOT SICK.
I HOPE THINGS GET BETTER TABATHA
MAYBE I'LL SEE YOU AGAIN SOME-TIME.... I'VE GOTTA GET GOING...
SILENCE = DEATH
BZZZ
BZZZZZ
DON'T EVEN THINK OF GIVING ME ANY MONEY BABE— KEEP IT FOR YOUR KID
THE END

Depressed Dora Comics
Boo-hoo-hoo... hoo.... Sob!... sob!!.. sob!!.... hoo... Sob! Sob!!
Sniff.....sob!!..... sniff... I don't know... what... sniff!... to do next!... I just don't know What!
Sniff!!
I don't have a place to live!!....
I don't know anybody here!!...
Sniff!!
I'm trying to study!!...
My money's running out!!
My car's on the blink
...and it needs to be fixed!!...
Sniff!!
I just can't stand this anymore!!!
I'm not even functioning right!!!
Sob!! I'm just... not... sob!!... ...Ohhh... sob!! sob!! sob!!... sob!!..sob!!...
!!!!!!!!!! I need to talk to someone... sniff!!!... now!!!!!
...Can I talk to you... please!! I ne...
..What!?! Oh!!!!
..Sob!.....fuckin! paranoid!... people.... (grumble!!) sob!!!
PHONE
TELEP
...Hello?!!...get me a crisis line... please!!! ...sob!!...sniff!!
Hello...
...Hello!!! Crisis line?!!...I need to talk with someone ...sniff!!!...sniff...
Yes!...I'll be glad to talk with you!... Are you a Christian?!!!
oh... Shit!
I don't need to deal with That now!!!... shit!...sniff!

TELEPHONE
Hello....... Suicide Prevention...
Hello!!...I need some Help!! I need to talk To somebody... and........
What's your name?!
What the "Fuck" is the difference What my name is!!?!!
...I just need to talk with somebody.....
...Don't use that kind of language with me.....and DON'T yell in the phone, or I am going to "hang-up"!......
What the!!
...you fucking asshole "You're suopposed to be a "crisis line".....not a jail matron.......even they.....
Click
Those.. !!#!! ?!!
sob!! sob!!
dangle! dangle!
sob!! sob!! sob!! sob!! sob!!
Hello ?!!!?!! This is the operator.... ...can I get you another number?!!
...I don't Know why Suicide Control hung-up ?!!
Those fuck... sob! sob!...they didn't like me! yelling in to the phone... sniff!...sniff!..
I can reconnect you with them?!...
...I hope you're not going to do anything silly!!?!
Ooohhhh
ha! ha! haw! haw! haw! haw! haw! haw!
haw! haw! haw!!!! reallll-yyyy!.... haw!..sniff!..sniff!...... Thank-you! That's just what I needed to hear!!! haw!! haw!! haw!
ha! ha! ha!
...I'll be o.k. now..
ha!
TELEPHONE
NO THANKS! .... the Operator just did it all.....
Hello... This is Suicide Prevention.... May I help you?!!
TELEPHONE
Elinore Norflus

all my relations
NINJA 68
i will release the pressure of truth inside you
give me a security diagram of your city
Names of your spies in our city
hey dumbass! can't you pump the gas faster! i've got important things to do!
yeah dude, your set was pretty cool, i mean, people aren't getting the connecti on, well, my band, you really should play with my band, it could be sre at, because, i played with Dog Nasty and Jerry Jiz back in that subway station, we improvised amazing and then Ritchie C. and Kimbo LP. came in and were real respons ive to my coaching, so like, you really should return my emails, the other night me and several of the best musicians around got together to break some new ground, i'll swing by your place to jam, should be cool
IN THE BASEMENT! LOCK THE CELLAR DOOR
your son is very beautiful
where did your city come from?
gay couples should Not enjoy the same rights as straight couples
will you drop your religion and take Jesus Christ into your heart?
i guess i pick joey for my team

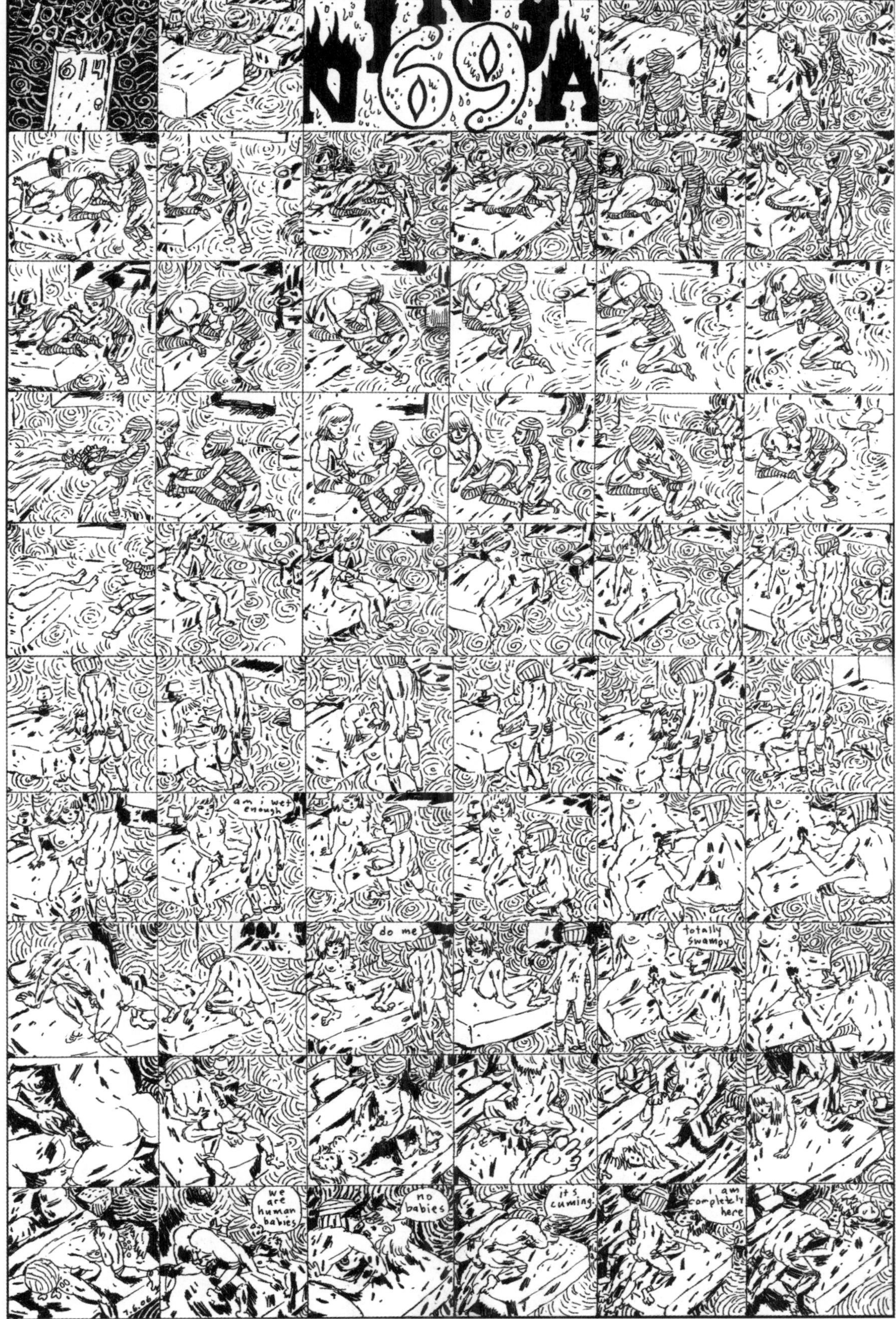

BRIAN CHIPPENDALE Ninja (Episode 69)

THAT'S THE OCEAN OUT THERE.

AT ONE TIME YOU COULD SWIM IN IT... BUT NOW IT'S FILLED WITH TRASH AND POISON

BUT THE WORLD'S ENDING ANYWAY...

THIS MIGHT BE OUR LAST CHANCE!

HERE GOES NOTHING

Near · Miss

SCREECH

STEVEN? IS THAT YOU?

IS SOMETHING WRONG AT WORK?

STEVEN...?
I WAS ALMOST KILLED.

OH, MY GOODNESS...
WHEN--?
LAST WEEK.

LAST WEEK? DEAR, WHAT HAPPENED?
IT JUST MISSED US, MA. THEY DIDN'T EVEN TELL US ABOUT IT. I COULDA BEEN OUT DRIVING, OR HAVING A BEER, AND WHAM!

DEAR, WHAT ARE YOU TALKING ABOUT?
THE ASTEROID, MA. I JUST HEARD IT ON THE RADIO. LAST WEEK AN ASTEROID MISSED HITTING THE EARTH. IT WAS JUST 450,000 MILES AWAY.

DEAR, 450,000 MILES IS A LONG WAY FROM HERE.
YOU DON'T UNDERSTAND, MA.

SURE, IT SOUNDS LIKE A LOT, BUT IN -- IN LIGHT YEARS, THAT'S LIKE... LIKE A FOUL TIP.
WELL..., BUT YOU SAID IT **MISSED** US.

YEAH, **THIS** ONE DID. BUT WHO KNOWS HOW MANY OF 'EM THERE ARE OUT THERE, SHOOTIN' AROUND THE UNIVERSE...
THERE COULD BE ANOTHER ONE COMING RIGHT NOW, AND WE DON'T EVEN KNOW ABOUT IT.

WE GOTTA BE READY, MA. I DON'T WANNA END UP LIKE THE DINOSAURS.

...**DINOSAURS?**
SCREEE

VOOMMM

UH...

UH... HELLO...

MISS...?
MA'AM...?

...I, UH...

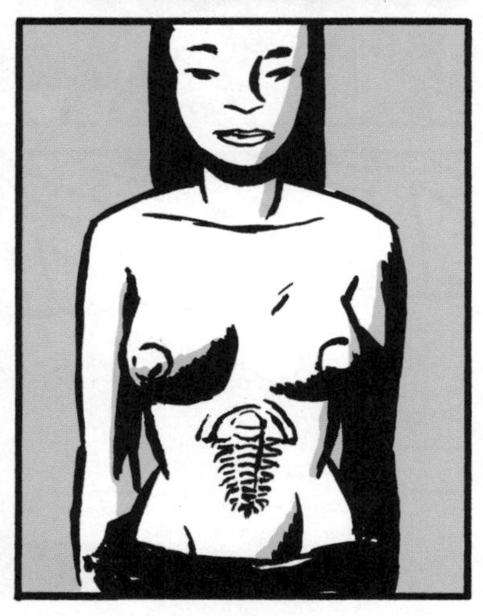

RRRRRRRRRRRRR

RRRRR

RRR

WOW, DID YOU SEE THAT?

...MA'AM?

BY: DAVID MAZZUCCHELLI

J J C A A A C C C K K K S S

SURVIVES

ROUND 6

NOW THERE'S TOO MANY GLOVES HITTING TOO MANY FACES

IT'S A KNOCK-DOWN

A KNOCKOUT

I MIGHT AS WELL HAVE WATCHED THE DAMN RADIO

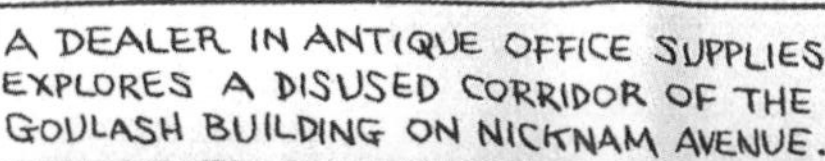

A DEALER IN ANTIQUE OFFICE SUPPLIES EXPLORES A DISUSED CORRIDOR OF THE GOULASH BUILDING ON NICKNAM AVENUE.
THESE DAYS I'M LUCKY TO FIND A PACKAGE OF DRIED-UP CARBON PAPER OR AN UNOPENED BOX OF NON-SKID PAPER CLIPS.
806
ROOMS 801-8

BUT HERE, WHAT'S THIS? AN UNUSED WATER-COOLER BOTTLE FROM 1962! THEY MUST'VE FORGOTTEN TO PICK IT UP.
817 NAXOS CORP.
NORTHWEST TERRITORY

IT'S GLASS AND IN FAIRLY GOOD CONDITION. THIS MAY BE WORTH SOMETHING. I'LL HAVE TO MAKE A FEW PHONE CALLS.

LATER THAT NIGHT IN HIS SHOP...
I SURMISE THAT IT CAME FROM A SUCCESSFUL LAW OFFICE OR ADVERTISING AGENCY – IN THOSE DAYS BOTTLED WATER WAS A LUXURY – MOST PEOPLE JUST REFILLED THE SAME BOTTLE WITH TAP WATER.

THE LABEL READS: "SVONNY RIVER PURE DRINKING WATER CO., 287 LATREEN AVE."
YES, YES, THAT'S THE REMARKABLE THING – IT WAS NEVER OPENED! WOULDN'T YOU BE CURIOUS TO HAVE A TASTE OF 1962 VINTAGE WATER?

THIS BOTTLE GOES WAY BACK BEFORE FLUORIDATION – WHEN THE UPSTATE RESERVOIR WAS REALLY UPSTATE. THIS IS THE SAME WATER NORMAN MELBAR MIXED WITH SCOTCH WHILE WRITING "THE DISPOSABLE MUSE" IN 1962. THIS IS WHAT WAS IN THE GLASS ON PRESIDENT DIAMINT'S LECTERN DURING THE FAMOUS TELEVISED DEBATE WITH SENATOR MILES HURON... NOT INTERESTED? NOT YOUR KIND OF THING? OKAY, I UNDERSTAND.
INDEX

UNLIKE WINE, THIS STUFF WAS NOT BOTTLED TO LAST – IT DOESN'T AGE WELL – PROBABLY SUBJECT TO ALL KINDS OF BACTERIAL CONTAMINATION. THERE SEEMS TO BE A SCUM ON THE TOP... BUT STILL, I'M TEMPTED TO HAVE A GLASS.

"KUROS VANDER, NOTED ANTIQUE DEALER, AGE 69, DIED LAST NIGHT OF COMPLICATIONS FOLLOWING A SEVERE BOUT OF DISILLUSIONMENT."
SPECIAL
©1996 BEN KATCHOR

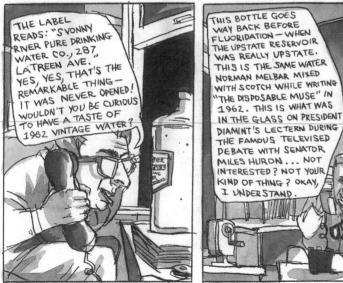

LOST IN THE CHEST-HAIR OF TEN THOUSAND BUSY MEN,
HERE, READ IT FOR YOURSELF.
NATURAL

DANGLING AT THE END OF A PHONY 18-CARAT GOLD CHAIN, IS A TINY AMULET OF DUBIOUS VALUE.
"THE SHORTEST DISTANCE BETWEEN TWO POINTS IS A STRAIGHT LINE."
SALE

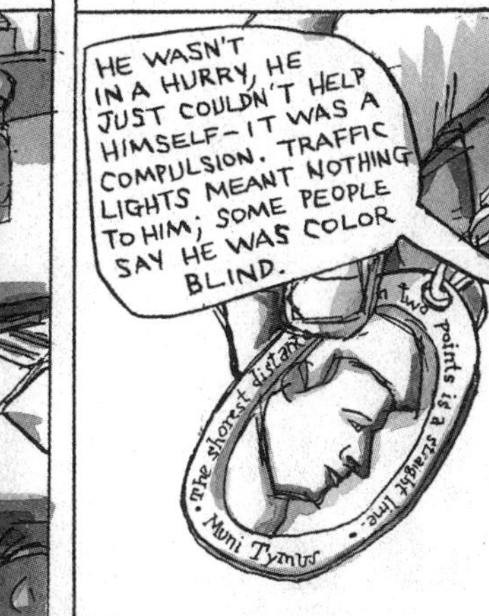
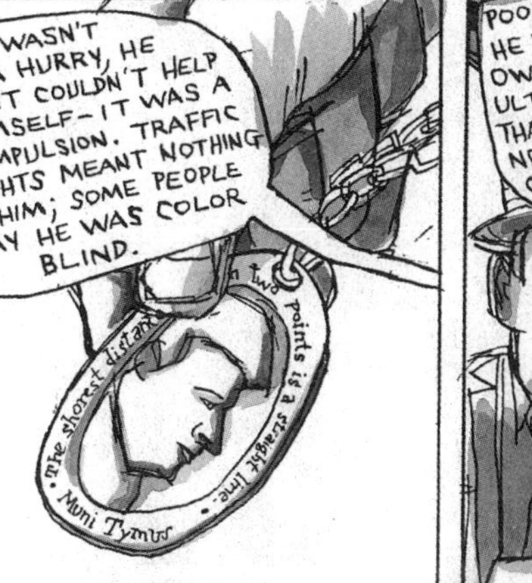
A THIN COPPER MEDAL STAMPED WITH THE HEAD-IN-PROFILE OF A PREMATURELY DECEASED YOUNG MAN:
HE WASN'T IN A HURRY, HE JUST COULDN'T HELP HIMSELF–IT WAS A COMPULSION. TRAFFIC LIGHTS MEANT NOTHING TO HIM; SOME PEOPLE SAY HE WAS COLOR BLIND.
Muni Tymus

MUNI TYMUS, THE UNOFFICIAL "PATRON SAINT" OF JAYWALKERS AND MID-BLOCK CROSSERS.
POOR GUY, HE WAS ON HIS OWN AND PAID THE ULTIMATE PRICE SO THAT ALL OF US CAN NOW CROSS WITH-OUT LOOKING.

HE'S WITH ME ALL THE TIME–EVEN IN THE SHOWER. HE LOOKS BOTH WAYS FOR ME.
BANK

WITH HIS HELP, WE CAN MAKE IT TO THE OTHER SIDE OF THE STREET– BUT MUNI'S NOT A LUCKY CHARM. MOST OF US END UP SICK, PENNILESS AND ESTRANGED FROM OUR FAMILIES. THE RECKLESSNESS OF OUR STREET-CROSSING HABITS EXTENDS INTO ALL AREAS OF OUR PRIVATE LIFE.

HE'S A SILENT COMPANION TO THE LONELY MAN WHO HAS ANTS IN HIS PANTS. HERE! NOW! LET'S GO!
'BEEP' 'BEEP'
'BEEP'

MY FATHER WORE "HIM" AND SO I WEAR "HIM," AND WHEN MY CHILD IS OLD ENOUGH TO CROSS BY HIMSELF, HE'LL WEAR "HIM" TOO.
'PANT' 'PANT'
©1996 BEN KATCHOR

THERE, JUST BELOW YOUR FILET OF SOLE OR BEEF CHOW FUN,
PLEASE STOP FIDGETING.
CLOAKED IN FINE LINEN OR SHEATHED IN THE CHEAPEST OF FORMICA,
I CAN'T HELP MYSELF.
ON THE UNDERSIDE OF EACH TABLE, IN EVERY RESTAURANT, OFFICE AND PRIVATE HOME,
I KNOW IT'S THERE
YOU'LL FIND A SHORT, CRYPTIC NOTE SCRAWLED IN CHALK OR BLACK CRAYON—
WAITING TO BE READ.
ONE OF AN ENDLESS SUCCESSION OF FOOTNOTES TO AN UNWRITTEN HISTORY OF SOCIAL UNREST AND DOMESTIC TRAGEDY.
THE INITIALS OF AN ASSEMBLY LINE WORKER WHO DIED OF GLUE POISONING?
THE FRANTIC INSTRUCTIONS OF A CATERER TO THE MANAGER OF A VANISHED BALLROOM?
A SECRETLY CODED LOVE LETTER FROM A MOVING MAN TO AN INTERIOR DECORATOR?
A FLASHLIGHT! WILL SOMEONE PLEASE GET THIS MAN A FLASHLIGHT!
©1996 BEN KATCHOR

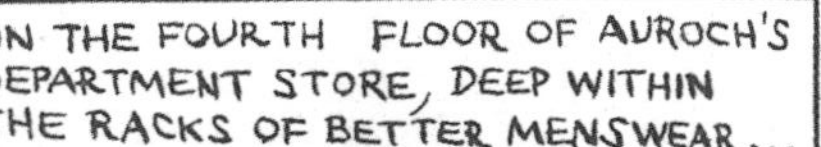

ON THE FOURTH FLOOR OF AUROCH'S DEPARTMENT STORE, DEEP WITHIN THE RACKS OF BETTER MENSWEAR...
THANK YOU FOR COMING WITH ME. WHEN WE'RE FINISHED, I'LL TAKE YOU FOR A NICE LUNCH AT "THE CARPATHIAN PEEPHOLE," ON ME.
TAKE YOUR TIME, I HAD A LATE BREAKFAST.
AUROCH

WILL A SALESMAN EVER FIND US HERE?
NO, WE'RE ON OUR OWN.

AH, THIS IS EXACTLY WHAT I'M LOOKING FOR—A DARK WOOLEN SUIT WITH TWO PAIRS OF PANTS.
HOW MUCH IS IT?

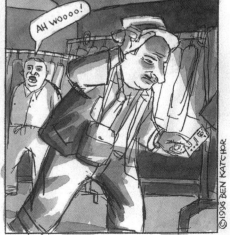

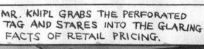

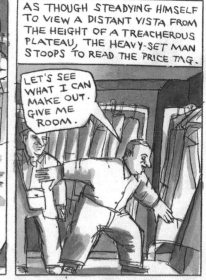

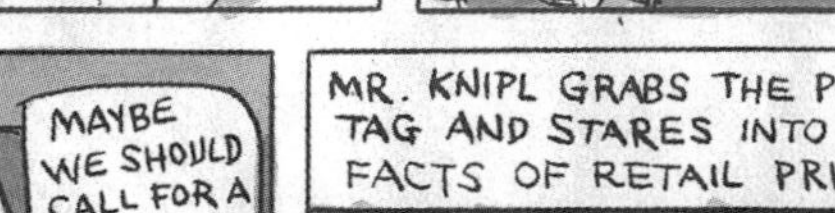
AS THOUGH STEADYING HIMSELF TO VIEW A DISTANT VISTA FROM THE HEIGHT OF A TREACHEROUS PLATEAU, THE HEAVY-SET MAN STOOPS TO READ THE PRICE TAG.
LET'S SEE WHAT I CAN MAKE OUT. GIVE ME ROOM.

HE PULLS THE TAG FROM THE JACKET SLEEVE, SHIELDS HIS EYES AND SQUINTS, WHILE FIGHTING A SUDDEN WAVE OF DIZZINESS.
LOOKS LIKE TWO HUNDRED AND SIXTY-FOUR DOLLARS AND NINETY-FIVE CENTS.

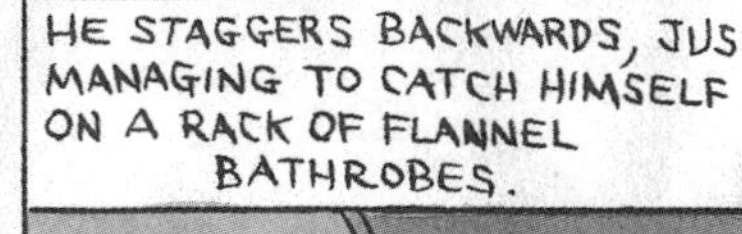

HE STAGGERS BACKWARDS, JUST MANAGING TO CATCH HIMSELF ON A RACK OF FLANNEL BATHROBES.
BETTER
THANK GOD YOU'RE HERE. NOW YOU SEE WHY I COULDN'T COME ALONE—I WOULD BE LOST.

PLEASE TAKE A LOOK, TELL ME WHAT YOU SEE. ARE THEY REALLY ASKING $264.95? I SOMETIMES DOUBT MY OWN EYES.
MAYBE WE SHOULD CALL FOR A SALESMAN.

MR. KNIPL GRABS THE PERFORATED TAG AND STARES INTO THE GLARING FACTS OF RETAIL PRICING.
AH WOOOO!
©1996 BEN KATCHOR

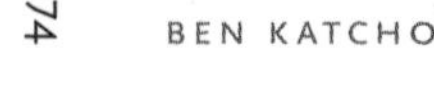

BY CHANCE, MR. KNIPL SITS NEXT TO A YOUNG MAN STRUGGLING TO READ A BATTERED PAPERBACK NOVEL.
"JUBILATION ALLEY" BY CONSTANTINE HOOPLE?
UPTOWN
PLAYTZER

HERE, THE TOP OF PAGE 218.
THANK YOU, THANK YOU. MOST PEOPLE DON'T UNDERSTAND.

THEY SAY "WHY NOT GO OUT AND BUY A FRESH COPY? YOU CAN FIND ONE IN ANY BOOKSTORE —IT MUST STILL BE IN PRINT."
BOOKS
NEW EDITION

WHY BOTHER RECOVERING THAT CRUMBLING COPY WITH CHRISTMAS WRAPPING PAPER? WHY WASTE TIME SHUFFLING THE LOOSE PAGES BACK INTO ORDER EACH TIME YOU PICK IT UP TO READ? WHY DEPEND UPON A RUBBER BAND TO HOLD THE ENTIRE FOUR-HUNDRED-PAGE MASTER-PIECE TOGETHER?"

BUT, YOU SEE, THIS COPY IS AN HEIRLOOM. PURCHASED ON AN IMPULSE BY MY GRANDMOTHER AT THE PORT AUTHORITY BUS TERMINAL IN 1958 ON HER WAY TO LAKE OLSWALO, IT WAS HER SUMMER READING MATERIAL. SHE GOT ONLY HALF WAY THROUGH, BUT FOREVER CONSIDERED IT HER FAVORITE BOOK.
BARGAIN
DRUGS

IT SAT FOR MANY YEARS ON THE BOTTOM SHELF OF HER TELEPHONE TABLE AND THEN, WHEN SHE DIED IN 1964, PASSED INTO THE POSSESSION OF MY MOTHER, WHO READ IT FOUR TIMES WHILE ON JURY DUTY IN THE EARLY 70S.
SECTION A

MY OLDER SISTER PREFERRED IT TO HER HIGH SCHOOL READING ASSIGNMENTS; THE BEGINNING OF CHAPTER THIRTY-TWO WAS ALREADY MISSING. IT WAS OF NO INTEREST TO ME; I WAS BUSY WITH THE TELEVISION BY THEN.

BUT NOW THAT I'M FINISHED WITH SCHOOL, I FEEL THAT IT'S TIME FOR ME TO TAKE THE PLUNGE AND SEE FOR MYSELF WHAT MADE THIS ONE BOOK ENDURE OVER THE YEARS WHILE OTHERS WERE LOST AND FORGOTTEN.
HERE, PAGE 378.
PLEASE
©1996 BEN KATCHOR

ON THE FLOOR OF A BUSY PHARMACY, FREDERICK MATINÉE WITNESSES A RARE MOMENT OF INSPIRATION IN A FELLOW POET,
SHE SWALLOWS CALMLY LIKE A QUEEN/ HER CHOSEN BRAND OF ASPIREEN...
AISLE 7
SPECIAL $2.95 OFFER
LAXATIVE

FOLLOWED BY AN AGONIZING DISCOVERY,
OUT OF INK! WITHOUT A SIGN, WITHOUT A SKIP!
SPECIAL $2.95 OFFER

HE RUSHES FORWARD WITH AN OFFER OF CONSOLATION.
THE PRODUCTION OF THESE CHEAP WRITING INSTRUMENTS HAS FAR OUT-STRIPPED THE DEMANDS OF POETIC INSPIRATION, AND SO, AS A RESULT, YOU HAVE HUNDREDS OF THOUSANDS OF PENS GOING DRY THROUGH DISUSE. REFILLS ARE SOLD IN PACKAGES OF A DOZEN, FURTHER WIDENING THE GAP.
WHAT DID I WRITE? A SHORT SHOPPING LIST, A FEW PHONE NUMBERS, A "BACK IN TEN MINUTES" NOTE FOR MY FRONT DOOR? AND THEN SUDDENLY, NOTHING.

NO, MY FRIEND, YOU DON'T UNDERSTAND. THE CHANNEL BETWEEN THE RESERVOIR AND THE BALL-POINT IS BLOCKED BY A MICROSCOPIC DAM OF STAGNANT INK. IF YOU HOLD IT UP TO THE LIGHT, YOU CAN SEE IT'S PERFECTLY FULL.

PURGATIVES
YOU CAN TRY APPLYING THE HEAT OF A MATCH OR RUNNING IT UNDER HOT WATER. SOME PEOPLE TAKE UP ABSENT-MINDED DOODLING JUST TO KEEP THE INK STREAM IN MOTION.
"YOUR SWALLOW FOLLOWS LIKE A QUEEN..." HOW DID IT GO?

WHOEVER SOLD THESE PENS SHOULD HAVE ISSUED A WARNING. DID YOU DO ANYTHING THAT MIGHT HAVE LED THE SALESMAN TO BELIEVE THAT YOU WERE A PROLIFIC AUTHOR?
NO, I WAS JUST TRYING TO SAVE MONEY.

IN DESK DRAWERS, ATTACHÉ CASES AND SHIRT POCKETS ALL OVER THE CITY, THESE EXPIRATION DATES COME AND GO WHILE PEOPLE WAIT FOR THE IMPULSE OR OCCASION TO WRITE.
ONE BOTTLE OF FEX-LAX AND SIX FINE-POINT PENS.
©1996 BEN KATCHOR

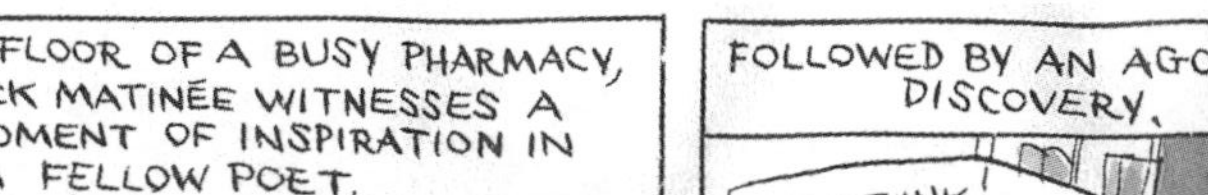

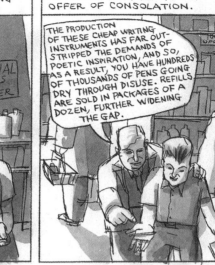

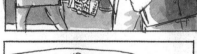

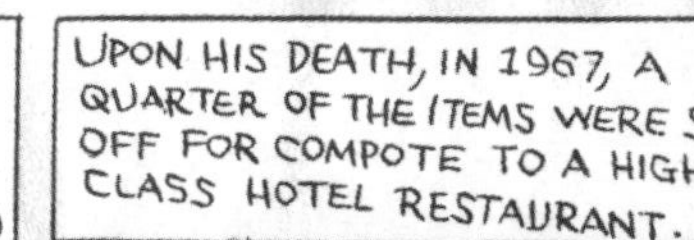

UNSUSPECTING GUESTS WERE SERVED STEWED, TURN-OF-THE-CENTURY TURKISH FIGS FOR BREAKFAST.

REST ROOM

MEN

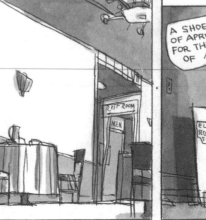

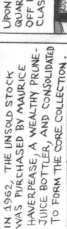

EACH MORNING, REGARDLESS OF MONTH OR DAY, THESE MIDDLE-AGED MEN RESOLVE TO CLAIM THEIR BIRTHRIGHT.
NOVEMBER 25th AT LAST!
NOV 25

A CASE OF ARRESTED DEVELOPMENT PLAYED OUT IN A BRUTAL ADULT WORLD.
ON THIS VERY DAY, FORTY-SEVEN LONG YEARS AGO, I WAS BROUGHT INTO THIS GLORIOUS WORLD.

A PATHETIC ATTEMPT TO REGAIN A BIT OF LEVERAGE NEVER FULLY USED DURING ONE'S CHILDHOOD.
HOW OLD DO YOU THINK I LOOK?
HERE, HAVE A DESSERT — ON THE HOUSE. HAPPY BIRTHDAY!
A CLAIM — OF SUCH TOTAL INNOCENCE THAT NO ONE WOULD EVER DOUBT IT —
I THROW IN THE NECKTIE AS A PRESENT — WHY NOT?!

REAPING BENEFITS OF SUCH MINUSCULE WORTH AS TO BE NEGLIGIBLE.
IMAGINE EATING HERE ALL ALONE ON YOUR BIRTHDAY.
YOUR BIRTHDAY?

THIS SO-CALLED "BIRTHDAY BOY SCAM" FALLS BELOW THE THRESHOLD OF SOCIETAL CENSURE; A CRIME HARDLY WORTH RECOGNIZING.
WE STOP THE METER NOW 'CAUSE IT'S YOUR BIRTHDAY.
ARGO CAB CO.

AND YET, THESE SMALL GAINS, COMPOUNDED OVER THE 365 DAYS OF A YEAR
I HAD A WONDERFUL BIRTHDAY — I DID.

AMOUNT, IN THE END, TO A GREAT WINDFALL — A VAST INHERITANCE JUST WAITING TO BE CLAIMED.
TOMORROW, NOVEMBER 26th AT LAST!
NOV 26
©1996 BEN KATCHOR

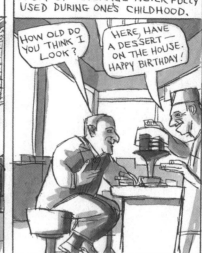

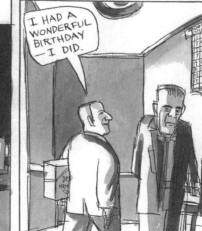

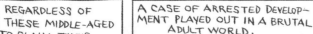

IT'S OKAY. IF YOU SAY SHE WAS AN ATTRACTIVE WOMAN, I BELIEVE YOU. I DON'T NEED PHOTOGRAPHIC PROOF.
I THOUGHT IT WAS RIGHT HERE.

A SMALL PHOTOGRAPH OF MY FIRST WIFE POSING ON THE BEACH. I DIDN'T WANT TO THROW IT OUT, BUT IT'S NOT THE KIND OF THING TO LEAVE LYING AROUND THE HOUSE, YOU UNDERSTAND, AND SO I HID IT.
WHY STIR UP TROUBLE UNNECESSARILY?

AT THE BOTTOM OF A CLOSET? UNDER SOME DRAWER? I PUT IT AWAY SIX YEARS AGO AND NOW I CAN'T REMEMBER WHERE.
RELAX, RELAX, IT'LL COME BACK TO YOU.

IN THIRTY YEARS, MY GRANDCHILDREN WILL FIND IT AND HAVE A GOOD LAUGH.
WHAT KIND OF BATHING SUIT WAS SHE WEARING?

I COULD HIRE A CONFIDENTIAL CLEANING SERVICE TO GO THROUGH THE APARTMENT, ROOM BY ROOM, BUT WHAT WOULD CELIA THINK?
IT WOULD LOOK SUSPICIOUS.

PEOPLE HIDE THEIR HIGH-SCHOOL REPORT CARDS, OLD LOVE LETTERS, POLITICAL LITERATURE —EVERYBODY HAS A SKELETON IN THEIR CLOSET.
DID YOU TRY THE HALL CLOSET?

SHE HAS A BROTHER WHO'S STILL LIVING— HE WAS THERE; HE TOOK THE PICTURE. I'D HATE TO GET INVOLVED, BUT I BET HE HAS A COPY.
HE HAS NOTHING TO HIDE.
TURVY
FURNITURE
SALE

SHE WAS A BLONDE... A LITTLE TALLER THAN YOU.
VERY ATTRACTIVE.
©1997 BEN KATCHOR

AS I APPROACHED MONTREAL, I FELT THAT EVERYTHING WOULD HAVE TO BE ALL RIGHT.
IT WAS JUST A MATTER OF FINDING THE REVEREND AND MAKING UP FOR LOST TIME.
I KNEW HE'D SET ME STRAIGHT. I KEPT GOING OVER IN MY MIND HOW I'D TELL HIM I WAS SORRY...
AND HOPING THAT HE'D BE SORRY, TOO.
12

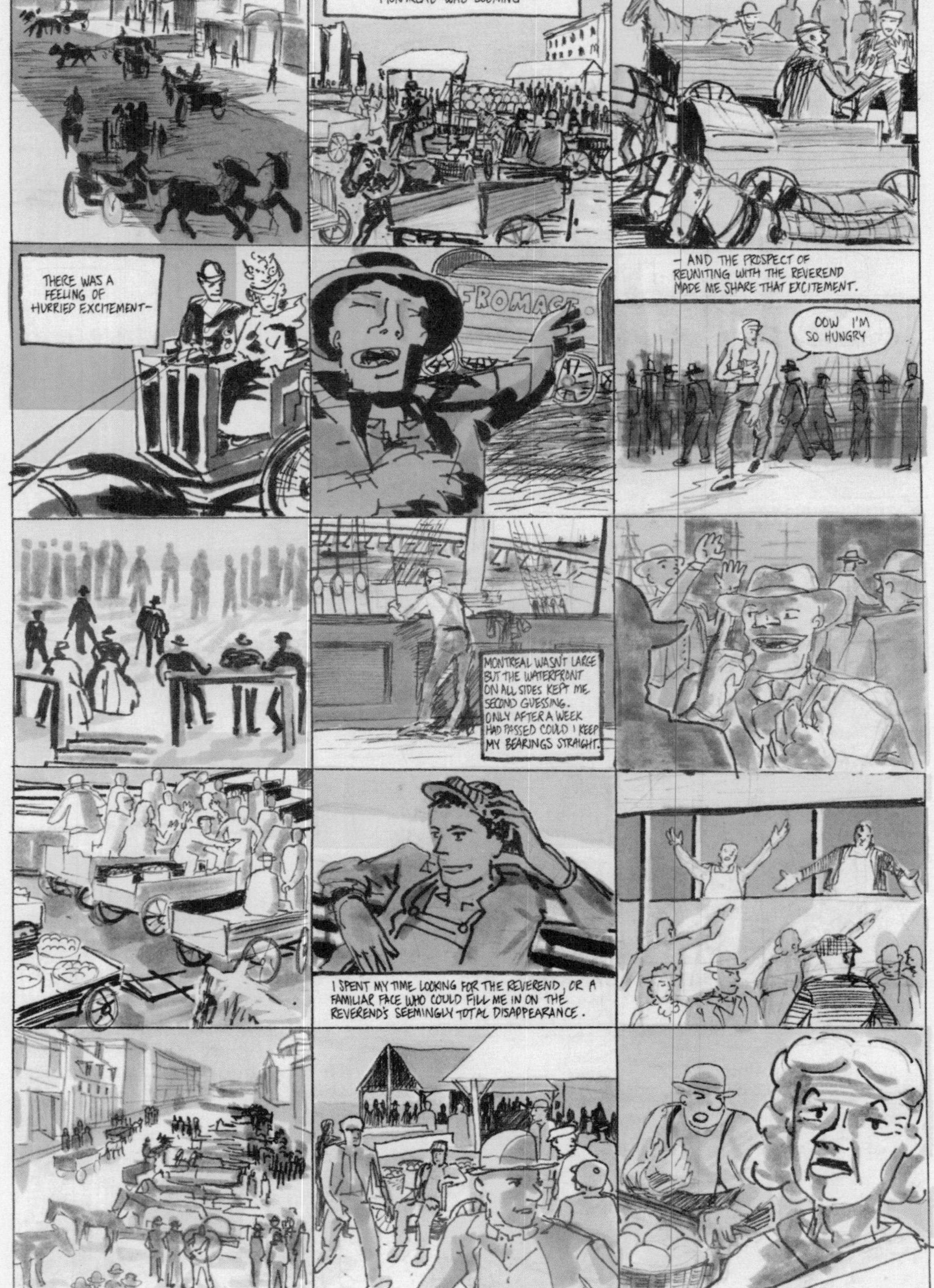
MONTREAL WAS BOOMING
THERE WAS A FEELING OF HURRIED EXCITEMENT–
FROMAGE
– AND THE PROSPECT OF REUNITING WITH THE REVEREND MADE ME SHARE THAT EXCITEMENT.
OOW I'M SO HUNGRY
MONTREAL WASN'T LARGE BUT THE WATERFRONT ON ALL SIDES KEPT ME SECOND GUESSING. ONLY AFTER A WEEK HAD PASSED COULD I KEEP MY BEARINGS STRAIGHT.
I SPENT MY TIME LOOKING FOR THE REVEREND, OR A FAMILIAR FACE WHO COULD FILL ME IN ON THE REVEREND'S SEEMINGLY TOTAL DISAPPEARANCE.
13

FRANK SANTORO *excerpt from* Storeyville

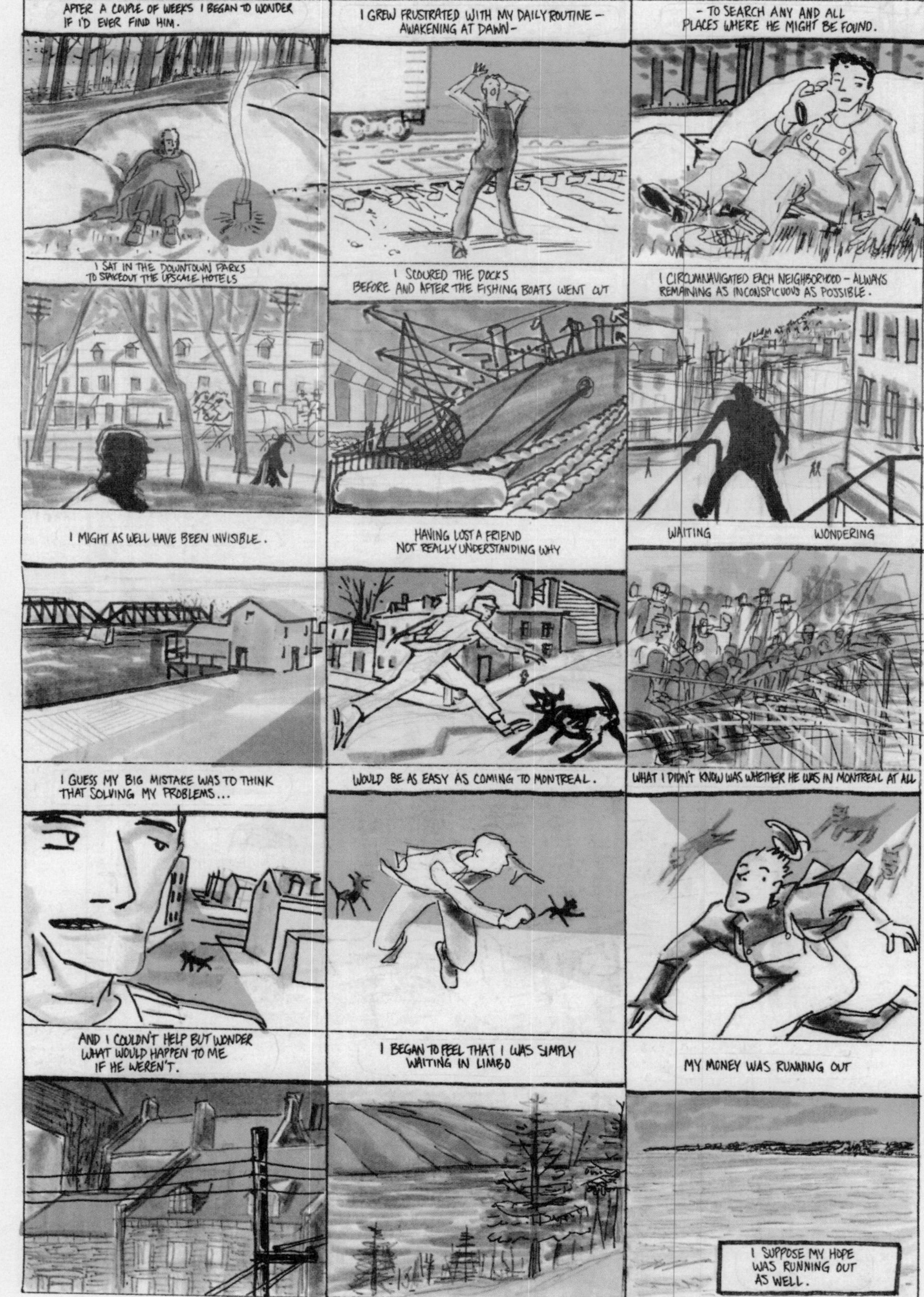

AFTER A COUPLE OF WEEKS I BEGAN TO WONDER IF I'D EVER FIND HIM.
I GREW FRUSTRATED WITH MY DAILY ROUTINE - AWAKENING AT DAWN-
- TO SEARCH ANY AND ALL PLACES WHERE HE MIGHT BE FOUND.
I SAT IN THE DOWNTOWN PARKS TO STAKEOUT THE UPSCALE HOTELS
I SCOURED THE DOCKS BEFORE AND AFTER THE FISHING BOATS WENT OUT
I CIRCUMNAVIGATED EACH NEIGHBORHOOD - ALWAYS REMAINING AS INCONSPICUOUS AS POSSIBLE.
I MIGHT AS WELL HAVE BEEN INVISIBLE.
HAVING LOST A FRIEND NOT REALLY UNDERSTANDING WHY
WAITING
WONDERING
I GUESS MY BIG MISTAKE WAS TO THINK THAT SOLVING MY PROBLEMS...
WOULD BE AS EASY AS COMING TO MONTREAL.
WHAT I DIDN'T KNOW WAS WHETHER HE WAS IN MONTREAL AT ALL
AND I COULDN'T HELP BUT WONDER WHAT WOULD HAPPEN TO ME IF HE WEREN'T.
I BEGAN TO FEEL THAT I WAS SIMPLY WAITING IN LIMBO
MY MONEY WAS RUNNING OUT
I SUPPOSE MY HOPE WAS RUNNING OUT AS WELL.
15

NOW THIS IS WHAT CONTROLS THE WHOLE THING.

CROSS-FADER

THIS IS WHAT TURNS OUR GIRL INTO GORILLA?

PRETTY MUCH. HERE, LOOK...

YOU CAN SEE I'VE TOOK TWO DIMMER SWITCH BOXES – EXTRAS FROM WHEN WE REDID THE WIRING OVER IN THE SANCTUARY–

EACH LEADIN' TO A DIFFERENT SET OF TRACK LIGHTING.

MRS. PEPPER McHENRY, 43, AKA "BUTCH". PLANT MANAGER/SECURITY GUARD, REDD RIVER CHURCH OF THE NAZARENE.

NOW I'VE TAPED THE KNOBS TOGETHER, SO THAT WHEN YOU'RE TURNIN' ONE OF 'EM, YOU'RE TURNIN' BOTH OF 'EM.

BUT LOOKIT HOW I'VE TURNED ONE OF THE SWITCHES BACKWARD, SO THAT ONE SET OF LIGHTS IS GETTIN' DIMMER ...

WHILE THE OTHER SET IS GETTIN' BRIGHTER. THIS IS CRUCIAL TO THE EFFECT.

MMM... YES I SEE!

(ACTUALLY HAS NO IDEA HOW IT WORKS)

REV. M CLIFF JACKSON, 55, PASTOR/ AMATEUR HAUNTED HOUSE GUIDE, REDD RIVER CHURCH OF THE NAZARENE.

HERE'S WHAT IT'LL LOOK LIKE. YOUR WIFE, LOOKIN' LOVELY AS ALWAYS, WILL STAND RIGHT HERE, WHERE THE FIRST SET OF LIGHTS WILL SHINE RIGHT ON HER, BRIGHT AS DAY.

SECRET BACK DOOR

THOSE TRACK LIGHTS I WAS TALKIN' ABOUT:

"SHROUD" BOXES KEEP BEAMS OF LIGHT SHOOTING FORWARD, AWAY FROM GLASS

EXIT

OVER THERE IN THAT BOX WILL BE YOUR GORILLA, STANDIN' IN THE DARK, BUT READY TO LOOK MEAN 'N SCARY.

INTERIOR WALLS PAINTED BLACK-DULL FINISH.

AH YES, I'VE GOT THE PERFECT FELLOW LINED UP FOR THE ROLE - BROTHER BIRDSONG - HE'S OVER IN MY OFFICE GETTING FITTED INTO THE SUIT RIGHT NOW.

AND HERE'S THE OTHER KEY PART. YOU MIGHT NOT BE ABLE TO SEE IT - I WIPED IT REAL CLEAN A FEW MINUTES AGO - BUT THERE'S A SHEET OF PLATE GLASS STANDIN' BETWEEN ME 'N YOU.

HMMM..."FROM BEAUTY TO BEAST... YOU WON'T BELIEVE YOUR EYES!"

SET INTO A GROOVE AT PRECISELY 45°

THE LID

ALSO NOTE: CRISS-CROSS DIAGONAL PATTERN PAINTED ON FLOOR TO DISGUISE BOTTOM EDGE OF GLASS

APE GIRL! IN THE FLESH! SHE'S ALIIIIIIIIVE!

OR HOW ABOUT: "BEHOLD! THE HORRORS OF EVOLUTION! I HOPE NO ONE HAS ANY BANANAS IN THEIR POCKETS!"

CROSS-FADER MECHANISM

OKAY, SO WHEN YOU WALK UP WITH THE KIDS AND PULL BACK THE CURTAIN, WHAT THEY'LL SEE IS...

WELL, NO, NOT YET REVEREND. THEY'LL JUST SEE ME- ERR - YOUR WIFE STANDIN' HERE, PURTY AS A PEACH. BUT IF YOU START TO TURN THE KNOB ON THE CROSS-FADER...

BLACK TAPE HINGES

... AND KEEP TURNIN', THE LIGHTS FADE FROM LEFT TO RIGHT, THE SHEET OF GLASS GOES FROM WORKIN' LIKE A WINDOW ...

TO WORKIN' LIKE A MIRROR.

FROM GIRL... TO ... GORILLA!!

RIGHT BEFORE YOUR EYES!

WOW!

IT REALLY WORKS LIKE A CHARM, BU— I MEAN, UH MRS. McHENRY.

Y'KNOW, ONE THING THOUGH, I'M NOT SURE MY WIFE IS THE BEST CHOICE FOR GETTIN' TRANSFORMED INTO THE APE. FOR ONE THING, SHE'S KIND OF A BIG-BONED GAL,

AND FOR A BIGGER LADY TO TURN INTO A SMALLER FELLA LIKE BROTHER BIRDSONG IN A GORILLA GET-UP, IT'S JUST NOT AS REALISTIC...

HM, SHE MIGHT NOT EVEN FIT THROUGH THE SECRET BACK DOOR!

... OR SCARY!

AND Y'KNOW, IT'S PROBABLY NOT GOOD P.R. FOR THE PASTOR'S WIFE TO GET MADE INTO A MONSTER, AFTER ALL. SOME OF THESE KIDS - THE YOUNGER ONES AT LEAST- MIGHT HAVE NIGHTMARES ABOUT THIS STUFF.

WHATEVER YOU DECIDE REVEREND, I'M SURE IT'LL BE FINE.

I'VE GOTTA GO MAKE SOME LAST-MINUTE ADJUSTMENTS TO THE ONCOMING SEMI. GIMME A HOLLER IF YOU NEED ANYTHING ELSE.

SURE THING, BUTC- MRS. McHENRY.

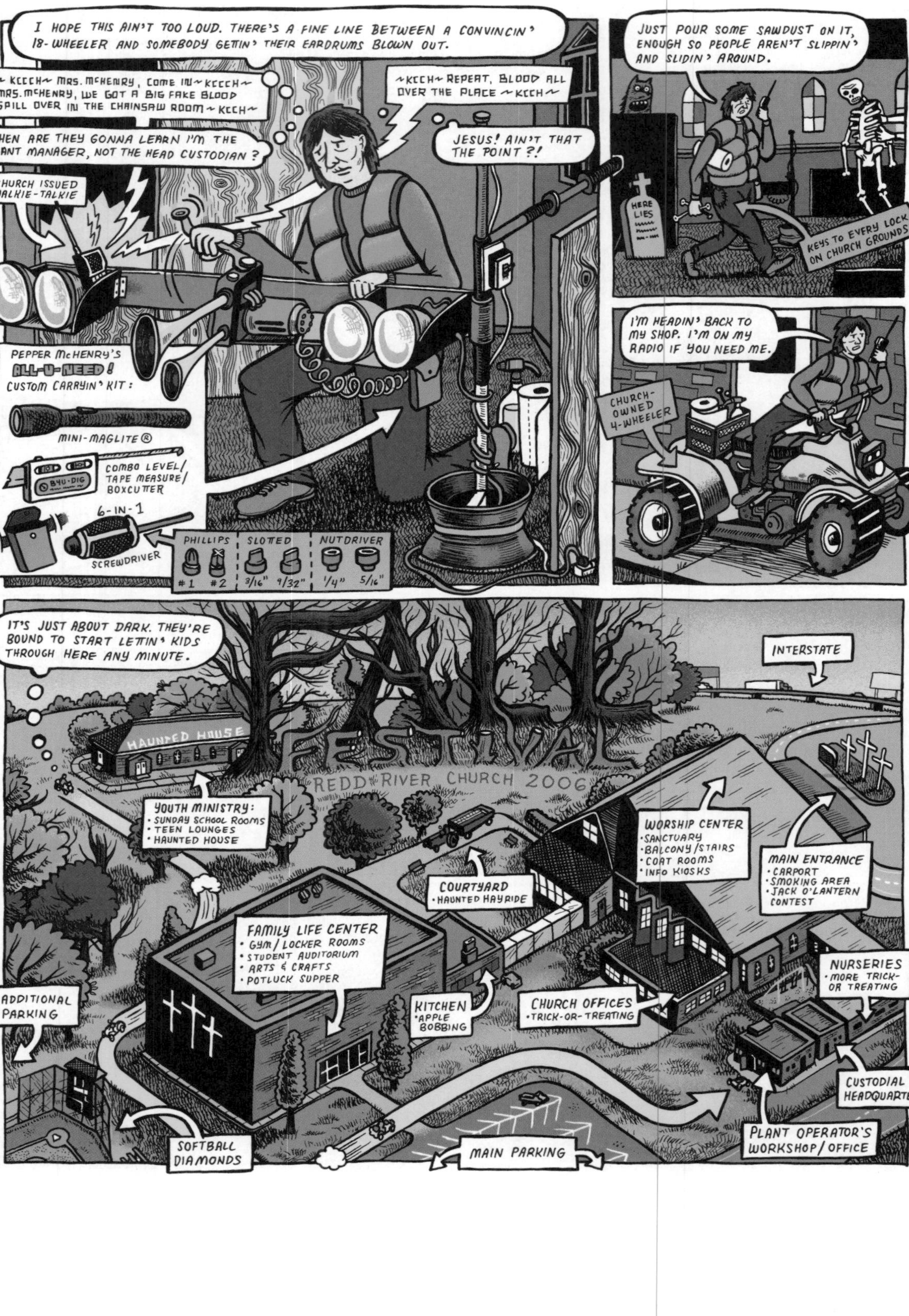

I HOPE THIS AIN'T TOO LOUD. THERE'S A FINE LINE BETWEEN A CONVINCIN' 18-WHEELER AND SOMEBODY GETTIN' THEIR EARDRUMS BLOWN OUT.

~KCCH~ MRS. McHENRY, COME IN ~KCCH~ MRS. McHENRY, WE GOT A BIG FAKE BLOOD SPILL OVER IN THE CHAINSAW ROOM ~KCCH~

~KCCH~ REPEAT, BLOOD ALL OVER THE PLACE ~KCCH~

WHEN ARE THEY GONNA LEARN I'M THE PLANT MANAGER, NOT THE HEAD CUSTODIAN?

JESUS! AIN'T THAT THE POINT?!

CHURCH ISSUED WALKIE-TALKIE

PEPPER McHENRY'S ALL-U-NEED! CUSTOM CARRYIN' KIT:

MINI-MAGLITE®

COMBO LEVEL/ TAPE MEASURE/ BOXCUTTER

6-IN-1 SCREWDRIVER

PHILLIPS		SLOTTED		NUTDRIVER	
#1	#2	3/16"	9/32"	1/4"	5/16"

JUST POUR SOME SAWDUST ON IT, ENOUGH SO PEOPLE AREN'T SLIPPIN' AND SLIDIN' AROUND.

HERE LIES

KEYS TO EVERY LOCK ON CHURCH GROUNDS

I'M HEADIN' BACK TO MY SHOP. I'M ON MY RADIO IF YOU NEED ME.

CHURCH-OWNED 4-WHEELER

IT'S JUST ABOUT DARK. THEY'RE BOUND TO START LETTIN' KIDS THROUGH HERE ANY MINUTE.

FALL FESTIVAL

REDD RIVER CHURCH 2006

HAUNTED HOUSE

INTERSTATE

YOUTH MINISTRY:
• SUNDAY SCHOOL ROOMS
• TEEN LOUNGES
• HAUNTED HOUSE

WORSHIP CENTER
• SANCTUARY
• BALCONY/STAIRS
• COAT ROOMS
• INFO KIOSKS

MAIN ENTRANCE
• CARPORT
• SMOKING AREA
• JACK O'LANTERN CONTEST

COURTYARD
• HAUNTED HAYRIDE

FAMILY LIFE CENTER
• GYM/LOCKER ROOMS
• STUDENT AUDITORIUM
• ARTS & CRAFTS
• POTLUCK SUPPER

NURSERIES
• MORE TRICK-OR TREATING

ADDITIONAL PARKING

KITCHEN
• APPLE BOBBING

CHURCH OFFICES
• TRICK-OR-TREATING

CUSTODIAL HEADQUARTERS

SOFTBALL DIAMONDS

MAIN PARKING

PLANT OPERATOR'S WORKSHOP/OFFICE

HONK!
BANANA SMOOTHIE!
GLUG GLUG
THAT'S RIGHT, OR YOU COULD ADD SOME STRAWBERRIES OR EVEN PROTEIN POWDER INTO THE MAGIC BULLET FOR AN INSTANT POWER
GLASS RACK: REGULAR & STAINED
PLUMBING & HEATING: •PIPES, BELTS, HOSES, •TOILET PLUNGERS/SNAKE
LONG TERM
A.S.A.P.
ILLUSION BOX
WAX FLOORS
CHART OF REQUESTS AND REPAIRS
BUTCH BUTCH!
WOODSHOP & SCRAP LUMBER
KCCCH WE NEED YOU OVER IN THE GORILLA BOOTH A.S.A.P.!
KCCH BUTCH! CAN YOU HEAR ME?!
FRENCH VANILLA CREAMER
MINI-FRIDGE
MISC PARTS: •RUSTED ORGAN PIPES •SOILED PEW LEATHER •UNDERINFLATED BASKETBALLS •ETC.
SUPER-BRAND™ BLACK CHERRY SODA (DIET)
LIGHTING & ELECTRICAL
FADER

YEAH- I'M HERE, I'M HERE.

KCH~ THE GIRL I HAD LINED UP FOR THE BOOTH FELL IN A PUDDLE OF FAKE BLOOD KCCH~ MY WIFE CAN'T FIT THROUGH THE SECRET BACK DOOR ~ KCCCHH ~

OKAY, OKAY, I'LL COME UP THERE WITH MY JIGSAW AND CUT A BIGGER HOLE-

~NO~

WE NEED YOU TO TURN INTO THE GORILLA! ~

COME UP HERE TO THE HAUNTED HOUSE AND SNEAK INTO THE BOOTH. I'M LEADIN' THE FIRST GROUP OF KIDS IN NOW~

I'M GETTIN' TOO OLD FOR THIS SHIT!

MY KIDS DON'T EVEN GO TO THIS CHURCH!

VROOM VROOM

VROOM

SOUNDS LIKE THE ONCOMING SEMI IS WORKING.

OUCH my EARDRUMS!

HONK

LAYPERSON/ GHOST

I'D BETTER GO IN THE BACK WAY.

CLICK

ALUMINUM SOFTBALL BAT

ONCOMING SEMI- SWIVEL ACTION

LAYPERSON/ TOILET PAPER MUMMY

SMOKY MAZE

BLACK LIGHT BULB

CHOIR-LEADER/ ORGANIST/ CRAZED CAVEMAN

ALRIGHT, WHO IS READY TO GET ... FREAKED OUT?

ENTER AT YOUR RISK

JINGLE JANGLE

HEAD-STEWARD/ WEREWOLF

PSSSSSHT.

PASTOR JACKSON (IN COSTUME)

AND FOLLOW THIS REAR HALLWAY ALL THE WAY DOWN TO THE BOX.

PUMPKIN GUTS

ME!

WHISKEY BOTTLE FILLED WITH MR. PIBB

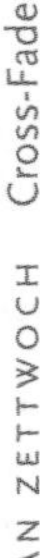

ALMOST THERE! I HOPE MY HAIR'S NOT TOO MESSED UP FROM MY LITTLE "POWER-NAP."
I GOTTA BE A CONVINCIN' GIRL BEFORE TURNIN' INTO A GORILLA.
OKAY, HERE WE GO...
BUS DRIVER/ ZOMBIE* (IN BEST SUNDAY SUIT)
TOP OF ILLUSION BOX BOLTED DOWN TO KEEP ALL OUTSIDE LIGHT OUT
BROTHER BIRDSONG
OOOGA BOOGA
OKAY, KIDS, ARE YOU READY...
SHEEE-IT!
WHOOAA
BLACK ELECTRICAL TAPE SEALS OUTER SEAMS
CLICK
VIBRATING FLOOR
HOUSE
* ON LOAN FROM THE HAUNTED HAYRIDE
** BLADE REMOVED FROM CHAINSAW
RUMBLE RUMBLE
... FOR THE GRAND FINALÉ, HORROR OF HORRORS?
I KNOW IT'S YOU, CHUCK.
STICK STICK
YOUTH MINISTER/ LEATHERFACE**
BEHOLD...
... THE BEAUTY!!
PSSSHT, JUST SOME DUDE IN A GORILLA SUIT.
WAIT A MINUTE! THEY'RE SEEIN' THE GORILLA?!
(OFF)
THAT MORON! HE TURNED THE WRONG SET OF LIGHTS ON FIRST!
I THOUGHT I MADE THIS THING IDIOT-PROOF!
MEANWHILE
UH... THAT'S RIGHT KIDS. BEHOLD, A REAL APE!
A REAL BEAUTIFUL APE!!!

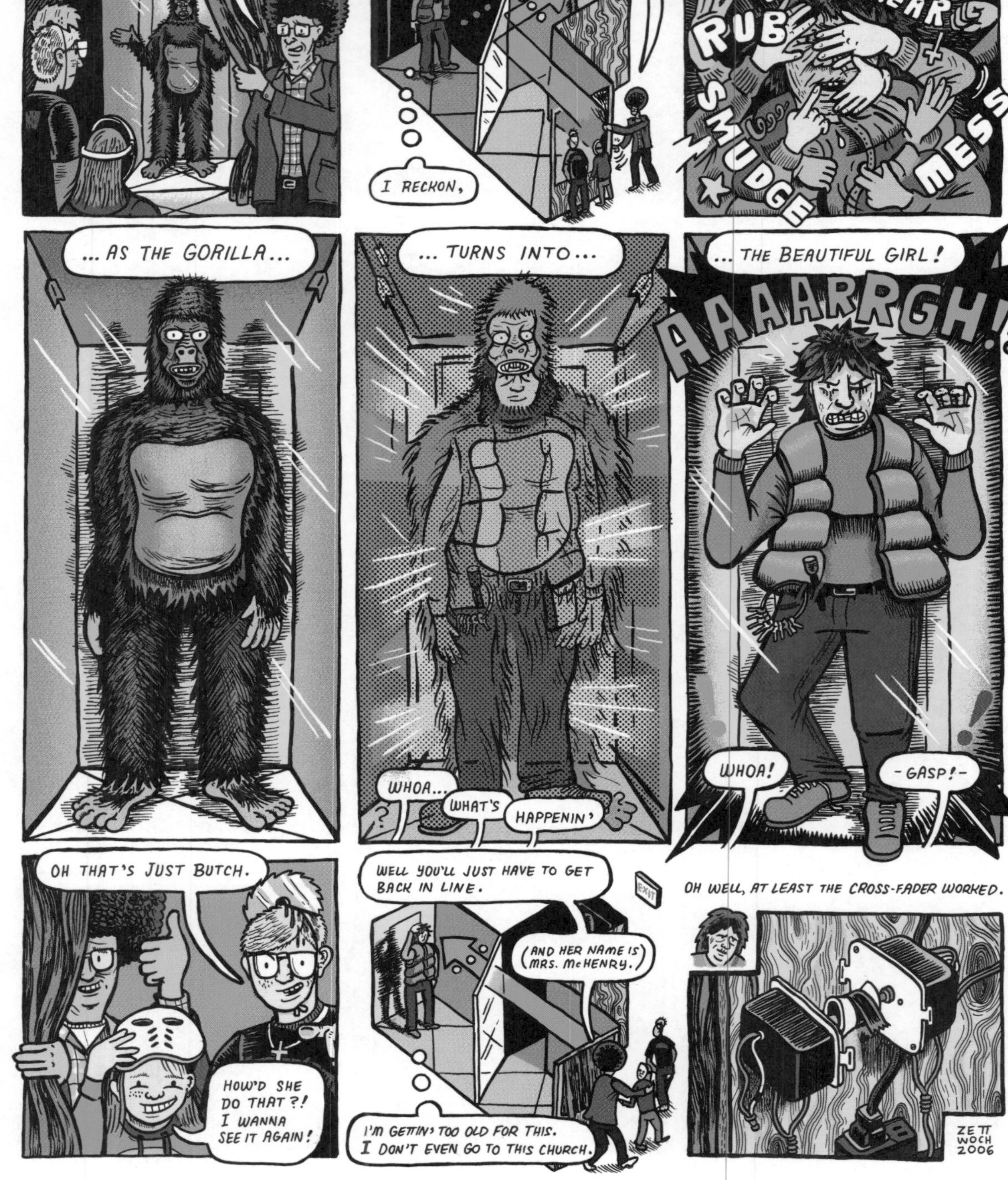
ONE OF GOD'S CREATIONS.
BUT WATCH CLOSELY...
I RECKON,
WE'LL DO THE BEST WE CAN HERE.
RUB
SMEAR
SMUDGE
MESS
...AS THE GORILLA...
...TURNS INTO...
WHOA...
WHAT'S
HAPPENIN'
...THE BEAUTIFUL GIRL!
AAAARRGH!!
WHOA!
-GASP!-
OH THAT'S JUST BUTCH.
HOW'D SHE DO THAT?! I WANNA SEE IT AGAIN!
WELL YOU'LL JUST HAVE TO GET BACK IN LINE.
(AND HER NAME IS MRS. McHENRY.)
I'M GETTIN' TOO OLD FOR THIS. I DON'T EVEN GO TO THIS CHURCH.
EXIT
OH WELL, AT LEAST THE CROSS-FADER WORKED.
ZETT WOCH 2006

GLENN GANGES

in:

"The Curse"

BASED ON A TRUE STORY

by KEVINH '03

EE
ARE YOU AWAKE?
HOW CAN I SLEEP?
CHIRP
CCURR SSSSS
CCKK
ZZKKCR
CCCCRR
EEE ZZ KK ZZZ
WAAA AAAA
KGC RRRR
ZZZ
CCKR RRZZ
BEEP
Oh my God
SUPER SUDZ CAR WASH
I CAN'T MOVE MY STUDIO OUT OF THE GARAGE...
OKAY, I'LL JUST HAVE TO PARK ON THE STREET.
THEY'VE STOPPED... THE RAIN HAS STOPPED THEM...
ZZZZ
LATER
THE SMELL!!
SHIT SOAKED GRASS!!
CHIRP! CHIRP! CHIRP!
SHUT UP SHUT UP SHUT UP PLEASE GOD
ZZKR CCURZ
I DON'T KNOW HOW MUCH MORE I CAN TAKE...
CCKUR ZZZ
CCKKR
SHHH SHHH
CKKC ZZZ
ZZ CK
FF SSHH

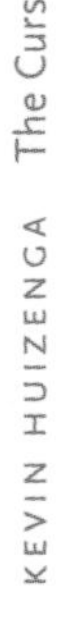

THE EUROPEAN STARLING (*STURNIS VULGARIS*) IS NOT NATIVE TO NORTH AMERICA. ON MARCH 6, 1890, EUGENE SCHIEFFLIN RELEASED BETWEEN 80 AND 90 STARLINGS IN NEW YORK CITY'S CENTRAL PARK.

EUGENE WAS A MEMBER OF THE AMERICAN ACCLIMITIZATION SOCIETY, WHOSE GOAL WAS "THE INTRODUCTION OF SUCH FOREIGN VARIETIES OF THE ANIMAL AND VEGETABLE KINGDOMS AS MAY BE USEFUL OR INTERESTING."

EUGENE'S PERSONAL GOAL WAS TO INTRODUCE TO AMERICA ALL THE BIRDS FOUND IN SHAKESPEARE. ACCORDING TO THE ORNITHOLOGY OF SHAKESPEARE (1871), THE STARLING APPEARS ONLY ONCE, IN I KING HENRY IV.

64 years old
Dies in 1909

servants

KING HENRY ORDERS HOTSPUR TO RELEASE HIS PRISONERS, BUT HOTSPUR REFUSES AND INSISTS THE KING FIRST PAY THE RANSOM OF HOTSPUR'S BROTHER-IN-LAW, MORTIMER, WHO IS A PRISONER OF THE ENEMY. THE KING REFUSES TO DO THIS AND LOSES HIS TEMPER, DECLARING THAT MORTIMER'S NAME NEVER BE MENTIONED AGAIN.

THE KING EXITS AND HOTSPUR IS LEFT FUMING:

He said he would not ransom Mortimer; Forbade my tongue to speak of Mortimer; But I will find him when he lies asleep, and in his ears I'll hollow Mortimer! Nay, I'll have a starling shall be taught to speak Nothing but "Mortimer," and give it him To keep his anger still in motion.

AS KIM TODD NOTES IN TINKERING WITH EDEN: A NATURAL HISTORY OF EXOTICS IN AMERICA (2001, W.W. NORTON), "MAYBE SCHIEFFLIN SHOULD HAVE READ HIS BELOVED BARD MORE CLOSELY.... THE STARLING WAS NOT A GIFT TO INSPIRE ROMANCE OR LYRIC POETRY."

They are dazed from their journey

"IT WAS A BIRD TO PROD ANGER, TO PICK A SCAB, TO SERVE AS A REMINDER OF TROUBLE."

There they go
Oh isn't it wonderful
Yes marvelous

DURING THE 20TH CENTURY, THOSE 80 OR SO BIRDS INCREASED TO OVER 200 MILLION, THE MOST POPULOUS SPECIES OF BIRD IN NORTH AMERICA.

AS OTHER NEWCOMERS SEVERELY ALTERED NORTH AMERICAN HABITATS, CLEARING LAND FOR FARMS, CITIES, AND SPRAWL, STARLINGS ALSO SPREAD RAPIDLY ACROSS THE CONTINENT.

FARMERS ORIGINALLY WELCOMED THE BIRDS, THINKING THEY WOULD CONTROL INSECT PESTS, BUT STARLING POPULATIONS SOON GREW OUT OF CONTROL AND BEGAN EATING SEED AND RUINING CROPS WITH THEIR DROPPINGS.

TO CONTROL THE STARLINGS FARMERS TRIED NOISEMAKERS, BALLOONS, ARTIFICIAL OWLS, LOUDSPEAKERS THAT MIMICKED STARLING DISTRESS CALLS, CHEMICALS THAT CAUSE KIDNEY FAILURE, AND BOMBS. NOTHING WORKS FOR LONG.

STARLINGS THRIVE IN CITIES AND SUBURBS. THEY'LL EAT ANYTHING — INSECTS, NUTS, FRUITS, TRASH. EVERY YEAR TONS OF STARLING EXCREMENT DO MILLIONS OF DOLLARS WORTH OF DAMAGE IN MAJOR CITIES.

THEY PRODUCE 2–4 BROODS A YEAR, NESTING EVEN IN WINTER INSIDE CREVICES AND HOLES — AN IDEAL ADAPTATION FOR DEFORESTED SUBURBAN SPRAWL — UNDER BRIDGES AND VIADUCTS, IN CABLE SPOOLS, GAS STATIONS, RADIATORS, AND AIR CONDITIONERS.

HUGE FLOCKS — CALLED "MURMURATIONS" — DARKEN THE SKY FOR MILES IN UNDULATING, SNAKE-LIKE FORMATIONS. IN THE LAST 15 YEARS, SOME WINTER ROOSTS HAVE BEEN ESTIMATED AT 15 MILLION BIRDS.

AIRPLANES SPRAY THESE HUGE WINTER MURMURATIONS WITH DETERGENT, WHICH DAMAGES WINTER PLUMAGE AND CAUSES HUNDREDS OF THOUSANDS TO FREEZE TO DEATH. BUT IN TIME THE STARLINGS ALWAYS RECOVER THEIR NUMBERS.

STARLINGS' SUCCESS HAS DEVASTATED MANY NATIVE POPULATIONS AND CONTRIBUTED TO THE EXTINCTION OF THE CAROLINA PARAKEET AND THE PASSENGER PIGEON. HUGE ROOSTING FLOCKS PRODUCE ENOUGH EXCREMENT TO HAVE KILLED GROVES OF PINE TREES.

ONE BIRD WATCHER REPORTED SEEING A STARLING DANGLE A PIECE OF FOOD IN FRONT OF A WOODPECKER'S NEST...

AND WHEN THE YOUNG WOODPECKER STUCK OUT ITS HEAD, THE STARLING KILLED IT WITH A QUICK STAB TO ITS SOFT SKULL.

THEY ARE NOTORIOUS NEST BANDITS, CHASING OTHER BIRDS OUT OF NESTS JUST BUILT.

THEY ARE ALSO KNOWN TO PUSH EGGS OUT OF NESTS AND TAKE THE SITE FOR THEMSELVES.

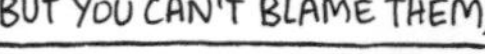

BUT YOU CAN'T BLAME THEM,

THEY'RE ONLY DOING WHAT COMES NATURALLY.

SUPER
SUDZ
CAR
WASH

I'M GOING TO GO AHEAD AND RECOMMEND YOU TO A GOOD ORNITHOLOGIST...

I'M GOING TO MY MOTHER'S.
GLENN?

OH NO
I DON'T UNDERSTAND IT – THEY STARTED UP AN HOUR BEFORE YOU GOT HERE...

CHARCOAL FILT
O.B.
Kentucky Straight Bourbon Whiskey

FLICK
FLICK

FFFFWIPP

BAM!

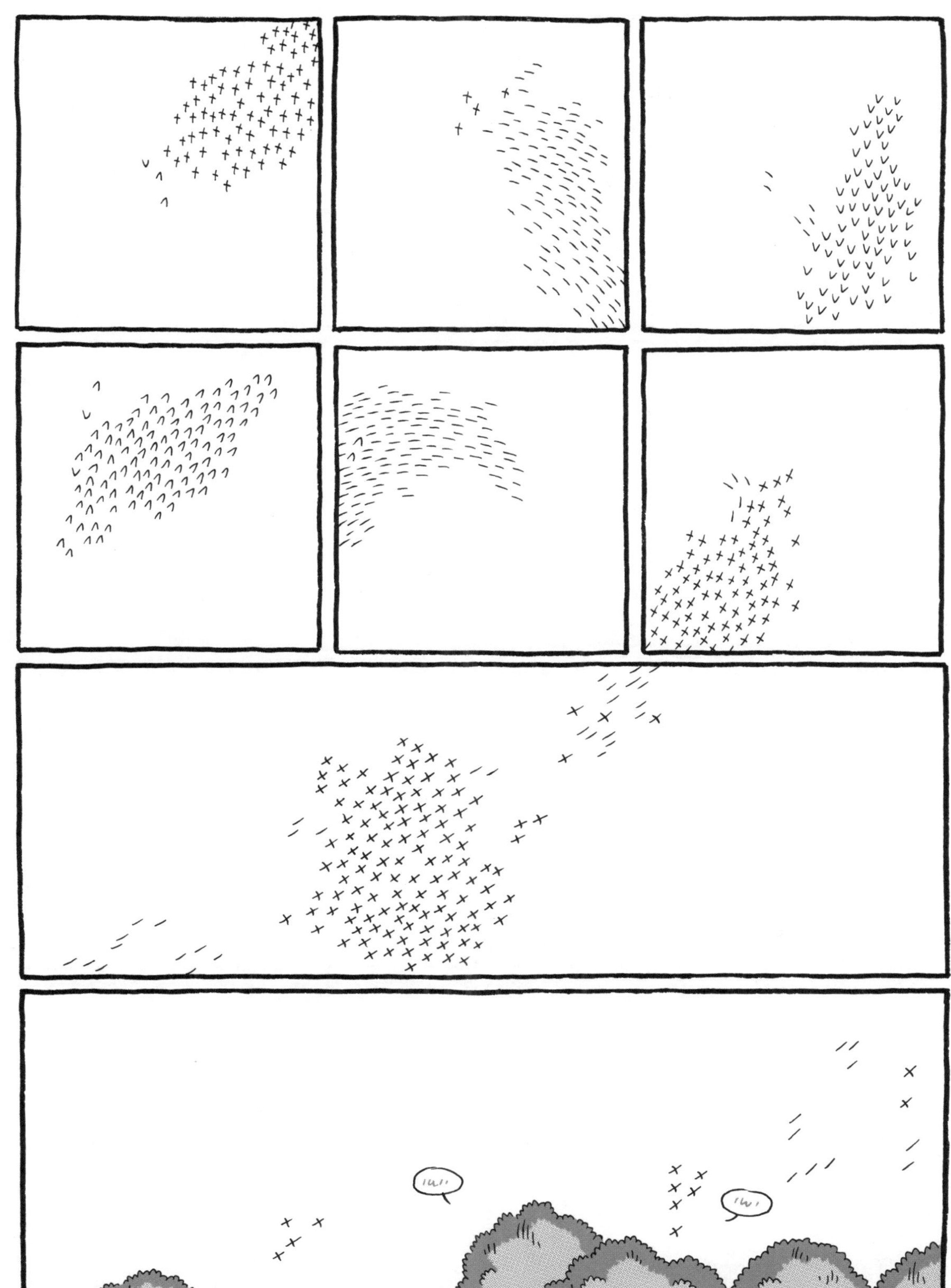

HIDDEN IN THE LOUD AND CONSTANT SQUAWKING, WHISTLING, CHIRPING, CLICKING, AND BUZZING ARE MIMICKED SOUNDS—THE SONGS OF PARAKEETS, COWBIRDS, AND KILLDEER, AS WELL AS ENVIRONMENTAL SOUNDS—DOGS BARKING, CAR HORNS, CELL PHONES...

"AS MEMBERS OF THE *STURNIDAE* FAMILY, STARLINGS ARE COUSINS OF THE MYNAH BIRD AND ARE OUTSTANDING MIMICS," SAYS DAVID IAN WITHERS, ZOOLOGIST.

THE EARLIEST RECORD OF STARLING MIMICRY IS FROM ANCIENT ROME. PLINY THE ELDER MENTIONS HEARING ONE RECITE IN BOTH LATIN AND GREEK.

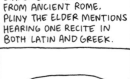

MOZART WAS SURPRISED TO OVERHEAR A CAGED STARLING WHISTLING ONE OF THE THEMES FROM THE FINAL MOVEMENT OF HIS OWN PIANO CONCERTO NO. 17 IN G MAJOR K. 453.

HE BOUGHT THE BIRD AND KEPT IT AS A PET FOR SEVERAL YEARS.

SOME MUSICOLOGISTS AND ORNITHOLOGISTS THINK THAT MOZART'S K. 522, "A MUSICAL JOKE," POSSESSES "THE COMPOSITIONAL AUTOGRAPH OF A STARLING" (WEST, KING, AMERICAN SCIENTIST VOL. 78, 113).

"ITS DRAWN OUT WANDERING PHRASES OF UNCERTAIN STRUCTURE ARE CHARACTERISTIC OF STARLING SOLILOQUIES" (ibid. 112).

WHEN THE BIRD DIED, MOZART ARRANGED A FUNERAL WITH A PROCESSION OF VEILED MOURNERS AND THE SINGING OF HYMNS. HE COMPOSED A POEM THAT HE READ AT THE GRAVESIDE.

"[MOZART] SHARED SEVERAL BEHAVIORAL CHARACTERISTICS WITH STARLINGS. HE WAS FOND OF MOCKING THE MUSIC OF OTHERS... HE ALSO KEPT LATE HOURS... [STARLINGS ALSO] INDULGE IN MORE THAN A LITTLE NIGHT MUSIC" (ibid. 112).

MOZART FINISHED K. 522 EIGHT DAYS LATER, PERHAPS AN "OFFBEAT REQUIEM OF SORTS" (ibid. 106).

ONE FLOCK IN WESTERN MICHIGAN WAS REPORTEDLY MADE UP OF STARLINGS WHOSE CALLS, "WHEN ISOLATED...

CONSISTED OF 30-50% SOUNDS RELATED TO AUTOMOBILES.

[THE ORNITHOLOGISTS] HEARD DISTINCTLY TIRES SCREECHING...

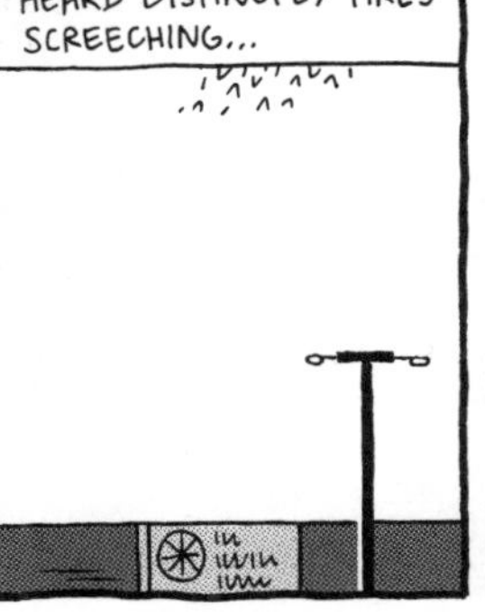

THE WHINE OF POWER WINDOWS..." (GROOT, 87).

THE SSSHHH OF TRAFFIC OUT ON 28TH STREET...

CCCURRS CHUGGG
DING BEEP SCREECH
PUFF CH
CHIRP! SQUAW SQUA
CCCKKUURRR

... A PASSING 747, A FREIGHT TRAIN IN THE DISTANCE...

EEEE CHHPPP FFFFF

FFFWIP CCCKKK
EEEEEE FFFFF

FFFWIPP BAM!
CREAK SLAM
CCR PUFF

cough

... THE HUM OF POWER LINES, AND A THOUSAND STARLINGS SINGING —

HOW CAN YOU SLEEP?

DO THEY EVER SLEEP, OR DO THEY SING IN THEIR SLEEP?
THE END

IS THERE LIFE AFTER LEVITTOWN?

"The little Levitt house is American Suburbia reduced to its logical absurdity."

– Eric Larrabee, Harper's Mag. Sept. 1948

BILL GRIFFITH

IN 1952 THE TREES WERE STILL AS SKINNY AS TELEVISION ANTENNAS AND THE HOUSES LOOKED NAKED AND NEW... I REMEMBER BEING UNABLE TO FIND MY STREET.. I REMEMBER KEEPING A LIST OF ALL THE LICENSE PLATES I SAW FOR TWO WEEKS...

FOR FUN, WE KICKED OVER GARBAGE CANS FROM OUR BIKES. WE HAD PAPER CLIP WARS. WE BROKE STREET LAMPS. WE CURSED AT PASSING CARS. AND WE EXPLORED THE SEWERS....
I STOLE A FLASHLIGHT FROM KRESGE'S— THEY ALMOST SAW ME !!
..YOU WANNA DIVIDE TH' SANDWICHES NOW ??

THE SEWERS
JEEZ.. IT'S DARK--
HOLY COW !! LOOKIT THIS! SOMEBODY PUT UP A WHOLE BUNCH OF PICTURES OF NUDE WOMEN IN HERE!! WOW...
KEEP OUT
TOWN OF HEMPSTEAD

UH.. LET'S GO BACK, LARRY.. WE GOT SIX COKE BOTTLES, A RING, A NICKEL.. IT'S TIME FOR SCHOOL ANYWAY..
YOU GO!! I'M WAITING FOR SUE PATTERSON TO WALK OVER THIS GRATING AGAIN!!

HOLY MACKEREL!! THERE'S AN OLD GUY AT TH' ENTRANCE.. HE'S SITTIN' DOWN LOOKIN' AT THE PICTURES..WHERE'S HIS PANTS?
WHAT'RE WE GONNA DO?? HE'LL PROB'LY MURDER US!!
..MAKE A RUN FOR IT!!

—WHA' TH' HELL?! GAWDAMN PUNKS!!
EVERYBODY OUTA THE POOL!!
WOW!!
KEEP OUT
DASH!

THE WISE GUY
..HOW YOU PEOPLE EVER EXPECT TO PASS THE ALGEBRA REGENTS EXAM... TSK, TSK..
..YOU'LL ALL WIND UP AS TRUCK DRIVERS, I'M WARNING YOU!!
GNNF!!
WE WERE MERCILESS BASTARDS.. WHO KNOWS HOW MANY NERVOUS BREAKDOWNS WE TRIGGERED IN OUR HAPLESS VICTIMS??

NOW, LET'S GET BACK TO.. HUH?
WHY, YOU LITTLE SON OF A BITCH!!!
HAW HAW!
SNIP!
HNNFF--
BILLY DID IT!!

MY SYMBOLIC CASTRATION PRANK DID NOT GO OVER BIG WITH MR. BRONOWSKY...
KRAK!
GET DOWN TO THE VICE PRINCIPAL'S OFFICE IMMEDIATELY!!!
YOW!!
I AM AN ASSHOLE
SNICK!!

..COUGH.. I'VE GOT QUITE A LIST HERE, BILLY— SOME THIRTY-ONE ITEMS...FROM UNHINGING DOORS TO THROWING CAFETERIA TRAYS OUT THE WINDOW.. DISOBEDIENCE OF TEACHERS.. I HAVE NO CHOICE BUT TO SUSPEND YOU, SON.. ..OF COURSE THIS WILL BE ON YOUR PERMANENT RECORD CARD.. ..NO COLLEGE WILL ACCEPT YOU, NO EMPLOYER WILL HIRE YOU.. THIS IS A LIFE-LONG BLOT.. IT WILL STAY WITH YOU FOR AS LONG AS YOU LIVE.. BLAH, BLAH, BLAH...
..I'LL RUN AWAY TO MIAMI AN' BECOME A BEACH BOY...
FILE
MR. GRANT

GHOST SHIP
MOM!! IT'S ME!! I HADDA STAY LATE FOR TH' POSTERITY CLUB..*
*DETENTION HALL
YOUR FATHER WANTS TO SPEAK TO YOU!!
SALK JUNIOR HIGH
MY FATHER LOST HIS JOB IN '57.. HE NEVER TALKED ABOUT IT.. BUT IT SURFACED IN OTHER WAYS. ..I TOOK REFUGE IN MY IMAGINATION—

DAD!! WHAT'RE YOU DOING HOME SO EARLY?!
HOW MANY TIMES HAVE I TOLD YOU TO NEATEN THE NEWSPAPER PILE?!
..AND YOUR ROOM'S A GYPSY NEST!! I WANT IT SHIPSHAPE BY SUPPER!!

UPSTAIRS IN MY ROOM, I DRIFTED OFF TO THE SOUTH SEAS, CAPTAIN OF A MENTAL OCEAN LINER—
WE SHOULD MAKE PAPEETEE BY MIDNIGHT.. COURSE IS SET AT 43° NORTH BY NORTH-WEST--
..I HOPE THAT SQUALL DOESN'T TURN NASTY!
BABY, LET ME TAKE YOU ON A SEA CROOZE!!
KOOL
HOPPY
GABBY HAYES

OH, CAPTAIN! CAN YOU SAVE US??
HAVE NO FEAR, MOM!! DAD, YOU SWAB TH' DECKS!
ULP!
RAVE ON, IT'S A CUH-RAZY FEELIN'- YOU KNOW IT'S-A GOT ME REELIN'..

WHO'S WHO
NANCY!!—IS THIS REAL?? IS THE LIVING ROOM REAL?
WHAT? IS WHAT REAL??
IT HAPPENED DURING A BOUT WITH SCARLET FEVER.. I WAS WATCHING 'AMERICAN BANDSTAND' AT THE TIME—

THESE "UNREAL" EXPERIENCES PERSISTED THROUGHOUT THE JUNIOR HIGH YEARS, OFTEN ENGULFING ME AT THE MOST AWKWARD MOMENTS—
..AM I DREAMING THIS WHOLE THING? HOW DO I KNOW I'M NOT MAKING EVERYTHING UP?..OH, GOD..
MR. GRIFFITH!! I BELIEVE THE CLASS IS AWAITING YOUR CONJUGATION OF THE VERB "MENSURARE"!!
LATIN II

LATER, IN MY BEATNIK PERIOD, [SATURDAYS IN GREENWICH VILLAGE COURTESY OF THE LONG ISLAND RAILROAD] I CONNECTED MY EPISODES OF DISSOCIATION TO GINSBERG'S AGONY IN "HOWL"—
"..I SAW THE BEST MINDS OF MY GENERATION.."
-SO THISH BROAD SHESH SHE DON'T SHUCK NO GUY WI' TH' CLAP SO I PUT TH' SHIV TO HER AN'.. VOMITED.. OH, MY SHTUMMIK, UNH.. ..AGH!!
AGH!
HUH?

SEARCHING—
HERE IT IS!! LIKE IT SAID IN TH' VILLAGE VOICE!!
-THEY'RE HAVIN' A HOOTENANNY!! WOW! THAT'S COOL! YOU DON'T HAFTA BE EIGHTEEN!!
YOU CATS GOT 49¢?
Downstairs
CAFE Wha
FOLK MUSIC
SALK
FOLK Poetr

JACKSON POLLOCK, JR.
WHAT'S IT S'POSED TO BE??
IT'S NOT SUPPOSED TO BE ANYTHING! I'M EXPLORING TH' PICTURE-PLANE!!
..BESIDES, IT'S NON-VERBAL!!
PRE-SPATTERED

I BECAME INTERESTED IN ART ABOUT THE SAME TIME I BECAME INTERESTED IN GIRLS—
...I WANTA SHOW YOU MY D-DRAWINGS --AND POETRY!!
UH--
REALLY?

--WHAT DO YOU THINK ABOUT MONDRIAN.. OR KANDINSKY.. OR FRANZ KLINE??
OHMYGOD! QUICK!! I THINK I HEARD MY MOTHER'S CAR PULL UP IN TH' DRIVEWAY!!

OPINIONATED UPSTART THAT I WAS, I CRITICIZED ANYTHING THAT DID NOT CONFORM TO MY WOBBLY AESTHETIC OF "NON-OBJECTIVITY"--
--YEH, BUT ED... DON'T YOU EVER JUST WANTA DO SOMETHING WILD AND SPONTANEOUS?!
ULTRA-REALISTIC
PATIENCE.. HE'S ONLY SIXTEEN...
OUR NEIGHBOR WAS A HIGHLY SUCCESSFUL SCI-FI ILLUSTRATOR-

HAIRY HAMBURGERS
UH--
WATCH THIS!!
HAW! HAW!
JEEZIS CHRIST, BARRY!! LOOKIT THAT KID!! HE'S MAKIN' HAMBURGERS UNDER HIS ARMPIT!!
CHOKE!
MY FIRST JOB WAS AT McDONALD'S..
[ONLY "2 BILLION SOLD" THEN..]

THE WISE GUY IN ME WAS STILL STRONG.. AND I VACILLATED CRAZILY BETWEEN MY 'ART-BOY' AND 'BRAT-BOY' SELVES-
ROTATE, DUMBO!!
-YOU'RE FIRED!! --WHAT KIND OF UPBRINGING DID YOU-- --BLUSTER!! PUFF--

WHEN GRADUATION DAY ROLLED AROUND, I ALMOST DIDN'T MAKE IT—
TAKE OFF THAT GOD-DAMNED PEACE BUTTON OR YOU DON'T GET YOUR DIPLOMA!!
ANGRY DAD
PROUD MOM
I WILL NOT!! IT IS A MATTER OF INDIVIDUAL CONSCIENCE!!

I SPENT MY LAST SUMMER BEFORE COLLEGE PAINTING BAN THE BOMB SLOGANS ON PUBLIC BUILDINGS —

MANY YEARS LATER, I RETURNED HOME FOR A VISIT--- -A REMARKABLE CHANGE HAD TAKEN PLACE.. THE TREES HAD GROWN TALL AND OBSCURED THE HOUSES.

..LEVITTOWN NEVER LOOKED BETTER...
END

HOW I QUIT COLLECTING RECORDS
AND PUT OUT A COMIC BOOK WITH THE MONEY I SAVED

Story by Harvey Pekar **Art by R. Crumb**

EVER SINCE I WAS A KID, IT SEEMS I COLLECTED SOMETHING.

AT ONE TIME IT WAS COMICS, THEN MAGAZINES AND BOOKS ABOUT SPORTS.

THEN, WHEN I WAS SIXTEEN, I STARTED COLLECTING JAZZ RECORDS.

AT FIRST, AND FOR A LONG TIME, IT WAS A HEALTHY THING TO DO.

I LOVED JAZZ, AND LISTENED TO IT CLOSELY AND ANALYTICALLY.

FOR A LONG TIME I COLLECTED IN A RATIONAL WAY. I ONLY BOUGHT RECORDS THAT I ENJOYED LISTENING TO, AND/OR THAT HAD A GREAT DEAL OF HISTORICAL SIGNIFICANCE.

THEN, FOR SOME REASON, I GOT OBSESSIVE ABOUT IT. I STARTED BUYING RECORDS I KNEW I'D SELDOM IF EVER LISTEN TO JUST FOR THEIR COLLECTOR'S VALUE.

IT GOT WORSE AND WORSE. I STARTED GETTING ALL THESE AUCTION LISTS AND SPENDING FANTASTIC AMOUNTS OF MONEY ON OUT-OF-PRINT L.P.'S.
DEAR MR. PEKAR
YOU HAVE WON THE FOLLOWING RECORDS.
PLEASE SEND
TOTAL

I WAS SPENDING ALL OF MY MONEY ON RECORDS I JUST FILED AWAY WITHOUT LISTENING TO. I HAD TO THINK TWICE ABOUT BUYING A HAMBURGER OR GOING TO A MOVIE.

I HUSTLED POP RECORDS THAT I GOT IN ALL SORTS OF WAYS TO PEOPLE AT WORK TO GET EXTRA DOUGH. THAT WAS A TIME-CONSUMING DRAG.

HEY MAN, YOU WANNA BUY THIS NEW DYLAN L.P. FOR TWO DOLLARS?

I WAS GOING BLIND GOING OVER ALL OF THE AUCTION AND SALES LISTS I GOT, I SPENT SO MUCH TIME READING THEM.

I BOUGHT SO MANY RECORDS IT WAS CRAZY. I WAS RUNNING OUT OF SPACE FOR THEM.

ONE DAY IN THE SPRING OF '75 I WAS GOING OVER A BUNCH OF AUCTION LISTS. THERE WERE RECORDS ON THEM THAT I WANTED TO BID ABOUT $600.00 ON WITHIN ABOUT SIX WEEKS.

SOME I WANTED REAL BAD. BUT WHERE WAS I GONNA GET THE BREAD FOR THEM? IT WAS FREAKING ME OUT!

WHILE I WAS THINKING ABOUT IT A BUDDY OF MINE CAME OVER TO ASK ME IF HE COULD BORROW A COUPLE OF RARE JOHN COLTRANE AIRSHOT L.P.S TO PLAY ON HIS COLLEGE JAZZ RADIO SHOW.

CAN YOU SPARE THEM FOR A FEW HOURS? I'LL TAKE GOOD CARE OF THEM AND RETURN THEM RIGHT AWAY.

THIS GUY WAS A REAL GOOD GUY. HE WAS INTO YOGA AND CAME ON SORT OF LIKE A HOLY MAN, BUT HE REALLY WASN'T SELF-RIGHTEOUS. HE WAS A RESPONSIBLE GUY, TOO, BUT I WAS PARANOID ABOUT LENDING OUT MY RECORDS.

WELL, YOU C'N USE 'EM, BUT I GOTTA COME DOWN TO THE STUDIO WITH YOU WHILE YOU DO IT.
JOHN COLTRANE

SO WE WENT DOWN TO THE STATION TOGETHER. WHILE HE WAS ON THE AIR I STARTED TO BROWSE THROUGH THE STATION'S RECORD LIBRARY.

I RAN ACCROSS ABOUT A HALF-DOZEN L.P.S I DIDN'T HAVE AND EVENTUALLY PLANNED TO GET.

THEY WERE STILL IN PRINT BUT THEY WOULDA' COST ME AROUND THIRTY BUCKS TO BUY.
$ $ $ $

I KNEW THAT ALOT OF PEOPLE RIPPED OFF RECORDS FROM THAT STATION.

SO I FIGURED, " FUCK IT, WHAT'S THE DIFFERENCE"! AND I DECIDED I WAS GONNA STEAL THE SIDES BUT I THOUGHT I'D BE SLICK ABOUT IT...

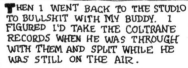

IT WAS SUNDAY, THE BUILDING WAS DESERTED. SO WHAT I DID, I SNEAKED THE SIDES OUT OF THE STUDIO AND STUCK 'EM IN A BATHROOM.
FIRST I CHECKED THE BATHROOM DOOR TO MAKE SURE IT WOULDN'T LOCK AUTOMATICALLY BEHIND ME SO I COULD GO BACK FOR THE SIDES. IT WAS O.K.
MEN

THEN I STUCK THE SIDES IN A BOX OF TOILET PAPER.
ACME TOILET TISSUE 100 ROLLS

THEN I WENT BACK TO THE STUDIO TO BULLSHIT WITH MY BUDDY. I FIGURED I'D TAKE THE COLTRANE RECORDS WHEN HE WAS THROUGH WITH THEM AND SPLIT WHILE HE WAS STILL ON THE AIR.

HE'D SEE ME WALKING OUT OF THE STUDIO WITH ONLY THE COLTRANE RECORDS IN MY HANDS, SO IF THE OTHER SIDES WERE MISSED HE WOULDN'T SUSPECT ME.

I MEAN, THE CAT TRUSTED ME AND I DIDN'T WANT HIM TO KNOW I WAS STEALING. LIKE HE WAS SUCH A MORAL DUDE, Y'KNOW. HE WAS EVEN AGAINST STEALING FROM STORES AND INSTITUTIONS.

SO HE FINISHES PLAYIN' THE COLTRANE SIDES, GIVES 'EM BACK TO ME AN' I SPLIT.

THANKS ALOT, MAN!

'S O.K. ...UH, LOOK, I GOTTA TAKE OFF NOW...

SO THEN I MAKE IT OVER TO THE BATHROOM TO GET TH' SIDES.

MEN

BUT THE DOOR IS LOCKED.

I COULDN'T BELIEVE IT. I HAD TESTED IT BEFORE TO MAKE SURE IT WOULDN'T LOCK ON ME. I YANKED ON IT AGAIN AND AGAIN. IT WAS LOCKED.

THAT BLEW MY MIND. I WAS ALREADY WONDERING ABOUT WHERE I WAS GONNA GET TH' $600.00 AND NOW I HAD THROWN AWAY ANOTHER $30.00 WORTH OF SIDES BECAUSE I'D DEVISED TOO ELABORATE A PLAN TO RIP THEM OFF.

IF I'D HAVE STUCK THEM IN THE HALL SOME PLACE THEY'D HAVE BEEN O.K. NO ONE WAS GONNA COME ALONG AND SEE THEM. BUT NO, I HADDA GET CUTE AN' STICK 'EM IN A TOILET PAPER BOX IN A BATHROOM.

I WALKED BACK HOME IN A DAZE.

HOW COULD I HAVE BEEN SO STUPID? IT WAS SO EASY TO STEAL THOSE SIDES! NOW I GOTTA COME UP WITH $30.00 MORE TO BUY THEM SOME DAY... WHAT IF THEY FIND THE SIDES IN THE TOILET PAPER BOX? WILL THEY SUSPECT ME ??

MY HEAD WAS ALL FUCKED UP. I SAT DOWN TO RELAX AND THINK ABOUT MY SITUATION.

THIS RECORD COLLECTING IS DRIVING ME NUTS. IT'S TAKING ALL OF MY TIME AND MONEY.

NO MATTER HOW MANY RECORDS I GET I'M NEVER SATISFIED; I GOTTA GET MORE. I'VE TRIED TO QUIT BUT I CAN'T. WHAT AM I GONNA DO? THIS IS LIKE BEING A JUNKY!!

I TRIED TO QUIT A FEW MONTHS AGO, I GOT SO DISGUSTED. I WENT TO BED THINKIN' I HAD IT TOGETHER, BUT I WOKE UP WITH THE SAME COLLECTOR'S ITCH.
BUS STOP

IT'S SO HARD FOR ANYBODY BUT ANOTHER COLLECTOR TO UNDERSTAND WHY YOU CAN'T KICK THE HABIT.
CLEVELAND T

RIGHT NOW I FEEL LIKE I WANT TO QUIT COLLECTING BUT TOMORROW I'LL PROB'LY FEEL DIFFERENT.
Home

BUT SURPRISINGLY THE NEXT DAY I STILL FELT FED UP WITH COLLECTING.
WOW, HEY MAYBE I CAN GIVE IT UP!

AND WHAT HAPPENED WAS THAT FOR SOME REASON I WAS ABLE TO GIVE IT UP.

IT'S FUNNY HOW YOUR MIND SOMETIMES WORKS. ONE DAY YOU CAN'T BRING YOURSELF TO DO SOMETHING, THE NEXT DAY YOU CAN DO IT. WHY IT HADN'T HAPPENED TO ME BEFORE I DON'T KNOW. ANYWAY, I'M GLAD IT DID, FOR A COUPLE OF MAJOR REASONS.

FOR ONE THING I WAS FREE FROM THE PRESSURES OF TRYING TO GET EVERY JAZZ SIDE EVER MADE AND ALL THE TIME AND EFFORT IT TOOK UP.

FOR ANOTHER, IT MEANT I COULD SPEND MY MONEY ON SOMETHING BESIDES FOOD, RENT AND RECORDS!

....SEE, I HAD BEEN WRITING THESE UNDERGROUND COMIC BOOK STORIES SINCE 1972. PEOPLE LIKED 'EM A LOT BUT I WAS HAVING TROUBLE GETTING 'EM PUBLISHED BECAUSE THE UNDERGROUND COMIC PUBLISHERS WERE IN BAD SHAPE FINANCIALLY. THEY WERE PRINTING VERY LITTLE.

ALL THEY WANTED TO HANDLE WERE SURE SELLERS, STUFF BY CRUMB AND SHÉLTON. IT REALLY BUGGED ME THAT I WAS HAVING SUCH A HASSLE GETTING STUFF PUBLISHED.

SO ANYWAY, I SUDDENLY HAD ALL THIS EXTRA DOUGH SINCE I WASN'T SPENDING IT ON RECORDS AND SINCE I WAS STILL HUSTLING L.P.S AT WORK...

I LIVE REAL SIMPLE AND CHEAP, Y' KNOW. I DON'T HAVE A CAR AND I EAT CHEAP FOOD, LIKE I MIGHT HAVE TWO HOT DOGS AN' SOME POTATO CHIPS FOR SUPPER.

SO I STARTED ASKIN' AROUND, TRYIN' TO FIGURE HOW MUCH IT WOULD COST TO PUBLISH A COMIC BOOK.

SO I FOUND OUT I COULD SAVE UP ENOUGH BREAD IN A YEAR TO PUBLISH ONE...

SO THAT SETTLED IT... I FIGURED, "FUCK IT, I'LL PRINT IT AND IF I LOSE MONEY ON IT, SO WHAT!

SO I PUBLISHED "AMERICAN SPLENDOR" AN' I'M REALLY GLAD I DID...
END

THAT'S LIFE

A HOT SUMMER DAY IN THE "COLORED" SECTION OF CRYSTAL SPRINGS, MISSISSIPPI IN THE YEAR 1931...

by R. CRUMB ©1975

PO-O' BOY—LO-ONG WAY F'UM HO-OME... PO' BOY, LONG WAY F'UM HOME....

MMM HMMM

WHEW... AH LIKES TA HEAR YOU SINGIN', TOMMY... SHO' IS PRETTY! AH WISH YE WOULD JOIN DE CHURCH AN' SING 'LONG WIF ME ON SUNDAY!

US DON' SEE EYE TO EYE ON DAT BUNCH OF GOSSIPIN' HYPOCRITES, ESTHER!!

PLUNK PLUNK

YEAH, AN' ANUTHA THING US DON' SEE EYE TO EYE 'BOUT IS DIS WORK WHAT'S GOTTA GIT DONE 'ROUND HERE... YOU S'POSE T'BE MINDIN' THEM BABIES AN' WHERE IS DEY, WHILE YOU SITTIN' HERE PICKIN' DAT GITTAR, AN'... ...WHAT'S DIS!? MAH SPESHAL SECRET MEDICINE!!

SHHEEIT...

AH WARNT YOU 'BOUT GITTIN' INTA MAH SPIRITS, MISTAH!!

AH'S GITTIN' TIRED O' YOU DRIVIN' ME, BITCH... AH KIN BEAT YOU PLENTY!

HA! AH KIN WALLOP YER SKINNY LI'L OL' BLACK ASS ANY DAY OB D'WEEK, HONEY CHILE...

GRRR... WE SEE 'BOUT DAT, SWEET!!

AH'M A PEEZABLE WOMIN BUT NOW YO' IS GOT ME RILED... AH'LL RIP DE FLESH OFF YOU BONES, NIGGUH!!

GUH!

MMUPGHHRR OOWLL...

UGH GHASP GAG

YOU FUCK WID ME AH'LL MAKE YOU EAT ALL DE DIRT IN DE YARD, BITCH!

AARNGH

CRUNCH

HEE HEE!

AH'LL DO A HOP-SCOP ON YO' HAID 'FO' AH LETS YOU GIT UP!

SPLUT SPUTTER PTOO!!

ALL DIS FUSSIN' AN' FIGHTIN' IS WEARYIN' ON ME... IT AIN' NO GOOD, ESTHER... ALLUS DISAGREEMENTS 'BOUT EVVA GODDAMN LI'L THING... DAT AIN' NO WAY TO LIVE!

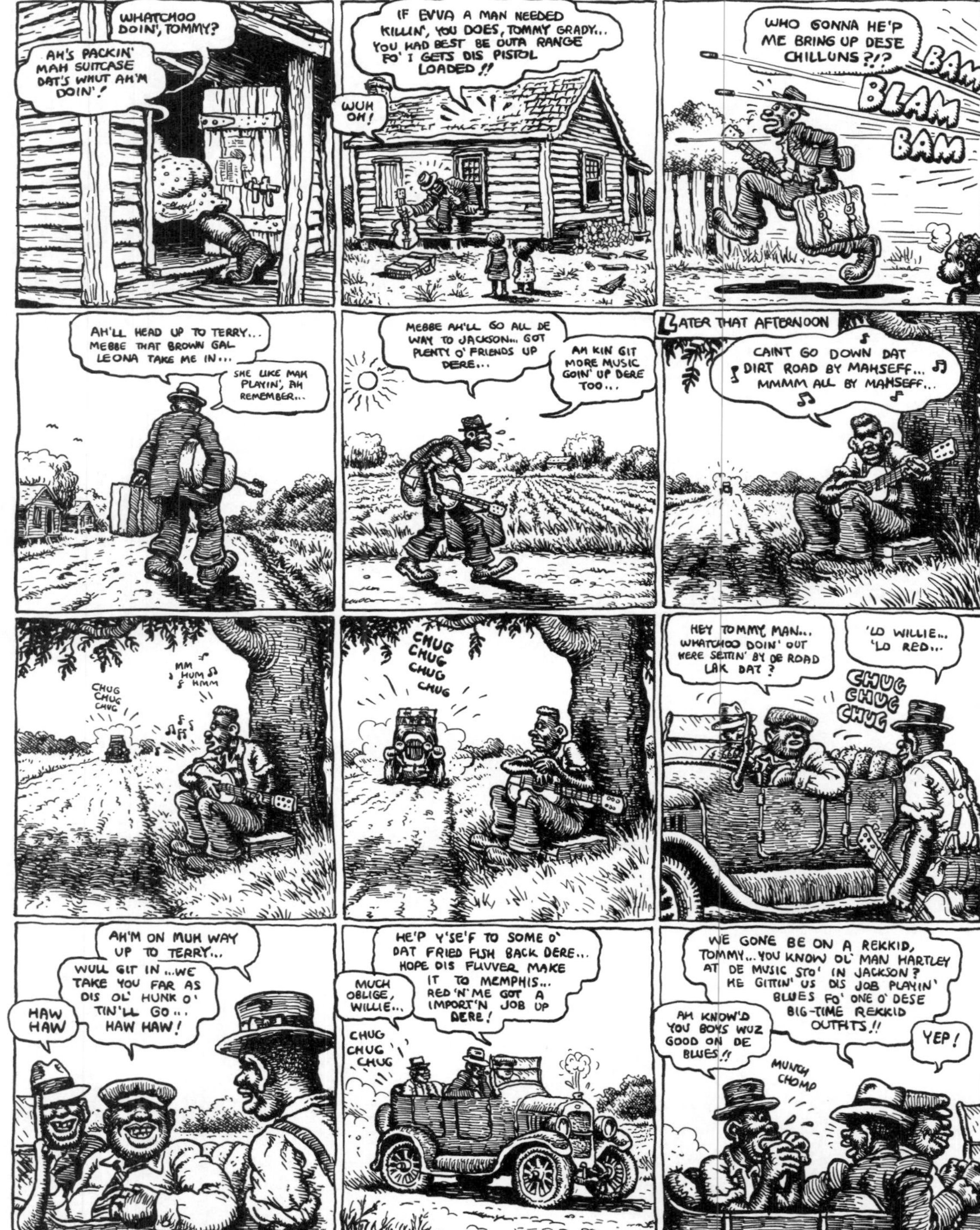

WHATCHOO DOIN', TOMMY?
AH'S PACKIN' MAH SUITCASE DAT'S WHUT AH'M DOIN'!
IF EVVA A MAN NEEDED KILLIN', YOU DOES, TOMMY GRADY... YOU HAD BEST BE OUTA RANGE FO' I GETS DIS PISTOL LOADED!!
WUH OH!
WHO GONNA HE'P ME BRING UP DESE CHILLUNS?!?
BAM
BLAM
BAM
AH'LL HEAD UP TO TERRY... MEBBE THAT BROWN GAL LEONA TAKE ME IN...
SHE LIKE MAH PLAYIN', AH REMEMBER...
MEBBE AH'LL GO ALL DE WAY TO JACKSON... GOT PLENTY O' FRIENDS UP DERE...
AN KIN GIT MORE MUSIC GOIN' UP DERE TOO...
LATER THAT AFTERNOON
CAINT GO DOWN DAT DIRT ROAD BY MAHSEFF... MMMM ALL BY MAHSEFF...
CHUG CHUG CHUG
MM HUM HMM
CHUG CHUG CHUG CHUG
HEY TOMMY, MAN... WHATCHOO DOIN' OUT HERE SETTIN' BY DE ROAD LAK DAT?
'LO WILLIE... 'LO RED...
CHUG CHUG CHUG
AH'M ON MUH WAY UP TO TERRY...
WULL GIT IN... WE TAKE YOU FAR AS DIS OL' HUNK O' TIN'LL GO... HAW HAW!
HAW HAW
HE'P Y'SE'F TO SOME O' DAT FRIED FISH BACK DERE... HOPE DIS FLIVVER MAKE IT TO MEMPHIS... RED 'N' ME GOT A IMPORT'N JOB UP DERE!
MUCH OBLIGE, WILLIE...
CHUG CHUG CHUG
WE GONE BE ON A REKKID, TOMMY... YOU KNOW OL' MAN HARTLEY AT DE MUSIC STO' IN JACKSON? HE GITTIN' US DIS JOB PLAYIN' BLUES FO' ONE O' DESE BIG-TIME REKKID OUTFITS!!
AH KNOW'D YOU BOYS WUZ GOOD ON DE BLUES!!
YEP!
MUNCH CHOMP

HOW MUCH YOU GOTTA PAY DESE PEOPLE TO MAKE DIS REKKID?
NO, TOMMY, MAN... DA PEOPLE PAYS YOU! OL' MAN HARTLEY TELL US DE MAN GIVE US TWENNY-FI' DOLLIZ FO' EVVY TUNE DAT YOU MAKE ON A REKKUD...
TWENNY FI' DOLLAH!! MAN, DAT'S PLENTY GOOD FO' ONE LI'L TUNE!
YOU GODDAMN RAHT DAS GOOD... AN' DEN IF YOU GET A HIT DEY GIT YOU BACK AN' MAKE A WHOLE SLEW O' MO' REKKUDS AN' YOU GITS BIGGER PAYMINTS... FITTY DOLLIZ A REKKUD OR MEBBE EVEN A HUNNID!!
DEN YOU GITS FAMOUS JUS' LAK OL' BLIND LEMON AN' PAPA CHARLIE JACKSON AN' ALL DE BLACK FOLKS IN DIS WHOLE WIDE WORL' KNOWS 'BOUT YOU!!
NEX' THING YOU KNOW YOU'S RIDIN' 'ROUN' IN LIMMAZINES WIT' YOU OWN SHO'FER.... YOU WEARIN' SILK SHOITS, AN' PAT'N LEATHA SHOES!
NO MO' WALKIN' BEHIND DAT PLOW STARIN' AT DAT MULE'S ASS! HEE HEE!!
JES' THINK OF ALL DEM BROWNS AN' YALLAS BE AFTA YOU DEN... MAN... HOPE AH MAKES A HIT REKKUD!
HEY WILLIE! YOU THINK DAT REKKID OUTFIT MIGHT COULD USE OL' TOMMY HERE?
MEBBE SO... AH DUNNO... HE PLAY DAT MEAN, DIRTY LOW-DOWN TYPE O' MUSIC... BUT HE DO GIT HOT ON DE GITTAR...
AW, DEY DON' WAN' NO OL' BACKWOODS COUNTRY NIGGUH ON NO REKKID... HAW HAW...
TOMMY, HEY MAN, US AIN' NO LESS COUNTRY BOYS DAN YOU IS... DEY GONNA GIVE US DE CHANCT... YOU COME ON WIT US, JES' FO' DE RIDE... MEBBE DE PEOPLE LAK YOU TYPE O' PLAYIN', MEBBE DEY DON'... YOU GOT NUTTIN' TO LOSE...
DAS RIGHT!
DAS' FO' SHO'... OKAY, AH COME 'LONG WIT Y'ALL... HEY, YOU BOYS GOT ANY OF DE GOOD STUFF IN DIS CAH SOMEWHERES?
SHO' IN HELL DON'T! DE WIMMEN MAKE US SWEAR ON DE BIBLE US'LL LAY OFF DE LIKKUH 'TIL AFTA WE MAKES DEM REKKUDS...
AMEN BRUTHA! HAW HAW HAW!
DEY DONT MISS A THING, BRUTHA!!
HAR HAR HAR!
LOOKIT... DERE'S A SAHN SAYIN "MEMPHIS, TWO-HUNNID AN' TWENNY MAHLS"...
MAN, WE GOT A LONG WAY TO GO!!
AH'S GLAD YOU KIN READ DEM SAHNS, WILLIE... ELSE WE'UD NEVER FIND DAT REKKID MAN!!
JACKSON .. 15 MILES
MEMPHIS 220 MILES
TWO DAYS LATER THE BOYS FINALLY ROLL INTO MEMPHIS, TENNESSEE...
MAN, DIS IS SOME BIG TOWN!!
AH BEEN IN MEMPHIS MANY TIMES 'FO' DIS... AH SHOW YOU 'ROUND ALL DE HOT SPOTS, TOMMY!!
HOPE WE GITS DAT MONEY SOON! AH'S FLAT BUSTED BROKE AFTAH ALL DAT GASOLINE AN' STUFF WE HAD T' BUY!!
NEXT DAY TOMMY GETS TO CUT FOUR TITLES AT A MAKE-SHIFT FIELD-RECORDING STUDIO IN A MEMPHIS HOTEL ROOM...
TOMMY, WILLIE & RED HANG AROUND THE ROWDY BEALE STREET AREA OF MEMPHIS, SPENDING ALL THEIR RECORD MONEY ON NEW SUITS, SHOES, HATS, TIES... THE REST ON BOOZE AND WOMEN...
BEING UNWISE TO THE WAYS OF THE BIG CITY, TOMMY UNWITTINGLY GETS INVOLVED WITH A WOMAN WHO HAS A JEALOUS HUSBAND. ONE NIGHT IN A JOINT, THE HUSBAND SHOOTS TOMMY IN THE HEAD, KILLING HIM INSTANTLY.

SIX MONTHS LATER, IN THE WINTER OF 1931-32, IN AN OFFICE OF THE "NOBLE" RECORD COMPANY, NEW YORK CITY...
WHEW...
HOW'D THE MEETING GO, ED?

FROM THE HANG-DOG EXPRESSION ON YOUR FACE, I'D SAY THINGS HAVE TAKEN A TURN FOR THE WORSE...
YOU SAID IT FRANK... MY WORST FEARS...
412

McENELLY AND SAUNDERS WERE AT THE MEETING... THOSE TWO OLD BUZZARDS HAVE ALWAYS BEEN AGAINST THE FIELD-TRIPS FROM THE BEGINNING...
WE FOUGHT THEM FOR EVERY PENNY SINCE OUR FIRST TRIP TO MISSOURRI IN 1925...

WELL PUSH HAS COME TO SHOVE, PODNER.. THEY'RE GOING TO DISCONTINUE THE RACE AND COUNTRY SERIES ENTIRELY... ALL FIELD RECORDING TRIPS ARE PERMANENTLY CANCELLED!
HM... TOO BAD.. I SUPPOSE IT HAD TO END SOONER OR LATER... THE MARKET'S BEEN DRYING UP.. THE HICKS ARE ALL STANDIN' IN LINE FOR A BOWL O'SOUP... WHO CAN AFFORD RECORDS?...
...AND THEN THERE'S THE RADIO..

YEAH, TH' WHOLE INDUSTRY'S IN THE WORST SHAPE IT'S EVER BEEN... NOBLE MIGHT NOT EVEN LAST THE YEAR...
AMERICAN RECORD CORPORATION IS PICKIN' UP ALL THE INDEPENDENT SMALL LABELS FOR A SONG... WE'RE PROBABLY NEXT...

LET'S TAKE CARE OF THIS BUSINESS... THE BIG BOYS WANT US TO CUT OUT ALL BUT THE BIGGEST NAME ARTISTS FROM THE CATALOGUE, AND DECIDE WHO MIGHT STILL HAVE ENOUGH COMMERCIAL VALUE FOR FUTURE RECORDING DATES...
...AND I'M SURE THEY WANT TO SEE A VERY SHORT LIST OF NAMES...
'FRAID SO, PAL!

OKAY, LET'S LOOK AT THE SALES FIGURES... CHARLIE HALL... 300 ON NOBLE 1761 230 ON 1780....
HE'S OUT...
TSK... A PITY... I THOUGHT HE WAS HOT... NEXT IS LITTLE JOE JENKINS... 650 ON 1624... 580 ON NOBLE 1605...
HMM... LOOKS LIKE HE'S OUT TOO... BOY, SALES ARE REALLY DOWN FROM LAST YEAR...

WELL, NOBODY'S DOING GREAT... I THINK WE CAN SAVE TIME BY FIRST ELIMINATING THE TOTAL LOSERS... LET'S SEE... HMM... HUMM... OKAY... TOMMY GRADY... HE'S GOT ONE COUPLING ON 1599... SALES: SIXTEEN COPIES!
SIXTEEN! IT'S HARD TO BELIEVE.. HA... WHEW...
MY SCALP ITCHES... G'DAMMIT...

THAT'S WHAT THEY SAID UPSTAIRS... THEY CAN'T AFFORD TO TAKE CHANCES ON THESE UNKNOWNS FROM THE WOODS ANYMORE... FROM NOW ON THE POLICY IS "TRIED AND TRUE" ONLY...
TIMES ARE TOUGH... ALOT OF GOOD TALENT IS GONNA GO DOWN THE DRAIN OUT THERE!
NOTHIN' WE CAN DO... WE MIGHT BE JOININ' 'EM ANY DAY NOW!
YEAH... HA HA HA...

SUMMER, 1975... AN OBSCURE RECORD COLLECTOR IS CANVASSING SMALL SOUTHERN TOWNS IN HOPES OF FINDING THE GOOD STUFF...
GEE, THIS TRIP HAS BEEN A WASH-OUT SO FAR... ALL THE OL' TIMERS ARE DYIN' OFF...
HMM... THIS PLACE LOOKS LIKE IT MIGHT YEILD SOMETHING.. WELL KEPT OLD HOUSE, LACE CURTAINS, FLOWER BEDS...

'MORNING MA'AM.. UH.. I'M LOOKING FOR OLD PHONOGRAPH RECORDS... I COLLECT THEM, YOU SEE, AND.. UH... IF YOU HAVE ANY OF THE KIND I'M LOOKING FOR, I'LL PAY GOOD MONEY FOR THEM...
?

YOU LOOKIN' FO' WHAT, SUH? OL' REKKIDS? HOW OLD YOU MEAN?
I'M AFTER THE REAL OLD STUFF... OL' TIME BLUES, JUG BANDS... THAT KIND OF THING... HEH HEH...
OH... UHUH.. AH SEE... YOU LAK DAT OL' BLUES... OH YES... NOW AH UNNASTAN'..

YEAH, I USETA LIKE DEM OL' BLUES MAHSE'F... ME 'N' MAH HUZZBIN'... HE'S PASSED AWAY... WE'UD WIND UP DAT OL' VIC-TROLA... AH STILL GOT DAT OL' THING 'ROUND IN BACK SOMEWHERE...

OH REALLY? D'YA THINK THE RECORDS MIGHT STILL BE IN IT?

OH... AH DON' KNOW... DEY MIGHT... DAT THING'S BURIED UNDER ALOTTA OL' JUNK... AH REALLY DON' WANNA MESS WIF ALL DAT STUFF TODAY... WHY DON' YOU STOP BACK 'ROUND HERE IN A COUPLA WEEKS, SUH... AH GIT TO IT IN D' MEANTIME... MAH BACK'S KILLIN' ME TADAY...

HMM... WELL, Y'SEE, I'M NOT FROM THIS AREA... I LIVE IN CALIFORNIA, AND... UH... I'M NOT GONNA BE AROUND THIS AREA VERY LONG...

...LIKE I SAID, I'LL PAY A GOOD PRICE FOR ANY RECORDS I FIND, IF THERE THE KIND I'M LOOKIN' FOR...

YOU LAK DEM OL' TIME BLUES, HUH?..

OH YES, MA'AM!

HOW MUCH DEY WUTH TO YOU?

OH... A DOLLAR, MAYBE MORE... IT DEPENDS...

DAT'S PRETTY GOOD FO' A OL' REKKID... DEY MUS' BE ANTEEKS, HUH?

YOU WAIT HERE ON DE PORCH... AH'LL GO AN' SEE IF DEM REKKIDS IS STILL IN DERE... DEM KIDS USETA BUST 'EM UP... BUT AH'LL LOOK ANYHOW... AH AINT LISTEN TO 'EM NO MO' FO' DE LONGEST TAHM...

HERE'S HOPIN'..

FIVE MINUTES OF SUSPENSE LATER...

OH YOU FOUND THEM...

HERE DEY IS, WHUT'S LEFT OF 'M, SUH... HERE, YOU TAKE A LOOK...

OH GOD... "HI" HENRY BROWN ON TOP OF THE STACK.. AN' WHAT'S THIS? CANNON'S JUG STOMPERS, BUT IT'S CRACKED! TOOBAD... WHAT ELSE IS HERE...

I'M SHAKING LIKE A LEAF!!

YEAH, WE USETA LIKE TA LISSEN TO DOSE REKKIDS ON DAT VICTROLA.. MAH HUZZBIN AN' ME... WE'D DANCE... WE DID HAVE SOME FINE TIMES INDEED...

KING DAVID'S JUG BAND... FRANK STOKES... I HIT IT THIS TIME... JOE CALICOTT... TOMMY GRADY... WHO'S HE? NEVER HEARD OF HIM... HERE'S A CHARLEY PATTON! MY HEART!

IS DEM DE TYPE YOU LOOKIN' FO', SUH? DEY KINDA BEAT UP... WE PLAYED 'EM ALOT, Y'KNOW... OH WE HAD DAT VICTROLA IN DE FRONT ROOM FO' YEARS AN' YEARS 'FO' WE GOT DAT RADIO... NOW, 'COURSE, AH GOT MAH TV...

THE COLLECTOR PAYS THE OLD WOMAN A QUARTER APIECE FOR THE RECORDS, BEING AS THEY WERE SOMEWHAT WORN... LATER, BACK HOME IN L.A., HE LISTENS TO HIS NEW FINDS...

WOW! THAT TOMMY GRADY IS TOP NOTCH! I'VE NEVER HEARD OF HIM BEFORE AND HE'S NOT LISTED IN THE DISCOGRAPHY... WONDER IF GARY SEIDEN KNOWS ANYTHING ABOUT HIM... HE'S THE BIGGEST BLUES COLLECTOR ON THE WEST COAST...

PO-O BOY LONG WAY F'UM HOME

I'LL CALL HIM...

TOMMY GRADY?? HM! THE NAME'S A COMPLETE MYSTERY TO ME... WHAT'S THE SERIAL NUMBER?

NOBLE 1599...

HM... COULD I COME OVER AND LISTEN TO IT?

SURE... COME ON OVER...

LATER

AMAZING! THE GUY'S ABSOLUTELY GREAT! EVIDENTLY YOU HAVE THE ONLY KNOW COPY OF THIS RECORD HERE... WOULD YOU CARE TO SELL IT?

MAKE ME AN OFFER...

SEVENTY FIVE...

HMM... I DON' KNOW... HOW 'BOUT A HUNDRED AND A COUPLE OF GOOD RECORDS?

CONDITION COULD BE BETTER, BUT SINCE IT'S THE ONLY COPY EVER FOUND... IT'S A DEAL!!

BEAUTIFUL GUITAR STYLE! TOTALLY UNIQUE!!

A WEEK LATER, GARY SEIDEN HOLDS A MEETING OF BLUES COLLECTORS AND SCHOLARS AT HIS HOME...

OKAY, YOU GUYS... NOW, LISTEN... THIS IS TOMMY GRADY... NOBODY'S EVER HEARD OF HIM... THIS IS THE ONLY COPY THAT'S EVER TURNED UP!

HOW'S CONDITION, GARY?

IT'S LISTENABLE!

LET 'ER ROLL!

PO-O BOY, LO-ONG WAY F'UM HOME... PO-O BOY, LONG WAY F'UM HOME..

...AND THAT'S LIFE!

MUCH TO-DO HAS BEEN MADE OVER THE U.S. ARMY GENERAL OF WORLD-WAR II, GEORGE S. PATTON. WELL, THIS STORY ISN'T ABOUT HIM. THIS ONE'S ABOUT CHARLEY PATTON, A HUMBLE MISSISSIPPI DELTA BLUES SINGER WHO DIED IN 1934. THE ONLY THING THIS PATTON HAD IN COMMON WITH THE RENOWNED GENERAL WAS THAT HIS NAME, TOO, WAS...

PATTON
by R.Crumb 1984
CHARLEY PATTON LIVED MOST OF HIS LIFE ON THE VAST DOCKERY PLANTATION IN THE BOTTOMLANDS OF THE MISSISSIPPI DELTA. HE WAS A RAMBLER, A SHIFTLESS NO-GOOD WHO LIVED OFF WOMEN AND PASSED HIS TIME IN TOTAL IDLENESS.
HE WAS ALSO A GREAT BLUES PERFORMER WHOSE POWERFUL EFFECT ON THE BLUES AND ROCK AND ROLL IS STILL FELT TODAY, THOUGH FEW PEOPLE EVER HEARD OF HIM. THE MUSIC HE PLAYED AND SANG CAN IN NO WAY BE DESCRIBED. IT MUST BE LISTENED TO.
RECOMMENDED LISTENING: "CHARLEY PATTON" YAZOO L-1020, A DOUBLE ALBUM WITH 28 OF HIS RECORDED SONGS
MOST OF THE TIME HE WORKED ALONE, AT PARTIES AND JUKE JOINTS ON THE PLANTATION, OR IN NEAR-BY TOWNS. HE WAS A POPULAR ENTERTAINER WITH THE FIELD-HANDS, WITH HIS DYNAMIC, DRIVING DANCE RHYTHMS, HIS THEATRICS, CLOWNING AND STUNTS LIKE PLAYING THE GUITAR BEHIND HIS BACK. WHEN THE GOOD TIMES WERE READY TO ROLL BACK IN "THE QUARTER," CHARLEY WAS THE MAN THEY WANTED!

For the poor, isolated black people who lived and worked on these plantations, it was a way of life little different from the days of slavery.

But every farm and every town had its musicians. There were songsters and guitar players, fiddlers and banjo pickers.

The blues was a new style of playing when Charley, as a teen-ager, first learned it from an older musician at Dockery's in the early 1900s. His name was Henry Sloan.

Henry Sloan may well have been the early bluesman that W.C. Handy heard while waiting for a train in Tutwiler, Mississippi in 1903.

Handy was a successful schooled musician who was so inspired by the music of the unknown blues singer that he went on to write "The St. Louis Blues," "Yellow Dog Blues," "Memphis Blues" and many other popular tunes using the blues form.

I HATE TO SEE-E-E...
THAT EVENING SUN
GO DOWN...
ST. LOUIS BLUES

THE NEW COMMERCIALIZED BLUES WERE SUNG IN THEATRES AND CABARETS BY REFINED BLACK WOMEN ENTERTAINERS, BACKED BY THE JAZZ BANDS THEN EMERGING ON THE SHOW BIZ SCENE.

THIS TIN-PAN ALLEY BLUES BARELY TOUCHED THE REMOTE RURAL BLACK PEOPLE OF THE DELTA REGION, WHERE THE REAL DOWN-TO-EARTH BLUES CONTINUED TO EVOLVE AS AN INTENSE AND ELOQUENT EXPRESSION OF THEIR LIVES.
AND THEY ALL CAME TO LEARN FROM CHARLEY PATTON. HE WAS RECOGNIZED AS THE HOTTEST BLUES PLAYER BY OTHER MUSICIANS AS WELL AS BY THE CROWDS HE PLAYED FOR.
ROSE CAFE
TOMMY JOHNSON, SON HOUSE, HOWLIN' WOLF, AND OTHER GREAT BLUES SINGERS CAME TO LISTEN AND LEARN FROM PATTON. SOME OF THEM WENT ON TO BECOME LEGENDS IN THEIR OWN RIGHT.

EDDIE "SON" HOUSE

HOWLIN' WOLF

TOMMY JOHNSON

BUKKA WHITE

FORTUNATELY FOR US, PATTON AND SOME OF THE OTHERS WERE APPROACHED BY COMMERCIAL RECORD COMPANY SCOUTS IN THE LATE '20s TO MAKE RECORDS.
SAY, I HEAR YOU PLAY A PRETTY MEAN GUITAR...
VARIETY STORE

THE MUSICIANS WERE PAID TO TRAVEL TO NORTHERN CITIES TO RECORD, OR BROUGHT TO TEMPORARY STUDIOS SET UP IN LOCAL HOTELS.
HERE, HAVE A LITTLE SOMETHIN'
THANK Y' SUH...

THE RECORD COMPANIES RECORDED THESE REGIONAL BLUES SINGERS IN THE HOPES OF SELLING PHONOGRAPH MACHINES TO BLACK PEOPLE.
AND WITH THE PURCHASE OF THIS FINE PHONOGRAPH YOU RECIEVE, FREE OF CHARGE, THREE OF THE LATEST BLUES HITS!!
WE GOT BLIND LEMON
LEROY CARR

WITH THE ONCOMING GREAT DEPRESSION, POOR PEOPLE STOPPED BUYING RECORD PLAYERS ALTOGETHER. WHAT WAS LEFT OF THE RECORDING INDUSTRY LOST INTEREST IN RURAL MUSICIANS AND STAYED WITH THE MORE PROFESSIONAL URBAN BLUESMEN LIKE WASHBOARD SAM, TAMPA RED AND BIG BILL BROONZY.

READY TO CUT SOME WAX TODAY, SAM?
YES SUH, MR. MELROSE...I GOT A COUPLA DOZEN NEW TUNES WORKED UP.

BUT THE EXTENSIVE RECORDING OF COUNTRY BLUES IN THE TWENTIES HAS LEFT US WITH A RICH CULTURAL HERITAGE. FORTUNATELY, MOST OF THE RARE OLD 78s HAVE BEEN REISSUED BY COLLECTORS ON SMALL LABELS, SO THAT WE CAN STILL ENJOY THIS GREAT MUSIC TODAY.

THAT MIGHTY BOY HE'S RUNNIN' WILD THAT MIGHTY BOY
A MAGNIFICENT PERFORMANCE!

ALMOST ALL THE ENTHUSIASM FOR PATTON'S MUSIC NOW COMES FROM WHITE, UPPER-MIDDLE CLASS AFICIONADOES AND A FEW ROCK MUSICIANS. ALL THE RESEARCH ON HIS LIFE HAS BEEN DONE BY WHITE ACADEMICS. IT SEEMS THE OLD BLUES IS STILL TOO VIVID A REMINDER TO BLACK PEOPLE OF AN OPPRESSIVE, "UNCLE TOM" PAST THEY'D RATHER FORGET ABOUT.

EXCUSE ME, MA'AM... THEY TELL ME YOU'RE THE NEICE OF CHARLEY PATTON...
YEH, I AM... MATTA FACT...

IF HE WERE STILL ALIVE, CHARLEY WOULD SURELY CONSIDER ALL THIS FUSS BITTERLY IRONIC. IN HIS TIME NO WHITE PEOPLE LISTENED TO THE RAW KIND OF BLUES HE PLAYED. IN FACT, CHARLEY HAD VERY LITTLE CONTACT WITH WHITES AT ALL.

NONE OF US GAVE MUCH THOUGHT TO THIS BLUES THING UNTIL A FEW YEARS AGO...WE NEVER HEARD THESE PEOPLE SING. WE WERE NEVER THE TYPE OF PLANTATION OWNERS WHO INVITED THEIR HELP TO COME IN AND SING FOR PARTIES....

MRS. KEITH DOCKERY IN AN INTERVIEW, 1979

EVEN RESPECTABLE, CHURCH-GOING BLACKS CONSIDERED HIM AND HIS KIND AS "BAD NIGGERS" AND THE BLUES WAS LOOKED UPON AS THE "DEVIL'S MUSIC".

COME ALONG OBEDIAH!
I GOTTA MOVE IN THE ALLEY

PATTON'S FATHER WAS A HARD-WORKING FARMER AND A DEVOUT CHRISTIAN. HE WAS NOT PLEASED WHEN HE FOUND OUT THAT HIS YOUNG SON WAS PLAYING THAT SINFUL MUSIC.

NO SON O' MINE GONNA PLAY MUSIC IN PLACES WHERE WHORES AN' PIMPS BE CONGREGATIN'!

WHEN STERN WARNINGS FAILED, CHARLEY WAS TAKEN TO THE WOODSHED FOR A HARSHER TASTE OF CHRISTIAN JUSTICE.
I TOLE YOU TO KEEP AWAY FROM THEM LOW-LIFE PEOPLES!

LATER HIS FATHER'S HEART SOFTENED TOWARD THE WAYWARD SON, AND HE BOUGHT CHARLEY A GUITAR.

IN THESE EARLY DAYS HE WAS PLAYING AROUND THE NEIGHBORHOOD WITH THE CHATMON FAMILY, A STRINGBAND GROUP THAT PLAYED RAGTIME, MINSTREL AND TIN-PAN ALLEY TUNES AT SOCIAL AFFAIRS, PICNICS AND PARTIES.

BUT EVEN THIS MUSIC WAS TOO TAME FOR THE INTENSE, SEETHING YOUNG PATTON. HE WAS IRRESISTABLY DRAWN TO THE MORE PASSIONATE AND LESS WHITE MUSIC OF HENRY SLOAN, WITH IT'S MORE COMPLEX RHYTHMS.

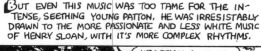

HEY, BOY, YOU WANNA PLAY SOME TUNES? COME ON IN THE HOUSE!

CHARLEY WAS UNDER THE SPELL OF THE BLUES AND FOLLOWED HENRY SLOAN AROUND FOR YEARS, TRYING TO GRASP THE RUDIMENTS OF THIS NEW MUSICAL APPROACH.

HIS FAMILY NEVER SAW HIM MUCH ANY MORE. HE WANDERED ABOUT, PICKING UP THE WAYS OF MIDNIGHT RAMBLERS, DRINKING HEAVILY, AND LIVING OFF WOMEN WHO COOKED IN WHITE PEOPLE'S KITCHENS.

SHE BRING ME TH'MEAT
SHE BRING ME LARD...

WHEN THINGS WENT BAD HE WOULD REPENT AND TAKE UP THE BIBLE, AND RESOLVE HENCEFORTH TO PUT HIS LIFE IN THE SERVICE OF THE LORD BY PREACHING THE GOSPEL.

THESE CONVERSIONS NEVER LASTED LONG. CHARLEY COULDN'T STAY AWAY FROM THE LOOSE WOMEN, THE GOOD TIMES, AND THE MOONSHINE LIQUOR.

PATTON WAS KNOWN FOR BEING "HIGH-TEMPERED," "FLIGHTY," AND FOR HAVING A "BIG MOUTH" WHICH OFTEN GOT HIM INTO FIGHTS, THOUGH HE WAS ILL-EQUIPPED TO DEFEND HIMSELF PHYSICALLY.

SOMETIME AROUND 1931 SOMEONE TRIED TO CUT HIS THROAT, BUT PATTON SURVIVED WITH AN UGLY SCAR.

IT IS ALSO WELL-KNOWN THAT HE FOUGHT VIOLENTLY WITH HIS WOMEN. "IF THOSE WOMEN MADE HIM MAD, HE'D JUS' FIGHT, AND, YOU KNOW, KNOCK 'EM OUT WITH THAT OLD GUITAR," CLAIMED AN OLD ACQUAINTANCE.

"I KNEW ONE OF HIS WIVES, NAMED LIZZIE, AND SHE SAID ONE DAY HE JUST WALKED OFF WITH HIS GUITAR AND NEVER CAME BACK. SHE HADN'T DONE NOTHIN' TO HIM. HE HADN'T DONE NOTHIN' TO HER."

"WELL, AFTER THAT SHE WOULD TALK ALOT ABOUT HOW MEAN HE WAS. BUT SHE KEPT HIS PICTURE RIGHT THERE ON HER MANTEL. SHE KEPT IT 'TIL THE DAY SHE DIED."

MOST OF THE BLUES RECORDED AT HIS FIRST SESSIONS IN 1929 WERE CELEBRATIONS OF THE WILD TIMES, BOASTS OF HIS SEXUAL ADVENTURES, JEALOUS WOMEN, TWO-TIMING WOMEN, DRINKING AND CAROUSING. IN "IT WONT BE LONG" PATTON SINGS, "GOT A LONG TALL WOMAN, TALL LIKE A CHERRY TREE, SHE GETS UP 'FORE DAY AND SHE PUT THE THING ON ME."

IN "TOM RUSHEN BLUES" HE SINGS ABOUT GETTING DRUNK AND THROWN IN JAIL. "I LAY DOWN LAST NIGHT, HOPIN' I WOULD HAVE MY PEACE, BUT WHEN I WOKE UP, TOM RUSHEN WAS SHAKIN' ME. WHEN YOU GET IN TROUBLE, NO USE TO SCREAMIN' AN' CRYIN', TOM RUSHEN WILL TAKE YOU BACK TO PRISON HOUSE FLYIN'."

ONE OF PATTON'S MOST POPULAR RECORDS, "HIGH WATER EVERYWHERE" WAS A WAILING LAMENT ABOUT THE MISSISSIPPI RIVER FLOOD OF 1927. THE GREAT RIVER OVERFLOWED THE LEVEES AND WASHED OVER THE LAND. "BACKWATER DONE ROSE AT SUMNER, DROVE POOR CHARLEY DOWN THE LINE, LORD, I TELL THE WORLD THE WATER DONE JUMPED THROUGH THIS TOWN."

"IT WAS FIFTY MEN AND CHILDREN COME TO SINK AND DROWN, OH LORDIE, WOMEN AND GROWN MEN DOWN, OH WOMEN AND CHILDREN SINKIN' DOWN."

"I COULDN'T SEE NOBODY HOME AND WASN'T NO ONE TO BE FOUND."

SEVERAL OF HIS SONGS WERE ABOUT MOVING ON, LEAVING A WOMAN, WANDERING... "I'M GOIN' AWAY, SWEET MAMA, DON'T YOU WANT TO GO? TAKE GOD TO TELL WHEN I'LL BE BACK HERE ANYMORE." (SCREAMIN' AND HOLLERIN' THE BLUES)
"SOME THESE DAY, YOU GONNA MISS YOUR HONEY, I KNOW YOU'RE GONNA MISS ME, SWEET DREAMS, FOR I BE GOIN' AWAY." (SOME THESE DAYS I'LL BE GONE)

MOSTLY HE SANG ABOUT HAVING A GOOD TIME; "I LIKE TO FUSS AND FIGHT, I LIKE TO FUSS AND FIGHT, LORD, AND GET SLOPPY DRUNK OFF A BOTTLE AND BALL AND WALK THE STREETS ALL NIGHT." (ELDER GREEN BLUES)

BUT THE WORDS WERE NOT THE MAIN POINT OF PATTON'S MUSIC. THEY ARE BARELY UNDERSTANDABLE MOST OF THE TIME AND IMPOSSIBLE SOMETIMES. EVEN SON HOUSE HAS SAID THAT CHARLEY'S WORDS WERE DIFFICULT TO MAKE OUT. CHARLEY WAS PLAYING DANCE MUSIC MOSTLY, FOR SATURDAY NIGHT PARTIES WHERE THERE WAS ALOT OF NOISE AND CARRYING ON, AND POTENT CORN LIQUOR FLOWED FREELY.

HIS VOICE WAS USED AS A MUSICAL INSTRUMENT. HE SHOUTED, SCREAMED, BELLOWED AND GROWLED. HE BEAT ON HIS GUITAR, POUNDING OUT HEAVY RHYTHMS FOR LONG STRETCHES, SOMETIMES HALF AN HOUR, WHILE THE CROWD DANCED.

HAYS McMULLEN, A CONTEMPORARY OF PATTON'S, REMEMBERS: "I'VE SEEN CHARLEY PATTON JUST BUMP ON HIS GUITAR 'STEAD OF PICKIN' IT... I BUMPED ON IT TOO. COLORED FOLKS GET DANCIN' GONNA DANCE ALL NIGHT AND I'D GET TIRED, SO I'D GET 'EM GOOD 'N' STARTED, YOU KNOW, I'D BE HOLLERIN', AND THEN I'D JUST BE KNOCKIN' ON THE BOX WHEN THE MUSIC GET GOING."

PATTON'S BEST FRIEND SEEMS TO HAVE BEEN WILLIE BROWN. AFTER YEARS OF HANGING OUT WITH CHARLEY AND STUDYING HIS WAY OF SINGING AND PLAYING, WILLIE BROWN BECAME A TOP-NOTCH DELTA BLUES MUSICIAN HIMSELF.

THEY SOMETIMES PLAYED TOGETHER FOR DANCES, WILLIE FILLING IN THE RHYTHM WHILE CHARLIE THREW HIS GUITAR UP IN THE AIR, CAUGHT IT BETWEEN HIS LEGS, AND RAN THROUGH HIS OTHER TRICKS TO AMUSE THE CROWD.

TOMMY JOHNSON, FROM SOUTHERN MISSISSIPPI, ALSO CAME TO LEARN FROM THESE TWO GREAT BLUES MASTERS. BACK HOME, HE TOLD HIS BROTHER LEDELL THAT HE HAD LEARNED THE BLUES BY SELLING HIS SOUL TO THE DEVIL.

"I ASKED HIM HOW," LEDELL LATER RECOUNTED. "HE SAID, IF YOU WANT TO LEARN HOW TO PLAY ANYTHING AND LEARN HOW TO MAKE SONGS YOURSELF, YOU TAKE YOUR GUITAR AND YOU GO TO WHERE A ROAD CROSSES THAT WAY, WHERE A CROSSROAD IS. BE SURE TO GET THERE JUST A LITTLE 'FORE TWELVE O'CLOCK THAT NIGHT...YOU HAVE YOUR GUITAR AND BE PLAYING A PIECE SITTING THERE BY YOURSELF."

"A BIG BLACK MAN WILL WALK UP THERE AND TAKE YOUR GUITAR, AND HE'LL TUNE IT AND THEN HE'LL PLAY A PIECE AND HAND IT BACK TO YOU. THAT'S THE WAY I LEARNED HOW TO PLAY ANYTHING I WANT."

ANOTHER GREAT DELTA SINGER WHO CAME TO KNOW CHARLEY PATTON WAS SON HOUSE. HOUSE HAD JUST GOTTEN OUT OF PARCHMAN, A MISSISSIPPI PENAL FARM, AFTER A TWO-YEAR TERM FOR SHOOTING AND KILLING A MAN IN A FIGHT IN 1928. PATTON LIKED SON HOUSE'S MUSIC AND INVITED HIM TO COME ALONG TO A RECORDING SESSION IN GRAFTON, WISCONSIN, WITH HIMSELF AND WILLIE BROWN.

ALSO GOING ALONG WAS LOUISE JOHNSON, A YOUNG GIRL WHO PLAYED A POWERFUL BOOGIE WOOGIE PIANO BLUES IN A LOCAL JUKE JOINT. PATTON WAS IMPRESSED WITH HER PLAYING AS WELL AS HER LOOKS AND HAD BEGUN COURTING HER.

HOUSE BRAGGED YEARS LATER HOW HE'D STOLEN THE GIRL PIANO PLAYER AWAY FROM CHARLEY ON THE TRIP UP TO GRAFTON; "CHARLEY, HE'S MAD. HE'S SITTING IN THE FRONT. RIGHT ALONG I COMMENCE TO LEANING OVER TALKING TRASH TO HER. I SAY, 'I REALLY KINDA LIKE YOU, GAL,' AND WE TAKE ANOTHER BIG SWALLOW."

"SO THEY HAVE A LITTLE HOTEL THERE IN GRAFTON WHERE THE RECORDERS STAY AT....SO I COME UP, AND THEY'S TELLING ME 'BOUT THE MAN DONE BEEN HERE AND GIVE US ALL THE KEYS. I SAID, 'WHERE DID HE GO, 'CAUSE HE AIN' GIVE ME NO KEY,' AND SO LOUISE SAY, 'YES HE DID.' I SAY, 'NO HE DIDN'T. SAY, 'I GOT ME AND YOUR KEY.' I SAY, 'OH, OH, THAT'S IT THEN'...AND THAT'S THE WAY IT HAPPENED...ME AND HER STAYED IN OUR LITTLE ROOM."

BY THE MID 'TWENTIES A YOUNGER CROP OF BLUES PLAYERS WERE COMING UP STRONG IN THE DELTA. AMONG THESE WAS A HIGH-STRUNG TEEN-AGER NAMED ROBERT JOHNSON. HE LIVED NEAR WILLIE BROWN AND STARTED COMING AROUND TO PICK UP THE BLUES FROM BROWN, PATTON, AND SON HOUSE.

THE OLDER MUSICIANS DISDAINED YOUNG JOHNSON'S FALTERING EFFORTS ON THE GUITAR. WHEN THEY WERE DRUNK AND FEELING MEAN, PATTON, BROWN AND HOUSE WOULD OFTEN RIDICULE HIS PLAYING, FINALLY FORCING HIM TO RUN AWAY FROM THE AREA.

A YEAR OR SO LATER, ROBERT JOHNSON RETURNED AND DAZZLED THEM ALL WITH A NEW BLUES GUITAR STYLE USING A DRIVING, HEAVY BASS BEAT THAT HE HAD CREATED ON HIS OWN. IN 1936 AND '37 JOHNSON WOULD RECORD SOME OF THE GREATEST COUNTRY BLUES OF ALL TIME.

PATTON'S HEALTH WAS SERIOUSLY FAILING BY 1930. A HARD, FAST LIFE OF DRINKING CORN LIQUOR AND CHAIN-SMOKING WAS BEGINNING TO TELL ON HIM. HE WAS PROBABLY ONLY IN HIS MID-FORTIES BY THIS TIME.

HIS SONGS BEGAN TAKING ON A MORE OMINOUS, DESPERATE NOTE. IN "BIRD NEST BOUND" HE SEEMED TO YEARN FOR SECURITY AND STABILITY. "IF I WAS A BIRD, MAMA, I WOULD FIND A NEST IN THE HEART OF TOWN, SO WHEN THE TOWN GET LONESOME, I'D BE BIRDNEST BOUND."

"OH I REMEMBER ONE MORNIN', STANDIN' IN MY BABY'S DOOR... BOY, YOU KNOW WHAT SHE TOLD ME? LOOKA HERE, PAPA CHARLEY, I DON'T WANT YOU NO MORE."

FROM 1930 ON PATTON LIVED WITH A WOMAN NAMED BERTHA LEE, WHO COOKED FOR WHITE FAMILIES IN THE NEIGHBORHOOD. THE COUPLE MOVED AROUND, HAD VIOLENT ARGUMENTS. PATTON BLAMED HIS FAILING HEALTH ON HER. HE ACCUSED HER OF STARVING HIM. THEY'D GET DRUNK AND GO AT EACH OTHER IN VIOLENT FITS OF RAGE.

BUT THEY STAYED TOGETHER, AND SANG TOGETHER AT PATTON'S LAST RECORDING SESSION IN 1934. IN JANUARY OF THAT YEAR W.R. CALAWAY OF THE AMERICAN RECORD CORPORATION BEGAN LOOKING FOR PATTON TO CUT SOME NEW RECORDS. THE INDUSTRY WAS BEGINNING TO REVIVE SOMEWHAT FROM THE DEPRESSION.

HE FINALLY LOCATED CHARLEY AND BERTHA LEE IN THE LITTLE TOWN OF BELZONI, MISSISSIPPI. THEY WERE BOTH IN JAIL, HAVING BEEN INVOLVED IN A DRUNKEN FRACAS AT A HOUSE PARTY. CALAWAY BAILED THEM OUT.

HE TOOK THEM WITH HIM BACK TO NEW YORK CITY. PATTON WAS IN VERY BAD SHAPE. HE WAS WEAK, SHORT OF BREATH, AND HAD LOST MUCH OF HIS PERFORMING POWER.
OMAT

HIS LAST RECORDINGS REVEAL HIS AWARENESS THAT HIS LIFE MAY BE CUT SHORT. IN "POOR ME" HE SINGS, "DON'T THE MOON LOOK PRETTY, SHININ' DOWN THROUGH THE TREE. I CAN SEE BERTHA LEE, LORD, BUT SHE CANT SEE ME."

HE AND BERTHA LEE SANG TOGETHER ON THE SONG "OH DEATH." ON THIS RECORD YOU CAN VIVIDLY HEAR THE NEARNESS OF DEATH AND CHARLEY'S HORROR IN THE FACE OF IT.

OH HUSH
OH HUSH
SOMEBODY IS CALLING ME...

OH HUSH
OH HUSH
SOMEBODY IS CALLING ME
OH LAWDY OH HUSH
OH HUSH
SOMEBODY IS—
CALLING YOU—
LORD I KNOW, LORD I KNOW, MY TIME AIN'T LONG

SEVERAL WEEKS AFTER THIS PATTON LAY ON HIS DEATH BED. FOR A WEEK HE LAID THERE PREACHING, REPEATING OVER AND OVER HIS FAVORITE SERMON, RECORDED BY HIM IN 1929 UNDER THE PSEUDONYM ELDER J.J. HADLEY; "WHEN HE COME DOWN HIS HAIR GONNA BE LIKE LAMB'S WOOL AND HIS EYES LIKE FLAMES OF FIRE, AND EVERY MAN GONNA KNOW HE'S THE SON OF THE TRUE LIVING GOD...'ROUND HIS SHOULDERS GOIN' TO BE A RAINBOW AND HIS FEET LIKE FINE BRASS... AND HE'S GONNA HAVE A TREE BEFORE THE TWELVE MANNERS OF FOOD, AND THE LEAVES GONNA BE HEALING DAMNATION, AND THE BIG ROCK THAT YOU CAN SIT BEHIND, THE WIND CAN'T BLOW AT YOU NO MORE, AND YOU GONNA COUNT THE FOUR-AND-TWENTY ELDERS THAT YOU CAN SIT DOWN AND TALK WITH, AND THAT YOU CAN TALK ABOUT YOUR TROUBLE THAT YOU COME— WORLD YOU JUST COME FROM."

CHARLEY PATTON DIED ON APRIL 28TH, 1934. HIS DEATH WENT UNREPORTED IN THE LOCAL AND NATIONAL PRESS.

A LARGE PORTION OF THE INFORMATION FOR THIS STORY CAME FROM ROBERT PALMER'S FINE BOOK, "DEEP BLUES," PUBLISHED IN 1981 BY VIKING PRESS.

HUNTING FOR OLD RECORDS

A TRUE STORY by R. CRUMB 1999

THE YEAR WAS 1960. THE AUTHOR WAS IN HIS LATE TEENS, LIVING WITH HIS PARENTS IN DOVER, DELAWARE.

I LOVE THIS OLD MUSIC! I MUST FIND MORE OLD BLUES AND JAZZ RECORDS FROM THE 'TWENTIES!

AFTER A FRUITLESS DAY OF KNOCKING ON DOORS IN THE BLACK SECTION, I WAS ABOUT TO CALL IT QUITS...

HAVEN'T SEEN A SINGLE WORTHWHILE RECORD TODAY... I'LL TRY ONE MORE HOUSE...

UHH... HM, WHY YES, IN FACT I *DO* HAVE SOME OLD RECORDS... HOW MUCH DO YOU PAY?

I CAN PAY TEN CENTS, MAYBE A QUARTER FOR A *REALLY* GOOD ONE...

THAT'S NOT MUCH... BUT I S'POSE YOU CAN HAVE A LOOK... YOU MAY COME IN...

...A BUNCH OF SWING BANDS FROM THE 'THIRTIES... NO INTEREST TO ME.... BUT *WHAT'S THIS!?!* "GOOFUS" AND "HAPPY" BY SLIM LAMAR'S SOUTHERNERS ON THE LATE 'TWENTIES VICTOR SCROLL LABEL!!

WELL, I—UH—I ONLY FOUND ONE THAT I'M INTERESTED IN... THIS ONE HERE...

HOW MUCH IS IT WORTH TO YOU?

WOULD YOU TAKE TEN CENTS FOR IT?

OH NO, DEFINITELY NOT! NOSSIR!

WELL, THEN, UM... HOW 'BOUT TWENTY-FIVE CENTS?

I *KNOW* THAT RECORD IS WORTH MORE'N *25 CENTS*! YOU THINK I WAS BORN YESTERDAY??

WULL, I JUST CAN'T *PAY* ANYMORE THAN THAT... I DON'T HAVE MUCH* MONEY, AND I—

I'M NOT GONNA SELL YOU THAT RECORD FOR NO 25 CENTS, YOU MAY REST ASSURED!

B-BUT—

SNATCH!

* TRUE—I HAD A HANDFUL OF CHANGE TO MY NAME! I HAD NEVER PAID MORE THAN 25 CENTS FOR A RECORD!

I WENT AWAY BUT RETURNED A WEEK LATER WITH A DOLLAR IN MY POCKET, DETERMINED TO POSSESS THAT RARE AND CURIOUS RECORD.

HELLO, IT'S ME AGAIN... HEH HEH... YOU REMEMBER THAT RECORD I WANTED TO BUY? I HAVE MORE MONEY NOW, SO, UM, WILL YOU TAKE A *DOLLAR* FOR IT??

ONE DOLLAR?! NO, I THINK NOT!

YOU KNOW IT'S NOT *RIGHT* WHAT YOU ARE DOIN'.. YOU THINK I'M JUST AN IGNORANT OLD COLORED WOMAN AN' YOU CAN TAKE ADVANTAGE, BUT I *KNOW* THAT RECORD IS WORTH ALOT OF MONEY AN' I'M NOT GONNA LET NO YOUNG WHITE BOY CHEAT *ME!!*

BUT A DOLLAR IS ALL I'VE GOT, THAT'S THE GOD'S HONEST TRUTH!

NOPE, SORRY... GOOD DAY TO YOU!

@★NW!!

BARBER SHOP

I NEVER *DID* GET THAT RECORD OFF OF THAT OLD LADY!

OVER THE YEARS I ASKED OTHER COLLECTORS ABOUT SLIM LAMAR'S SOUTHERNERS.

THE TUNES WERE "GOOFUS" AND "HAPPY"...

SLIM LAMAR? DOESN'T RING A BELL...

DID I DREAM IT??

TWENTY-FIVE YEARS LATER I FINALLY FOUND ANOTHER COPY ON A DEALER'S AUCTION LIST.

IT COST ME FIFTY DOLLARS TO WIN THIS BABY— LET'S PUT IT ON THE MACHINE AND FINALLY HEAR WHAT IT SOUNDS LIKE!

THIS IS A *GREAT* RECORD!!

CRAZY, ECCENTRIC JAZZ!

HERE'S THE LABEL TO PROVE THAT I OWN THIS AMAZING RECORD!

VE

Orthophonic Recording

VICTOR

For best results use Victor Needles

21710-A

GOOFUS

(Bob Nolan)

Slim Lamar's Southerners

under the direction of Bob Nolan

Dance Orchestra with vocal refrain

VICTOR TALKING MACHINE CO.

VE

...AND IT'S ALMOST *MINT!*

STRANGE, THOUGH—EVERY TIME I LISTEN TO IT, I SEE THAT OLD BLACK LADY'S ANGRY FACE...

YOU THINK I'M JUST AN IGNORANT OLD COLORED WOMAN...

END

SPENCER, Tn.
My Grandparents lived a simple life way the hell out in the middle of nowhere no distractions, no electricity.. It was so quiet there. And they never said much — I like to think it was because they were so content with their little piece of paradise.
follow panel number sequence:
PANEL
①

WHOOH! IT SURE IS QUIET!
YE-UH
SHORE IS.
bzt
②

They were like a couple of Zen Masters
hmm
③
COUNTRY
The "PROGRESS" Song
4u
4me
C'MON CUZINS 'N SING ALONG
⑧
This piece of heaven's gone. I'm sure you know the tune

CIRCA 1970.
LOOKING BACK, I see now that this was Nirvana, out there with them. Although back then, when I'd visit, I found the silence unsettling and kinda scary. Until the day I began to listen very carefully..
scree
woo
twink
nee-a nee-a
erwa
zurp
fs
dzzt
chip
snep
oka
moo
caw caw caw
dku
riss-sheru
boop eee
R-R RRR
tett
hiss
QUIET MY FOOT! IT'S....
COUNTRY MUSIC
nrk
ahg
scritch scratch
heh heh heh heh
inch inch
COUNTRY MUSIC!
pt
WHY, THAT'S A GOOD IDEE, CARILUN! WE COULD DO FER SOME COUNTRY MUSIC. GO ON IN THERE AND FIRE-UP THE OLD VICTROL-Y!
IT'S BEEN TOO AWFUL QUIET.
OH, I GET IT... COUNTRY,
AS IN SOUSA!
as in The Stars and Stripes forever
DA-DAAA DAT-DAT DAAA DAT-DAT-DAAA
YE-UH
WOOH
MUSIC
CARRY ON.
they pushed the old folks out · to bring the new road thru ___ ___ ___.
© C. Tyler 2002/3

Maurice Vellekoop

SNAp

July 6, 1966
8:30 AM

The leg pulls itself out of the bed and sets the foot down on the floor

Soon it is joined by the other foot. They rest a moment.

Together, with the aid of the arms, they raise the tired, ungraceful body from the bed.

Slippers slide onto the feet and the figure lopes along toward the bathroom.

The head, like a periscope, swivels on the neck and peers into the mirror.

A face is reflected back.

Long seconds pass before recognition strikes in the brain.

Finally the brain sends out an urgent message-- "I am Simon Matchcard."

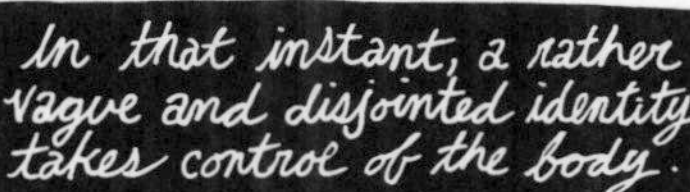

In that instant, a rather vague and disjointed identity takes control of the body.

"I am Simon Matchcard."
CLICK

Mother--it's me. I'm coming in with your breakfast.
KNOCK KNOCK

SETH *excerpt from* Clyde Fans

SETH *excerpt from* Clyde Fans

They were bothering me again.

Who? Who was bothering you?
The people who visit my room.

There are no people in your room. What are you talking about?

The ones who come every night--out of the light socket.

Not this nonsense again.
The doors are locked. The windows are locked. There are no people coming in here at night.

I already told you--they don't come in through the window, they use the light socket!

And they steal from me. They take my best things.

SETH *excerpt from* Clyde Fans

Where are you getting this from? I've never heard you say that before.
Oh, don't be stupid! I've always said it.
ISSUES

All right, all right--calm down. You were saying that your father always yelled at you.

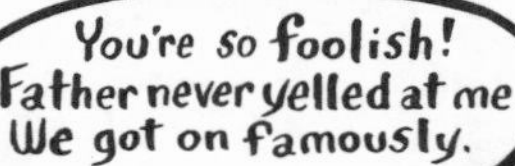
You're so foolish! Father never yelled at me. We got on famously.

I can see you're in one of your moods. Let's just forget it.

Where is the little fellow?

What little fellow? What are you talking about now?

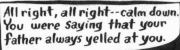

SETH
excerpt from Clyde Fans

SETH *excerpt from* Clyde Fans

I'm a stupid fool... losing my mind.

No mother, no! It's not true! It's just a spell. We all get them when we get older.

Here--let me put your radio on for you.
KLIC

You rest. I'm going to take these dishes downstairs.

I have some things to do this morning but we'll play a game of cards later.

Five years ago, when I thought of mother passing on... I thought it would kill me.

Now, if I honestly look into myself, I realize (rather sadly) that my terror has eased.
1966

Month by month, year by year, she has been drifting.

Where is the mother I knew? And who knew me?
TSSS

I can't seem to touch her with words anymore.

It's as if she's being viewed through frosted glass.

I suppose I've already done some mourning. Much of her has already died.

When she does finally go... it will almost be like something that had happened in the past.

SETH *excerpt from* Clyde Fans

HAZEL
EYES

AFTER FORTY-FIVE MINUTES OF WAITING, TARA McLAUGHLIN CHECKS HER PHONE TO MAKE SURE SHE TURNED THE RINGER BACK ON WHEN SHE WOKE UP EARLIER THIS EVENING. SHE THEN LIFTS THE RECEIVER AND, UPON CONFIRMING THAT THE LINE HAS NOT GONE DEAD, PLACES IT BACK ON THE CRADLE.

IN THE PAST, TARA WOULD HAVE SIMPLY CALLED NICOLE OR COREY IF THEY DIDN'T PHONE WHEN THEY WERE SUPPOSED TO, BUT NOW IT'S BECOME A MATTER OF DIGNITY. SHE'S BEEN TESTING THEM LATELY, COUNTING THE DAYS THAT PASS BEFORE ONE OF THEM CALLS OR STOPS BY.

SHE DOESN'T SPEND TIME WITH EITHER OF THEM INDIVIDUALLY ANYMORE, THOUGH SHE SUSPECTS THE TWO OF THEM ARE STILL AS INSEPARABLE AS THEY ALL WERE BEFORE.
R-RING!

HI.
SURE, OKAY. YEAH. UH-HUH... 9:30.

SHE WAITS FOR NICOLE AND COREY AT THE DOWNTOWN BAR THEY SUGGESTED, SURROUNDED BY BUSINESSMEN AND LAWYERS WATCHING FOOTBALL AND THROWING DARTS.

HER FRIENDS SHOW UP TOGETHER, HALF AN HOUR LATE.
HEY TARA!
SORRY, SORRY, SORRY.

YEAH, SORRY WE'RE LATE, BUT NICOLE HAD TO CHANGE HER OUTFIT LIKE FIVE TIMES.
I CAN'T HELP IT!

THAT'S WHAT HAPPENS WHEN I'M P.M.S.-ING. BESIDES, YOU'RE THE ONE WHO HAD TO SEE THE END OF "NASH BRIDGES."
I WAS **WAITING** FOR YOU!
HAPPY HOUR

AFTER A FEW MINUTES OF SMALL TALK, TARA LOSES INTEREST IN HER FRIENDS' CONVERSATION AND IMAGINES THE FASCINATING DISCUSSIONS TAKING PLACE ELSEWHERE IN THE BAR.

AT THIS POINT, I'M NOT SURE THAT SETTLING DOWN IS WHAT I WANT.
OF COURSE NOT. I AGREE, BUT...
YOU CAN'T JUST COMPLETELY WRITE OFF AN ARTIST OF THAT CALIBER WHEN THEY FALTER...

SHE BECOMES DESPONDENT AS THE TALK TURNS TO NICOLE AND COREY'S BOYFRIENDS. BEING SINGLE, TARA CONSIDERS HER EXPECTED ROLE IN THIS EXCHANGE TO BE THAT OF THE ATTENTIVE AUDIENCE.

I WAS SO PISSED AT HIM, BUT THEN HE DID THE **SWEETEST** THING.
FOOT MASSAGE?

ALTHOUGH THE BREAK-UP OCCURRED OVER A YEAR AGO, TARA'S LAST BOYFRIEND AL HAS, MUCH TO HER CHAGRIN, REMAINED IN CLOSE CONTACT WITH NICOLE AND COREY, AS WELL AS THEIR BOYFRIENDS.

HE BROUGHT OVER HIS KEYBOARD AND PLAYED THIS NEW SONG HE WROTE.
CUTE! THAT REMINDS ME OF WHEN...

DISCRETION WAS NEVER HIS STRONG SUIT, AND TARA WORRIES OFTEN ABOUT AL REGALING HER FRIENDS WITH THE SORDID DETAILS OF THEIR RELATIONSHIP. IN PARTICULAR, SHE REGRETS EVER CONFIDING IN HIM HER EROTIC ATTACHMENT TO THE SCENT OF OLD BOOKS.

...AND ONCE SHE ACTUALLY WANTED TO LAY AN OPEN COPY OF BAUDELAIRE ACROSS HER FACE WHILE WE FUCKED!

AT A LULL IN THE CONVERSATION, TARA ATTEMPTS TO RE-FOCUS HER ATTENTION AND RECTIFY HER CONSPICUOUS SILENCE.

YOU KNOW, I HAD THE WEIRDEST DREAM THE OTHER NIGHT.

"IT WAS ABOUT AL. HE'D COMMITTED SOME CRIME AND WAS BEING SENT AWAY TO LIVE ON A DESERTED ISLAND SOMEWHERE. WE HAD JUST A FEW MINUTES TO TALK BEFORE THE COPS WERE GONNA HAUL HIM AWAY."

"HE TOLD ME THE THING HE WAS GONNA MISS THE MOST WAS LOOKING AT MY HAZEL EYES. I TOLD HIM THE THING I WAS GONNA MISS THE MOST WAS FEELING HIS SMOOTH SKIN."

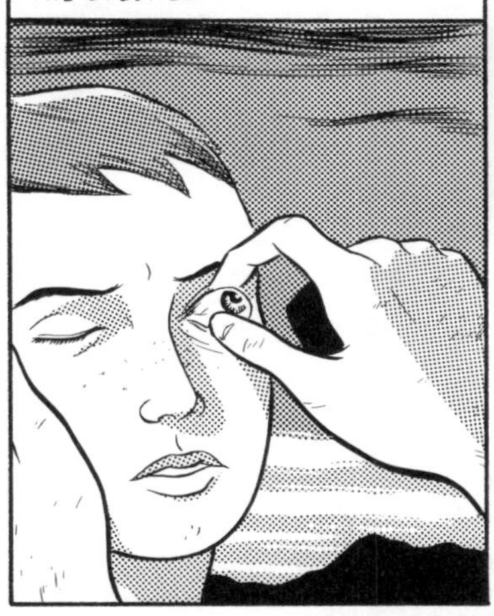
"SO WE AGREED TO TRADE. HE STUCK HIS FINGERS INTO MY LEFT SOCKET AND PULLED OUT THE EYEBALL."

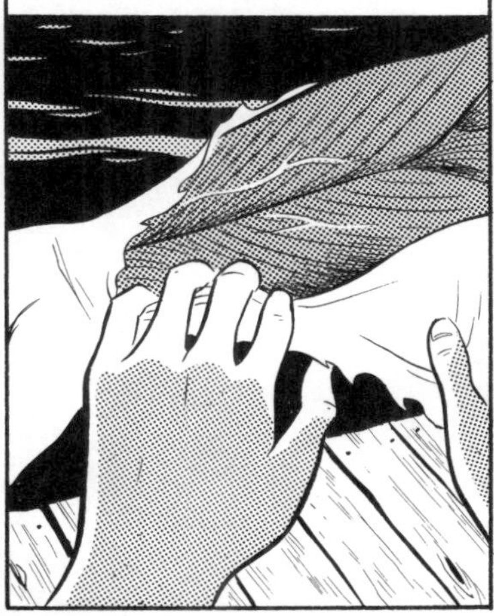
"THEN I DUG MY NAILS INTO HIS ARM AND PEELED OFF A CHUNK OF SKIN. THERE WASN'T ANY BLOOD OR ANYTHING..."

TARA'S VOICE TRAILS OFF AS SHE NOTICES NICOLE AND COREY EXCHANGE BRIEF, KNOWING GLANCES.
WHAT?
WHAT WAS THAT LOOK FOR?

NOTHING! IT'S JUST... YOU'RE ALWAYS HAVING THESE FREAKY DREAMS. THEY'RE SO... VIVID.
YEAH, I HARDLY EVER HAVE DREAMS LIKE THAT. IT'S ALMOST LIKE A MOVIE OR SOMETHING.

TARA FEELS A SWELL OF DEFENSIVENESS, BUT MAKES A CONCERTED EFFORT TO REMAIN AGREEABLE.
WELL, I TOLD YOU IT WAS PRETTY WEIRD.

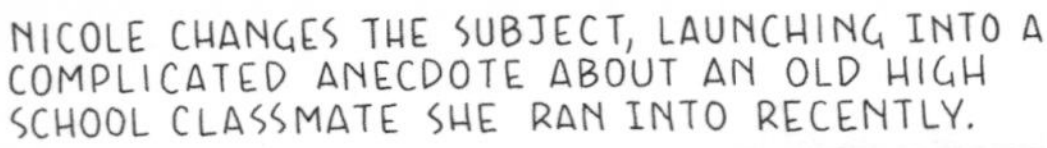
NICOLE CHANGES THE SUBJECT, LAUNCHING INTO A COMPLICATED ANECDOTE ABOUT AN OLD HIGH SCHOOL CLASSMATE SHE RAN INTO RECENTLY.

...AND SHE WAS LIKE, "I HEAR YOU'RE MODELING," AND I WAS LIKE, "YEAH? I HEAR YOU'RE A *BITCH!*"
HAHAHA

GOD... YOU REALLY SAID THAT TO HER?

WELL, I MEAN, THAT'S WHAT I WAS *THINKING*, OKAY TARA?
OH.

I-I SHOULD PROBABLY GET GOING. I'M TEMPING TOMORROW.

AFTER LESS THAN AN HOUR AND A HALF, THE THREE FRIENDS DECIDE TO CALL IT A NIGHT.

AS SHE DRIVES AWAY, TARA CAN'T HELP BUT CONSIDER THE CONVERSATION THAT IS UNDOUBTEDLY TAKING PLACE IN NICOLE'S CAR AT THAT MOMENT.

...SHE DOESN'T SAY ANY-THING ALL NIGHT, THEN SHE GOES ON AND ON ABOUT THAT CREEPY DREAM.

RIGHT... YOU MEAN HER QUOTE UNQUOTE *DREAM*.
HAHAHA! I KNOW... IT'S LIKE, IF YOU WANNA MAKE SHIT UP, WRITE A BOOK OR SOMETHING!

"AND PLUS, QUIT PATHETICALLY TALKING ABOUT A GUY WHO **DUMPED** YOU!"
"YEAH...LIKE TWO YEARS AGO!"
...FUCKING **HATE** YOU...

TARA DRIVES TO AN OLDER, EMPTIER BAR ON THE OUTSKIRTS OF TOWN AND EMBARKS ON A SERIES OF DRINKS, ALTERNATING VODKA GIMLETS AND BEER.
...BUT I MEAN, BACK IN SCHOOL, ME AND THIS GIRL AMBER WERE **CLOSE**. THAT'S WHY IT PISSED ME OFF SO MUCH.
MM-HMN?

SO ANYWAY, LAST WEEK I'M OVER AT LUCKY'S, AND GUESS WHO I BUMP INTO? IT'S AMBER, AND SHE JUST MOVED BACK FROM BOSTON.

SO SHE STARTS TALKING TO ME AND SHE'S LIKE, "I HEAR YOU'RE MODELING," AND I'M LIKE, "YEAH? I HEAR YOU'RE A **BITCH**!"
HMM.

HEY, LOOK AT MY EYES. SOMEBODY TOLD ME ONCE, "I CAN OVERLOOK ALL YOUR SHIT BECAUSE OF THEM."
HA HA
EXIT

YOU EVER HAVE THAT? WHERE JUST ONE GOOD THING ABOUT SOMEONE IS ENOUGH?
I DON'T KNOW... I GUESS...

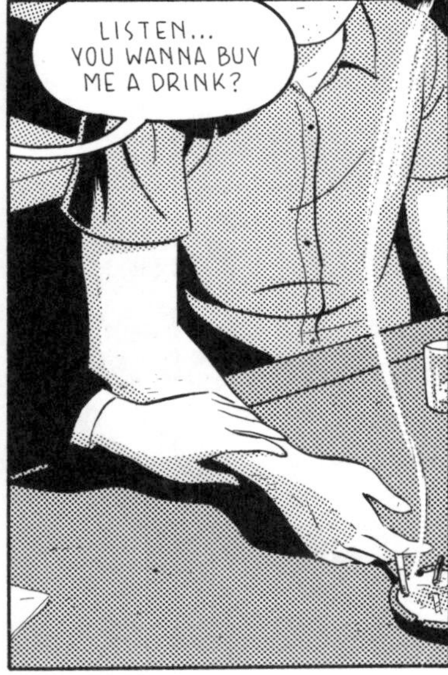
LISTEN... YOU WANNA BUY ME A DRINK?

I BETTER NOT. SORRY...

THE ROAD BLURS IN AND OUT OF FOCUS AS TARA DRIVES AWAY FROM THE BAR. SHE TRIES TO CONCENTRATE ON THE LINES AND REFLECTORS, BUT BEGINS IMAGINING HERSELF ON A DIFFERENT ROAD, A HIGHWAY.

IT WAS ALMOST SIX YEARS AGO THAT SHE LOADED UP HER CAR AND DROVE AWAY FROM SEATTLE. AS SHE SPED THROUGH OREGON, HER MIND BEGAN TO RACE. CHANGES THAT SEEMED TOO MONUMENTAL, TOO CONSPICUOUS BACK HOME COULD BE DECIDED UPON RIGHT THEN.

AS SHE BROKE THROUGH THE HILLS NEAR VALLEJO, A PHRASE STARTED REPEATING INSIDE HER HEAD. IT WAS SOMETHING SHE'D WRITTEN SEVERAL TIMES IN HER JOURNAL JUST BEFORE SHE LEFT.

SHE MOUTHED THE WORDS SILENTLY: "I CAN BE WHOEVER I WANT WHEN I STOP THIS CAR." SHE LET UP ON THE GAS AT THAT INSTANT, TO GIVE HERSELF TIME TO THINK.

TARA PULLS INTO HER PARKING SPACE IN THE GARAGE BELOW HER APARTMENT. SHE SITS THERE, GRIPPING THE WHEEL TIGHTLY, FEELING THE ALCOHOL BUZZ AND THE RATTLING IDLE OF THE ENGINE. SHE CAN'T BRING HERSELF TO KILL IT.

AT 97

THE HAPPY HOUR
NO CLASH, SEX PISTOLS OR THE RAMONES IN 1987!
JERUSALEM CRICKETS
THE DIRT CLODS
THRAS
WEEKEND SURF PARTY!!!
40 THIEVES
BEERGUTS • LA LLORONA
ACTIVE THOUGHTS • RADDD
come + support the cause!!!
hippie
JPA PARK • SAT10 • 1 PM
$5 w/FLYER $7 WITHOUT $100 HIPPIES
JAIME 1987
BLAST
APE SEX

SOMEWHERE ABOUT TWO THOUSAND MILES FROM HOME...
GASS
67
80
UHAUL
1

DID YOU CALL HER?
NO, I WAS GETTING CIGARETTES.

TWO WEEKS ON THE ROAD AND YOU STILL HAVEN'T CALLED HER. SHE MUST BE MIGHTY SORE BY NOW.
I DIDN'T WANNA LEAVE HER BEHIND. YOU HIPPIES WANTED TO LEAVE AT FOUR O'CLOCK IN THE MORNING.

ALL YOU HAD TO DO WAS TELL HER WE WERE LEAVING EARLIER THAN PLANNED.
OH, SO NOW IT'S MY FAULT SHE COULDN'T COME.

IT'S NOBODY'S FAULT. ALL I'M SAYING IS THAT YOU SHOULD CALL HER AND EXPLAIN IT TO HER. I'M SURE SHE'LL UNDERSTAND.
WHY DON'T YOU CALL HER AND EXPLAIN IT TO HER?

JESUS CHRIST. IF I'D HAVE KNOWN YOU WERE AFRAID OF HER...
YEAH, YOU KNOW EVERYTHING, DON'T YOU?

WHAT ARE THESE GUYS CALLED AGAIN?
LA LLORONA. THEY'RE TOURING WITH THE 40 THIEVES.
OH, WELL. AT LEAST THEY LOOK NICE ON STAGE.
2

I CAN'T BELIEVE WE ACTUALLY GOT PAID TODAY. NOW WE CAN EAT.
WE SHOULD SAVE MOST OF THIS MONEY IN CASE THE CAR BREAKS DOWN.
FUCK THE CAR! LET'S GET A MOTEL TONIGHT! I'LL JUST DIE IF I HAVE TO SLEEP IN THAT DEATHTRAP OR ON SOMEONE'S COLD FLOOR ANOTHER NIGHT STRAIGHT!

NO WAY! WE CAN'T TAKE A CHANCE ON THE CAR FUCKING UP!
C'MON, ZERO! JUST ONE LOUSY MOTEL ROOM...
WE WOULDN'T BE IN THIS BIND IF MAGGIE THE MECHANIC WAS WITH US.

YEAH, HOW COME SHE DIDN'T COME AFTER ALL?
DON'T YOU FUCKERS LOOK AT ME! I MEAN IT!
LET'S GET A MOTEL ROOM!

MMM... SORT OF MAKES YOU FORGET YOU'RE A MILLION MILES FROM HOME.

HEY! YOU SPILLED ALL THE FUCKIN' WINE, YOU ASSHOLE!
WELL, WHY DID YOU PUT IT WHERE I'D TRIP OVER IT?
!!!
3

CHECK IT OUT. THIS GUY CRACKS ME UP.
ZERO, WHO ARE THESE PEOPLE?
LOCAL SCENE MAKERS. I DIDN'T KNOW THIS STATE GREW PUNKS.

HEY, WHY DON'T YOU PEOPLE PARTY SOMEWHERE ELSE? SOME OF US HAVE TO DRIVE TWO HUNDRED MILES IN THE MORNING.
LET'S GO. IT'S A RERUN, ANYWAY.

ROCK STARS.
I KNOW. TSK!
HEY, KID. I'LL GIVE YOU MY LAST CIGARETTE IF YOU MAKE A PHONE CALL FOR ME.
NYEH! I DON'T SMOKE.
PHONE

I'LL GIVE YOU THE REST OF MY BEER, THEN...
NYEH! I DON'T DRINK.

C'MON! JUST MAKE THIS CALL FOR ME. THERE'S THIS REALLY HOT CHICK IN CALIFORNIA THAT...
CALIFORNIA?? DOUBLE NYEH!

TAKE THE BEER ANYWAY, YOU FUCKIN' STRAIGHTEDGE FAGGOT!

DID YOU...?
SHUT UP.
APE SEX
4

SIX FLAGS
OVER
HARDCORE
SHORES

SO, WE'RE KICKED OFF TONIGHT'S SHOW. IT'S NOT THE FIRST TIME, ZERO.
BUT THAT MAKES OUR NEXT GIG IN THREE DAYS. WHAT ARE WE GONNA DO FOR MONEY TILL THEN?
OK, THEN, WHAT DO YOU SUGGEST?

I SAY FUCK IT, AND LET'S GO HOME.
I GUESS THAT'S ALL WE CAN DO.
LUCKY DOG. NOW YOU DON'T HAVE TO CALL MAGGIE.
YOU KNOW WHERE TO PUT THIS...

OH, WELL. I WAS SORT OF LOOKING FORWARD TO WATCHING THE SUN RISE OVER THE OCEAN.
I'D RATHER SEE MY OWN BED RISE OVER THE OCEAN.

OH, C'MON, TERRY. YOU HAD FUN AND DON'T DENY IT.
OH, YES. I ESPECIALLY LOVED ALL THAT BOOING...

IT SURE BEAT SELLING COSMETICS AT MONTY'S.
FOR YOUR INFORMATION, LITTLE ONE, I QUIT THAT JOB SO I COULD GO ON THIS FUCKING TOUR!
5

YOU WOULDA ROTTED IN THAT FUCKING JOB ANYWAY.
LISTEN YOU...
OH, PLEASE! MUST YOU TWO CONSTANTLY QUARREL SO?

I SWEAR, IT'S LIKE TRAVELING WITH A BUNCH OF JERUSALEM CRICKETS.
A BUNCH OF WHATS??
YOU CAN TALK, MONICA...
HEY, LISTEN UP! I GOT US A GIG FOR TOMORROW!
U HAU

SATAN'S LAW NEED AN OPENING BAND AND THEY'LL GUARANTEE AT LEAST A HUNDRED BUCKS.
THEY'RE SPEED METAL, ZERO!
SO WHAT? WE CAN INSULT THEIR FANS.

YEAH, TERRY. WHERE'S THAT ROCK 'N' ROLL SPIRIT YOU OL' JERUSALEM CRICKET?
OK, THAT MEANS YOU HAVE TO CALL THE MAGPIE! AND I MEAN TONIGHT!
I JUST MAY SEE THAT SUN RISE OVER THAT OCEAN AFTER ALL.

IF YOU WERE REALLY HARD CORE, YOU'D HAVE THROWN A FULL BOTTLE.
EXIT

BLUE ITALIAN SHIT

BY D. CLOWES

SO ANYWAY, MY NAME IS RODGER YOUNG, ETC., ETC. I'M EIGHTEEN YEARS OLD AND STILL A VIRGIN AT THIS POINT. I'VE JUST MOVED TO THE BIG CITY. THIS IS ABOUT FIFTEEN YEARS AGO. IT'S THE FALL OF 1979...

UP TO THIS POINT IN MY LIFE THINGS HAVEN'T GONE TOO WELL. SO NOW, FINALLY, HERE'S MY BIG CHANCE TO CREATE A NEW PERSONA. IT'S THE PERFECT PLACE TO BEGIN A STORY...

AS WE BEGIN, OUR CITY HAS ENTERED AN ERA OF EXTREME SQUALOR AND DECAY... WE'RE USED TO IT NOW, BUT AT THAT TIME THE UNYIELDING FILTH CARRIED WITH IT A MYSTICAL, ALMOST BIBLICAL QUALITY...

YO DEVO!

A FEW YEARS LATER, I'M SITTING ON A STOOP WITH MY BEST FRIEND'S GIRLFRIEND. I FEEL THAT WE'VE FALLEN IN LOVE DURING THE COURSE OF THE AFTERNOON. A BUM PICKS UP ON THIS AND STARTS TALKING TO US...

YOU TWO ARE BEAUTIFUL... I KNOW WHAT IT'S LIKE BECAUSE I'M IN LOVE, TOO...

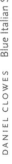

THEN HE LEANS TOWARD US AND VOMITS THREE HEAVES OF WHAT LOOKS LIKE BEER AND CHEERIOS, AND WALKS AWAY LIKE NOTHING HAPPENED. THAT'S WHAT I MEAN BY BIBLICAL... IT'S LIKE THEY SENT AN ANGEL TO PUNISH US FOR OUR ADULTEROUS THOUGHTS.

BUT THAT WAS LATER. WE'RE STILL IN 1979. SATURDAY NIGHT FEVER WAS STILL THE BIG CULTURAL REFERENCE... WHEN I FIRST GOT THERE I WENT TO THE BARBER SHOP. THE WHOLE TIME I'M WORRYING ABOUT HOW MUCH IT'S GOING TO COST AND NOT PAYING ATTENTION AND THE NEXT THING I KNOW, THERE I AM WITH A JOHN TRAVOLTA HAIRCUT!

I JUST PAID AND GOT OUT... I ALWAYS THINK ABOUT THAT--THERE WERE FIFTEEN MINUTES ON THIS EARTH WHEN I HAD A JOHN TRAVOLTA HAIRCUT!

SKRITCH SKRITCH
79¢
DISCOUNT
I GOT ANOTHER HAIRCUT (IN THE SUBWAY-4 BUCKS) LATER THAT WEEK.

HORROR WAS IN THE AIR IN THOSE DAYS. WE HAD TO REGISTER AGAIN FOR THE DRAFT, REAGAN WAS ABOUT TO BE ELECTED, THE NUCLEAR CLOCK WAS AT 11:57... I GAVE IN TO IT WITHOUT A FIGHT... BEYOND THAT, EVEN...

HEY, Y'WANNA TAKE SOME OF THESE FLYERS-- IT'S FOR A NO NUKES ASSEMBLY ON FRIDAY.
FUCK OFF! YOU SHOULD BE HONORED TO BE PART OF THE LAST GENERATION!
WHAT?

IT WAS COMFORTING TO EMBRACE MY DOOM IN FRONT OF OTHERS, BUT EVERY NIGHT I WOULD LIE AWAKE, SCARED SHITLESS OF ALL SORTS OF THINGS THAT WOUND UP NEVER HAPPENING...

COME WITH US, SON... YOU'RE UNDER ARREST FOR DRAFT EVASION!

DURING THIS TIME I WAS LIVING WITH TWO ROOMMATES...

...SO THERE I AM, ALL FUCKED-UP IN MY UNCLE'S 'VETTE AND NOBODY AROUND FOR MILES...
DAVID
NAT

NAT WAS A TOTALLY WORTHLESS, DISGUSTING IDIOT. HE LISTENED TO KANSAS, WALKED AROUND NAKED, AND HIS FAVORITE SNACK WAS WONDER BREAD SMOTHERED IN RANCH DRESSING.

I TOOK IT UP TO 120 FUCKIN' M.P.H., MAN... I CAN HONESTLY SAY IT WAS A SEXUAL FEELING --AS GOOD AS BANGIN' A CHICK... BETTER...
THANK GOD THAT COP WAS INTO 'VETTES!

DAVID WAS A PRETTY INTERESTING CASE... WAS HE GAY? I MEAN, HE WAS A FASHION STUDENT, HE SPOKE IN AN AFFECTED WAY, LIKE A DISAPPROVING MATRON, AND HE WAS REALLY INTO MOTOWN... BUT HE NEVER HAD A BOYFRIEND OR ANYTHING...

THE ONLY THING MORE DISGUSTING THAN EATING OR SHITTING IS HAVING A BABY!

WHO KNOWS? MAYBE HE WAS JUST ASEXUAL, OR WHATEVER... THERE WAS JUST NO WAY YOU COULD EVER IMAGINE HIM EVEN KISSING A WOMAN...

I SHOULD HAVE SAID, "HONEY, MY ADVICE IS TO SPRAY YOUR ENTIRE BODY WITH F.D.S.!"

I GUESS HE MADE IT PRETTY CLEAR... IN POINT OF FACT, HE WAS THE MEANEST GUY I EVER MET, POSSESSING A FORMIDABLE KNACK FOR HONING IN ON ONE'S WEAK POINTS (ALWAYS IN THE THIRD PERSON--ALL THE MORE DANGEROUS) AND ENLARGING THEM...

...I TOLD HER SHE LOOKED NICE, BUT I WAS THINKING "TELL ME: IN WHAT EXACT YEAR WAS IT FASHIONABLE TO WEAR BLUE ITALIAN SHIT?"

THE ONLY TIME I EVER SAW BEYOND HIS CULTIVATED FACADE WAS WHEN I CAME HOME EARLY ONCE AND FOUND HIM GYRATING STIFFLY ON HIS BED TO A CONNIE FRANCIS RECORD...

♫ KISS 'N' TWIST IT'S THE LATEST CRAZE IT'S THE HAP-HAP-HAPPIEST DANCE ♫

I DIDN'T HANG OUT WITH MY ROOMMATES MUCH, BUT EVEN SO, AFTER A FEW MONTHS I BEGAN TO ADOPT SOME OF DAVID'S VOCABULARY, MOSTLY ONLY WHEN I WAS TALKING TO HIM... I'VE OFTEN INGRATIATED MYSELF TO BULLIES AND CREEPS LIKE THAT, COME TO THINK OF IT...

OH MY GOD, LOOK AT HER!
SHE LOOKS LIKE AN OBESE, WET CLOWN!

OUTSIDE THE APARTMENT I HAD A DIFFERENT PERSONA ENTIRELY... THE PUNK SCENE WAS PRETTY MUCH OVER IN 1979 BUT IT WAS NEW TO ME. I IMAGINED MYSELF AS SORT OF A ROGUISH TOUGH-GUY (!) PRETTY PATHETIC, BUT I MANAGED TO TEMPORARILY ATTRACT A FEW DRUNKEN GIRLS WITH IT...

...I SAW THEM OPEN FOR THE DICTATORS.. THEY FUCKIN' STUNK!
NO SHIT!

THIS WORKED UP TO A POINT, BUT IT WAS ESSENTIAL TO GET AWAY BEFORE I SAID SOMETHING TO DESTROY THE ILLUSION...

HEY, WHERE Y'GOIN'? FUCK YOU!!

UP TO THIS POINT, I HAD NOT TAKEN DRUGS OF ANY KIND... I GUESS I HAVEN'T REALLY *SINCE* THEN EITHER... I PROBABLY WOULD HAVE TAKEN MORE DRUGS, BUT I COULDN'T STAND THE IDEA OF LOOKING LIKE A NOVICE... IT WAS KINDA THE SAME REASON I HADN'T HAD SEX YET... ANYWAY, ONE NIGHT THIS OLDER COUPLE CONVINCED ME TO TAKE ACID...

IT TURNED OUT IT WAS ONLY SOME REALLY BAD SPEED... I DECIDED TO RIDE THE SUBWAY WHILE I WAS WAITING FOR MY "TRIP" TO BEGIN BUT I ONLY GOT A WEIRD, NERVOUS TINGLING IN MY SCALP... FOR SEVERAL HOURS I CONTINUOUSLY COMBED BACK ONE SIDE OF MY HAIR WITH MY FINGERS...

I REMEMBER LOOKING AROUND AND BEING ACUTELY AWARE OF HOW HOPELESS EVERYONE LOOKED... I MEAN *REALLY* HOPELESS, AS IN *NO HOPE EVER*... THOSE OF YOU WHO HAVE RIDDEN THE SUBWAY WILL RECOGNIZE THAT THIS WAS NOT JUST SOME HALLUCINATION...

I WALKED AROUND FOR SEVERAL HOURS AND DECIDED TO GO TO A LAME "ROCK" CLUB... THREE BANDS I'D NEVER HEARD OF BUT NO COVER... AT THIS POINT I WAS EXTREMELY JITTERY, BUT SOME NEOPHYTE, OUT-OF-IT PUNK GIRL STARTED TALKING TO ME ANYWAY...

I REALLY LOVE YOUR HAIR!
?

AH, PUNK GIRLS... THEY SAVED MY LIFE... NOT THE KIND OF PUNK GIRLS WHO ARE SCARY DRUG ADDICTS AND LIVE IN ABANDONED BUILDINGS, BUT A DIFFERENT TYPE OF LONELY, NAIVE, URBAN MISFIT-GIRL...

WHERE DID YOU GET THOSE SHOES?

I'M NOT SURE THEY EVEN EXIST ANYMORE, BUT ANYWAY, GOD LOVE 'EM! NOT THAT I'D GOTTEN LAID AT THIS POINT, BUT IT WASN'T THEIR FAULT...

ANYWAY, AS I SAID, THE PUNK THING WAS JUST ABOUT OVER. BUT I WAS STILL TOTALLY INTO IT... I SPENT EVERY PENNY I HAD ON RECORDS... I STILL HAVE 'EM ALL...

ACTUALLY, I GUESS I'VE SOLD A LOT OF THEM...

I REMEMBER ONE TIME ON THE SUBWAY THIS GUY WAS HASSLING ME ABOUT JESUS AND I TOLD HIM I WAS BROKE AND HE HANDED ME A 20 DOLLAR BILL... THAT WAS LIKE 80 DOLLARS NOWADAYS...

NO, THAT'S OKAY...
TAKE IT, MAN, TAKE IT!

HE SAID, "NOW DO YOU BELIEVE THAT THERE AT LEAST *MIGHT* BE SOME HIGHER POWER LOOKING OUT FOR YOU?" I SAID "YES!" AND WENT DOWNTOWN AND BOUGHT 20 DOLLARS WORTH OF SINGLES...

AS I GOT OFF THE SUBWAY I HEARD A GUY SAY, "HEY YO, WHAT ABOUT ME, MAN? I DON'T BELIEVE THAT SHIT!"

ANYWAY, BOTH OF MY ROOMMATES SPLIT. NAT JUST DROPPED OUT OF SIGHT AND DAVID, I THINK, GOT TIRED OF ME IMITATING HIM AND TOOK OFF. I CAN'T SAY I BLAME HIM; IT EMBARRASSES ME TO THINK ABOUT IT NOW... IT'S JUST THAT I COULDN'T STAND THE IDEA OF HIM TALKING ABOUT ME BEHIND MY BACK THAT WAY... I GUESS I'VE ALWAYS BEEN A PRETTY IMPRESSIONABLE GUY...

SO I MOVED TO ANOTHER ROOM WITH THE SADDEST AND MOST FASCINATING OF ALL ROOMMATES...

LARRY WAS THE TEXTBOOK DEFINITION OF A CREEP. HIS CREEPINESS WAS IMMEDIATELY APPARENT AND NOT ONLY BECAUSE OF HIS EXTREMELY CREEPY APPEARANCE. FOR INSTANCE, HE KEPT A SPYGLASS IN HIS DRESSER WITH WHICH HE WOULD SCRUTINIZE EVERY WOMAN WHO ENTERED THE BUILDING...

HE WAS A 28-YEAR OLD ENGINEERING STUDENT. HE WAS (AND I'M SURE STILL IS) A VIRGIN. HE MADE HIS OWN FURNITURE OUT OF CARDBOARD (COULD I MAKE THAT UP?) AND SHOWED NO DISTASTE FOR MY DECOR (WHICH COULD NOT HAVE BEEN LESS LIKE HIS AND WAS CHOSEN SPECIFICALLY TO OFFEND HIM)...

I'M GLAD YOU DON'T HAVE A *BOOB-TUBE*... THE LAST GUY IN HERE COULDN'T KEEP HIS FACE OUT OF THE *BOOB-TUBE*!

The Ventures

AFTER A FEW DAYS OF TORTURE, I KNEW THAT THIS WAS THE OPPORTUNITY OF A LIFETIME AND VOWED TO STICK IT OUT. IF THIS SEEMS LIKE A POINTLESS DETOUR IT'S ONLY BECAUSE I REFUSE TO LET SACRIFICE GO TO WASTE.

HE HAD AN INCORRUPTIBLE, MANNERED CHEAPNESS PERFECTLY SUITING HIS MARTYR-LIKE PERSONALITY. HIS DIET CONSISTED OF FROZEN JONES SAUSAGES AND CORN FLAKES WHICH HE ATE WITH A GROTESQUE, SOGGY, SLURPING GUSTO...

HE WAS A DEVOTED REPUBLICAN (OFTEN REFERING TO OUR SOON-TO-BE-FORMER PRESIDENT AS "MR. PEANUT") AND AN ATHEIST, BUT WAS ODDLY UNABLE TO SWEAR WITHOUT USING AWKWARD, HOMEMADE EUPHEMISMS, WEIRDEST OF WHICH WAS "SUCK" IN PLACE OF "FUCK"...

ONLY ONE TIME DO I REMEMBER HIM PURSUING A "MATE". SHE WAS A HOMELY GIRL WHO WORKED AT THE STORE ACROSS THE STREET WHO HE INSISTED WAS SMILING AT HIM. I KNEW SHE WAS JUST THAT SMILEY TYPE, BUT STILL I EGGED HIM ON... IT APPARENTLY WENT LIKE THIS:

He was entirely without charm and I talked to him only in the spirit of morbid fascination, which made the sudden revelation of this horrible fact all the more chilling:

Y'know, now that I'm no longer on speaking terms with "The Moose", I guess that makes you my best friend...
Yow!
He wouldn't have numbered among my fifty best friends and I'm a loner!

I constantly made fun of poor Larry behind his back while appearing to be his pal... what a callous bastard! Fortunately, whenever I start to feel bad about it, I have a backlog of memories that justify my cruelty...

I can get along with anybody, but I draw the line with coons and fags!
SIZZLE

Not that I can claim I really cared about such transgressions at the time... it took me another 4 or 5 years before I developed any sort of a conscience (and to be honest, I'm not even sure that's what it is) ... I'm a late bloomer, I guess... Anyway, the last time I saw Larry was 7 or 8 years ago. I was living in a different place and he stopped by. The minute he got inside, he started tapping on the walls with his fingertips...

During that summer with Larry I went out every night. It's like I knew that nothing was going to happen at home so I went out to improve my chances. I spent the whole summer waiting for something to happen. It was really hot but I never took off my leather jacket...

There were hundreds of beautiful girls in those days... in retrospect, it seems like they were all flirting with me only I didn't know how to read the signs... it was a tragic season of missed opportunities... this was even before AIDS...

What does your button say?
Uh... I-it's a band...
PO

This was also the summer I started drinking heavily... I strongly recommend it for anyone who has trouble talking to the opposite sex... I'd probably still be a virgin if not for alcohol...

I remember one night I was at this bar... some girl told me to meet her there, but then she showed up with a bunch of friends and ignored me. It was pretty awkward so I drank a lot -- partly to make her think I was a hard-drinkin' bad-ass...

AFTER SHE AND HER FRIENDS LEFT, I TOOK THE SUBWAY DOWNTOWN AND STARTED WALKING AROUND THE BUSINESS DISTRICT... IT WAS TOTALLY DESERTED...

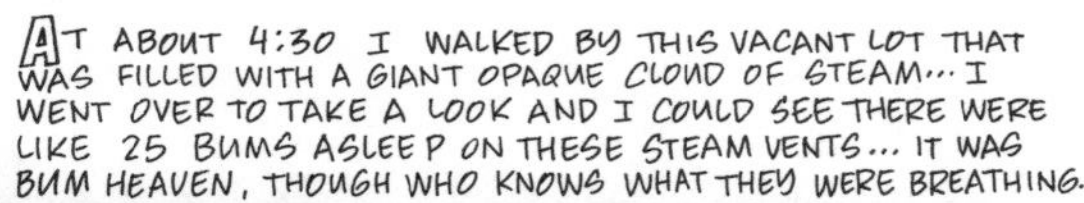

ABOUT AN HOUR LATER IT WAS MORNING. I HADN'T SEEN ANYBODY SINCE THE BUMS. OUT OF NOWHERE THIS BEAUTIFUL GIRL COMES FROM AROUND THE CORNER AND WALKS PAST ME... WE SMILED AND LOOKED BACK AT EACH OTHER... I'LL NEVER FORGET THAT LOOK ON HER FACE...

IT WAS ONE OF THOSE RARE MOMENTS WHERE LIFE DELIVERS ON THE PROMISES OFFERED BY HOLLYWOOD... I JUST STOOD THERE AND WATCHED HER DISAPPEAR LIKE THE PATHETIC, "ROMANTIC" COWARD I WAS (AND STILL AM, I GUESS)... IN A WAY, IT WAS A PERFECT MOMENT -- EVERYTHING I HAD BEEN WAITING FOR... PEOPLE LIKE ME PROBABLY DON'T WANT ANYTHING TO ACTUALLY HAPPEN TO THEM, ANYWAY...

IT'S LIKE WHEN I WAS A TEENAGER, I USED TO HANG OUT AT THE BEACH WITH THIS KID NAMED BEMIS, A DUMB SOCIAL DEVIANT WHO WAS INTO RUSH AND EVEL KNIEVEL... THIS BEACH WAS TOTALLY DESERTED AND WE WERE ALWAYS WAITING... AT LEAST ONCE A DAY WE'D GO THROUGH THIS RITUAL:

WHAT WOULD YOU DO IF THREE NAKED CHICKS CAME OVER THAT HILL?
...FUCK 'EM.

THE LEATHER JACKET I USED TO HAVE -- I GAVE IT TO A GIRL I WAS IN LOVE WITH IN 1983... ONLY ONE OF MANY REGRETS...

ANYWAY, TOWARD THE END OF THE SUMMER, I FUCKED A GIRL I MET AT A BUZZCOCKS CONCERT. SHE DIDN'T KNOW IT WAS MY FIRST TIME AND I DIDN'T TELL HER.

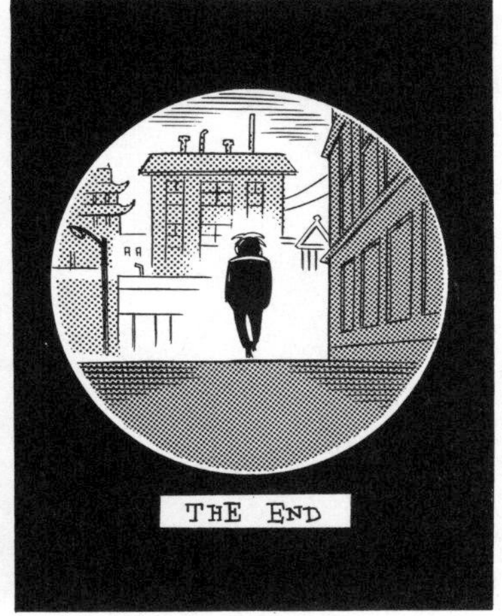

GO ON, DAVID, PLAY WITH CHARLES...
Our Children
AND THEIR FRIENDS
BOK BOK

THAT'S IT, DAVID... GO ON, HONEY...
BOK BOK BOK

PLAY WITH CHARLES, DAVID...
BOK BOK BOK

OH DAVID, WHAT'S WRONG WITH YOU?
BOK BOK BOK

PA-THOK

WERE YOU TALKING TO THAT DAVID GOLDBERG?
NO.
BOK BOK BOK

BOK BOK BOK

ARE YOU GOING TO PLAY FOR THE BABY GIANTS NEXT YEAR?
NO.
BOK BOK

ME NEITHER. SPORTS ARE IGNORANT.

DO YOU LIKE PAULA?
NO.
THUT

THAT'S BECAUSE YOU HAVEN'T MADE LOVE TO HER.
BOK BOK

DANIEL CLOWES *excerpt from* Ice Haven

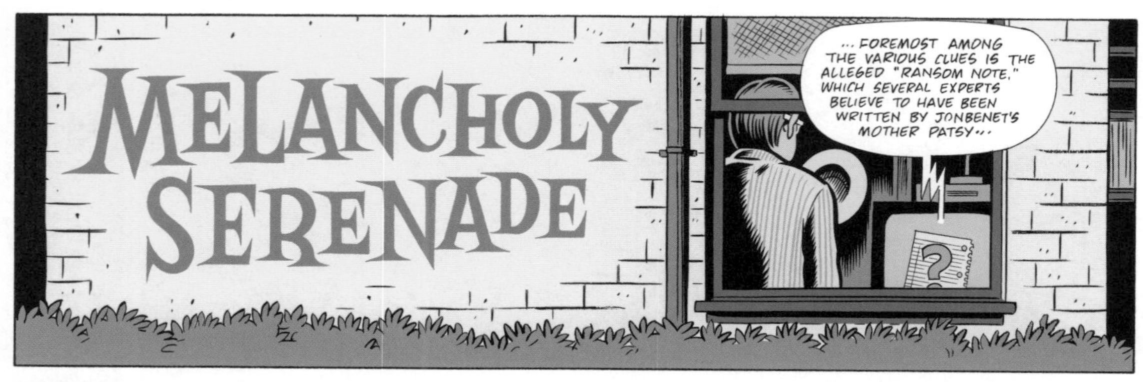

MELANCHOLY SERENADE
...FOREMOST AMONG THE VARIOUS CLUES IS THE ALLEGED "RANSOM NOTE," WHICH SEVERAL EXPERTS BELIEVE TO HAVE BEEN WRITTEN BY JONBENET'S MOTHER PATSY...

THIS DOCUMENT HAS BEEN STUDIED IN MICRO-SCOPIC DETAIL BY A TEAM OF HIGHLY TRAINED PRO-FESSIONALS, AND YET NO CONCLUSIONS HAVE BEEN--
CLICK

IS THAT WHAT IT TAKES TO GET A CAREFUL READING OF YOUR WORK THESE DAYS-- CHILD MURDER?

TWO OF YOUR BEWITCHING RIB-EYES, MR. KNUDSON!
ENTERTAINING TONIGHT ARE WE, WILDER?

THAT'S RIGHT!

I WAS YOUR BUTCHER, YOUR SOMETHINGSOMETHING, YOUR SOMETHING CAVEMAN... YOUR...

I WAS YOUR BUTCHER, SOMETHINGSOMETHING, SOMETHING SLAUGHTER...
SIGH
WHY CAN'T I CONCEN-TRATE?

IF THE PUBLIC ONLY HAD A CHANCE TO READ MY POEMS... HOW COULD THEY EVER AGAIN FIND MERIT IN THE LIKES OF MRS. WENTZ AND HER TIRESOME BEGONIAS?
SIZZLE

WHICH ONE SHALL I WATCH TONIGHT?
HA!

WHADDYA HAVE TO BE, AN EINSTEIN TO OPEN UP A HOT DOG STAND? IT RUNS BY ITSELF!
LISTEN, RALPH--
SHEER PERFECTION!

DANIEL CLOWES *excerpt from* Ice Haven

I WILL NOT ALLOW YOU Y--
BLANG BLA
WHAT!

GOD DAMN THEM!
BLA BL

TSK! TIME FOR ANOTHER NOTE!
BLANG B

DEAR MRS. AURELIO,
I WOULD LIKE TO STRANGLE YOUR HORRIBLE, INSOLENT CHILDREN
EASY, WILDER...

DEAR MRS. AURELIO,
DESPITE PREVIOUS MISSIVES, YOUR CHILDREN (ALL OF WHOM SHOULD HAVE LEFT HOME BY NOW, DON'T YOU THINK?) CONTINUE TO ANNOY WITH THEIR PUERILE "MONKEY MUSIC"
BETTER!

MUCH LATER...
AND SO YOU CAN SEE THAT I SPEAK FOR THE ENTIRE NEIGHBORHOOD WHEN I CALL FOR THIS "BEAT-A-DIDDLE" MUSIC TO STOP AT ONCE!
SIGNED, A NEIGHBOR

DONE.

MAIL

OOF!
MA

AN ANONYMOUS NOTE SPEAKS FOR EVERYONE!

WHAT'S THIS? A LIGHT AT THE WENTZ PLACE--AT THIS HOUR?

WHO COULD IT BE? HER GRAND-DAUGHTER?

SHE'S KIND OF A HOMELY GIRL, ISN'T SHE...

OOPS, LEFT THE TV ON.
STOPPED MAN WITH STRING OF UNKNOWN CANINE UN NOTHIN

...THE DISCOVERY OF THE TORSO SENT POLICE ON A BLOODY SCAVENGER HUNT THAT LED THEM TO THIS REMOTE EMBANKMENT. SHOCKING DETAILS WERE TO FOLLOW...
DEAR GOD, HOW CAN A HUMBLE POET HOPE TO CAPTURE A PUBLIC IMAGINATION AWASH IN SUCH VULGARITY?

IT WAS 2 PM. WE HAD BEEN CALLED TO **ICE HAVEN** BY MRS. NATALIE GOLDBERG TO INVESTIGATE THE DISAPPEARANCE OF HER SON...

WHY DID YOU TELL HIM TO MEET US HERE WHEN YOU KNOW I HATE CHINESE FOOD?
PAN

MAYBE I'D LIKE CHINESE FOOD ONCE IN A WHILE.
WELL WE'RE HERE -- LIVE IT UP!

SEEMS LIKE A CUTE TOWN.

THEY ALL DO AT FIRST...

IT'S JUST ANOTHER SHITHOLE, FILLED WITH WORTHLESS PIGS.

AT 2:13 WE MET WITH OFFICER KAUFMAN OF THE IHPD. HE GAVE US SEVERAL LEADS AND A COPY OF THE RANSOM NOTE -- IT WAS A WEIRDIE.

WE WENT BACK TO THE HOTEL WHERE I FAXED THE NOTE TO OUR LAB GUYS. AFTER DINNER, I SAT DOWN TO TAKE A CLOSE LOOK AT IT MYSELF. IT WAS 8:40 PM...

JOE, LET'S GO DO SOMETHING...

MY CHIQUITA BABY
GOD DAMN THAT GUY -- WHY DOES HE HAVE TO HAVE IT SO LOUD?

SHOW SOME RESPECT TO OTHERS!
SHE'S SOUTH OF THE BORDER...
JOE...

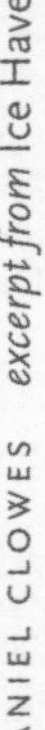

YOU DIRTY-- TURN IT DOWN!!
MY CHIQUITA BAY-BEE
JOE, DON'T.

SHE'S SOUTH OF THE
STOP IT, JOE...

I HAVE ALWAYS TRIED TO OBEY THE LAW AND TO SEE TO IT THAT MY PRESENCE IS IN NO WAY OBTRUSIVE TO THOSE AROUND ME. IN RETURN, I EXPECT FROM OTHERS THE SAME COURTESY.

YOU WOULD THINK THAT ALL OF THE DISCUSSIONS BETWEEN MRS. AMES AND MYSELF IN REGARD TO THIS MATTER WOULD HAVE HAD SOME EFFECT ON MY ACTIONS. WHO COULD BLAME HER FOR WALKING OUT?

I NEED TO WATCH MYSELF AND KEEP MY EMOTIONS IN CHECK, BECAUSE DEEP DOWN I'M REALLY A VERY EMOTIONAL PERSON. HELL, I CAN CRY LIKE A BABY OVER A DAMNED TV COMMERCIAL.

TELL ME, FRIEND, ARE YOU A MARRIED MAN?
NO, SIR.

IT'S A LOT OF TROUBLE, BUT IT CAN SURE BE WORTH IT IF YOU FIND THE RIGHT GIRL.

I'M SORRY.

IT'S OKAY.

WHAT?

I SAID, "THIS WORLD WOULD BE ABSOLUTELY UNBEARABLE WITHOUT YOU."

DANIEL CLOWES *excerpt from* Ice Haven

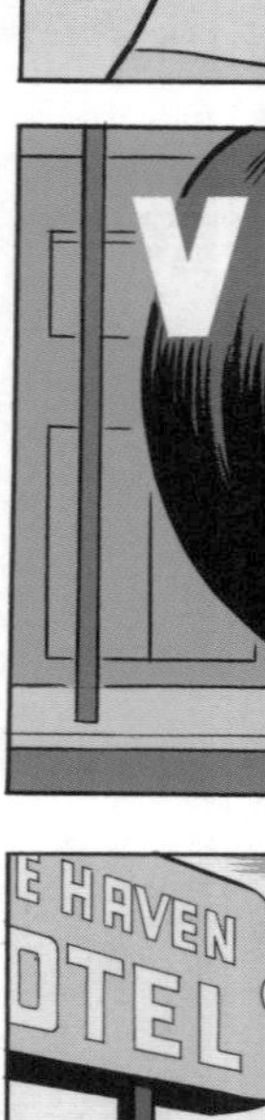

I EXPECT TO SEE YOU HOME BY 3:30, VIOLET.
NOT TODAY-- I HAVE FRENCH CLUB UNTIL SIX, REMEMBER?

VIOLET IN LOVE

E HAVEN
OTEL

NO, PENROD...

VIOLET... I CAME ALL THIS WAY TO SEE YOU...

I KNOW IT'S STUPID, BUT I WANT US TO GET MARRIED FIRST.

I'LL MARRY YOU WHENEVER YOU WANT.

YOU REALLY WILL?

OH GOD, I'M SORRY...

DON'T BE SCARED...
I DON'T WANT YOU TO SEE ME...

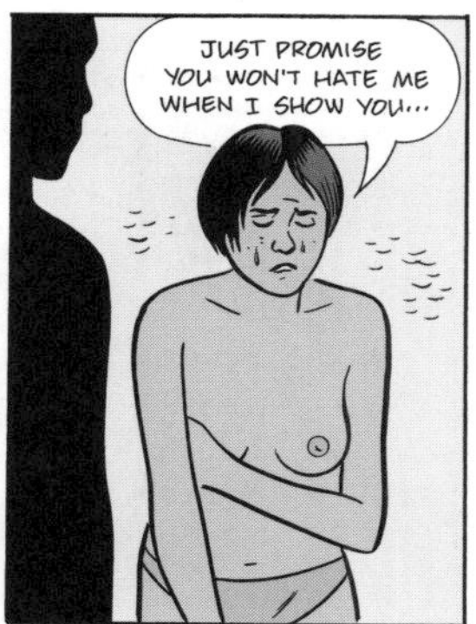
JUST PROMISE YOU WON'T HATE ME WHEN I SHOW YOU...

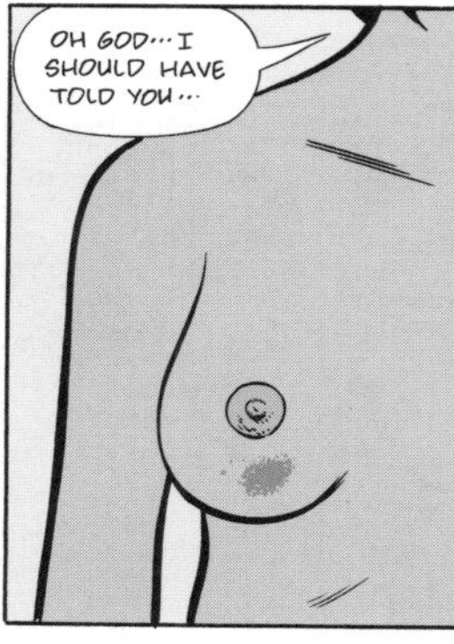
OH GOD... I SHOULD HAVE TOLD YOU...

YOU'RE NUTS...

THE FIRST THING I DID WHEN I GOT HOME WAS I WENT THROUGH ALL OF MY STUFF. I THREW AWAY ALL OF MY STUPID CDS AND MAGAZINES, AND ABOUT TWO THIRDS OF MY CLOTHES.

THE NEXT DAY I WENT OUT AND BOUGHT A CD OF FREDERIC CHOPIN, MOSTLY FOR "NOCTURNE #9" WHICH IS MY FAVORITE. I FEEL LIKE THIS MUSIC IS CLEANSING ME OF ALL THE CRAP IN MY LIFE UP TO THIS POINT. IT'S LIKE LISTENING TO ICE WATER.

THE FOLLOWING MORNING I GOT UP EARLY AND WENT OVER TO THE ALTMANS', WHO WERE ALWAYS ON VACATION, AND WENT SWIMMING NAKED IN THEIR POOL (WHICH WAS TOTALLY FREEZING!). THEN I WENT HOME AND STUDIED MYSELF IN THE MIRROR FOR A LONG TIME. I'M NOT SUCH A FREAK, I GUESS.

I WAS JUST THINKING.. I HAVE TO BE BACK AT WORK ON TUESDAY. MAYBE WE SHOULD WAIT UNTIL SUMMER...

I'M NOT EVEN GOING TO LOOK AT YOU UNTIL WE GET THERE.. IT'S BAD LUCK.

I GUESS I DON'T NEED TO TELL YOU BUT MY LIFE HAS BEEN PRETTY HORRIBLE UP TO THIS POINT. MY REAL DAD LEFT WHEN I WAS LIKE FOUR AND MY MOM IS PRETTY MUCH A TOTAL SELFISH BITCH.

MY FRIEND JULIE THINKS IT'S CRAZY TO GET MARRIED, BUT SHE'S KIND OF BIASED AGAINST MEN. I DON'T KNOW, I MEAN, I DON'T BELIEVE IN GOD AND ALL THAT, BUT DESPITE ALL THE CRAP I'VE BEEN THROUGH IN MY LIFE, I STILL BELIEVE IN TRUE LOVE.

I'M SURE THAT SOUNDS REALLY STUPID, BUT I REALLY DO. SO MAYBE I'M STUPID.

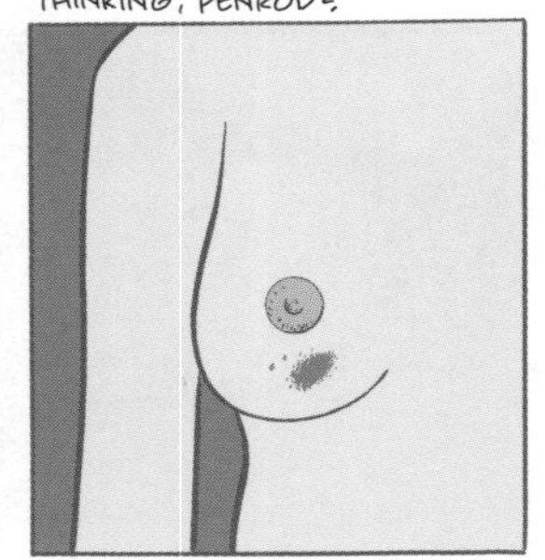

MAYBE THIS IS A BIG MISTAKE. I WONDER WHAT PENROD IS THINKING? WHAT ARE YOU THINKING, PENROD?

I GUESS HE WOULDN'T BE HERE IF HE DIDN'T REALLY LOVE ME. I LOVE YOU TOO, PENROD.

I FEEL SO WEIRD. DON'T YOU FEEL WEIRD?
YEAH.
"MRS. PULASKI."

I DON'T KNOW WHAT I SHOULD DO. I KNOW I SAID I WAS GOING TO STAY HERE UNTIL THE END OF SCHOOL, BUT I WANT TO COME WITH YOU NOW...
IT'S ONLY TWO MONTHS.
I GUESS...

I CALLED JULIE'S MOTHER AND SHE SAID YOU DIDN'T GO OVER THERE AT ALL TONIGHT.

YOU DON'T KNOW ANYTHING, SO SHUT THE FUCK UP.

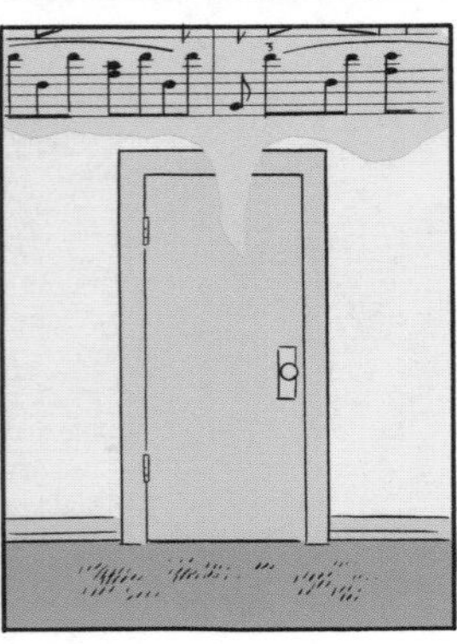

DANIEL CLOWES *excerpt from* Ice Haven

Charles

I WON'T LET IT HAPPEN TO ME, GEORGE··· YOU DON'T HAVE TO LET SEXUAL DESIRE CONTROL YOUR LIFE. DESIRE IS NATURE'S WAY OF FURTHERING THE SPECIES AT THE COST OF THE INDIVIDUAL, AND WHAT GOOD IS A SPECIES OF THWARTED INDIVIDUALS?

I SUPPORT ANYTHING THAT GOES AGAINST NATURE. NATURE IS EVIL. ONLY HUMAN CONSCIOUSNESS IS HEROIC, ESPECIALLY WHEN IT FINDS A WAY TO OUTWIT NATURE.
CHARLES'S LITTLE NEIGHBOR, GEORGE

HAVE YOU EVER WITNESSED A SPECTACLE AS AWFUL AS THAT OF A NOBLE STALLION BEING ATTACKED BY A SWARM OF HORSEFLIES? THE POOR BEAST, UNABLE TO ELUDE THE BLOODSUCKERS, CAN DO NOTHING BUT SUFFER AS THEY HAVE THEIR WAY WITH HIM -- THAT'S NATURE!

NATURE IS NOT BEAUTIFUL. ONLY THE ARTIFICIAL AND THE MAN-MADE CAN BE TRULY BEAUTIFUL.
GEORGE!

WHEN I GROW UP, I WON'T NEED TO GET MARRIED. THERE WILL BE VIRTUAL REALITY GOGGLES TO TAKE CARE OF MY SEXUAL NEEDS, AND WHO KNOWS WHAT ELSE. WHEN OUR DNA LEARNS THAT IT CAN NO LONGER RELY ON PROGRAMMED URGES TO FURTHER THE SPECIES, IT WILL GIVE UP IN DEFEAT, AND SEXUAL DESIRE WILL RECEDE LIKE POLIO OR SMALLPOX.

WILL THIS PUT AN END TO OUR ONGOING SELF-DESTRUCTION? DOES ALL VIOLENCE RISE FROM DISTORTED SEXUAL IMPULSES? AND WHAT IS THE EQUIVALENT OF VIRTUAL REALITY WHEN IT COMES TO REROUTING VIOLENT INCLINATIONS?
BYE CHARLES!

MURDER IS THOUGHT TO BE A "CRIME AGAINST NATURE." HOW ABSURD! SENSELESS VIOLENCE IS AS NATURAL AS AN OAK TREE! NATURE WANTS US TO DIE! NATURE LAUGHS AT OUR SUFFERING!

IF WE, BELIEVING IN OUR OWN VIRTUE, FIND OURSELVES IN A PITILESS UNIVERSE THAT FAVORS CRUELTY AND MAYHEM, WE HAVE NO CHOICE BUT TO UPSET IN WHATEVER WAY WE CAN THE STRUCTURE OF THAT UNIVERSE!

REJECT INSTINCT AND DESIRE! EMBRACE TECHNOLOGY AND THE BEAUTY OF THE INDIVIDUAL HUMAN CONSCIOUSNESS!

CHARLES, DO YOU KNOW WHERE YOUR DAD AND MY MOM WENT?

THE EYE DOCTOR'S.
DO YOU KNOW WHEN THEY'LL BE BACK?

5:00.
THANKS.

CLICK

HOW CAN I HAVE THE STRENGTH TO ENDURE WHEN I KNOW THAT SHE WILL NEVER RECOGNIZE THE DEPTH OF MY LONGING?

The End

DANIEL CLOWES *excerpt from* Ice Haven

WHILE I WAS STILL IN ART SCHOOL, I DEVELOPED A REPUTATION AMONGST SOME OF THE FACULTY AS A READILY AVAILABLE CAT-, DOG-, AND HOUSE-SITTER. I WAS PERFECT FOR THE JOB: SINGLE, RELIABLE, WELL-SPOKEN, AND AMBITIONLESS... PLUS, I WAS HANDICAPPED, SO IT MADE THEM FEEL GOOD TO GIVE ME MONEY.

I ACTUALLY ENJOYED IT... MOST OF THEIR HOUSES AND LOFTS REMINDED ME OF MY PARENTS' PLACE, WHERE I'D GROWN UP... VERY 'NINETEEN SEVENTIES,' A LINGERING HIPPYNESS UNDER IT ALL: SECOND-HAND FURNITURE, DUSTY ABSTRACT PAINTINGS, THE ODOR OF THE DECOMPOSING GLUE IN USED PAPERBACK BOOKS... ALL, NONETHELESS, GRADUALLY BEING BURIED BY THE TRAPPINGS OF A CREEPING MIDDLE CLASS PROSPERITY...

EXHIBITION ANNOUNCEMENTS FROM WASHED-UP FRIENDS

VIDEO TAPES

AUTOMATIC CAT WATER BOWLS

I GUESS IT WAS MY REPUTATION FOR TRUSTWORTHINESS THAT BROUGHT ME TO THE ATTENTION OF THE ACADEMIC DEAN, WHO CONTACTED ME TOWARDS THE END OF MY LAST SEMESTER WITH THE NEWS THAT A GOOD FRIEND OF HIS WAS GOING TO BE MOVING SOMEWHERE TEMPORARILY WITH HIS FAMILY FOR THE SUMMER, AND WOULD I BE INTERESTED, POSSIBLY, IN WATCHING OVER THEIR HOME WHILE THEY WERE AWAY?

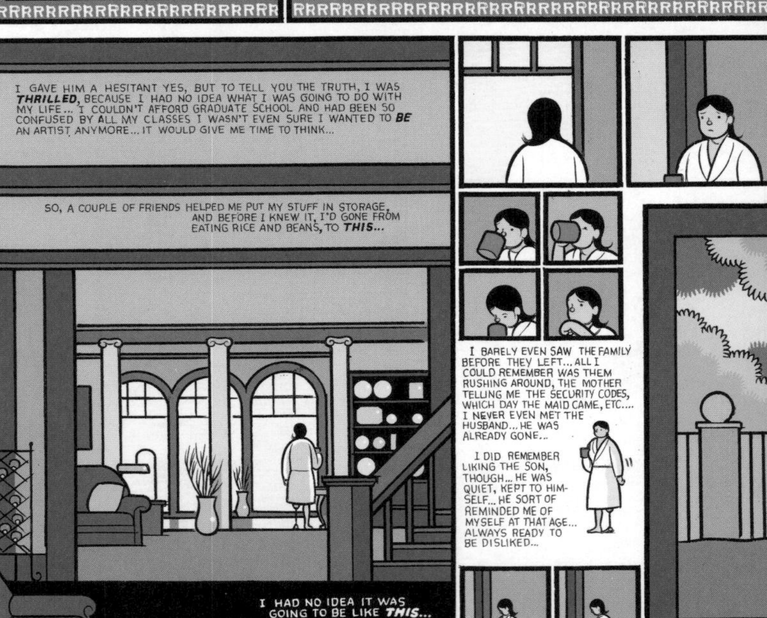

I GAVE HIM A HESITANT YES, BUT TO TELL YOU THE TRUTH, I WAS ***THRILLED***, BECAUSE I HAD NO IDEA WHAT I WAS GOING TO DO WITH MY LIFE... I COULDN'T AFFORD GRADUATE SCHOOL AND HAD BEEN SO CONFUSED BY ALL MY CLASSES I WASN'T EVEN SURE I WANTED TO ***BE*** AN ARTIST ANYMORE... IT WOULD GIVE ME TIME TO THINK...
SO, A COUPLE OF FRIENDS HELPED ME PUT MY STUFF IN STORAGE, AND BEFORE I KNEW IT, I'D GONE FROM EATING RICE AND BEANS, TO ***THIS...***
I HAD NO IDEA IT WAS GOING TO BE LIKE ***THIS...***
I BARELY EVEN SAW THE FAMILY BEFORE THEY LEFT... ALL I COULD REMEMBER WAS THEM RUSHING AROUND, THE MOTHER TELLING ME THE SECURITY CODES, WHICH DAY THE MAID CAME, ETC.... I NEVER EVEN MET THE HUSBAND... HE WAS ALREADY GONE...
I DID REMEMBER LIKING THE SON, THOUGH... HE WAS QUIET, KEPT TO HIMSELF... HE SORT OF REMINDED ME OF MYSELF AT THAT AGE... ALWAYS READY TO BE DISLIKED...

AT FIRST I WAS AFRAID TO TOUCH ANYTHING... I JUST KEPT ALL MY STUFF IN MY SUITCASE... AFTER A WHILE, THOUGH, I STARTED TO LOOSEN UP A BIT, AND BEFORE I KNEW IT, I ACTUALLY BEGAN TO FEEL ODDLY COMFORTABLE... I MEAN, HERE I WAS... I HAD THIS WHOLE PLACE TO ***MYSELF!***

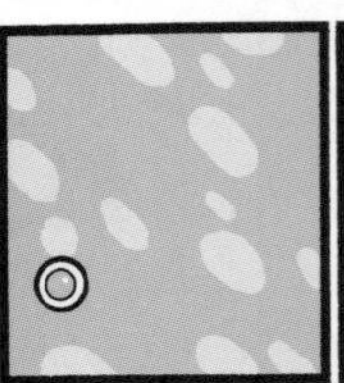

I GOT SO I'D WALK AROUND IN MY UNDERWEAR OR MY BATHING SUIT WITHOUT THINKIN THING OF IT... IT FELT LIKE ANOTHER PLANET TO ME... NO ***WONDER*** RICH PEOPLE ARE SO

THING IS, I DIDN'T HAVE TO DO ***ANYTHING...*** I MEAN, NOT EVEN SURE WHY I WAS THERE; THE MAID (THURS CLEANED EVERYTHING, THE POOL SERVICE (MONDAYS) N AND FILTERED AND WHATEVERED, THE LAWN GUYS (SAT MOWED, RAKED, AND FERTILIZED... OTHER THAN MY BI-WE CALL TO THEIR ANSWERING SERVICE TO LET THE FAMILY KN PLACE HADN'T BURNED DOWN, IT SEEMED LIKE MY ONLY PURPOSE WAS TO WATCH SATELLITE TELEVISION, SNOOP THEIR DRAWERS, AND MAKE SURE NO BLACK PEOPLE B IN AND STOLE EVERYTHING...

I WAS CONSCIENTIOUS AND RESPONSIBLE... I SUPPOSE ANY OTHER ONE-LEGGED 22-YEAR OLD WHO STILL WASN'T THAT FAT YET WOULD'VE BEEN INVITING THE BOYS OVER IN DROVES... I DIDN'T, THOUGH... I DIDN'T REALLY ***KNOW*** ANYONE I COULD ASK ANYMORE...

MY FEW FRIENDS FROM SCHOOL HAD EITHER GONE HOME FOR THE SUMMER OR MOVED AWAY FOREVER... I FELT COMPLETELY ALONE, LIKE A GHOST BANISHED SOME PAMPERED PURGATORY WITH CENTRAL AIR AND A WELL-STOCKED LIQUOR CABINET...

OKAY, ONE TIME I **DID** INVITE THIS ONE GUY OVER... HE WAS ONE OF THE ONES WHO'D HELPED ME PUT MY STUFF IN STORAGE, AND I WANTED TO COOK HIM DINNER TO PAY HIM BACK...

HE WAS NICE ABOUT IT, BUT I THINK I MADE HIM SORT OF UNCOMFORTABLE...

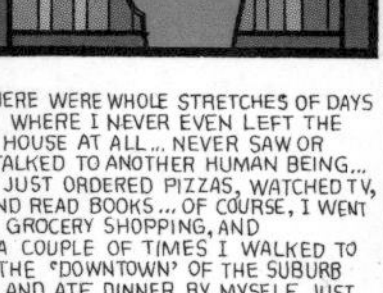

HERE WERE WHOLE STRETCHES OF DAYS WHERE I NEVER EVEN LEFT THE HOUSE AT ALL... NEVER SAW OR TALKED TO ANOTHER HUMAN BEING... : JUST ORDERED PIZZAS, WATCHED TV, ND READ BOOKS... OF COURSE, I WENT GROCERY SHOPPING, AND A COUPLE OF TIMES I WALKED TO THE 'DOWNTOWN' OF THE SUBURB AND ATE DINNER BY MYSELF, JUST FOR VARIETY'S SAKE...

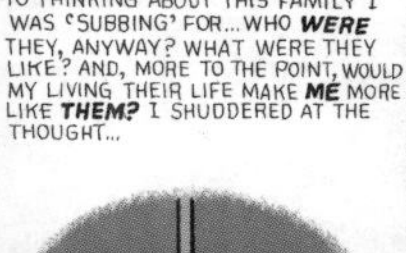

SOMETIMES, THOUGH, I'D REALLY GET TO THINKING ABOUT THIS FAMILY I WAS 'SUBBING' FOR... WHO **WERE** THEY, ANYWAY? WHAT WERE THEY LIKE? AND, MORE TO THE POINT, WOULD MY LIVING THEIR LIFE MAKE **ME** MORE LIKE **THEM?** I SHUDDERED AT THE THOUGHT...

I IMAGINED THEM, THE DAD ALWAYS BUSY, DISINTERESTED IN BOTH HIS WIFE AND HIS CHILD... A SPORTS FAN WHO PROBABLY SLEPT AROUND ON BUSINESS TRIPS...

SHE WAS PROBABLY AT HEART A VERY NICE PERSON WHO JUST GOT SCARED IN COLLEGE, SAW AN OPPORTUNITY IN HER LAW STUDENT BOYFRIEND, AND JUMPED.

WHO COULD BLAME HER? WHAT GIRL, DEEP DOWN, WOULDN'T WANT TO LIVE LIKE A PRINCESS FOR THE REST OF HER LIFE?

EVEN SO, IT MUST'VE BEEN ITS OWN LONELY SORT OF HELL...

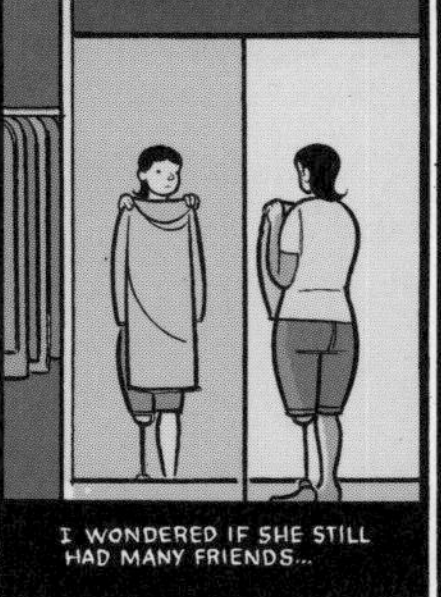

BVIOUSLY, SHE SPOILED HIM SILLY... E HAD ALL THE REQUISITE TOYS... CTION FIGURES, PLASTIC SPACESHIPS... HOUGH NO SPORTS EQUIPMENT... GUESS 'DAD' MORE THAN MADE UP OR THAT...

IT WAS SOME SORT OF STORAGE CLOSET, BUILT INTO THE EAVES OF THE HOUSE... BUT HE'D MADE IT INTO A KIND OF 'SECRET HEADQUARTERS,' WITH CARDBOARD COMPUTERS AND 'CRIME CHARTS' OF THE NEIGHBORHOOD TAPED TO THE WALLS... THERE WERE MAPS OF THE YARD WITH NOTES ABOUT HIS PARENTS' ACTIVITIES ("MOM: OUTSIDE 4:30 PM") AS IF HE WAS A PRIVATE DETECTIVE... THOUGH HIS 'YEARLY DIARY' WAS ONLY FOUR DAYS LONG HE SEEMED TO BE VERY INTERESTED IN WHEN HIS DAD CAME HOME AND WHEN HIS MOM WENT SHOPPING...

AS THE SUMMER WOUND DOWN, AND I REALIZED I WAS NO CLOSER TO HAVING A JOB OR A LIFE THAN WHEN IT BEGAN, I SORT OF STARTED TO PANIC...

I CIRCLED WANT ADS AND MADE A COUPLE OF CALLS HERE AND THERE, BUT IT WAS HARD TO FOCUS... I FELT LIKE I WAS ON A TRAIN, HEADING FOR A DISTANT MOUNTAIN, BUT THERE WAS NO TUNNEL THROUGH THE MOUNTAIN, JUST SOLID ROCK.

THEN, ONE DAY, A TELEGRAM ARRIVED ADDRESSED TO ME... THAT CHANGED EVERYTHING.

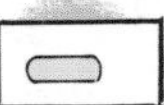

OUR NANNY IS CANCELLING OUT ON US. WOULD YOU CONSIDER STAYING ON TEMPORARILY (WITH PAY) AFTER WE RETURN UNTIL WE CAN SOLVE THE SITUATION? WE THINK IT WOULD BE GREAT. WILL CALL IN A COUPLE OF DAYS TO DISCUSS. PLEASE CONSIDER!

DON'T CARRY THAT.. I CAN GET IT...
THAT'S OKAY... I'M OKAY...
JUST DON'T ASK ME TO RUN A MARATHON...
K-KLK
JEFFREY! DON'T **RUN!**
JEFFREY!
THE POWER RANGERS ARE ALMOST **OVER,** MOM, AND NANNA AND I WATCH IT EVERY **DAY!**
KRNKL
GO AHEAD AND WATCH IT WITH HIM... I'VE GOT EVERYTHING HERE...
ARE YOU SURE?
I WAS ACCEPTED INTO THEIR LIFE SO QUICKLY IT WAS ALMOST DIZZYING... IN PRACTICALLY NO TIME I WAS HELPING THE MOTHER SHOP, TAKE HER SON TO SCHOOL... EVERYTHING. SHE ACTED AS IF WE'D BEEN BEST FRIENDS FOR YEARS, AND I LIKED HER. WE GOT ALONG WELL TOGETHER.
OF **COURSE...** HE LOVES WATCHING T.V. WITH YOU...
WELL O**KAY...**
DID YOU HEAR THAT, JEFFREY?
I FEEL A **TICKLE ATTACK** COMING ON!
HELLO!
NO! **NO!** HAHA STAY AWAY STAY AWAY!

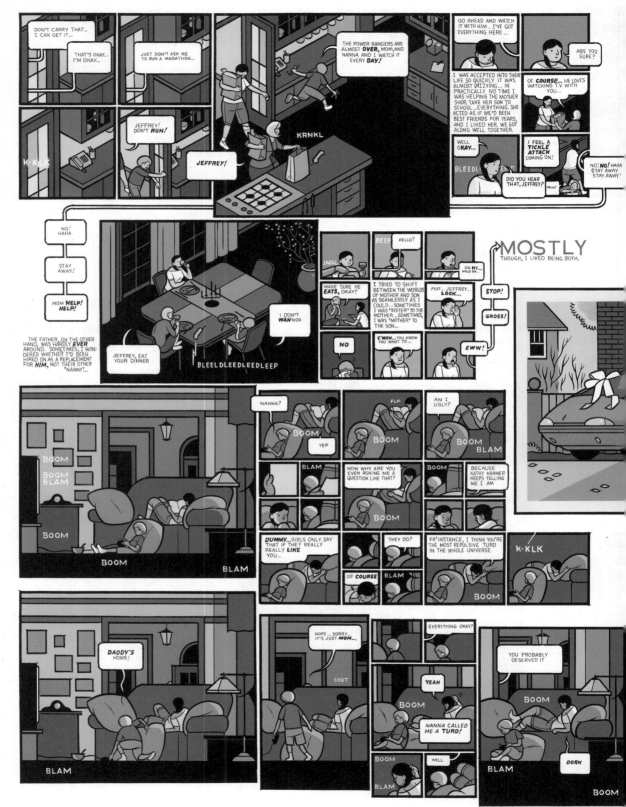

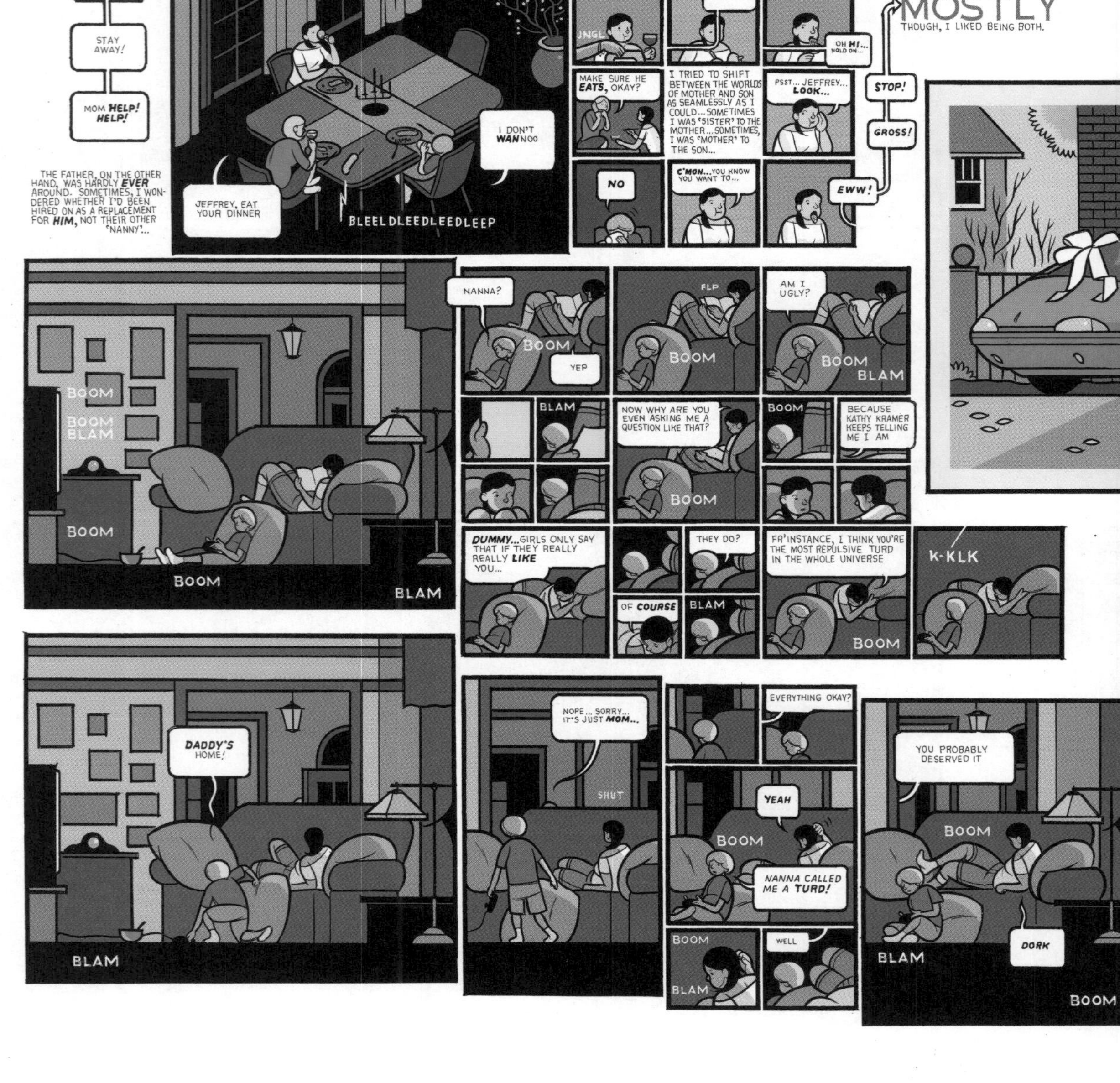

I WAS SURE

OF COURSE I WAS WRONG. COMPLETELY. I COULDN'T BELIEVE I COULD BE SO WRONG. **SHE** WAS THE ONE, NOT HIM.

HOW COULD SHE DO SUCH A THING TO HER SON? AND TO HER HUSBAND, WHO WAS NOW, I KNEW, PRACTICALLY WORKING HIMSELF TO DEATH TO SUPPORT HER SHOPPING HABITS?

ALL OF A SUDDEN, EVERYTHING CHANGED.

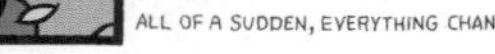

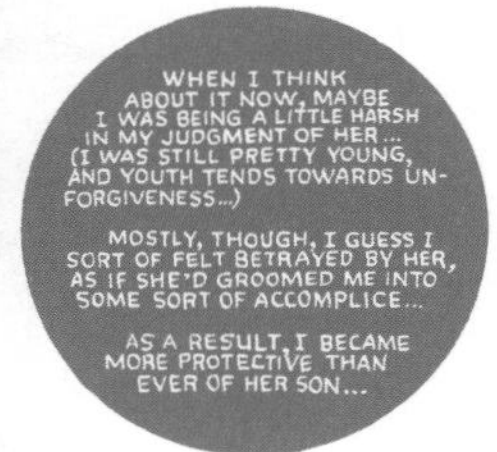

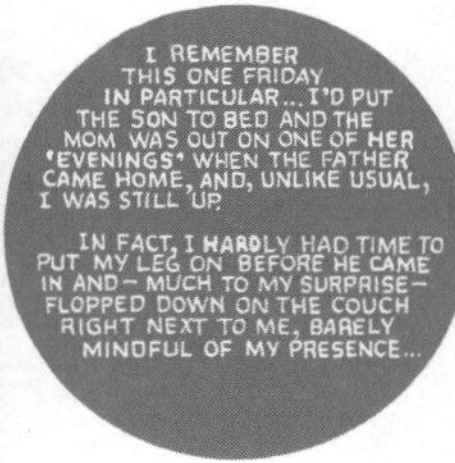

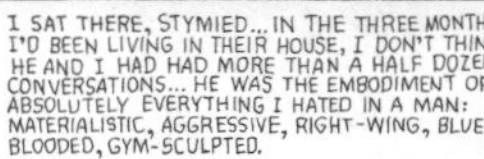

CONTINUED.

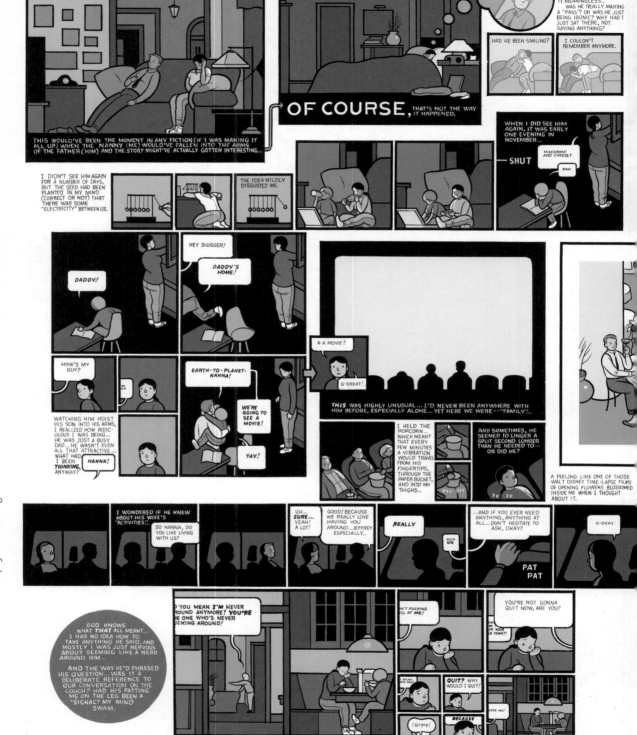

BUT I COULDN'T GET THAT "LOOK" HE'D GIVEN ME OUT OF MY MIND... I KEPT REPLAYING IT, OVER AND OVER, UNTIL I'D ALMOST RENDERED IT MEANINGLESS...
WAS HE REALLY MAKING A "PASS"? OR WAS HE JUST BEING IRONIC? WHY HAD I JUST SAT THERE, NOT SAYING ANYTHING?

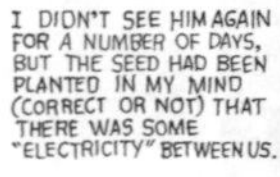

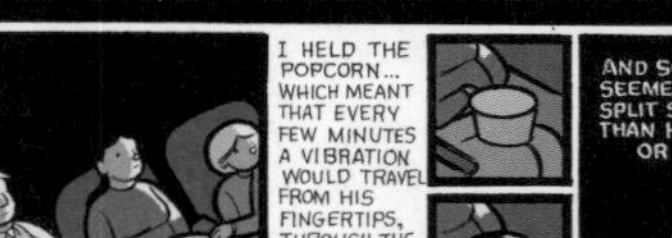

I HELD THE POPCORN... WHICH MEANT THAT EVERY FEW MINUTES A VIBRATION WOULD TRAVEL FROM HIS FINGERTIPS, THROUGH THE PAPER BUCKET, AND INTO MY THIGHS...

A FEELING LIKE ONE OF THOSE WALT DISNEY TIME-LAPSE FILMS OF OPENING FLOWERS BLOSSOMED INSIDE ME WHEN I THOUGHT ABOUT IT.

GOD KNOWS WHAT *THAT* ALL MEANT... I HAD NO IDEA HOW TO TAKE ANYTHING HE SAID, AND MOSTLY I WAS JUST NERVOUS ABOUT SEEMING LIKE A NERD AROUND HIM...

AND THE WAY HE'D PHRASED HIS QUESTION... WAS IT A DELIBERATE REFERENCE TO OUR CONVERSATION ON THE COUCH? HAD HIS PATTING ME ON THE LEG BEEN A "SIGNAL"? MY MIND SWAM.

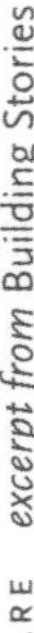

I GUESS I'D EXPECTED SOME SORT OF FANCY FAMILY GATHERING... CATERERS, WAITERS, CHAMBER MUSIC -- LIKE YOU'D SEE IN A MOVIE... BUT IT WASN'T THAT WAY AT ALL... WE JUST GOT DRESSED UP AND DROVE DOWNTOWN TO A FANCY RESTAURANT THAT THE MOTHER HAD READ ABOUT IN A SOCIETY MAGAZINE... ON THE WAY THOUGH, WE PASSED THROUGH THE NEIGHBORHOOD I'D LIVED IN WHEN I WAS IN ART SCHOOL, WHICH WAS MORE EXCITING FOR ME THAN I THOUGHT IT WOULD'VE BEEN... IT WAS LIKE MEETING UP WITH AN OLD FRIEND...

I DIDN'T TRY TO MAKE SENSE OF ANY OF THESE THOUGHTS AS THEY SPUN THROUGH MY HEAD...

I JUST KEPT UP MY USUAL SUNNY DEMEANOR... I DON'T REMEMBER A SINGLE WORD THAT WAS SAID, I'M SURE.

ISN'T THIS CRANBERRY SAGE RELISH SIMPLY TO **DIE** FOR?

LOVE IT LOVE IT LOVE IT LOVE IT

I FELT MYSELF DRIFTING IN AND OUT OF IT ALL...

WHAT, REALLY, WAS I **DOING** WITH MY LIFE? A YEAR AGO I THOUGHT I WANTED TO BE AN ARTIST, BUT HERE I WAS, NOTHING MORE THAN A BABYSITTER, A SURROGATE SISTER... OR, I DON'T KNOW...

WHAT THE FUCK DID THEY **WANT** FROM ME, ANYWAY? WHO WOULD EVEN **HAVE** A KID IF THEY DIDN'T WANT TO **RAISE** HIM? PEOPLE LIVE IN MUD HUTS AND SHACKS THE WORLD OVER AND HAVE **DOZENS** OF CHILDREN... DO **THEY** NEED NANNIES?

I KNEW WHAT IT WAS (IT ALL OF A SUDDEN OCCURED TO ME) -- THEY COULDN'T **STAND** EACH OTHER ANYMORE... THEY NEEDED SOMEONE TO "PLAY TO"... AN AUDIENCE... SOMEONE TO ACT AS "BUFFER"... WELL, FUCK THAT... I DIDN'T WANT TO BE "BUFFER"...

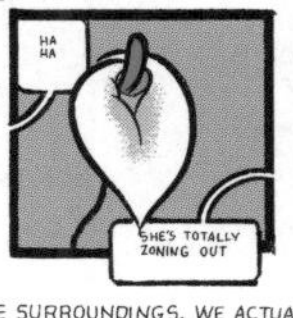

IRONICALLY, FOR ALL OF MY MENTAL TURMOIL AND THE ARTIFICIALITY OF THE SURROUNDINGS, WE ACTUALLY ENDED UP HAVING A "PRETTY GOOD TIME." AS WE DROVE HOME THROUGH THE NEW SNOW, MY IRE RELAXED SOMEWHAT, TOO, AS I THOUGHT ABOUT EVERYTHING... REALLY, HOW ELSE WERE THEY SUPPOSED TO ACT TOWARDS ME, REALLY? THEY WERE PAYING ME TO WATCH THEIR KID, AND PAYING ME WELL... AT LEAST I HAD A **JOB,** RIGHT?

I DON'T KNOW WHAT WAS WRONG WITH ME... I GUESS I WAS JUST AVOIDING MY LIFE, AND I WAS BLAMING THEM FOR IT...

BUT THAT NIGHT, AS I WAS PUTTING THE SON TO BED, USING THE SAME PLOYS AND GAMES I USUALLY DID TO GET HIM THERE, A DISTURBING THING HAPPENED...

(RATHER THAN ALWAYS BEING "THE AGGRESSOR," I'D FREQUENTLY ALLOW HIM TO "GET THE BETTER OF ME," JUST SO THAT HE DIDN'T EVER END UP FEELING THREATENED OR IMPOTENT, OR SOMETHING...

SOMEWHERE I GUESS I'D READ THIS WAS A GOOD IDEA...)

BUT HE WAS **REALLY** SMUSHING DOWN ON ME, AND SOMEHOW ONE OF HIS ACTION FIGURES HAD GOTTEN LODGED BETWEEN US AND WAS POKING ME IN THE STOMACH, SO I REACHED DOWN TO MOVE IT...

...BUT IT WASN'T AN ACTION FIGURE.

I THINK THAT'S WHEN I DECIDED IT WAS PROBABLY TIME FOR ME TO LEAVE.

BESIDES, MY VISIT HOME THAT YEAR HAD BEEN SO **STRANGE...** UNCOMFORTABLE... IT WAS THE FIRST CHRISTMAS I'D REALLY FELT LIKE A GUEST IN MY PARENT'S HOUSE...

I DUNNO... I GUESS I'D NEVER NOTICED HOW... **SHABBY** IT WAS BEFORE... DUSTY... THE LITTLE RUTS THEY'D FALLEN INTO WEREN'T ENDEARING ANYMORE, BUT... IRRITATING...

I MEAN, WHY DID THEY CONTINUE TO **LIVE** THAT WAY?

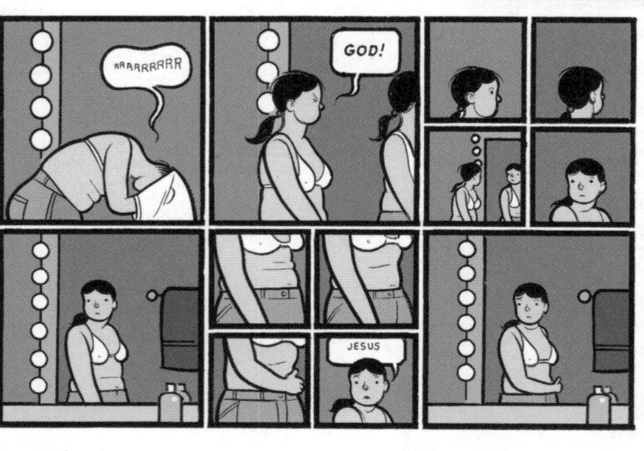

I WAS PRETTY CONFUSED THEN, ANYWAY... I WENT THROUGH A PERIOD FOR A COUPLE OF MONTHS WHERE LITERALLY ALL I COULD THINK ABOUT WAS HAVING KIDS... HAVING KIDS, HAVING **KIDS...** IT WAS LIKE A **THIRST,** MADE ALL THE MORE UNQUENCHABLE BY MY UTTER LACK OF PROSPECTS... HAS ANYONE ELSE EVER GONE THROUGH THIS IN THEIR EARLY TWENTIES? I REALLY FELT LIKE I WAS GOING **CRAZY** FOR A WHILE...

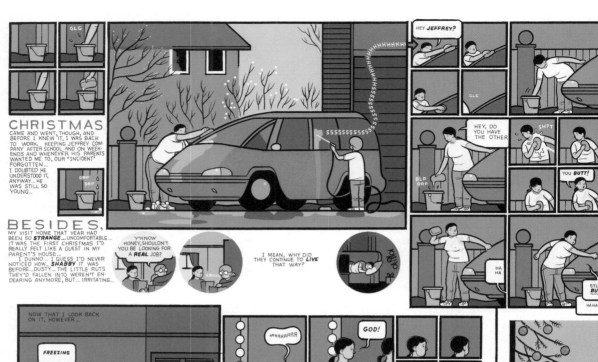

CHRIS WARE *excerpt from Building Stories*

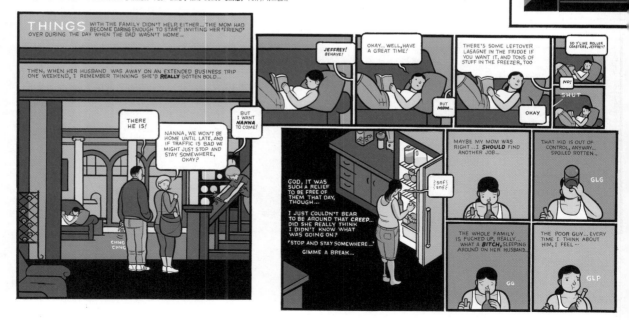

THERE, STUFFED UNDER A RUG IN JEFFREY'S CLOSET, WERE DOZENS OF DRAWINGS, ALL ON 3"x5" INDEX CARDS...

ALL THESE LITTLE MAGIC MARKER DRAWINGS, FOCUSING ON WHAT I GUESS A NINE YEAR-OLD BOY MIGHT, UM, WONDER ABOUT...

SOME WERE SCRAWLS, SOME WERE MORE CAREFULLY COMPOSED, SOME WERE SCRIBBLED OUT, BUT ALL HAD A DESPERATE SORT OF INTENSITY TO THEM, A SENSE OF FUMBLING, REFINING...

HOW HAD HE EVEN FOUND OUT **THIS** MUCH, ANYWAY? I MARVELLED AT HIS DEDICATION AND HIS CREATIVITY... (MY FAVORITE ONE WAS NOTHING MORE THAN A SLIT CUT IN THE PAPER, SURROUNDED BY SCRIBBLES OF CURLY HAIR..)

AND Y'KNOW, IT DIDN'T EVEN BOTHER ME... IN FACT, IT WAS ALMOST SWEET, IN A WAY... FLATTERING (IF I CAN SAY THAT WITHOUT SOUNDING WEIRD)... BUT HOW WAS I SUPPOSED TO **ACT** AROUND HIM NOW, KNOWING THIS? IT WASN'T LIKE OUR EARLIER ENCOUNTER, WHICH WAS AN INNOCENT ACCIDENT... THIS SHOWED AN ACTIVE CURIOSITY, WHICH I WOULDN'T HAVE SUSPECTED AT HIS AGE (THOUGH I HAD TO ADMIT TO SIMILAR SUCH 'RESEARCH' AS A KID)...

I STARTED TO WORRY THAT MAYBE OUR 'ACCIDENT' HADN'T SEEMED SO INNOCENT TO HIM, AFTER ALL, AND MAYBE **THIS** WAS THE RESULT... GOD, WAS THIS **BAD?**

NOW,

I REALLY HADN'T EXPECTED ANYONE TO COME HOME FOR A LONG TIME... IN FACT, I'D THOROUGHLY ANTICIPATED HAVING THE HOUSE TO MYSELF FOR THE NEXT FEW HOURS, IF NOT UNTIL THE FOLLOWING DAY...

QUICKLY, I GATHERED UP ALL OF THE INDEX CARDS AND PACHED THEM BACK UNDER THE CARPET, SHUTTING THE CLOSET AS SOFTLY AS I COULD...

RIGHTING MYSELF, I SHUFFLED TOWARD THE DOOR, AND THEN, TO THE EDGE OF THE STAIRS, AND LISTENED:

SOME KEYS HIT A TABLE... THEN, A SIGH... STEPS TO THE KITCHEN... A CABINET OPENED AND CLOSED...

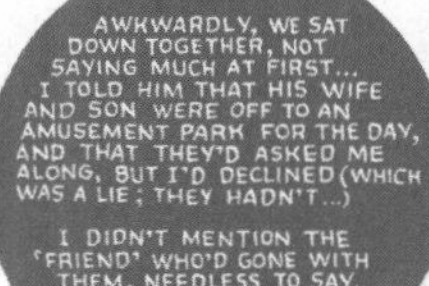

AWKWARDLY, WE SAT DOWN TOGETHER, NOT SAYING MUCH AT FIRST... I TOLD HIM THAT HIS WIFE AND SON WERE OFF TO AN AMUSEMENT PARK FOR THE DAY, AND THAT THEY'D ASKED ME ALONG, BUT I'D DECLINED (WHICH WAS A LIE; THEY HADN'T...)

I DIDN'T MENTION THE 'FRIEND' WHO'D GONE WITH THEM, NEEDLESS TO SAY...

I FELT SORRY FOR HIM, SITTING THERE.

HE'D STARTED OUT TALKING ABOUT HIS BUSINESS TRIP AND HOW LONELY IT'D BEEN BUT THEN SOMEHOW GOT ONTO THE SUBJECT OF RELATIONSHIPS... HOW THEY CHANGE, HOW PEOPLE CHANGE... HOW SOMETIMES EVEN THOUGH YOU WANT THINGS TO GO ONE WAY, THEY WENT THE OTHER... THAT'S JUST THE WAY THE WORLD WAS... THE HEART COULDN'T BE TOLD WHAT TO DO -- Y'KNOW WHAT I MEAN?

THE POSSIBILITY OF THE EMPTY HOUSE ENVELOPED ME LIKE A SLEEPING BAG AND TUGGED THE DRAWSTRINGS OF MY CROTCH TIGHT... I FELT AS IF I WAS AT THE EDGE OF A CLIFF, TEETERING...

DID... **DID** HE POSSIBLY KNOW HIS WIFE AND SON WERE GOING TO BE GONE? DID HE **HOPE** TO FIND ME HERE ALONE, WAITING FOR HIM, WELCOMING HIM, NOW AND FOREVER?

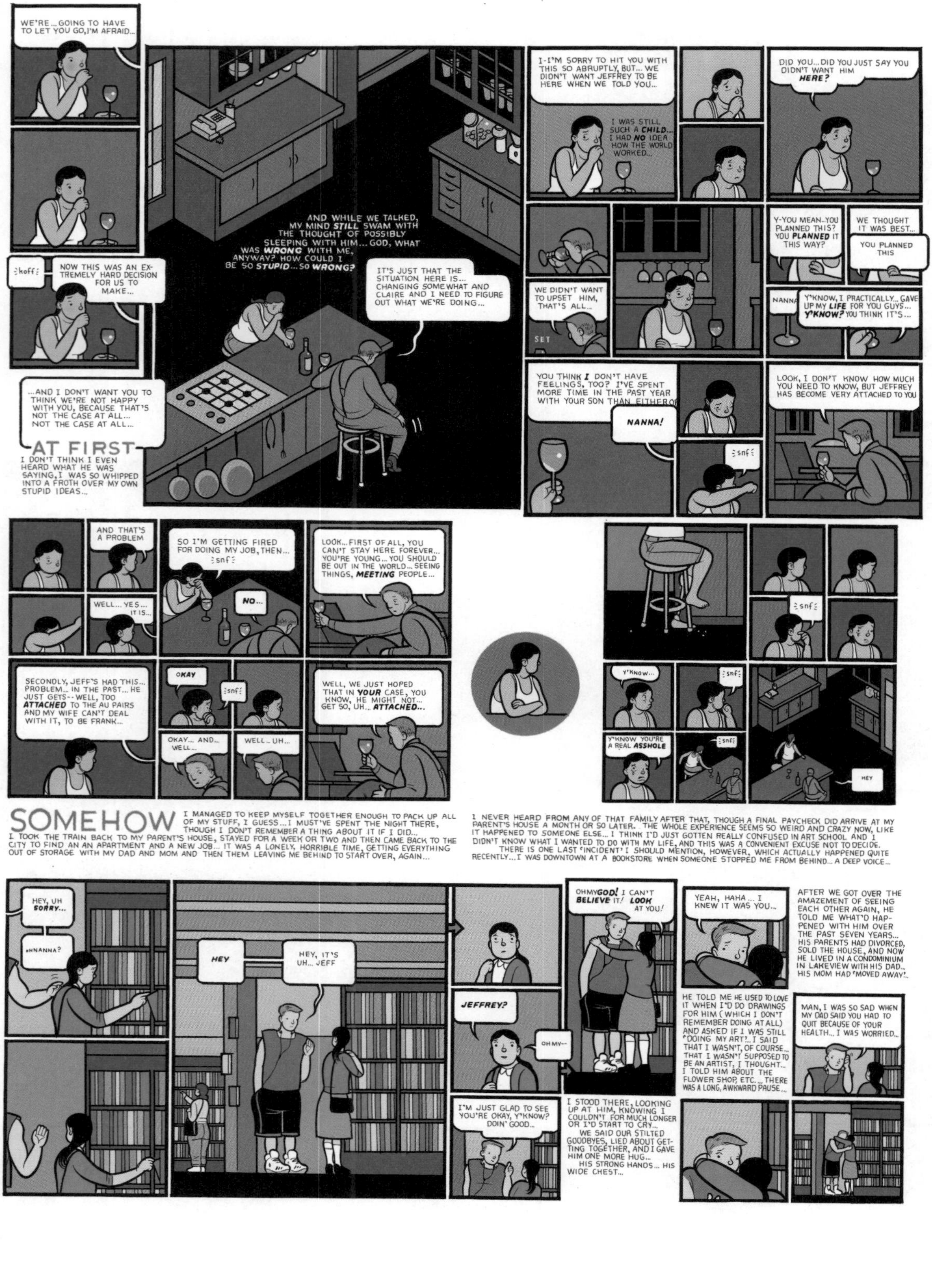

WE'RE... GOING TO HAVE TO LET YOU GO, I'M AFRAID...

AND WHILE WE TALKED, MY MIND *STILL* SWAM WITH THE THOUGHT OF POSSIBLY SLEEPING WITH HIM... GOD, WHAT WAS **WRONG** WITH ME, ANYWAY? HOW COULD I BE SO ***STUPID***... SO **WRONG?**

koff

NOW THIS WAS AN EXTREMELY HARD DECISION FOR US TO MAKE...

IT'S JUST THAT THE SITUATION HERE IS... CHANGING SOMEWHAT AND CLAIRE AND I NEED TO FIGURE OUT WHAT WE'RE DOING...

...AND I DON'T WANT YOU TO THINK WE'RE NOT HAPPY WITH YOU, BECAUSE THAT'S NOT THE CASE AT ALL... NOT THE CASE AT ALL...

AT FIRST I DON'T THINK I EVEN HEARD WHAT HE WAS SAYING, I WAS SO WHIPPED INTO A FROTH OVER MY OWN STUPID IDEAS...

I-I'M SORRY TO HIT YOU WITH THIS SO ABRUPTLY, BUT... WE DIDN'T WANT JEFFREY TO BE HERE WHEN WE TOLD YOU...

I WAS STILL SUCH A **CHILD**... I HAD **NO** IDEA HOW THE WORLD WORKED...

DID YOU... DID YOU JUST SAY YOU DIDN'T WANT HIM ***HERE?***

WE DIDN'T WANT TO UPSET HIM, THAT'S ALL...

SET

Y-YOU MEAN... YOU PLANNED THIS? YOU **PLANNED** IT THIS WAY?

WE THOUGHT IT WAS BEST...

YOU PLANNED THIS

NANNA

Y'KNOW, I PRACTICALLY... GAVE UP MY **LIFE** FOR YOU GUYS... ***Y'KNOW?*** YOU THINK IT'S...

YOU THINK *I* DON'T HAVE FEELINGS, TOO? I'VE SPENT MORE TIME IN THE PAST YEAR WITH YOUR SON THAN EITHER OF

NANNA!

snf

LOOK, I DON'T KNOW HOW MUCH YOU NEED TO KNOW, BUT JEFFREY HAS BECOME VERY ATTACHED TO YOU

AND THAT'S A PROBLEM

WELL... YES... IT IS...

SO I'M GETTING FIRED FOR DOING MY JOB, THEN... snf

NO...

LOOK... FIRST OF ALL, YOU CAN'T STAY HERE FOREVER... YOU'RE YOUNG... YOU SHOULD BE OUT IN THE WORLD... SEEING THINGS, ***MEETING*** PEOPLE...

SECONDLY, JEFF'S HAD THIS... PROBLEM... IN THE PAST... HE JUST GETS-- WELL, TOO ***ATTACHED*** TO THE AU PAIRS AND MY WIFE CAN'T DEAL WITH IT, TO BE FRANK...

OKAY

snf

OKAY... AND... WELL...

WELL... UH...

WELL, WE JUST HOPED THAT IN **YOUR** CASE, YOU KNOW, HE MIGHT NOT... GET SO, UH... ***ATTACHED...***

snf

Y'KNOW...

snf

Y'KNOW YOU'RE A REAL **ASSHOLE**

snf

HEY

SOMEHOW I MANAGED TO KEEP MYSELF TOGETHER ENOUGH TO PACK UP ALL OF MY STUFF, I GUESS... I MUST'VE SPENT THE NIGHT THERE, THOUGH I DON'T REMEMBER A THING ABOUT IT IF I DID... I TOOK THE TRAIN BACK TO MY PARENT'S HOUSE, STAYED FOR A WEEK OR TWO AND THEN CAME BACK TO THE CITY TO FIND AN AN APARTMENT AND A NEW JOB... IT WAS A LONELY, HORRIBLE TIME, GETTING EVERYTHING OUT OF STORAGE WITH MY DAD AND MOM AND THEN THEM LEAVING ME BEHIND TO START OVER, AGAIN...

I NEVER HEARD FROM ANY OF THAT FAMILY AFTER THAT, THOUGH A FINAL PAYCHECK DID ARRIVE AT MY PARENT'S HOUSE A MONTH OR SO LATER. THE WHOLE EXPERIENCE SEEMS SO WEIRD AND CRAZY NOW, LIKE IT HAPPENED TO SOMEONE ELSE... I THINK I'D JUST GOTTEN REALLY CONFUSED IN ART SCHOOL AND I DIDN'T KNOW WHAT I WANTED TO DO WITH MY LIFE, AND THIS WAS A CONVENIENT EXCUSE NOT TO DECIDE.

THERE IS ONE LAST 'INCIDENT' I SHOULD MENTION, HOWEVER, WHICH ACTUALLY HAPPENED QUITE RECENTLY... I WAS DOWNTOWN AT A BOOKSTORE WHEN SOMEONE STOPPED ME FROM BEHIND... A DEEP VOICE...

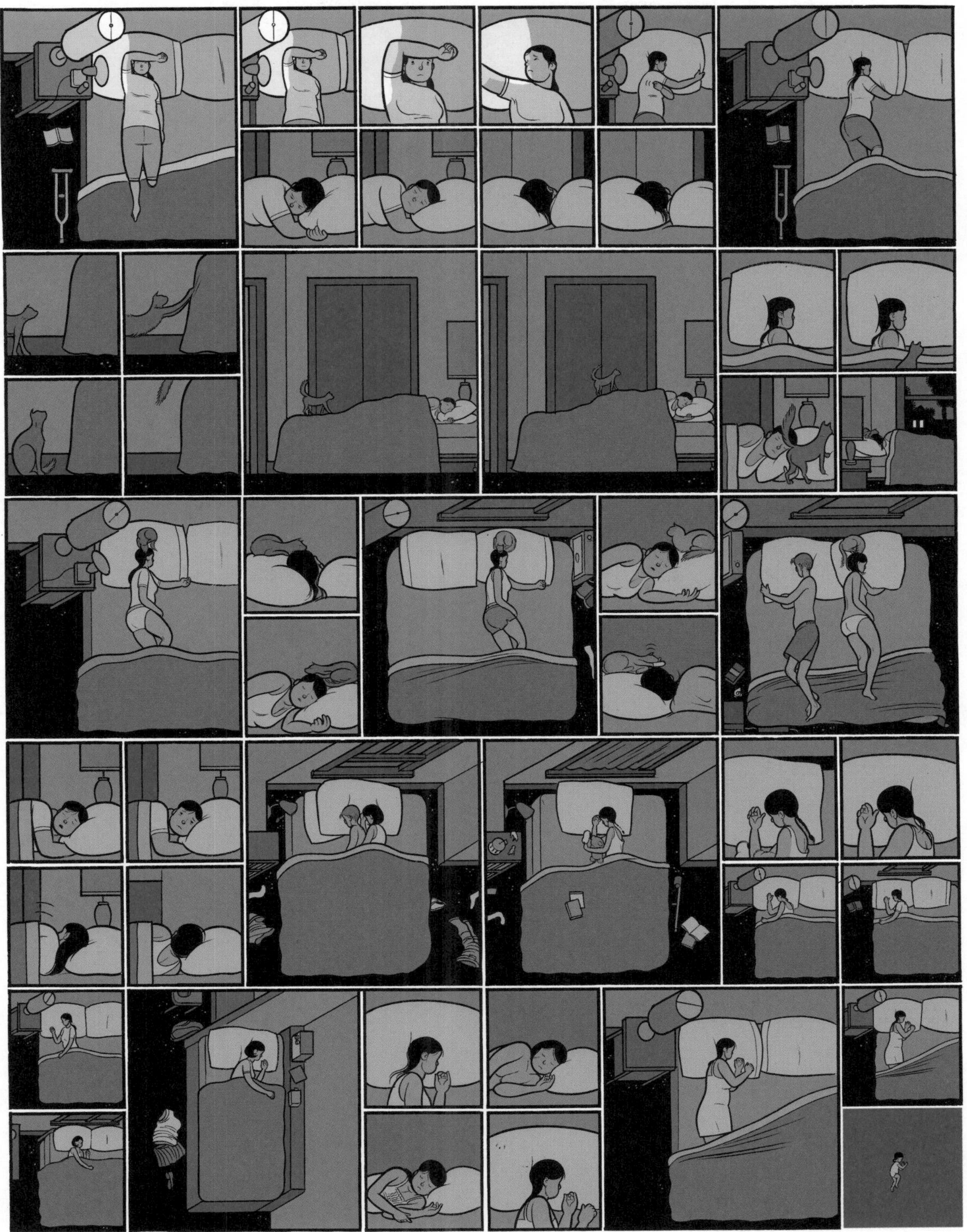

Excerpted from the forthcoming September 2008 publication of My Brain Is Hanging Upside Down *by David Heatley*

PARKING LOT

RECIPE FOR STRUVELLA

1. COMBINE EGGS, FLOUR, SUGAR, OIL AND SALT.
2. DEEP FRY.
3. TOAST ALMONDS IN OVEN.
4. POUR HOT HONEY OVER ALMONDS AND STRUVELLA, THEN ADD SPRINKLES.

MOM'S BLACK EYE

HOLD STILL, DAVID.

PHOTOGRAPHIC EVIDENCE

FOUND*

* MY MOM WEPT WHILE RECOUNTING THIS STORY TO ME 30 YEARS LATER.

CLAY

IT'S A SCULPTURE I MADE.

BATHROBE

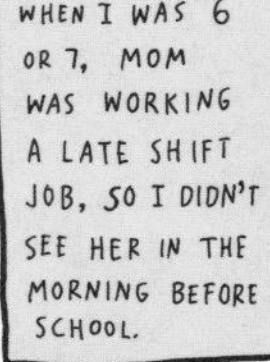

HAM

BIDDIE BASKETBALL

EXPLAINING HITLER

TEN

BEST BIRTHDAY PARTY EVER!

LUCKY

I FEEL SO LUCKY THAT I GET TO HANG OUT WITH YOU BOYS.

I DON'T THINK WE WOULD'VE BEEN FRIENDS IF I WASN'T YOUR MOTHER.

TEMPS

X-MAS CRECHE

ONE YEAR MOM DESIGNED THIS NATIVITY SCENE AS A CHRISTMAS PRESENT FOR ME AND MY BROTHERS. SHE HAD MY GRANDMOTHER SEW THE FIGURES TOGETHER USING DECADES' WORTH OF OLD DRESS MATERIAL. WE MOSTLY PILED THE DOLLS INTO THE MANGER AND PLAYED "JESUS IN SPACE."

HUGS

AMY

TICKLE TORTURE

MY BLACK EYE

HAIRCUT

PORNO

* SHE ALWAYS GASPED IN TERROR WHENEVER I WOKE HER UP.

SAFE

LATE NIGHT

AT LOUIE'S CHARCOAL PIT

...AND I'LL HAVE THE GREEK SALAD. HOLD THE ANCHOVIES.

DAVID, I KNOW YOU'VE BEEN MESSIN' AROUND WITH DRUGS.
TCHH
MOM! THAT'S NOT EVEN TRUE!

YOU'RE 2 HOURS LATE...

YEAH... I'M SORRY. I LOST TRACK OF TIME.

HONEY, I KNOW IT'S TRUE. AND I KNOW YOU'VE BEEN LYING TO ME.

WELL, IF YOU DON'T WANT TO BELIEVE ME, THEN FINE!

YOUR EYES ARE ALL RED.

I'M JUST TIRED, MOM. I'M GOING TO BED.

DAVID, I AM FIGHTING FOR YOUR LIFE!!!

I'M WORRIED ABOUT YOU.

DON'T WORRY. I'M FINE. I PROMISE.

BEEN CAUGHT STEALING

SIGH KYLE STILL ISN'T DONE WITH HIS GOD DAMNED CLARINET LESSON.
POWER RECORDS
I'M SO BORED.
SALE
I WANT THIS TAPE!
INSIDE POCKET
PEEL
MAGNETIC STRIP
I'LL TAKE THIS TOO.
SOON
3RD TAPE
OH. THERE HE IS.
KYLE
THAT'S HIM!
SHOW ME WHAT'S IN YOUR COAT.
NO!
I KNOW MY RIGHTS.
WE HAVE YOU ON VIDEO TAPE AND WE HAVE THE SHRINK WRAP YOU LEFT BEHIND.
SO YOU'RE COMING WITH ME!
"I KNOW MY RIGHTS." HA HA YOU'RE FUNNY!
KNOCK
IF YOU STEP FOOT INTO ANY OF OUR STORES, YOU'LL BE ARRESTED ON THE SPOT.
OKAY, MRS. HEATLEY.
CLICK
YOUR MOM'S EXPECTING YOU AT HER OFFICE.
SOON
I'VE BEEN WAITING FOR SOMETHING LIKE THIS TO HAPPEN.
YEAH...
I THOUGHT I'D GIVE IT TO YOU.

THERAPY, NJ

FOR THE NEXT 6 YEARS (MOSTLY AT MY MOM'S URGING) I STARTED SEEING

JIM

↪ ACTUAL OIL PAINTING I DID FOR HIM IN '97

HE WAS A LEGALLY BLIND SOCIAL WORKER/HYPNOTIST / PRIEST-IN-TRAINING WITH A BLACK BELT IN KARATE WHO SWORE LIKE A SAILOR.

SOME TIMES WHEN YOU ACT LIKE AN ASSHOLE, THE ONLY THING TO DO IS BEND OVER AND WIPE!

MY LITTLE BOY

JUST TELL YOUR LITTLE BOY INSIDE HE'S OKAY.
I WISH I COULD JUST HOLD THAT LITTLE BOY AND TELL HIM I'M SORRY.

HER LITTLE GIRL

I TOLD MY LITTLE GIRL TO GO PLAY WHILE I TOOK CARE OF BUSINESS.
I JUST NEEDED TO HUG MY LITTLE GIRL AND TELL HER NOT TO BE SCARED ANYMORE.

JOB HERSTORY

1955	1958-59	1960	1961	1964	1970	1971	1972-78
SALESGIRL AT THE FIVE AND DIME, NUTS, BOLTS AND SCREWS DEPARTMENT.	SWITCH BOARD OPERATOR. ONCE SET FIRE IN OFFICE WHILE SMOKING.	BLOOMINGDALE'S. SOLD SCARVES.	PINKUS REALTY. RECEPTIONIST. WELL-LOVED BY EVERYONE.	GEYER, MORREY, BALLARD. SECRETARY AT THIS AD AGENCY. BORED OUT OF HER MIND.	HOTEL MAID IN SAN DIEGO. LOST A LOT OF WEIGHT.	ASSOC. FOR THE RETARDED. SECRETARY FOR AN INSPIRING EXECUTIVE WOMAN (ROLE MODEL).	DIRECTOR OF RELIGIOUS EDUCATION FOR VARIOUS CATHOLIC CHURCHES, CALIFORNIA AND NJ.
1979-81	**1982**	**1983**	**1984-85**	**1986**	**1987-1999**	**2000-present**	**2008**
ESSEX WEIGHT-LOSS CENTER, NJ. WROTE CURRICULUM AND DID TRAINING.	CO-FOUNDER OF COLORFUL IMAGES, LTD. - DID COLOR ANALYSIS AND SOLD MAKEUP.	SECRETARY FOR A CHAUVINIST ASSHOLE. FIRED FOR STANDING UP FOR OTHER WORKERS.	SUN CHEMICAL. SECRETARY. GIVEN MORE RESPONSIBILITY BY FEMALE BOSS.	COFFEE ASSOC. PR DIRECTOR. COMPANY'S SPOKESPERSON, STAFF LIAISON.	SENIOR VICE PRESIDENT OF A LARGE NYC COMPANY. DID PR ON TV, RADIO AND LOBBIED CONGRESS.	STARTED OWN COMPANY. PR, CRISIS MANAGEMENT, STRATEGIC THINKING.	AFTER AN EXCRUCIATINGLY SLOW COUPLE OF YEARS, BUSINESS IS NOW BOOMING.

COMMUTING TO MANHATTAN

OKAY, DAVE. TIME TO GO.

THE SIDEWALK IS SO SLIPPERY.

CAN I HOLD ON TO YOUR ARM?

SHE'S ACTING LIKE A HOBBLING OLD LADY!

TWO PLEASE.

IT'S SO FUNNY. PUTTING ON MY MAKE-UP ALWAYS MAKES ME FEEL MORE AWAKE.

I ALWAYS FEEL LIKE I WANT TO START READING THE TIMES, BUT I DON'T KNOW ANYTHING ABOUT WHAT'S GOING ON.

THIS IS HOW I READ IT.

I BROWSE THE HEADLINES, THEN START READING THE ARTICLES THAT LOOK INTERESTING.

I ONLY TURN THE PAGE AND CONTINUE THE STORY IF I'M REALLY HOOKED!

HERE, YOU CAN READ THE SECTIONS I'M DONE WITH.

WORKING AT MOM'S OFFICE

HI, KRISTY.

SECRETLY SEXUALLY ATTRACTED TO HER

I CAN'T STOP PLAYING THIS GAME WHERE I TYPE "KRISTY IS A CUNT" AND LEAVE IT ON MY SCREEN UNTIL RIGHT BEFORE SHE CHECKS ON ME.

EVEN IF SHE CAUGHT ME, I KNOW SHE'D NEVER SAY ANYTHING SINCE MY MOM'S A BIG EXECUTIVE.

I JUST NEED A LITTLE NAP.
EMPTY CONFERENCE ROOM

SEE YOU AT HOME, MOM.

FUCKING LOSERS.

DATA ENTRY

GOOD MORNING.

WHAT A MISERABLE EXISTENCE.

OBERLIN DROP-OFF

AFTER A 10-HOUR DRIVE

HERE WE ARE!

OBERLIN DROP-OUT

REBECCA AND I BROKE UP, MY FAVORITE PAINTING TEACHER GOT FIRED. I'M TAKING ONE CLASS AND WORKING FULL-TIME AS A DISHWASHER.

SCENES FROM A DIVORCE

"You still think you're leaving..."

"Bye, Dad."

"Let me get that for you, sir."

CHAIRS

CENTRAL PARK WALK

NEVER SAW THAT DRAWING AGAIN.

CLASS DIVIDE

THERAPY, CA

BIG YEAR AND A HALF

OAKLAND VISIT

HARD LINE

PETE INTRODUCES HIS FIRST BOYFRIEND TO THE FAMILY

ANNOUNCEMENT

DAVID, YOU HAVE A CONNECTION WITH HER THAT YOUR FATHER AND I NEVER HAD.

MONTHS PASS AND THAT X-MAS REB & I DECIDE TO GET ENGAGED.

THIS IS WHY I LOVE MY MOM. TWO SECONDS AGO SHE WAS SOUND ASLEEP!

RESTAURANT SEARCH

* WHERE WE WOUND UP GETTING MARRIED.

REHEARSAL DINNER

MOM, WHY DID YOU JUST HUG US THEN?!?

SLEEPOVER AT MOM'S

HAIR APPOINTMENT

DRIVING TO THE BIG DAY

* HELPING AN ELDERLY RELATIVE TO HER SEAT.

MOM'S BLESSING

SPIRITUAL TEAM

SO I'M WRITING MY BOOK ABOUT CEOs RIGHT NOW.

H. CIXOUS

"THE WESTERN HISTORY OF WRITING IS SYNONYMOUS WITH THE SEPARATION OF THE BODY FROM THE TEXT. THE BODY ENTERING THE TEXT DISRUPTS THE MASCULINE ECONOMY OF SUPER-IMPOSED LINEARITY AND TYRANNY. THE FEMININE IS THE OVERFLOW OF 'LUMINOUS TORRENTS,' A MARGIN OF 'EXCESS' EROTICISM AND FREE-PLAY NOT DIRECTLY ATTRIBUTABLE TO THE FIXED HIERARCHIES OF MASCULINITY."

-Helene Cixous' theory of "L'ecriture Feminine" as summarized by Chiara Brigante and Robert Con Davis.

AT MY GALLERY SHOW IN BOSTON

JUDY CHICAGO'S DINNER PARTY

BODY MEMORY THEORY

THIS NEW BODY WORK SPECIALIST I'M SEEING IS AMAZING! I'M REALIZING I HAVE ALL THESE MEMORIES STORED IN DIFFERENT PARTS OF MY BODY!

≡PFFT!≡ THAT'S RIDICULOUS. IT'S OBVIOUSLY ALL TAKING PLACE IN YOUR BRAIN! YOUR MEMORIES ARE TRIGGERED BY FAMILIAR SENSATIONS WHICH CALL UP OLD ASSOCIATIONS. MEMORIES AREN'T STORED IN YOUR MUSCLE TISSUE.

IDIOTS.

THIRTY

AT JACKSON HOUSE RESTAURANT

MAYBE YOU SHOULDN'T READ ANY OF MY COMICS...

MOM, THE COMIC IS GOING TO BE ALMOST ENTIRELY ABOUT YOU AND ME.

I GUESS SOMETIMES I DON'T BELIEVE THERE EVEN IS A YOU AND ME.

AN HOUR LATER
I'M GLAD WE TALKED IT ALL THROUGH.

BLAH BLAH INTUITION, SPIRITUALITY, BLAH BLAH MAN-MADE DISASTERS.

END.

THE UNIVERSE

*EYE MOVEMENT DESENSITIZATION AND REPROCESSING THERAPY

Portrait of My Dad

AT LOUIE'S CHARCOAL PIT, PART 1

SO, DAD, I JUST GOT THOSE SLIDES OF MY PAINTINGS TAKEN, SO NOW I JUST HAVE TO...

ALWAYS ASKS FOR 6 SYRUPS

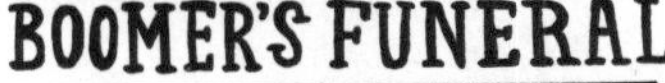

BOOMER'S FUNERAL

I FEEL COMPLETELY BETRAYED!

WHAT ARE YOU TALKING ABOUT??

YOU WERE SUPPOSED TO BE HERE AN HOUR AGO. YOUR MOTHER AND BROTHERS WILL BE HERE SOON!

CRUNCH

I GUESS YOU'RE A LOT STRONGER THAN ME. THIS WOULD HAVE TAKEN ME ALL AFTERNOON.

I'M SORRY I SNAPPED AT YOU. IT WAS HARD FOR ME SEEING POOR LITTLE "BOO" AT THE VET LIKE THAT. THEY HAD HIM IN THIS PLASTIC FREEZER BAG.

CHOKES

CAN I SHOW YOU MY BEGONIAS?

HUMP

HARVEY

I'LL NEVER KNOW HOW TRUE THIS IS, BUT APPARENTLY, SOON AFTER MY FATHER WAS BORN, HIS MOTHER (WHO HAD TWO CHILDREN FROM A PREVIOUS MARRIAGE) OVERHEARD MY DAD'S FATHER (WHO WAS ORPHANED AT A YOUNG AGE) SAY IN A DIABOLICAL VOICE:

DAD'S CARS

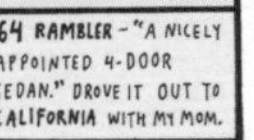

1984

"THE BIG BLUE VAN" – DAD GOT TO KEEP THE COMPANY CAR-POOL VAN ON WEEKENDS.* I GOT TO BE COOL FOR SIX MONTHS.

2005 - PRESENT

2001 BUICK REGAL
"THE DEALERSHIP MUST HAVE SOLD IT TO ME BECAUSE I LOOK LIKE A KING."

WHAT DID YOU THINK I WOULD DO AT THIS MOMENT?

THIS IS A SONG THAT MY FRIEND JASON GAVE TO ME, AND IT REMINDS ME OF MY FATHER. IT HELPS ME TO GET IN TOUCH WITH ALL THE PAIN AND TO CRY ABOUT HIM.

RACQUET SPORTS

* WE NEVER TOOK IT ON ANY TRIPS. ** I HAVE A PRETTY GOOD PING-PONG GAME TO THIS DAY, THANKS TO MY DAD.

FIRESTARTERS

AROUND 13

I SAW YOU PLAYING YOUR GAME IN THE BACKYARD, THE ONE WHERE ONE OF YOU SETS THE GRASS ON FIRE AND THE OTHER TRIES TO PUT IT OUT.

WELL I JUST WANT TO TELL YOU THAT IT'S OKAY SOMETIMES TO USE YOUR PENIS AS A LITTLE "TUB TOY."

THE PITCHER

ONE OF DAD'S FAVORITE SNACKS WHILE WATCHING TV IN HIS ROOM WAS A SPOONFUL OF PEANUT BUTTER FOLLOWED BY A SPOONFUL OF JELLY. HE KEPT A PITCHER FULL OF WATER TO SOAK THE SPOONS ON HIS BEDSIDE TABLE, BUT EVENTUALLY THE WATER EVAPORATED. (P.S.- I WASHED ALL THOSE SPOONS.)

CALIFORNIA

AT LOUIE'S CHARCOAL PIT PART 2

...AND THEN FINANCIAL AID TELLS ME THAT PARENTS WHO TAKE OUT LOANS FOR THEIR KIDS' TUITION, USUALLY GIVE ANY LEFTOVER MONEY TO THE KIDS FOR THEIR EXPENSES! THEY DON'T JUST KEEP IT!!!

GAS ATTENDANT

RESUME

1966

CONSTRUCTION LABORER- WORKED W/HIS FATHER ON BUILDING HE LATER TOOK CLASSES IN.

1967

STAFF MEMBER AT COUNTRY CLUB- SOLD COCKTAILS TO LADIES PLAYING MAH JONG.

1968

CAMP COUNSELOR FOR DISADVANTAGED KIDS IN ALBANY, NY.

1968
CAMPUS SECURITY GUARD ("CHASED COUPLES OFF OF PARK BENCHES")

1970

DISHWASHER AT UNSPECIFIED RESTAURANT IN SAN DIEGO, CA.

1972-78

DIRECTOR OF RELIGIOUS ED. FOR THE CATHOLIC CHURCH IN SAN DIEGO AND NEWARK, NJ.

1978-80

INDUSTRIAL ENGINEER AT OTIS ELEVATOR.

1980-81

PLAY TEX, INT'L "I COMPUTERIZED THE SPECIFICATION DEPARTMENT."

1981-82

DREXEL, BURNHAM & LAMBERT- DID COMPUTER STUFF FOR THIS NYC BROKERAGE FIRM.

1982-85

CRUMB & FORSTER- CHIEF OFFICER OF OFFICE AUTOMATION SPECIALISTS.

1985-87
XEROX- DID TRAINING, SET UP NETWORKS, TROUBLESHOOTING, ETC.

1987-98

SELF-EMPLOYED CONSULTANT & COMPUTER TRAINER FOR AT&T, NOVA SCOTIA TEL CO., MTV, ETC.

1998-2000

FULL-TIME CONSULTANT & MANAGER OF TRAINING CENTER AT A NYC AD AGENCY.

2000-03

SELF-EMPLOYED.

2003

MENTAL HEALTH ADVOCATE FOR AN UNSPECIFIED SERVICE GROUP IN NJ. "I'M SEMI-RETIRED."

GAIUS JULIUS

CAN YOU TELL ME ABOUT THAT ANCIENT ROME WEBSITE YOU BELONG TO?

SURE. IT'S CALLED 'ANCIENT WORLDS.' I'M A ROMAN CITIZEN NAMED GAIUS JULIUS CAECILIUS.

I'M A LEGATE UNDER CAESAR, A GOVERNOR OF THE AFRICAN PROVINCE.

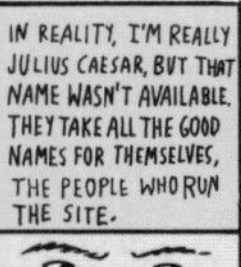

...OR DOPEY AND ANNOYING AND HAVE NAMES LIKE "JED CAESAR."

SO DO THEY POST OBNOXIOUS MESSAGES TO YOU?

VOCAB

SOME WORDS MY DAD MADE UP, MANY OF WHICH ARE STILL IN USE (IN NO PARTICULAR ORDER):

1. SCHNARKY
2. SKALALABATCH
3. SCHNARKY FLARGET
4. DING DAO DAY
5. CHING CHAO CHAY (THE ABOVE TWO SUNG IN DOO-WOP SOUNDING SONGS)
6. HAPPY, DAPPY DAN
7. *PORK!* (AS A CURSE AGAINST THE HUMAN RACE)

D.Q.

IN THE BATH

DREAMT BY ME

DEATH BED

JULY 2003

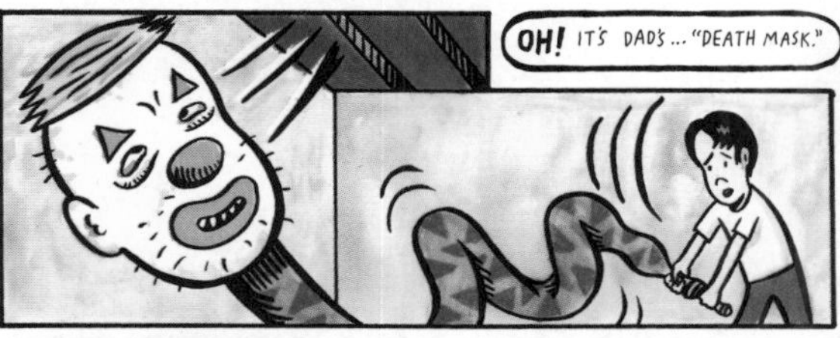

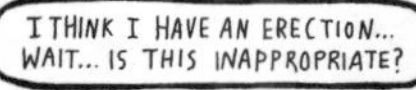

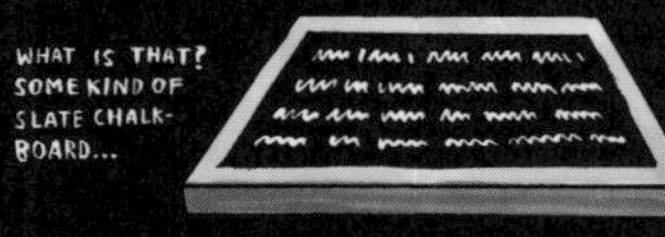

AT LOUIE'S CHARCOAL PIT, PART 3

SEE THAT WOMAN OVER THERE? HER HUSBAND JUST PASSED AWAY AND SHE'S BEEN REALLY DEVASTATED.

L.O.D.I., NJ

I THINK I'M GOING TO REALLY LIKE LIVING HERE. I'VE BEEN AROUND ITALIANS ALL MY LIFE!

GENERATION Y FINDS CHRIST

I'D SEE THESE POOR YOUNG KIDS DRESSED ALL IN BLACK, WEARING T-SHIRTS WITH CORPSES AND SNAKES ON THEM.

BEAM ME UP

ISAAC ASIMOV

DAD DISCOVERED "I, ROBOT" IN JR. HIGH SCHOOL AND HAS SINCE READ ALL OF ASIMOV'S SHORT STORIES AND NOVELS MULTIPLE TIMES.

STAR WARS

SAW THIS IN THE THEATRE IN 1977 AND WAS "AMAZED." HE NOW OWNS ALL THE MOVIES AND QUOTES FROM THEM CONSTANTLY. "IF OUR FAMILY WASN'T CHRISTIAN, OUR RELIGION WOULD BE 'STARWARSIAN.'"

STAR TREK

DAD LOVES ALL THE MOVIES, SOME OF THE ORIGINAL TV SHOW AND ALL OF THE "NEXT GENERATION" SERIES. HE FOUND THE SPINOFF NOVELS TO BE "INSTANTLY FORGETTABLE." HE DOESN'T CONSIDER HIMSELF A "TREKKIE."

BATTLESTAR GALACTICA ('78)

"THEY HAD A BUDGET OF A MILLION DOLLARS PER EPISODE AND SPENT HALF OF IT ON SPECIAL EFFECTS ALONE. TRULY, TRULY AWESOME!"

LORD OF THE RINGS

WHILE LIVING ALONE IN CALIFORNIA FOR SIX MONTHS, DAD DISCOVERED J.R.R. TOLKIEN. HE QUICKLY DEVOURED ALL OF HIS BOOKS. DECADES LATER, HE OWNS ALL THE MOVIES AND WATCHES HIS FAVORITE SCENES WEEKLY. "IT'S A BIG PART OF MY LIFE."

STAR GATE

DAD HAS ALL 10 YEARS OF THE SHOW COPIED ON DVDs. HE ATTENDED 3 CONVENTIONS, MET 5 CAST MEMBERS AND SAW 3 MORE UP CLOSE. HE ALSO PAID TO HAVE BREAKFAST WITH MICHAEL SHANKS AND HAVE HIS PICTURE TAKEN WITH HIM.

HAIRLINE

MY FATHER WAS BALD ALL MY LIFE. I DON'T WANT TO LOOK IN THE MIRROR EVERY DAY AND SEE HARVEY.

WE'LL SEE

AT VICTORIA'S CAFÉ

SO I'VE GOT THIS NEW FRIEND THAT I'VE BEEN HELPING. HE'S HAD A VERY ROUGH LIFE.

RECREATION

VHS TAPES

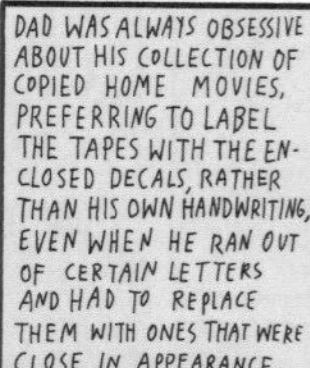

DAD WAS ALWAYS OBSESSIVE ABOUT HIS COLLECTION OF COPIED HOME MOVIES, PREFERRING TO LABEL THE TAPES WITH THE ENCLOSED DECALS, RATHER THAN HIS OWN HANDWRITING, EVEN WHEN HE RAN OUT OF CERTAIN LETTERS AND HAD TO REPLACE THEM WITH ONES THAT WERE CLOSE IN APPEARANCE.

X-MAS VILLAGE

DAD'S HOLIDAY "CHRISTMAS VILLAGE," WHICH STAYED SET UP ON HIS DINING ROOM TABLE FROM NOVEMBER 2001 UNTIL APRIL 2003.

DREAMT BY DAD

HOW GREAT THOU ART

SOME TIME IN 1993

How Great Thou Art

O LORD MY GOD, WHEN I IN AWESOME WONDER, CONSIDER ALL THE WORLDS THY HANDS HAVE MADE: I SEE THE STARS, I HEAR THE ROLLING THUNDER, THY POWER THROUGHOUT THE UNIVERSE DISPLAYED.

WHEN THROUGH THE WOODS, AND FOREST GLADES I WANDER, AND HEAR THE BIRDS SING SWEETLY IN THE TREES. WHEN I LOOK DOWN FROM LOFTY MOUNTAIN GRANDEUR AND SEE THE BROOK AND FEEL THE GENTLE BREEZE.

AND WHEN I THINK THAT GOD, HIS SON NOT SPARING; SENT HIM TO DIE, I SCARCE CAN TAKE IT IN. THAT ON THE CROSS, MY BURDEN GLADLY BEARING, HE BLED AND DIED TO TAKE AWAY MY SIN.

WHEN CHRIST SHALL COME, WITH SHOUT OF ACCLAMATION, AND TAKE ME HOME, WHAT JOY SHALL FILL MY HEART. THEN I SHALL BOW, IN HUMBLE ADORATION, AND THEN PROCLAIM, "MY GOD, HOW GREAT THOU ART!"

END.

CONTRIBUTORS

Jessica Abel's most recent work includes *Drawing Words & Writing Pictures*, a textbook on comics, and the script for the graphic novel *Life Sucks*. She's also the author of *La Perdida* and two collections of comics short stories, *Soundtrack* and *Mirror, Window*. She lives in Brooklyn with her husband Matt Madden and daughter Aldara.

The author of *Utility Sketchbook* (PictureBox) would like to remain **Anonymous**.

Lynda Barry is a writer and cartoonist whose comic strip *Ernie Pook's Comeek* celebrated its 30th year in print in 2007. She is a recipient of the Washington State Governor's Award for her novel *The Good Times Are Killing Me*, which she adapted into a long-running off-Broadway play. The *New York Times* called her second novel, *Cruddy*, "a work of terrible beauty." She received the 2003 Eisner Award for Best Graphic Album and an American Library Association Alex Award for her book *One! Hundred! Demons!* She lives and works in southern Wisconsin.

For security reasons **Mark Beyer** is unable to provide any personally identifiable information regarding his current whereabouts or activities.

Ariel Bordeaux studied art at the Museum School in Boston, and throughout the 1990s self-published the acclaimed minicomic *Deep Girl*. Drawn & Quarterly published her novella *No Love Lost* in 1997. Ariel recently collaborated with her cartoonist husband Rick Altergott on the comic book series *Raisin Pie*, published by Fantagraphics. Ariel and Rick currently live in Rhode Island with their son, Edwin.

Chester Brown was born in Montreal, Canada, in 1960. His fifth and latest graphic novel is *Louis Riel: A Comic-Strip Biography*. He is currently drawing his next book in a very small apartment in Toronto.

Jeffrey Brown is a cartoonist best known alternately for his autobiographical comics such as *Clumsy* and humorous parodies like *Incredible Change-Bots*. Simon & Schuster published his latest collection of comics *Little Things* and will next publish his longest work to date, *Funny Misshapen Body*. He lives in Chicago with his partner Jennifer and their son, working on more autobiographical comics as well as the comic series *Sulk* from Top Shelf.

Charles Burns (Philadelphia) is the author of *Black Hole* (Pantheon) as well as *Big Baby*, *El Borbah*, and *Skin Deep* (Fantagraphics). He has done covers for such magazines as *Time* and the *New Yorker*, and he is the regular cover artist for *The Believer*. A book of recent photographs, *One Eye*, was published by Drawn & Quarterly in 2006.

Martin Cendreda's comic leavings have stained the pages of such well-known publications as *Dang!*, *Mome*, *Drawn & Quarterly Showcase*, *Kramers Ergot*, and *Giant Robot*. He currently lives in his hometown of Los Angeles with his wife Jenny, daughter Margot, and a pair of mismatched cats.

C.F. (Providence) makes music under the name "Kites." He also self-publishes his *Fantasy Empire* magazine monthly and regularly contributes to the comics anthology *Kramers Ergot*. He is currently working on his multi-volume *Powr Mastrs* comics series and a new book collection titled *Pioneer Trash*.

Brian Chippendale (Providence) is a part-time cartoonist slightly known for his books *Ninja* and *Maggots*. He spends much of his time drumming for the band Lightning Bolt or for no reason at all. He was born and bred in Fort Thunder, Rhode Island. His most recent work includes the ongoing minicomic *Galactikrap* and the solo music project *Black Pus*.

Daniel Clowes (Oakland) is the creator of the *Eightball* series, which has been collected in the books *Like a Velvet Glove Cast in Iron*, *Pussey!*, *Caricature*, *David Boring*, *Ice Haven*, and *Ghost World*, among others (the latter was adapted by Clowes and Terry Zwigoff into an Oscar-nominated screenplay). He also wrote the screenplay for *Art School Confidential*, loosely adapted from one of his comics. His serial *Mister Wonderful* recently completed a 20-episode run in the *New York Times Magazine*.

David Collier (Hamilton, ON) has written a travelogue of a trip to Iceland (www.cbc.ca/arts/books/icelanddiary.html) and was awarded a Chalmers Fellowship for his work as a soldier-artist. He is currently working on his ongoing series *Collier's*.

Robert Crumb was born in Philadelphia in 1943, created *Zap Comix* in 1967, and continues to produce "adult" comic books, including collaborations with Harvey Pekar and his wife Aline Kominsky-Crumb. In the 1980s he was editor of *Weirdo* magazine's first nine issues. He has also done many album and CD covers and other types of illustration work. He is presently working on a long-term project, a comic-book version of the Book of Genesis.

Vanessa Davis lives in Santa Rosa, California. *Spaniel Rage*, a collection of her daily diary comics, was put out in 2005 by Buenaventura Press. Her work has also appeared in such publications as *Kramers Ergot*, *The Best American Comics 2007*, and the *New York Times*. She is currently working on her next book of short stories.

Kim Deitch: I was born in 1944 and have been at this comics thing for forty years. I still like it and am still evolving even as the medium itself is. The story printed in this volume can be found along with nine others in *Shadowland*, published by Fantagraphics. Also from Fantagraphics, just out, is *Deitch's Pictorama*, by me and my two brothers in various combinations between us. And check out my books from Pantheon, *The Boulevard of Broken Dreams* and *Alias The Cat*.

Debbie Drechsler (Santa Rosa) created comics for a while and now has a thing for traipsing through the woods and drawing and photographing fungi. Go figure.

Charles Forbell's (1884–1946) *Naughty Pete* strips, which ran only during the last five months of 1913, can be found in *Art Out of Time*, edited by Dan Nadel.

Renée French has been writing and illustrating comics since the early 1990s. She is the creator of the Top Shelf books *The Ticking*, *Micrographica*, and *The Soap Lady*, the collection *Marbles in My Underpants* for Oni Press, and most recently *Edison Steelhead's Lost Portfolio*, published by Sparkplug. She is presently working on a graphic novel for PictureBox and lives and works on the right coast of Australia and the left coast of the U.S.

Drew Friedman's comics and drawings have been collected in six books, the most recent being *The Fun Never Stops!* and *More Old Jewish Comedians*, both from Fantagraphics. His work can be seen regularly in the *New Republic* and the *New York Observer*, among others.

Phoebe Gloeckner is perhaps best known for her book *A Child's Life and Other Stories* and her illustrated novel *The Diary of a Teenage Girl*. She was awarded a Guggenheim Fellowship in 2008 for a graphic narrative about a Mexican girl murdered at the turn of this century in Ciudad Juarez, a major U.S.-Mexico border crossing adjacent to El Paso, Texas.

Leif Goldberg lives in Providence and produces *National Waste* zines and books. He was co-editor of *Paper Rodeo* during its five-year existence. His new book is *Watch Out for Watch Out*, a child's introduction to paranormal awareness.

Carrie Golus has written five nonfiction books for children, including biographies of Tupac Shakur and Muhammad Ali. She is currently collaborating on a picture book with Patrick W. Welch.

Adam Gopnik has been writing for the *New Yorker* since 1986. He is a three-time winner of National Magazine Awards for essays and for criticism and winner of the George Polk Award for magazine reporting. His books include *Paris to the Moon*, *The King in the Window*, *Americans in Paris: A Literary Anthology*, and *Through the Children's Gate*.

Bill Griffith is best known for the strip *Zippy*, syndicated by King Features to around 100 daily newspapers. In 2000 Fantagraphics published the first *Zippy Annual*, the latest of which are *From Here to Absurdity*, *Type 'Z' Personality*, and *Walk a Mile in My Muu-Muu*. Griffith is married to cartoonist and editor Diane Noomin; they live in Connecticut.

Milt Gross (1895–1953) is perhaps most famous for the strips *Gross Exaggerations*, *Dave's Delicatessen*, and *Count Screwloose of Tooloose*, as well as books such as *Nize Baby*, *Dunt Esk*, and his masterpiece, *He Done Her Wrong* (the latter reprinted by Fantagraphics in 2006). He is also one of the featured artists in *Art Out of Time*, edited by Dan Nadel.

John Hankiewicz (Westmont, IL) is the author of *Asthma*, a collection of short comics. He is slowly making new minicomics and booklets, as well as etchings and lithographs.

In 2007, Fantagraphics published a collection of comics by **Fletcher Hanks** (1879–*c.*1970s) entitled *I Shall Destroy All the Civilized Planets*, edited by Paul Karasik.

Sammy Harkham (b. 1980, Los Angeles) has edited seven volumes of the comics anthology *Kramers Ergot*, and his book *Poor Sailor* was published by Gingko Press in 2006. He is currently working on his ongoing series *Crickets*.

David Heatley is a cartoonist who lives in Queens with his wife, the writer Rebecca Gopoian, and their children, Maya and Sam. His comics and illustrations have appeared in the *New Yorker*, the *New York Times*, and numerous anthologies. A collection of his autobiographical work, *My Brain Is Hanging Upside Down*, will be published in the fall of 2008. For more information: www.davidheatley.com and www.drawger.com/heatley.

Tim Hensley (Hollywood) is a graduate of the prestigious California State University at Northridge. He is currently serializing a story called "Gropius" in the anthology *Mome*.

Gilbert Hernandez is co-creator of the still ongoing *Love and Rockets* comic book as well as the mind behind the graphic novels *Sloth*, *Chance in Hell*, and *Speak of the Devil*. He has been creating comics for the adult reader for 25 years now.

Jaime Hernandez (Pasadena) has been writing and drawing his half of *Love and Rockets* for over a quarter century and has no plans of stopping. It has won him numerous awards in and outside of the U.S. He is a genius. Just ask him.

Bill Holman (1903–1987) drew *Smokey Stover* from 1935 until he retired in 1973, coining such words as "Foo" and "Notary Sojac" along the way. The strip was the longest lasting of the "screwball comedy" genre. See www.smokey-stover.com for a generous sampling of his work.

Kevin Huizenga (St. Louis) happily writes and draws comics for the ongoing series *Or Else* for Drawn & Quarterly and also *Ganges* for Fantagraphics.

Jess Collins (1923–2004) was known professionally as **Jess**. A retrospective *(Jess: A Grand Collage, 1951–1993)* toured the U.S. in 1993–1994, accompanied by a book of the same title. More recently, the Independent Curators International published *Jess: To and From the Printed Page* (2007).

Cole Johnson (San Antonio) has published strips in anthologies such as *40075km*, *Blood Orange*, and *Hi-Horse Omnibus*. He is currently working on a book called *Beige Floral Pattern*.

J. Bradley Johnson (San Francisco) has contributed to several anthologies over the years but has yet to make a whole comic book. He enjoys drawing and long late-night walks.

Ben Katchor (New York City) publishes his picture-stories and drawings in the English-language *Forward*, *Metropolis* magazine, and the *New Yorker*. He was the recipient of a Guggenheim Memorial Foundation Fellowship and a MacArthur Foundation Fellowship, and he was a fellow at the Cullman Center for Scholars and Writers at the New York Public Library. He collaborated with composer Mark Mulcahy on two music-theater productions: *The Slug Bearers of Kayrol Island* and *The Rosenbach Company*. He teaches at Parsons, the New School. For more information visit www.katchor.com.

Kaz has been drawing comics since he attended New York's School of Visual Arts in the early 1980s. An original contributor to *Raw* magazine and a cartoonist for the *New York Rocker*, he has also done illustrations for numerous magazines and appeared in many comics collections. In 1991 he created the Harvey-nominated weekly alternative newspaper strip *Underworld* (which he continues to draw). In 2001, Kaz wrote for Nickelodeon's *SpongeBob SquarePants*, and in 2002 he won France's Prix Alph-Art Award for his *Underworld* collection *Cruel and Unusual*. In 2004 he joined the staff of Cartoon Network's *Camp Lazlo*, for which he received an Emmy nomination. In 2007 he created the animated short *Zoot Rumpus, the Junkyard Dog*.

Megan Kelso's (Seattle) most recent book of short stories, *The Squirrel Mother*, was published by Fantagraphics in 2006. In the summer of 2007, she had a serialized story called "Watergate Sue" published in the *New York Times Magazine*. She is currently finishing a graphic novel called *Artichoke Tales*, which will be published by Fantagraphics in 2008.

Dave Kiersh (Massachusetts) is the author of *A Last Cry for Help* (Bodega Books, 2006). His work is partly the result of growing up on Long Island and reading way too many Young Adult novels. More samples of his work can be found at www.davekiersh.com.

Aline Kominsky-Crumb is one of the grandmothers of kvetching and whining in comic form. Her most recent book is *Need More Love* (2007)—the publisher went bankrupt during the dazzling book tour. Her next book is *Dream House* from W.W. Norton. She collaborates with her husband Robert for the *New Yorker* and *Dirty Laundry*. Their daughter Sophie is the best artist in the family! (Not objective.)

Michael Kupperman's illustrations and comics have appeared in publications such as the *New Yorker* and *Fortune* and have been collected in his book *Snake 'n' Bacon's Cartoon Cabaret*, as well as his ongoing comic series *Tales Designed to Thrizzle*, available from Fantagraphics.

Harvey Kurtzman (1924–1993) is probably best known as the comic genius who created *Mad;* he also wrote, edited, and contributed to *Two-Fisted Tales* and *Frontline Combat*, war comics that refused to glorify war.

Joe Matt's recent book *Spent* chronicles his ongoing addiction to pornography and masturbation in a way that's more appetizing than it sounds. And to his delight, his previous book *The Poor Bastard* is currently being adapted into a Broadway musical. Joe Matt lives in Los Angeles without a car, cell phone, or computer.

David Mazzucchelli has been making comics his whole life. His graphic novel *Asterios Polyp* should be out any day now.

Winsor McCay's (1867–1934) two best-known creations are the newspaper comic strip *Little Nemo in Slumberland*, which ran from 1905 to 1914, and the animated cartoon *Gertie the Dinosaur*, which he created in 1914. An expanded edition of John Canemaker's authoritative biography *Winsor McCay: His Life and Art* was published in 2005 (Abrams).

Richard McGuire recently designed and directed part of an animated feature film called *Puer(s) Du Noir* [Fear(s) of the Dark]. He is a regular contributor to the *New Yorker* and known to cult music fans as the founder and bass player of the "no wave" band Liquid Liquid. *Comic Art* No. 8 features his cover artwork, a career overview, and an interview with him.

James McShane (Providence) has appeared in *Paper Rodeo*, *Kramers Ergot*, *Orang Magazin*, and *Whatcha Mean, What's a Zine?* He has been making minicomics since 2001.

Jerry Moriarty (New York City) did *Jack Survives* in 1984, to be published with much more Jack stuff as *The Complete Jack Survives* by Buenaventura Press in 2008. He has had paintings in shows curated by Art Spiegelman and Chris Ware in 2004, 2007, and 2008; has been published in *Kramers Ergot*, *Uninked*, and *Comic Art* in 2006, 2007, and 2008; and is currently working on *Sally's Surprise*, which has morphed into *Sally Chevy*, a strip about a girl and her car.

Anders Nilsen is the author and artist of *Dogs and Water*, *Don't Go Where I Can't Follow*, and *Monologues for the Coming Plague*. He's received two Ignatz Awards and has had his comics translated into several languages. He is currently working on an ongoing graphic novel, *Big Questions*. He lives in Chicago.

Diane Noomin was born in Brooklyn and attended the High School of Music and Art, Brooklyn College, and Pratt Institute. She is the creator of *DiDi Glitz* and editor of the *Twisted Sisters* anthologies of women cartoonists. One of the early contributors to *Wimmen's Comics*, Noomin created the first issue of *Twisted Sisters Comics* with Aline Kominsky-Crumb in 1976. In 1981, she collaborated on the musical comedy *I'd Rather Be Doing Something Else: The DiDi Glitz Story* with the San Francisco–based women's theater group Les Nickelettes. Noomin has been nominated for Harvey and Eisner Awards and was given the Ink Pen Award in 1994. She has curated and shown work in exhibits in New York, San Francisco, and Los Angeles. Noomin is currently working on a graphic memoir detailing her parents' involvement with the Communist Party in the 1950s. She lives in Connecticut with her husband, cartoonist Bill Griffith, and three cats.

Any information about **Elinore Norflus** may be sent to the editor of this volume, care of the publishers.

Onsmith (Chicago) has published several minicomics, such as *Spit-Toons* and *Baka-Geta*, and edited an anthology of one-panel cartoons, *Gag-Hag*. He is currently a student and is working on his first major book, tentatively titled *Bad Math*.

A three-time Emmy Award–winner for his production design on *Pee-wee's Playhouse* and the recipient of the 2000 Chrysler Award for design excellence, graphic artist **Gary Panter** has drawn inspiration from diverse vernacular and traditional art arenas over the course of the past four decades. Closely associated with the underground comics and music scenes on both coasts, he is responsible for designing the Screamers iconic 1970s poster, many record covers for Frank Zappa, the Red Hot Chili Peppers, and The Residents, and the ongoing comic character Jimbo. Most recently, Panter has performed psychedelic light shows at the Hirshhorn Museum in Washington, DC, and at New York's Anthology Film Archives. PictureBox has just released a 700-page collection of his work, titled simply *Gary Panter*.

Paper Rad (New England): see www.paperrad.org. New books out in 2008 from pictureboxinc.com. New videos out in 2008 from loadrecords.com.

Laura Park (Chicago) is working on a collection to be published whenever she can finish it. She is trying her best. See www.flickr.com/photos/featherbed/.

Harvey Pekar was born in Cleveland in 1939, graduated high school in 1957, and worked as a file clerk for the federal government for 37 years. The subject of the Oscar-nominated film *American Splendor,* his American Book Award–winning series of the same name has been published since 1976. Pekar's music and book reviews have been published in the *Boston Herald*, the *Austin Chronicle*, *Jazz Times*, and *Down Beat.* He is the author of the recent graphic novels *Ego & Hubris*, *The Quitter*, and *Students for a Democratic Society: A Graphic History*. Due in 2008 is *The Beats*, illustrated by Ed Piskor.

John Porcellino has been self-publishing his zine, *King-Cat Comics & Stories*, since 1989. Several books collecting his work are available from the publishers La Mano, Drawn & Quarterly, and Hyperion, among others. For more information please visit www.king-cat.net.

Jayr Pulga: Not much artwork done in the last 20 years. Best things I've done are start a family and avoid subprime loans. Everything else is still a mystery.

Archer Prewitt (Oak Park, IL) works as a cartoonist when he isn't recording and touring with his solo project or the indie band The Sea and Cake. His comic *Sof' Boy and Friends* is published by Drawn & Quarterly, and his *Funny Bunny* cartoons appear in a variety of publications. He is currently working on new album projects and a *Sof' Boy* collection.

Ron Regé, Jr.'s new book *Against Pain* (Drawn & Quarterly 2008) collects 20 years' worth of his experimental cartoons that had previously appeared buried deep inside books like this one, or in obscure fanzines like *Wingnut,* and the *New York Times Magazine.*

Joe Sacco is the author of *Palestine*, *Safe Area Gorazde*, and other works of comics journalism. He is currently working on a book about the Gaza Strip.

Richard Sala (Berkeley) is currently finishing up his miniseries *Delphine* for Fantagraphics Books/Coconino Press. His books include *Hypnotic Tales*, *Peculia*, *Mad Night*, and *The Chuckling Whatsit*.

Souther Salazar (Los Angeles) has exhibited his paintings, sculptures, and installations in Tokyo, New York, Los Angeles, and Brazil. He regularly contributes his comics work to the anthology *Kramers Ergot*. He is currently working on further chronicling the adventures of Fervler 'n' Razzle in comics form.

Frank Santoro (Pittsburgh) was born and raised in Pittsburgh, moved to San Francisco on an art school scholarship, and quit to create and self-publish *Sirk* zines and comics—some in conjunction with Katie Glicksberg—culminating in the publication of *Storeyville*. He moved to New York City, returned to painting, worked five years as Francesco Clemente's assistant, met Dan Nadel, and began a project to integrate painterly and poetic values into comics, starting with *Chimera* and *Incanto* and continuing in collaboration with Ben Jones on *Cold Heat*.

Kevin Scalzo (Northampton, MA) is currently working on art for the next *BLAB!* anthology and will have his first solo painting show in Los Angeles in 2008. He can be reached at info@kevinscalzo.com.

Seth is the nom de plume of Canadian cartoonist Gregory Gallant. He is currently plodding along toward the finish of his *Clyde Fans* "picture novella." His most recent book is *George Sprott (1894–1975)*, much of which was serialized in the *New York Times Magazine*.

R. Sikoryak (New York City) is working on a collection of his classics adaptations, to be published by Drawn & Quarterly in 2009.

Art Spiegelman (New York City) was awarded a Pulitzer Prize in 1992 for his two volumes of *Maus*, which was first serialized in *Raw*, the influential comix magazine he co-founded with his wife, Françoise Mouly, in 1980. His most recent book, *In the Shadow of No Towers* (Pantheon), was listed as one of the New York Times 100 Most Notable Books of 2004. A new edition of his 1978 anthology *Breakdowns* will be published in fall 2008; it will include an autobiographical comix-format introduction almost as long as the book itself, titled *Portrait of the Artist as a Young %@&*!* Also in 2008 a new children's book, *Jack and the Box*, will be published by Toon Books, and in 2008, *McSweeney's* will publish a 72-page sketchbook titled *Auto Phobia*. Additionally, in preparation is a book with a DVD about the making of *Maus*, titled *Meta Maus*.

William Steig (1907–2003) sold his first cartoon to the *New Yorker* in 1930. Over the following decades he published over 1,600 cartoons in the magazine, including 117 of its covers, leading *Newsweek* to dub him the "King of Cartoons." In 1968 he wrote his first children's book, *C D B!* His third book, *Sylvester and the Magic Pebble* (1970), won the prestigious Caldecott Medal. He went on to write more than 30 children's books, including *Shrek!*

Saul Steinberg (1914–1999) was one of America's most beloved artists, renowned for the covers and drawings that appeared in the *New Yorker* for nearly six decades and for the drawings, paintings, prints, collages, and sculptures exhibited internationally in galleries and museums. The traveling retrospective and accompanying book, *Saul Steinberg: Illuminations*, is a comprehensive look at Steinberg's extraordinary contribution to 20th-century art.

Any information about **Eugene Teal** may be sent to the editor of this volume, care of the publishers.

Matthew Thurber lives in Brooklyn. His printed works include *1-800-MICE*, *Carrot for Girls*, and *Mining the Moon*.

Adrian Tomine (Brooklyn) is the writer-artist of *Optic Nerve*, *Sleepwalk and Other Stories*, *Summer Blonde*, and *Shortcomings*. His work appears with some regularity in the *New Yorker*, and he is also the editor-designer of the English-language editions of Yoshihiro Tatsumi's comics.

H. J. Tuthill (1886–1957) created George and Josephine Bungle in 1918. His strip, originally titled *Home Sweet Home*, was renamed *The Bungle Family* seven years later. He wrote and drew the strip until his retirement in 1945. More samples can be seen in Dan Nadel's *Art Out of Time*.

Carol Tyler is an American cartoonist born into a working-class family in 1950s Chicago. She attended Catholic school for K-12, went to college in Tennessee, and finally received a master's degree in fine art from Syracuse University in the 1980s. Her work has appeared in many publications since that time. *Late Bloomer*, her most recent book, was published by Fantagraphics in November 2005. She teaches comics at the University of Cincinnati College of Design, Art, Architecture, and Planning (DAAP). Currently, she is working on a story about her dad and WWII, which will be published in 2009. See www.bloomerland.com.

Maurice Vellekoop was born in 1964 in the suburbs of Toronto. Since 1986, he has been illustrating for major magazines and books in North America and Europe. Among his books are *Vellevision: A Cocktail of Comics and Pictures*, *Maurice Vellekoop's ABC Book: A Homoerotic Primer*, and *A Nut at the Opera*. He lives on Toronto Island with his cat Fred.

Chris Ware is the author of *Jimmy Corrigan—The Smartest Kid on Earth* and was editor of the 13th issue of *McSweeney's Quarterly Concern*. His work was the focus of an exhibit at the Museum of Contemporary Art, Chicago, in 2006, and his ongoing series *The Acme Novelty Library* attained its 19th issue in 2008.

Patrick W. Welch is an artist and professor based in Chicago. He is regarded as the Founding Father of the Micromentalist art movement. He has collaborated with Carrie Golus for over a decade. He likes small things.

Mack White (Austin) has published many comics, including his series *Villa of the Mysteries* and *The Bush Junta*, an anthology he co-edited. His most recent comic story, "Trouble in Tascosa," appeared in the Fantagraphics anthology *Hotwire*.

Karl Wirsum (Chicago), a member of the Chicago artistic group The Hairy Who, has recently appeared in *The Ganzfeld* 3 and 4. He teaches at the Art Institute of Chicago and is represented by the Jean Albano Gallery. In 2007, the Chicago Cultural Center published a catalog in conjunction with its retrospective exhibition, *Karl Wirsum: Winsome Works (Some)*.

Basil Wolverton (1909–1978) was a self-professed "Producer of Preposterous Pictures of Peculiar People Who Prowl this Perplexing Planet." A generous selection of his work is featured in the 2007 book *The Original Art of Basil Wolverton: From the Collection of Glenn Bray* (Last Gasp).

Jim Woodring is the author of *The Frank Book*, *The Book of Jim*, and *Seeing Things*, all published by Fantagraphics. He works in pen and ink, charcoal, watercolor, oil, plastic, wax, tin, and chitta to get his ideas across. His multimedia collaborations with the musician Bill Frisell won them a United States Artists Fellowship in 2006. He lives in Seattle and on jimwoodring.blogspot.com.

Dan Zettwoch (St. Louis) has self-published several comics, including *Ironclad* and *Schematic Comics*, and has had stories published in many anthologies, including *Drawn & Quarterly Showcase* and *Kramers Ergot*. He is hard at work on his comic *Redbird* for Buenaventura Press.